HOUGHTON MIFFLIN SOCIAL STUDIES

Oh, California

*O*h, California,

That's the land for me!

I'm bound for San Francisco

With my washbowl on my knee.

J. Nichols

Beverly J. Armento
Gary B. Nash
Christopher L. Salter
Karen K. Wixson

Oh, California

Houghton Mifflin Company • Boston

Atlanta • Dallas • Geneva, Illinois • Princeton, New Jersey • Palo Alto • Toronto

Consultants

Program Consultants

Edith M. Guyton
Associate Professor of Early
  Childhood Education
Georgia State University
Atlanta, Georgia

Gail Hobbs
Associate Professor of Geography
Pierce College
Woodland Hills, California

Charles Peters
Reading Consultant
Oakland Schools
Pontiac, Michigan

Cathy Riggs-Salter
Social Studies Consultant
Hartsburg, Missouri

Alfredo Schifini
Limited English Proficiency Consultant
Los Angeles, California

George Paul Schneider
Associate Director
  of General Programs
Department of Museum Education
Art Institute of Chicago
Chicago, Illinois

Twyla Stewart
Center for Academic Interinstitutional
  Programs
University of California—Los Angeles
Los Angeles, California

Scott Waugh
Associate Professor of History
University of California—Los Angeles
Los Angeles, California

Teacher Reviewers

David E. Beer (Grade 5)
Weisser Park Elementary
Fort Wayne, Indiana

Jan Coleman (Grades 6–7)
Thornton Junior High
Fremont, California

Shawn Edwards
  (Grades 1–3)
Jackson Park Elementary
University City, Missouri

Barbara J. Fech (Grade 6)
Martha Ruggles School
Chicago, Illinois

Deborah M. Finkel
  (Grade 4)
Los Angeles Unified
  School District,
  Region G
South Pasadena,
  California

Jim Fletcher (Grades 5, 8)
La Loma Junior High
Modesto, California

Susan M. Gilliam
  (Grade 1)
Roscoe Elementary
Los Angeles, California

Vicki Stroud Gonterman
  (Grade 2)
Gibbs International
  Studies Magnet School
Little Rock, Arkansas

Lorraine Hood (Grade 2)
Fresno Unified School
  District
Fresno, California

Jean Jamgochian
  (Grade 5)
Haycock Gifted and
  Talented Center
Fairfax County, Virginia

Susan Kirk-Davalt
  (Grade 5)
Crowfoot Elementary
Lebanon, Oregon

Mary Molyneaux-Leahy
  (Grade 3)
Bridgeport Elementary
Bridgeport, Pennsylvania

Sharon Oviatt
  (Grades 1–3)
Keysor Elementary
Kirkwood, Missouri

Jayne B. Perala (Grade 1)
Cave Spring Elementary
Roanoke, Virginia

Carol Siefkin (K)
Garfield Elementary
Sacramento, California

Norman N. Tanaka
  (Grade 3)
Martin Luther King Jr.
  Elementary
Sacramento, California

John Tyler (Grades 5, 8)
Groton School
Groton, Massachusetts

Portia W. Vaughn
  (Grades 1–3)
School District 11
Colorado Springs,
  Colorado

Acknowledgments

    Grateful acknowledgment is made
for the use of the material listed below.
    The material in the Minipedia is
reprinted from *The World Book*
Encyclopedia with the expressed permission of the publisher. © 1990 by World
Book, Inc.

–Continued on page 349.

From Your Authors

The January morning began like many others. James W. Marshall walked down to the American River to check on the sawmill he was building for John Sutter. At the water's edge, a flash of light caught Marshall's eye. Then he saw another flash and another.

So begins the exciting account of the discovery of gold at Sutter's Mill in 1848. By the year 1849, thousands of men and women had rushed to California, hoping to strike it rich. In Chapter 5 of this book, you will read more about those exciting days, which had so much impact on California's history.

Most of the people you will meet in this book lived long ago in places that may seem very different to you now. But they all had feelings just like yours and faced many of the same challenges you will face in your life. And whether they were great leaders or ordinary people, their decisions and actions helped shape California and the world you live in.

As you read about these people, places, and events, we hope you will ask many questions. Some questions may be about history: "What caused these people to come to California?" or "How do we know about these events?" Other questions may be about geography: "What are the land and weather like in that place?" or "Why did people choose to settle there?" Still other questions may be about economics: "How did people meet their needs for food and shelter?" or "How did people work out ways for using limited resources?"

Most of all, we hope you catch the excitement of thinking, questioning, and discovering answers about your world—now and in the twenty-first century.

Beverly J. Armento
Professor of Social Studies
Director, Center for Business and
Economic Education
Georgia State University

Christopher L. Salter
Professor and Chair
Department of Geography
University of Missouri

Gary B. Nash
Professor of History
University of California—Los Angeles

Karen K. Wixson
Associate Professor of Education
University of Michigan

Contents

Understanding Skills

Each "Understanding Skills" feature gives you the opportunity to learn and practice a skill related to the topic you are studying.

Understanding Concepts

Each "Understanding Concepts" feature gives you more information about a concept that is important to the lesson you are reading.

Making Decisions

Much of history is made of people's decisions. These pages take you step-by-step through fascinating problems from history and today. What will you decide?

Exploring

The story of the past is hidden all around you in the world of the present. "Exploring" pages tell you the secrets of how to find it.

Literature

Throughout history people have expressed their deepest feelings and beliefs through literature. Reading these stories, legends, poems, and shorter passages that appear in the lessons will help you experience what life was like for people of other times and places.

Primary Sources

Reading the exact words of the people who made and lived history is the best way to get a sense of how they saw themselves and the times in which they lived. You will find more than 50 primary sources throughout this book including the following:

A Closer Look

Take a closer look at the objects and pictures spread out on these special pages. With the clues you see you'll become a historical detective.

A Moment in Time

A person from the past is frozen at an exciting moment. You'll get to know these people by reading about where they are, what they're wearing, and the objects around them.

Charts, Diagrams, and Timelines

These visual presentations of information help give you a clearer picture of the people, places, and events you are studying.

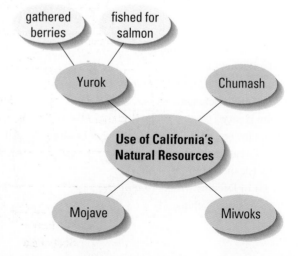

Maps

The events of history have been shaped by the places in which they occurred. Each map in this book tells its own story about these events and places.

Starting Out

What makes this textbook so much more interesting than others you've used? In this book, the people of California's past speak to you, through their words and the objects they used. You'll walk inside their houses and look inside their cooking pots. You'll follow them as they settle the wilderness, build cities, fight wars, develop a modern state.

When and what? The timeline at the beginning of each lesson tells you when these events took place. The lesson title tells you what the lesson is about.

From unit to chapter to lesson—each step lets you see history in closer detail. The photos show you where events happened. The art introduces you to the people.

Right from the beginning the lesson opener pulls you into the sights, the sounds, the smells of what life was like at that time, in that place.

Like a road sign, the question that always appears here tells you what to think about while you read the lesson.

Look for these key terms. They are listed here so that you can watch for them. The first time they appear in the lesson they are shown in heavy black print and defined. Key terms are also defined in the Glossary.

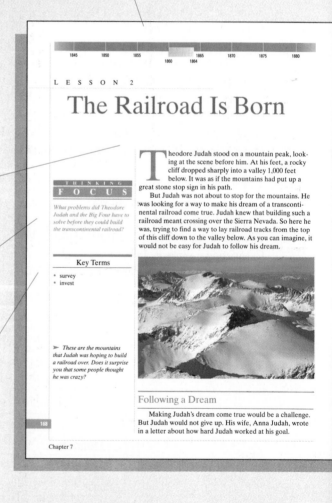

LESSON 2

The Railroad Is Born

THINKING
FOCUS

What problems did Theodore Judah and the Big Four have to solve before they could build the transcontinental railroad?

Key Terms

* survey
* invest

➤ *These are the mountains that Judah was hoping to build a railroad over. Does it surprise you that some people thought he was crazy?*

Theodore Judah stood on a mountain peak, looking at the scene before him. At his feet, a rocky cliff dropped sharply into a valley 1,000 feet below. It was as if the mountains had put up a great stone stop sign in his path.

But Judah was not about to stop for the mountains. He was looking for a way to make his dream of a transcontinental railroad come true. Judah knew that building such a railroad meant crossing over the Sierra Nevada. So here he was, trying to find a way to lay railroad tracks from the top of this cliff down to the valley below. As you can imagine, it would not be easy for Judah to follow his dream.

Following a Dream

Making Judah's dream come true would be a challenge. But Judah would not give up. His wife, Anna Judah, wrote in a letter about how hard Judah worked at his goal.

168

Chapter 7

Frozen at a moment in time, this gold miner almost jumps off the page in his excitement. You learn all about him by reading about his clothes, the objects he has with him, and the place he's working.

Forty-niner
2:30 P.M., August 15, 1850
A mountain stream near Sacramento

Blistered Hand
Swinging his pick since dawn has raised new blisters on this miner's rough hands. He was a bookkeeper from Maine, and all this stooping and digging is harder work than he thought it would be.

Wild Grapes
He found these grapes as he moved downstream to get away from other miners. His food is rarely exciting — flapjacks and bacon every day.

Backpack
He bought this pack in San Francisco for 50 dollars — 10 times what it would have cost back East. Strapped to the top are the first letters he's received from home.

Nugget
"Yahoo! Now that's more like it!" This is the biggest nugget he's ever seen. He'll build a lean-to right here, set up camp, and stake his claim.

Goldmining Pan
He has been working on his twenty-sixth panful of dirt since this morning. The cloudy water just cleared. Until now, he has only seen flakes of gold at the bottom of the pan.

Boots
His cold toes are pressed against soaking wet leather. These boots haven't been dry in weeks.

Letters, diaries, books—short passages from these primary sources let people from the past speak to you. When you see a tan background, a red initial letter, and a gray bar, you know that the quotation is a primary source.

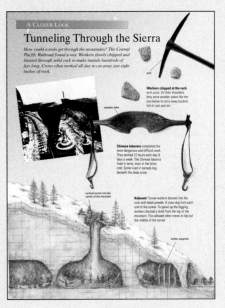

Tunneling Through the Sierra
How could a train get through the mountains? The Central Pacific Railroad found a way. Workers slowly chipped and blasted through solid rock to make tunnels hundreds of feet long. Crews often worked all day to cut away just eight inches of rock.

Workers chipped at the rock with picks. On their shoulders they wore wooden yokes like the one below to carry away buckets full of rock and dirt.

Chinese laborers completed the most dangerous and difficult work. They worked 12 hours each day, 6 days a week. The Chinese laborers lived in tents, even in the bitter cold. Some lived in tunnels dug beneath the deep snow.

Kaboom! Tunnel workers blasted into the rock with black powder. A crew dug from each end of the tunnel. To speed up the digging, workers blasted a shaft from the top of the mountain. This allowed other crews to dig out the middle of the tunnel.

Take a closer look, in this case at a tunnel through the mountains. Look at the tools the laborers used to carry away the dirt. Find the air shafts that allowed them to breathe under ground.

---

*E*verything he did from the time he went to California to the day of his death was for the great continental Pacific Railway. Time, money, brains, strength, body and soul were absorbed. It was the burden of his thought day and night, largely of his conversation, till it used to be said, "Judah's Pacific Railroad crazy."

—Anna Judah, 1889

At times, Anna Judah was one of the few people who believed in her husband's ideas. But Judah was not concerned that he did not have a lot of people behind him. "We must keep the ball rolling," he would tell his wife.

Finding a Route

Judah knew that before others believed in him, he would have to show them that his dream could work. He would have to prove that a railroad could cross the Sierra Nevada.

To find an answer to this difficult problem, Judah and his assistant, Daniel Strong, climbed deep into the Sierra Nevada. Judah and Strong stopped often to **survey**, or measure, the height of the mountains.

After weeks of searching, the men found the railroad route they were looking for. By following this route, Judah figured, the tracks would not rise too steeply or cross too many deep valleys. Judah and Strong were so excited by their discovery that they did not notice the coming of a winter storm. A sudden blizzard forced them from their camp in the middle of the night. Fighting snow and darkness, Judah and Strong barely made it to safety.

How Do We Know?

HISTORY Theodore and Anna Judah traveled to many places. Wherever they went, Anna wrote letters to her family and friends. Many of these letters described her husband's thoughts, words, and work. Anna Judah's letters give valuable information about the man who helped build the first transcontinental railroad.

⬆ *This is the compass Theodore Judah used to help him survey the mountains. Below is a map Judah made of his idea for a route through the mountains. Judah drew this map by hand.*

The Transcontinental Railroad

169

Giving you the inside story is the purpose of two special paragraphs. How Do We Know? tells you where information about the past comes from. Its companion, Across Time & Space, connects what you're reading to things that happened centuries ago or continents away. (See page 171 for an example.)

A picture is worth a thousand words. But just a few words in a caption can help you understand a picture, or a photograph. In this case, the caption tells you about a map and the compass Theodore Judah used while drawing it.

The things people make and use tell a great deal about them. In this book you'll find lots of photographs of the paintings, statues, and maps people made. You'll also see the tools, jewelry, and weapons they used.

Continuing On

As you get to know the people of the past, you'll want ways of understanding and remembering them better. This book gives you some tools to use in learning about people and places and remembering what you've learned.

You're in charge of your reading. See the red square at the end of the text? Now find the red square over in the margin. If you can answer the question there, then you probably understood what you just read. If you can't, perhaps you'd better go back and read that part of the lesson again.

The titles outline the lesson. The red titles tell you the main topics discussed in the lesson on "The Railroad Is Born." (Judah was the founder of the Central Pacific Railroad Company.) The blue titles tell you the subtopics.

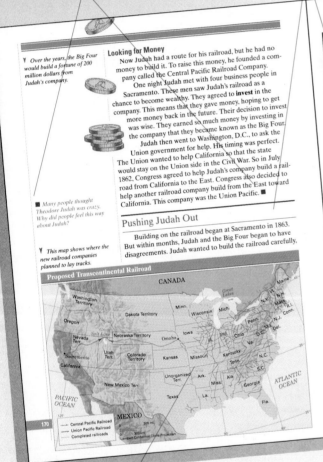

Every map tells a story. The large maps in this book tell their own story of where people like the builders of the first railroads went and what the land was like.

After you read the lesson, stop and review what you've read. The first question is the same one you started out with. The second question connects the lesson to what you've studied earlier. Other questions and an activity help you think about the lesson you've read. Chapter Review questions help you tie the lessons together. (See pages 182 and 183 for an example.)

Some tools you'll always use.
The Understanding pages walk you through skills that you will use again and again, as a student and later on in life. On this page you learn about the different time zones in the United States.

A special kind of Understanding
page looks at concepts—the big ideas that help put all the pieces together. This section helps you understand ideas like Resources, the Nation, and in this case, Justice.

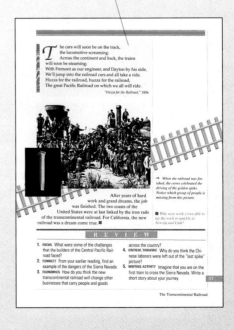

Diagrams make clear things that are hard to understand. Here the diagram shows how night follows daylight as the earth revolves around the sun. Other illustrations, charts, and graphs tell you how things work and how one bit of information relates to another.

Every age has its great storytellers.
Each chapter includes short examples of fine writing from or about the period. The literature is always printed on a tan background with a blue initial letter and a multicolored bar.

Sample page: Understanding Justice

Mining Town Trouble

Law and order was also a problem in California's many mining towns. Stealing and fighting were common in these busy, crowded camps. Police or sheriffs often lived a day's horseback ride away. Miners did not want to spend time guarding prisoners while they waited for the sheriff. The miners wanted to dig for gold, so they often took care of problems themselves. Because they were in a hurry, they quickly punished people they thought had committed a crime. Like the vigilantes, the miners ignored justice.

UNDERSTANDING JUSTICE

The vigilantes in California were trying to protect themselves and their belongings. They took strong action to catch and punish people who they believed had broken the law. But in doing this, the vigilantes treated many citizens unfairly. The vigilantes ignored justice.

Our Justice System
In the United States, we have a special way to decide fairly who has broken the law. It is called the justice system. At the head of this system is the Supreme Court. Sandra Day O'Connor, seen here, is a member of that court.
The justice system would not be fair if a person who was robbed decided who was guilty. That is why a judge or a group of people called a jury decides who is guilty. During the trial the victim and the suspect tell their sides of the story. Then the judge or jury decides whether the suspect committed the crime. If the person is guilty, then he or she is punished.
Our justice system helps make sure that there is justice, or fair treatment, for everyone. People who steal, for example, are punished. That's because taking something that belongs to another person is unfair. But it is also unfair to punish people for crimes they did not do. (Have you ever been blamed for something your brother or sister did?) So our justice system gives suspects a chance to tell their stories to someone who will be fair.

Vigilantes Ignore Justice
California's vigilantes thought that they were helping to stop crime. But they ignored the justice system. They did not give suspects the chance to tell their stories to a fair judge. As a result, many people in California did not receive justice. And many people were punished unjustly.

148

Sample page: Understanding Time Zones

UNDERSTANDING TIME ZONES
Reading a Time Zone Map

Here's Why
The earth rotates from west to east. As the earth rotates, sunlight hits different places at different times. Each day, sunlight hits the East Coast of the United States three hours earlier than it hits the West Coast.

In the 1800s, each community set its own clocks by the sun. Clocks in different places did not agree. This system was confusing, and problems arose. When the transcontinental railroad was finished in 1869, the trains needed to run on a set time schedule. Finally, in 1883 the United States was divided into four time zones. The clocks in one zone all said the same time. This system solved the railroad's time-schedule problem. By understanding time zones on a map, you can figure out what time it is in different parts of the country.

Here's How
There are four time zones in the mainland of the United States. They are the Eastern, Central, Mountain, and Pacific Time Zones. Alaska and Hawaii also have time zones. Look at the map

on page 331 of the Atlas. It shows which states are in each of the time zones. The clock in the Eastern Time Zone says 7:00. The clock in the Central Time Zone says 6:00. It is one hour earlier. As you go west from the Eastern Time Zone, subtract one hour for the Central Time Zone, one more hour for Mountain Time, and another hour for Pacific Time. There is a difference of three hours between the East and West Coasts.

Try It
Look at the time zone map on page 331 and answer the questions below:
1. Name one state in each time zone.
2. Name three states that are in more than one time zone.
3. Name the time zone that is just to the east of the Mountain Time Zone.
4. When it is 7:00 A.M. in Iowa, what time is it in Vermont? Louisiana? Colorado? Nevada? New York?
5. As you go east from Sacramento, does the time get earlier or later?

Apply It
Using the Atlas, plan a trip to six U.S. towns or cities. Begin in Los Angeles and end up in Washington, D.C. Be sure to include places that are located in each time zone. Trace your route on the map on page 324. If it is 4:00 P.M. when you arrive in Washington, D.C., what time is it in each of the other cities?

172

Sample page: The Transcontinental Railroad

The cars will soon be on the track,
the locomotive screaming;
Across the continent and back, the trains
will soon be steaming;
With Fremont as our engineer, and Dayton by his side,
We'll jump into the railroad cars and all take a ride.
Huzza for the railroad, huzza for the railroad,
The great Pacific Railroad on which we all will ride.

"Huzza for the Railroad," 1856

◄ When the railroad was finished, the crews celebrated the driving of the golden spike. Notice which group of people is missing from this picture.

After years of hard work and grand dreams, the job was finished. The two coasts of the United States were at last linked by the iron rails of the transcontinental railroad. For California, the new railroad was a dream come true. ■

▶ Why were work crews able to lay the track so quickly at Nevada and Utah?

REVIEW
1. **FOCUS** What were some of the challenges that the builders of the Central Pacific Railroad faced?
2. **CONNECT** From your earlier reading, find an example of the dangers of the Sierra Nevada.
3. **ECONOMICS** How do you think the new transcontinental railroad will change other businesses that carry people and goods

across the country?
4. **CRITICAL THINKING** Why do you think the Chinese laborers were left out of the "last spike" picture?
5. **WRITING ACTIVITY** Imagine that you are on the first train to cross the Sierra Nevada. Write a short story about your journey.

177

The Transcontinental Railroad

Also Featuring

Some special pages show up only once in every unit, not in every lesson in the book. These features continue the story by letting you explore an idea or activity, or read a story about another time and place. The Time/Space Databank in the back of the book brings together resources you will use again and again.

School isn't the only place where you can learn social studies. This feature gives you a chance to explore history and geography outside the classroom—at home or in your own neighborhood.

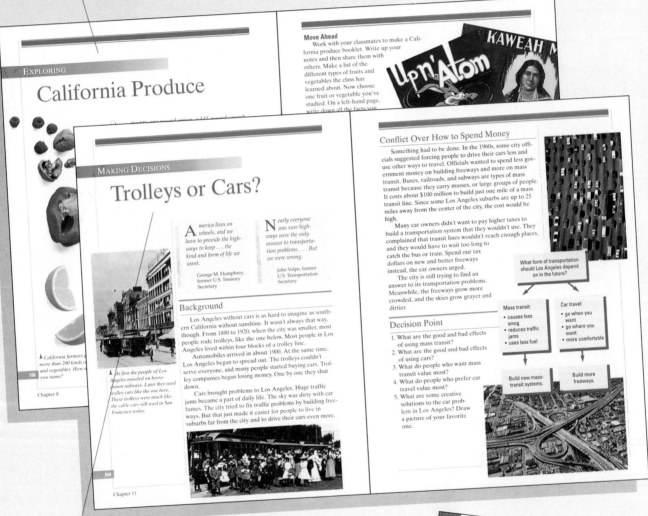

EXPLORING

California Produce

MAKING DECISIONS

Trolleys or Cars?

A merica lives on wheels, and we have to provide the highways to keep . . . the kind and form of life we want.

George M. Humphrey, former U.S. Treasury Secretary

N early everyone was sure highways were the only answer to transportation problems. . . . But we were wrong.

John Volpe, former U.S. Transportation Secretary

Background

Los Angeles without cars is as hard to imagine as southern California without sunshine. It wasn't always that way, though. From 1880 to 1920, when the city was smaller, most people rode trolleys, like the one below. Most people in Los Angeles lived within four blocks of a trolley line.

Automobiles arrived in about 1900. At the same time, Los Angeles began to spread out. The trolleys couldn't serve everyone, and many people started buying cars. Trolley companies began losing money. One by one they shut down.

Cars brought problems to Los Angeles. Huge traffic jams became a part of daily life. The sky was dirty with car fumes. The city tried to fix traffic problems by building freeways. But that just made it easier for people to live in suburbs far from the city and to drive their cars even more.

▲ *At first the people of Los Angeles traveled on horse-drawn railways. Later they used trolley cars like the one here. These trolleys were much like the cable cars still used in San Francisco today.*

Chapter 11

Move Ahead
Work with your classmates to make a California produce booklet. Write up your notes and then share them with others. Make a list of the different types of fruits and vegetables the class has learned about. Now choose one fruit or vegetable you've studied. On a left-hand page, write down all the facts you...

Conflict Over How to Spend Money

Something had to be done. In the 1960s, some city officials suggested forcing people to drive their cars less and use other ways to travel. Officials wanted to spend less government money on building freeways and more on mass transit. Buses, railroads, and subways are types of mass transit because they carry masses, or large groups of people. It costs about $100 million to build just one mile of a mass transit line. Since some Los Angeles suburbs are up to 25 miles away from the center of the city, the cost would be high.

Many car owners didn't want to pay higher taxes to build a transportation system that they wouldn't use. They complained that transit lines wouldn't reach enough places, and they would have to wait too long to catch the bus or train. Spend our tax dollars on new and better freeways instead, the car owners urged.

The city is still trying to find an answer to its transportation problems. Meanwhile, the freeways grow more crowded, and the skies grow grayer and dirtier.

What form of transportation should Los Angeles depend on in the future?

Decision Point

1. What are the good and bad effects of using mass transit?
2. What are the good and bad effects of using cars?
3. What do people who want mass transit value most?
4. What do people who prefer car travel value most?
5. What are some creative solutions to the car problem in Los Angeles? Draw a picture of your favorite one.

Mass transit:
• causes less smog
• reduces traffic jams
• uses less fuel

Car travel:
• go when you want
• go where you want
• more comfortable

Build new mass-transit systems.

Build more freeways.

What would you do? The Making Decisions pages show you an important decision from the past. Then you practice the steps that will help you to make a good choice.

Stories have always been important parts of people's lives. Each unit in the book has at least one story or group of poems about the time and place you're studying. In this case, it's a story about pioneers crossing the mountains in California.

LITERATURE

Patty Reed's Doll

Rachel Laurgaard

The Sutter's Fort Historical Museum has a wooden doll that belonged to a girl named Patty Reed in 1846. In this story, Patty's doll tells the adventures of the Donner Party on their journey from Illinois to California. Here you join the frightened pioneers as they climb the frozen Sierra Nevada in a dangerous snowstorm. As you read, ask yourself, "What were these pioneers feeling as they tried to cross the mountains?"

In Lesson 1 you learned about the Donner Party. These early pioneers faced many hardships as they crossed the Western frontier.

A s we traveled up toward Truckee Lake, snow began to fall. When the clouds lifted from the summits of the mountains and the folks saw that they were covered with white, I could tell that they were frightened.

"Oh, it will be awful if we are snowed in," Patty said to Puss.

"We won't be. Papa will be...

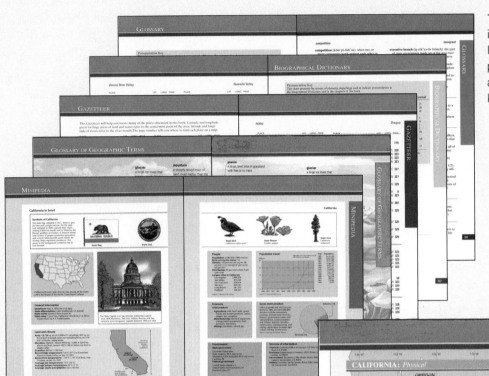

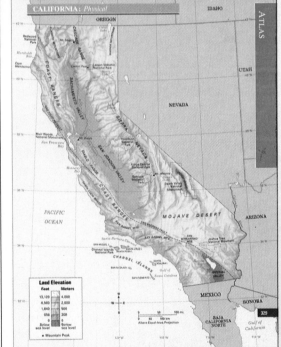

The Time/Space Databank is like a reference section of a library at your fingertips. It's the place to go for more information about the places, people, and key terms you meet in this book.

What's a minipedia? It's a small version of an encyclopedia, one that you don't have to go to your library to use. It's bound right into the back of your book so you can quickly look up its articles, charts, and graphs.

The Atlas maps out the world. Large maps show you the political divisions of your world, your country, and your state. Special maps tell you about the climate, vegetation, population, and time zones of the United States.

"The rain will melt the snow, won't it?" Patty's mother asked.

"It may not be rain up on the pass," Mr. Stanton answered in a worried tone. "When it rains lower down, it snows up above, they say."

He was right. Floundering through the drifts next day, we were able to advance only a mile or two before nightfall. Wet and cold from plunging into the deep snow, the folks gathered around a blazing log fire that night in frightened consultation.

"We'll have to abandon the wagons, there's no doubt of that," someone said. "If we strap our provisions to the backs of the oxen, we may be able to pack through."

"It will be slow going with all the children," someone else said. "Every grownup will have to carry a child. The snow's much too deep for the little ones to make it alone."

The next day they tried to carry out this plan. The oxen were not very co-operative. The children laughed to see them wallowing in the snow. But it was no laughing matter to the men who were trying to salvage enough food to get their families safely across the mountains

It was late after—

consultation discussion

provisions supplies and food

sal—

Unit 1

People and Place

California's land has always helped shape the way people live. The first people found California to be a land rich in plants and animals. They used these and other resources in many ways. In the desert, Indians made this 150-foot painting. No one knows the meaning of the figures. But we do know that early people depended on the land just as we do today.

14,000 YEARS AGO

Indian geoglyph constructed by ancestors of the Yuma near Blythe, California. c. post-1700. Southwest Museum, Los Angeles, California.

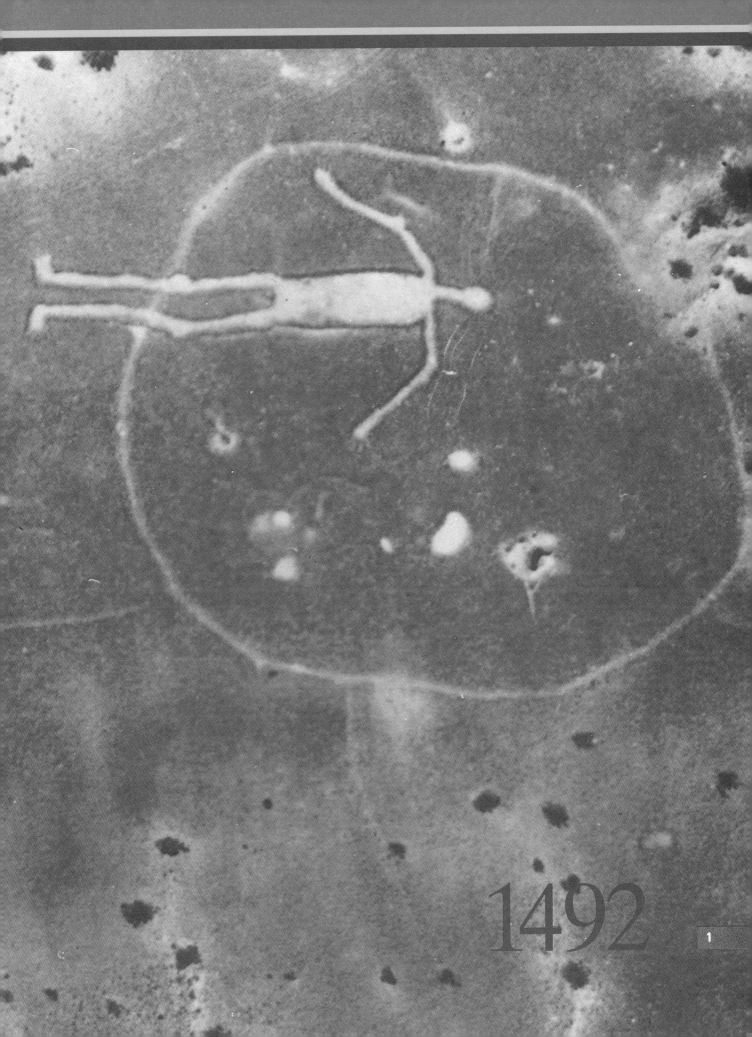

1492

Chapter 1

Geography of California

Question: Where is it rainy and dry, hilly and flat, noisy and quiet, hot and cold? Answer: California. You live in a state with many types of land, people, wildlife, and weather. That's why California has so much to see and do. So pack your snow boots and your bathing suit. You're about to take a trip through the Golden State.

The ocean is a big part of life along the California coastline. Here, children touch starfish in a tank at the Monterey Bay Aquarium.

Carrots are one of hundreds of vegetables and fruits grown in California's Central Valley.

A hang glider rides the blasts of warm air that rises from the desert. What a way to see the geography of California!

This looks like a rock, but it's not. It's a piece of wood from the Petrified Forest in Sonoma.

Much of the state is covered with mountains. The hiker above looks down on the Yosemite Valley and the Sierra Nevada.

Where on Earth Is California?

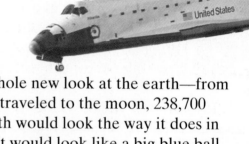

What states, countries, and continents are closest to California?

Key Terms

- globe
- continent
- border

➤ *This picture of the earth was taken from thousands of miles away.*

Imagine getting a whole new look at the earth—from outer space. If you traveled to the moon, 238,700 miles away, the earth would look the way it does in the picture below. It would look like a big blue ball wrapped in white clouds. But you don't have to go that far away to get a thrilling view of the planet. Just take a ride in the space shuttle.

From high up in the shuttle, you can see the earth stretching for hundreds of miles. It fills your window with its colors—blue of ocean, white of clouds, green and brown of land. If you look closely, you can see mountains, large rivers and lakes, icebergs, and farmland. You can even see some cities, bridges, and airports.

Your speeding shuttle circles around the side of the earth away from the sun. Suddenly, all is as black as night. You can barely see the earth against the black sky. Astronaut Sally Ride, the first woman to travel in the space shuttle, described the view like this:

"The lights of cities sparkle; on nights when there was no moon, it was difficult for me to tell the earth from the sky—the twinkling lights could be stars or they could be small cities."

Your shuttle circles back into the light and you spot your home state, California. You can see miles of its curving coastline against the blue ocean. Suddenly, you feel very far from home.

Looking at the Earth

The space shuttle circles the earth every 90 minutes. It goes so fast that sometimes you lose track of what country or ocean you are flying over. But it's easy to find out where you are by looking at a globe or a map.

A **globe** is a ball that has all of the earth's areas of land and bodies of water drawn on it. The earth does not really have lines drawn on it or the names of oceans and lands written across it. But a globe does. A globe gives you much more information about the earth than you can get from looking at a picture.

If you turn a globe around, you can see all of the earth's seven great areas of land, or **continents.** You can also see the bodies of water that cover much of the earth.

Now look at the map at the bottom of this page. A map also shows the earth's lands and oceans. But a map is different from a globe. Because it is flat, and not round, a map lets you see all the continents and oceans at once.

You can see California on the globe and on the map. Compared to the whole earth, California looks very tiny. ■

How Do We Know?

GEOGRAPHY *Satellites are special spacecraft sent into outer space. They help scientists make maps of the earth. There are no astronauts on satellites, but cameras on board can take pictures of the continents and the oceans. Satellites also send back information about the weather. They can also search for lost ships.*

■ *In what ways is a map of the world different from a globe?*

▼ *This map shows the earth's seven continents.*

Map of the World

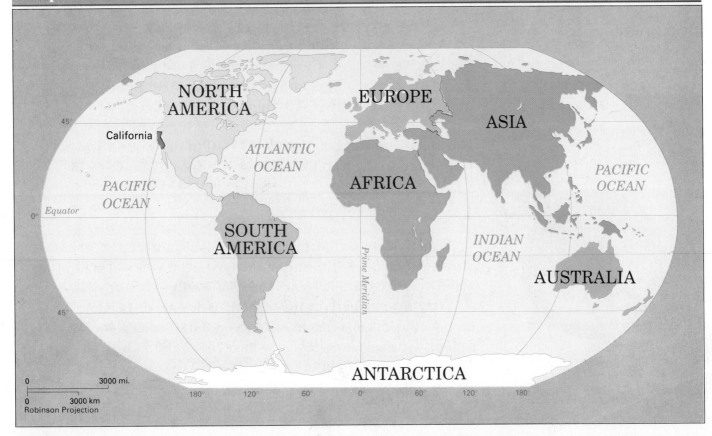

NORTH AMERICA
EUROPE
ASIA
California
ATLANTIC OCEAN
PACIFIC OCEAN
AFRICA
PACIFIC OCEAN
Equator
SOUTH AMERICA
INDIAN OCEAN
AUSTRALIA
Prime Meridian
ANTARCTICA

45°
0°
45°

0   3000 mi.
0   3000 km
Robinson Projection

180   120   60   0   60   120   180

Looking at North America

As your shuttle circles the earth, you fly over the continent of North America. The map below shows that many countries make up this large continent. In the middle of North America is the United States. Its neighbor countries are Canada to the north and Mexico to the south. Find the borders that separate the United States from its neighbors.

A **border** is the line where one area ends and another begins. The border of a country may follow the natural line of mountains or a river. Or it may cut across a piece of land to divide one country from another.

Look at the border between the United States and Canada. Part of it is a straight line. But another part follows the natural line of the five Great Lakes. Now look at the border between the United States and Mexico. What natural feature makes up part of this border?

You can see the borders of several smaller countries on this map. South of Mexico is an area called Central America. This area includes the countries of Guatemala, Belize, Honduras, El Salvador, Nicaragua, Costa Rica, and Panama. Farther east, in the Caribbean Sea, is a group of island countries called the West Indies. And at the top of the map is the country of Greenland.

The map shows that California is on the continent of North America and on the West Coast of the United States. Compared to the whole continent, California looks tiny. ■

▼ *What countries and bodies of water touch the border of the United States?*

North America

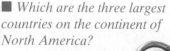

■ *Which are the three largest countries on the continent of North America?*

Looking at California

You fly over California each time the shuttle crosses North America. At the end of the next orbit you will land in California. You lean close to the window for a better view.

You have been flying over the Pacific Ocean, heading east. California appears ahead of you. First, you fly over the famous Golden Gate Bridge, which crosses San Francisco Bay. A few minutes later you can see Lake Tahoe. The lake

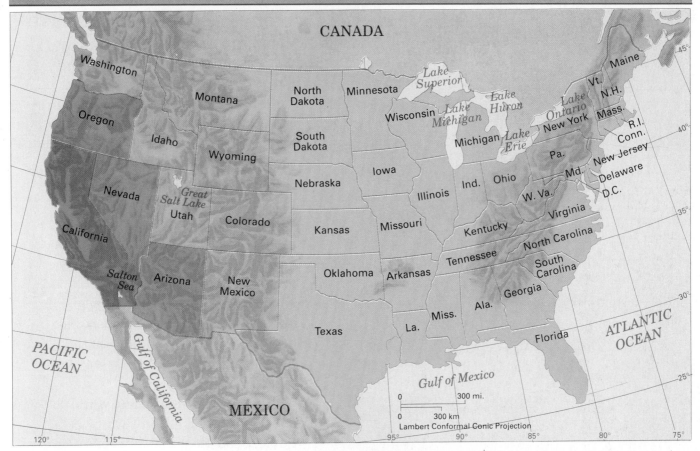

CANADA

Washington
Montana
North Dakota
Minnesota
Lake Superior
Maine
Oregon
Idaho
Wyoming
South Dakota
Wisconsin
Lake Michigan
Lake Huron
Lake Ontario
Vt.
N.H.
New York
Mass.
Nevada
Great Salt Lake
Utah
Colorado
Nebraska
Iowa
Michigan
Lake Erie
Pa.
R.I.
Conn.
New Jersey
Delaware
Md.
D.C.
California
Kansas
Missouri
Illinois
Ind.
Ohio
W. Va.
Virginia
Salton Sea
Arizona
New Mexico
Oklahoma
Arkansas
Kentucky
Tennessee
North Carolina
South Carolina
PACIFIC OCEAN
Gulf of California
Texas
La.
Miss.
Ala.
Georgia
Florida
ATLANTIC OCEAN
MEXICO
Gulf of Mexico

0   300 mi.
0   300 km
Lambert Conformal Conic Projection

120°   115°   95°   90°   85°   80°   75°
45°   40°   35°   30°   25°

is so large that you spot it easily, shining like a jewel far below. Next, you fly over a long strip of snowy mountains.

California's Neighbors

If you look at the map on this page, you can see that these mountains mark the border between California and Nevada. The map is shaded to show bumps and ridges. This shading on the map makes the mountains seem to rise above the flatter land nearby.

Besides Nevada, California has three other neighbors—two states and one country. Oregon lies on California's northern border. To the south of Nevada is Arizona, touching California's eastern border. California shares its southern border with the country of Mexico. ■

Zooming in on California

Now you are buckled in for the landing. The shuttle races downward. This time you are heading toward the hot, flat southern California desert. There you will land at Edwards Air Force Base.

As your shuttle dips closer and closer to the ground, you can see California's beautiful landscape more clearly.

▲ *California is on the western border of the United States.*

■ *Name the states, country, and body of water on California's borders.*

7

Geography of California

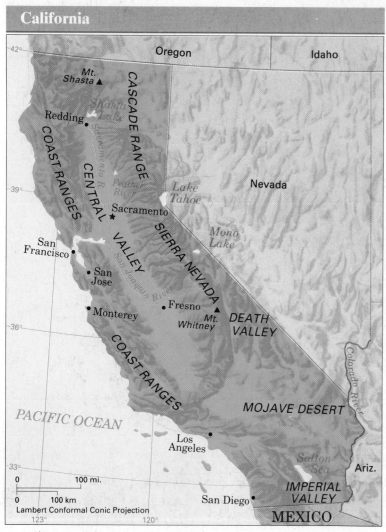

California

Oregon
Idaho
Mt. Shasta ▲
CASCADE RANGE
Redding
Shasta Lake
Sacramento River
Nevada
Feather River
Lake Tahoe
COAST RANGES
CENTRAL VALLEY
Mono Lake
Sacramento ★
SIERRA NEVADA
San Francisco
San Jose
San Joaquin River
Monterey
Fresno
Mt. Whitney
DEATH VALLEY
COAST RANGES
MOJAVE DESERT
Colorado River
PACIFIC OCEAN
Los Angeles
Salton Sea
Ariz.
San Diego
IMPERIAL VALLEY
MEXICO

0   100 mi.
0   100 km
Lambert Conformal Conic Projection

▲ *Locate and name two cities, two rivers, a bay, and a lake in California.*

■ *What geographic features of California does the space shuttle pass over as it is landing?*

The California coast curves inward where you pass over Monterey Bay, a little south of San Francisco. Now you are flying southeast down California's long Central Valley. The fields of the valley's rich farmland look like green and brown square patches on a quilt. You can see some rivers weaving through the valley. Then you leave the valley behind, and fly over rows of mountains. The ridges of the mountains make curving patterns across the brown earth. As you enjoy this view, you can't help agreeing with Robert Crippen, one of the astronauts who flew on the first space shuttle: "What a way to come to California!"

East of the mountains, you fly over the desert. At Edwards Air Force Base, the crews are ready for your arrival. Television cameras and hundreds of people are searching the sky for their first view of the space shuttle. From far above, you can see the field where you'll be touching down. As your shuttle glides lower to the ground, the landing field seems to grow larger. The shuttle shakes as waves of rising desert heat pound against it. Finally, the back wheels touch the ground. The nose wheel drops down, and the shuttle glides to a stop. On the radio an excited voice from mission control cries, "Welcome home!" ■

R E V I E W

1. **FOCUS** What states, countries, and continents are closest to California?

2. **GEOGRAPHY** Look at the map of California. Name the land features such as mountains and rivers you might see most clearly from the space shuttle.

3. **GEOGRAPHY** Why do you think borders for countries and states often follow rivers, lakes, and mountains?

4. **CRITICAL THINKING** From which country outside of the United States would you guess California gets most of its visitors? Give the reason for your answer.

5. **WRITING ACTIVITY** Pretend you're an astronaut floating above the earth in a space shuttle. Write a one-page story describing how you feel being so far from home and what the earth looks like from where you are.

Identifying Main Ideas

Here's Why

In 1971 a baby gray whale was caught by scientists and raised at Sea World in San Diego. The scientists named the whale Gigi.

Suppose you want to read more about gray whales. How will you remember the new information you learn?

You cannot remember every detail, but you can remember the most important ideas. Identifying main ideas will help you to organize information and to remember more of what you read.

Here's How

In a paragraph, one sentence often states the main idea or tells what the whole paragraph is about. The main idea in the paragraph below is stated in the first sentence: *Gray whales grow most rapidly in their first year of life*. The main idea is often stated in the first sentence of a paragraph. The other sentences in the paragraph give details that support the main idea.

Gray whales grow most rapidly in their first year of life. When the gray whale Gigi came to Sea World, she was only two months old and was already 18 feet long. Eventually she became too big to fit in her tank. A year later, when scientists returned her to the ocean, she was 26 feet long. Gigi would grow only 20 feet more before she would reach her full size.

Try It

Read the paragraph below. Ask yourself these questions: What one thing is the whole paragraph about? Which sentence states the main idea? Which sentences give details that support the main idea?

Gray whales spend their summers feeding in the cold waters of Alaska. When these northern waters begin to freeze, the whales travel south. They swim along the coast of California to the warm waters of Mexico. There they mate and have their young. Gray whales travel long distances each year, sometimes over 10,000 miles.

Apply It

Now read the first paragraph of the next lesson in your book. What is the whole paragraph about? Which sentence states the main idea? What two examples do the other sentences give to support the main idea?

Mojave

Diane Siebert

The Mojave Desert in southern California is a large dry area of sandy soil and extinct volcanoes.

Throughout her poetry, Diane Siebert gives the desert the voice of a very old woman. She reminds us that the desert—and the earth itself—are living things. As you read the poem, ask yourself, "How can a desert be like a person?"

I am the desert.
I am free.
Come walk the sweeping face of me.

Through canyon eyes of sandstone red
I see the hawk, his wings outspread;
He sunward soars to block the light
And casts the shadow of his flight
Upon my vast and ancient face,
Whose deep arroyos boldly trace
The paths where sudden waters run—
Long streams of tears dried by the sun.

arroyos dry, narrow valleys

I feel the windstorm's violent thrust;
I feel the sting of sand and dust
As bit by bit, and year by year,
New features on my face appear.

Great mountain ranges stretch for miles
To crease my face with frowns and smiles.
My lakes are dry and marked by tracks
Of zigging, zagging, long-eared jacks.
Dust devils swirl and slowly rise;
They whistle, whirling to the skies,
While tossed and blown in great stampedes
Are stumbling, bumbling tumbleweeds.

stampedes sudden rushing movements

10

. . . .

And as the desert seasons change,
The hands of Nature rearrange
My timeworn face with new designs
Of colors, shadows, shapes, and lines:

In wintertime the north winds blow;
My mountain peaks are capped with snow;
But resting, waiting patiently
Beneath the frost that covers me,
I dream of spring, when I can wear
The blossoms of the prickly pear,
Along with flowers, wild and bright,
And butterflies in joyful flight.

My summer face is cracked and dry,
All blotched and flecked with alkali,
Until the coming of a storm
When thunderclouds above me form,
And bursting, send their rains to pound
Across my high, unyielding ground
Where walls of water grow, and flow
Toward my valleys far below.

But soon the blazing sun breaks through,
And then, beneath skies wide and blue,
My features shimmer, blurred by heat,
Till autumn breezes, cool and sweet,
Caress my face, now brown and burned,
To tell me autumn has returned,
To touch the land where coyotes prowl,
Where coyotes lift their heads and howl;
At night they sing their songs to me:

We are the desert.
We are free. . . .

alkali (AL kuh ly)
a salty mineral sub-
stance found in dry
soil

unyielding hard and
dry

Further Reading

This Is the Desert. Philip H. Ault

11

California's Regions

THINKING FOCUS

How are California's geographic regions different from one another?

Key Terms

- region
- geography
- climate
- mountain range

▼ *A rope and a canteen are some of the tools used by explorers in California's mountains and deserts.*

Some people love a challenge. A high mountain begs them to climb it. A burning desert dares them to cross it. In California, adventurers can find two of nature's toughest challenges—Mount Whitney and Death Valley. Nowhere else on earth can you find two places so close together, yet so different from each other.

Mount Whitney is a snow-topped mountain that touches the clouds. It is 14,491 feet high, the highest point in the United States outside of Alaska. State officials came upon Mount Whitney in 1864, when they were mapping the state. In 1873 several groups of climbers made the dangerous journey to its peak. Then they argued over who got there first. A group of five fishermen is given the credit.

Less than 100 miles away from Mount Whitney is Death Valley. It is the lowest point in North America. There the desert sinks to 282 feet below the level of the oceans. On July 10, 1913, the temperature in Death Valley hit a blazing 134 degrees Fahrenheit. That is the highest temperature ever measured in the United States.

During the gold rush of 1849, a group of miners and their families tried to cross the 130-mile-long valley. Some got lost, ran out of water, and died. The people who made it out alive gave Death Valley its scary name.

Frightening stories were told about the valley. One writer called it "the loneliest, the hottest, the most deadly and dangerous spot in the United States." "Once you enter it," the writer said, "there is no escape." Today, however, many people visit Death Valley to see its strange and lonely beauty.

Four Regions

On any one day in California, you can swim in the ocean, ski in the mountains, pick fruit on a farm, or drive across the desert. California is the only state in the country where you can do so many activities in so many regions. A **region** is an area of land whose features set it apart from other areas. The number of people, the kinds of business, and the weather are some features that can make one region different from another. A region's geography may also set it apart. **Geography** is all of the land and water features, such as mountains, lakes, meadows, and rivers, that are found in an area. If you look at California's geography you can see four main regions. They are the coast, the Central Valley the mountains, and the deserts.

People and the Regions

For early settlers, each region held different challenges. The first explorers came by sea and braved the storms of the coast. Later, families in covered wagons crossed the hot desert and rugged mountains. Still later, farmers in the Central Valley, had to find ways to bring water to their land.

Each region also offered many advantages to early settlers. Features such as natural beauty, rich soil, and the kind of weather drew different people to different areas. A scientist named Luther Burbank described California's beauty in a letter he wrote after arriving in California in 1875. ■

The map below shows the four regions of California. To find out more about California's land, climate, and people, see the Minipedia, pages 310–311.

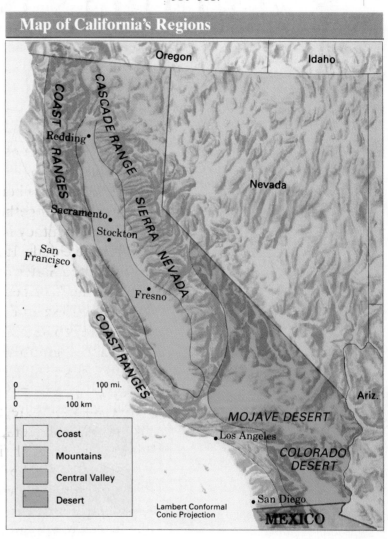

Map of California's Regions

- Coast
- Mountains
- Central Valley
- Desert

Lambert Conformal Conic Projection

100 mi.
100 km

■ *Name four geographic regions in California and give one word to describe each region.*

> I firmly believe from what I have seen that it is the chosen spot of all this earth as far as nature is concerned. . . . The sunshine is pure and soft, the mountains . . . are very lovely. The valley is covered with majestic oaks placed as no human hand could arrange them for beauty.

The Coast

It's like entering a gray, misty tunnel. The water whispers as the ferryboat cuts slowly through the soupy fog. Out of nowhere, seagulls cry out.

"You're really sensitive to sound when you're on fog watch," says Nancy MacLean. As the ferry's lookout, she listens and watches for the sailboats, fishing boats, and oil tankers that travel across the busy San Francisco Bay. Each morning, MacLean's ferry carries people from their homes in Marin County to their jobs in San Francisco.

The Northern and Southern Coast

Most mornings, ocean mists cover much of the northern coast. But later in the day, the fog usually burns off with the heat of the sun. The general condition of the weather in an area is called its **climate.** On the northern coast the climate is cool and damp. San Francisco usually gets about 23 inches of rain a year. The wet climate along the northern coast helps thick forests grow there. The northern coast attracts lots of visitors to places like Big Sur and Redwood National Park.

The southern coast has another kind of beauty. Rainfall is very low. San Diego gets less than 10 inches a year. The sunshine attracts many people who want to live in a warm climate. It is also perfect for television and movie filming, as well as sports such as surfing, biking, running, and sailing. Tourists enjoy visiting aquariums, theme parks, and the many beaches.

So many people like the coast region that more than half of all Californians live either in the Los Angeles area or, like Nancy MacLean, in the San Francisco Bay area. ■

State fish: the golden trout

■ *How is the northern coast of California different from the southern coast?*

➤ *Many people enjoy sailing in San Diego's natural harbor. San Pedro's fishermen earn a living from the sea.*

The Central Valley

You don't have to be a farmer to know what crops grow in the Central Valley. Just use your nose. As you pass each farm, the air fills with the thick scent of the fruit or vegetable planted there. A grove of orange trees fills the air with a sweet scent. The smell of an onion field is so sharp it makes your eyes water.

The land in the Central Valley is some of the most productive farmland in the world. Almost every kind of crop is grown on the farms in this valley. These crops are shipped all over California, the United States, and the world. A child on the East Coast might drink juice from Central Valley oranges on a frosty winter day. A Japanese family can enjoy avocados grown nearly halfway around the world.

▲ State flower: the golden poppy

Crops and Climate

The climate in the Central Valley is hot and dry in the summer and cooler and wetter in the winter. The winter rains and summer sun make the region perfect for growing the 200 different kind of crops produced there. Farmers grow cotton, grapes, walnuts, wheat, potatoes, tomatoes, and cherries, as well as many other kinds of fruits, vegetables, and nuts. Other farmers raise dairy cows, chickens, or beef cattle. The region gets its water from the Sacramento and the San Joaquin (*san waw KEEN*) rivers. Most of the people who live in the Central Valley are farmers or do work connected to farming.

Most Central Valley farms are run by big companies. But there are some small family farms too. Lupe Villarreal and his family raise peaches, almonds, and walnuts on their 70-acre farm in Hughson. Villarreal loves farming in the Central Valley. He says, "I think the most beautiful thing is when I'm driving down the road and I see so many different varieties of crops. That really makes me feel good. That's why I think we're very lucky to have the Central Valley." ■

▲ *These fields of flowers are one of the Central Valley's many crops. Across the valley farmers use machines like the one you see here harvesting a crop of lettuce.*

■ *Why is the Central Valley such a good farming area?*

15

The Mountains

The rains that fall on the mountaintop trickle into small streams. These streams of fresh water join together and gather speed as they rush down the mountainside. Suddenly, there is a roar like thunder. The stream has become a giant waterfall. It races over a cliff and pounds into the valley over 2,000 feet below.

The valley is the Yosemite *(yoh SEHM ih tee)* Valley, one of the most beautiful spots in California. There are more waterfalls here than in any other place in the world. Visitors are amazed by the sound and size of these giant waterfalls.

Yosemite is in the Sierra Nevada, an area whose name means "snowy mountain range" in Spanish. A **mountain range** is a long row of mountains. The Sierra Nevada is just one of many mountain ranges in California. In fact, over half of the land in the state is covered with mountains.

John Muir and the Sierra Nevada

The Sierra Nevada was the favorite spot of John Muir, a famous man who wrote about nature. Muir spent many years hiking through this mountain range. After his first visit to Yosemite in 1868, he wrote in his journal:

> As long as I live, I'll hear waterfalls and birds and winds sing. I'll interpret the rocks, learn the language of flood, storm, and the avalanche. I'll acquaint myself with the glaciers and wild gardens, and get as near the heart of the world as I can.

Today, rangers at Yosemite National Park continue Muir's work of teaching people about nature. One Yosemite ranger, Althea Robison, especially likes working with children. She walks children through the woods and shows them the plants and animals. "Children really respect rangers," Robison says. "When you tell them they shouldn't feed wildlife, or whatever the message is, they teach other people." See Making Decisions on page 26 to learn about John Muir's efforts to save California's forests. ■

▲ *State animal: the California grizzly bear*

■ *Why do you think California's mountain region attracts visitors from all over the world?*

▼ *The natural beauty of the Sierra Nevada brings many visitors to camp, hike, and ski.*

The Deserts

Compared to the busy coast, the Central Valley's rich cropland, and the mountains filled with wildlife, the desert might seem very empty. But actually, California's desert region is full of life too.

The two big deserts in the region are the Mojave (*moh HAH vee*) Desert and the Colorado Desert. In these areas the climate is very extreme. You can fry an egg on a flat rock in the heat of summer and freeze a glass of water on a winter night. But hundreds of types of plants and animals have found ways to live with these hard conditions. Cactus plants, for instance, can stay alive during long dry spells. Many of them store moisture in their thick skins. Their sharp spines keep animals from raiding their storehouses of water. One type of desert lizard has a special feature like windshield wipers to wipe blowing sand from its eyes. The tiny bush rabbit never drinks water. Instead, it gets the water it needs from the plants that it eats.

▲ *State bird: the California valley quail*

▼ *Even though much of California's desert region looks empty, many plants, animals, and people live there.*

The Fort Mojave Indians

People have found ways to live in the desert too. The Fort Mojave tribe of Native Americans has lived in the Mojave Desert for thousands of years. "This is where the Almighty has placed us," says Llewellyn Barrackman, a leader of the tribe. The desert is not an easy place to live. But Barrackman believes that God "protects us and gives us food from the river or the land or the desert." The Fort Mojave people fish for rainbow trout and catfish in the Colorado River. They hunt rabbits in the desert and get some of their medicine from the desert plants.

Desert dwellers become attached to the strange and special beauty of the rainbow-colored sunsets, the soaring hawks, and the cries of the coyote. They look forward to spring, when the dry, brown land blooms with brightly colored wildflowers. ■

■ *How are desert plants and animals well suited to their climates?*

17

The Four Regions of California

Region	Cities	Industries	Natural Features	Interesting Facts
The Coast	• Los Angeles • San Diego • San Francisco • Oakland	• oil • film and television • shipping and fishing • aviation • computers	• San Francisco Bay • San Diego Harbor • Big Sur • The redwood forests	• 1 in 18 Americans live within about 200 miles of downtown Los Angeles.

The Central Valley	• Sacramento
	• Fresno
	• Stockton
	• Modesto
		• Agriculture:
		  fruit
		  vegetables
		  cotton
		  dairy products
		  poultry
		  cattle
			• Sacramento River
			• San Joaquin Valley
			• Kern River
			• Flat-topped hills
				• The Central Valley leads the nation in sales of such crops as raisin grapes, walnuts, almonds, peaches, and olives.

The Mountains	• South Lake Tahoe • Ridgecrest • Susanville • Placerville	• recreation (skiing, hiking) • gold and copper mining • lumber • sand and gravel excavation	• Mount Lassen • Lake Tahoe • Merced River • Mount Whitney	• Yosemite Falls, at 2425 feet, is the highest waterfall in the United States.
The Deserts	• Palm Springs • Lancaster • El Centro • Indio	• borax mining • natural gas drilling • aviation • recreation (golfing, camping)	• Owens Lake Bed • Salton Sea • Mono Lake • Red Rock Canyon	• The town of Bagdad in the Mojave Desert holds the nation's record for the longest period without rain: 767 days.

REVIEW

1. **FOCUS** How are California's geographic regions different from one another?
2. **CONNECT** The Sierra Nevada spreads into one of California's neighboring states. Which state do you think that is?
3. **GEOGRAPHY** Why have the Fort Mojave Indians been able to live for so long in the dry and hot desert?
4. **CRITICAL THINKING** What could you learn from growing up in one of California's four regions that you couldn't learn in another region?
5. **WRITING ACTIVITY** Find your city or town on a map of California. Then write a two-paragraph description of the region your town is in. Describe the region's landscape and climate and the activities you can do there.

Identifying Regions on a Map

Here's Why

In Lesson 2 of this chapter, you learned that a region is an area of land whose features set it apart from other areas. You also learned that a region can be set apart by its geography, climate, people, or businesses.

Maps that show different regions can give you important information about places on the earth. If you learn to read maps that show regions, you will be able to compare the places they show.

Here's How

Different colors are often used on maps to stand for different regions. The map on this page shows yearly precipitation in California. Rain and snow are called precipitation. The different colors on the map show how much precipitation falls in different areas of the state each year. The legend tells how many inches of precipitation each color stands for.

On the map legend, you can see that dark green stands for 66-96 inches of precipitation. The dark green areas receive this much rain and snow in a year. There are six dark green areas on the map. Locate them. These areas have the same feature that makes them different from other regions. They all receive the same amount of precipitation each year.

Now turn to the map of California's four geographic regions on page 13. What four regions does it show? What color stands for each region?

Try It

Use the map of California's yearly precipitation and its legend to answer these questions.

1. What feature makes each region different from all the other regions?
2. What color stands for 32-66 inches of precipitation? for 16-32 inches?
3. How much rain and snow do the dark yellow areas on the map receive?
4. How much precipitation falls in Yosemite National Park each year?
5. Find your town on the map on page 328. How much rain and snow fall each year where you live?

Now compare the precipitation map with the map of California's four geographic regions on page 13, and answer the following questions.

1. Which geographic region gets the least amount of precipitation?

California's Yearly Precipitation

Legend:
- 0-8 inches
- 8-16 inches
- 16-32 inches
- 32-66 inches
- 66-96 inches

42° N
40° N
38° N
36° N
34° N

COAST RANGE
SIERRA NEVADA
COAST RANGE
Sacramento River
San Joaquin River
Sacramento
Yosemite National Park
San Francisco
Mt. Whitney
Death Valley
PACIFIC OCEAN
Mojave Desert
Los Angeles
Colorado Desert
San Diego

0   100   200 mi.
0   100   200   300 km
Lambert Conformal Conic Projection
124° W   122° W   120° W   118° W

19

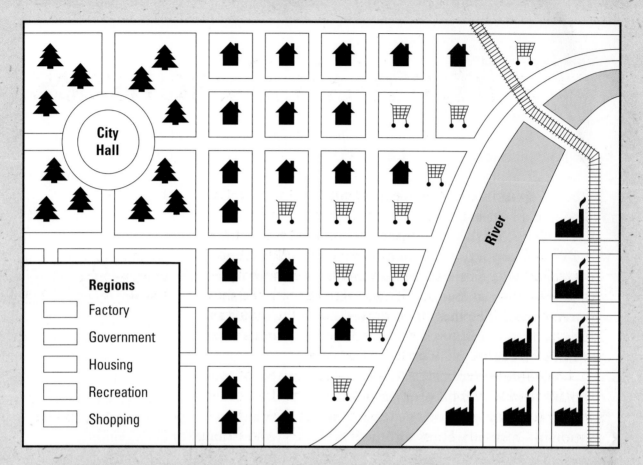

2. Which geographic region receives more precipitation, the northern mountains or the Central Valley?

3. Suppose you want to visit one of California's beaches. Will you find more sunshine on the northern or the southern coast? How do you know?

4. How do you think the different amounts of precipitation that fall in each geographic region affect the regions' plant life?

Apply It

Above is an outline map of an imaginary city. The pictures on the map stand for the activities that take place in different areas of the city.

Make a copy of the map and its legend. Then draw boundaries for these five regions: factory, government, housing, recreation, and shopping. Choose colors to stand for each region, and color in each region on your map. Be sure to show on the legend which color stands for each region. Give your map a title.

Use the following questions to help you decide where to draw boundaries for the five different regions.

1. Where are the shopping areas on the map? Choose a color to stand for this region of the city.

2. Parks are places people visit for recreation. Where are the parks located on the map? What color will you choose for the recreation region?

3. The mayor meets with city leaders at City Hall. What will you call this region of the city?

4. Where are the factory and housing areas on the map? What colors will you choose for these regions?

California's Resources

Mount Lassen went off with a bang. The California volcano erupted in a series of explosions between 1914 and 1917. It threw out tons of hot ash, boulders, and melted rock called lava. The boiling lava melted the snow at the top of Mount Lassen. It made the earth beneath the snow turn into mud. The thick mud flowed down the mountainside like a river. It mowed down miles of trees in its path and filled meadows with up to 20 feet of mud.

The explosion of Mount Lassen is an example of the fiery forces felt along the "Ring of Fire." The Ring of Fire, shown on the map below, is a large crack in the earth's crust. Volcanoes are formed when hot liquids burst through this crack and force a hole in the surface of the earth. These fiery volcanoes give the ring its name. Earthquakes happen when the sides of the crack move and rub against each other. This makes the ground tremble and quake. Places along the Ring of Fire, including the state of California, feel and see these quakes and fires.

Mount Lassen's inner fires still burn. But California's other volcanoes have all cooled down. Earthquakes, on the other hand, are still common. Over millions of years, earthquakes have changed California's surface with their powerful force.

THINKING FOCUS

What natural resources are found in California?

Key Terms

- mineral
- natural resources
- human resources

◄ *Mount Lassen exploded on June 14, 1914.*

21

Geography of California

Mining California's Resources

Across Time & Space

Thousands of years ago, great sheets of thick ice from the North Pole moved down and covered much of North America, including California. These ice sheets, sometimes thousands of feet thick, are called glaciers. Because of changes in the earth's climate, the glaciers grew and shrank several times. Each time, they left their mark on the land. They carved out valleys, rounded the sides of mountains, and left large pools of melted water that became lakes.

■ *How did changes in the land help to create California's natural resources?*

➤ *Many important minerals and other goods come from California.*

Millions of years ago, much of California was under water. In fact, you can still find seashells and whale bones on the tops of some of California's highest mountains. The same forces that make earthquakes today pushed mountains like the Sierra Nevada up out of the ocean long ago.

The heat and force that changed the land also caused substances like oil and other minerals to form underground. **Minerals** are natural substances usually found by digging in the ground. California is rich in minerals. Each year, the state's oil fields pump out more than 365 million barrels of oil. Many other minerals, such as gold, copper, iron, clay, and borax lie among layers of rock and earth in California. Borax is a type of salt used in laundry detergent. It is mined from the hot earth of Death Valley.

Minerals are some of California's natural resources. Materials that are found in nature and can be used by people are called **natural resources.** The map below shows a few of California's most important natural resources.

California's 28 million people use many of its natural resources. But people are resources too. They are **human resources.** Everyone who can do a job or service is a human resource. You are one of California's human resources. ■

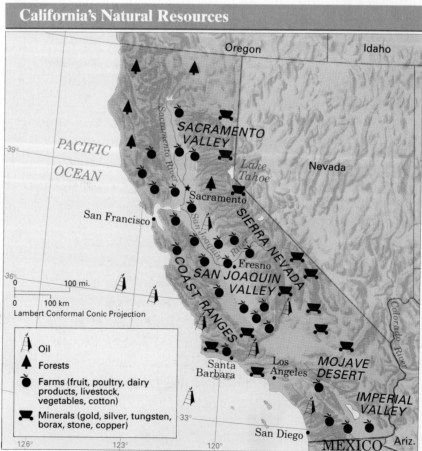

California's Natural Resources

Legend:
- Oil
- Forests
- Farms (fruit, poultry, dairy products, livestock, vegetables, cotton)
- Minerals (gold, silver, tungsten, borax, stone, copper)

0   100 mi.
0   100 km
Lambert Conformal Conic Projection

UNDERSTANDING HUMAN RESOURCES

*D*id you know that you are a resource? So is Nancy MacLean, the ship's lookout. So is Mojave leader Llewelln Barrackman.

You have just read about some of the natural resources that people can use and enjoy. But people are resources as well. We call them human resources.

The term "human resources" has to do with the value, or importance, of people. Every person is valuable in some way. So all Californians are a part of the state's human resources. That includes everyone from bankers to bee-keepers. It includes scientists, ballet dancers, janitors, children, basketball players, dentists, and teachers. Some of California's human resources help to develop its natural resources. People are needed to drill for oil, for example.

The skills and talents people provide make them valuable resources. But you don't have to have a job to be

a good resource. People are also important for how they help their friends, family, or community. They are valuable for their ideas, sense of humor, kindness, or honesty. California's interesting mix of people makes the state rich in human resources.

Caring for California's Resources

Some of California's natural resources are probably around you right now. Think of sunshine, for example. Sunshine, soil, and water are resources that help living things grow. These living things, including some plants and animals, are resources too. Some of these resources are important not only when you use them, but also when you leave them alone. California's forests are a good example. Each year, thousands of people come to see the mighty sequoias *(sih KWOI uhz)*. They are the largest and one of the oldest kinds of trees on earth. Sequoias can grow as high as 30-story buildings and as wide as trucks. They can live for thousands of years.

But trees are not just beautiful to look at. They provide homes for wildlife like birds, deer, beavers, and bears. When a fire burns down a large forest, many animals lose their homes. A Moment in Time on the next page tells about smokejumpers, the firefighters of the forest who risk their lives to save trees and animals.

▲ *The cones of the giant sequoia are only two to three inches long, and the seeds they carry weigh less than a feather. From these tiny seeds grow the largest trees on earth.*

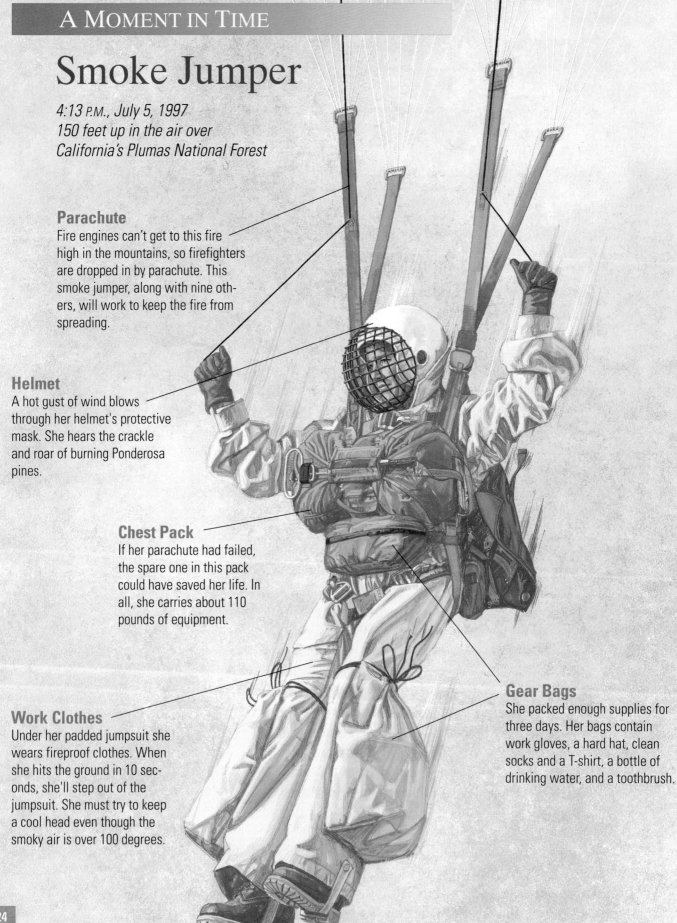

Smoke Jumper

4:13 P.M., July 5, 1997
150 feet up in the air over
California's Plumas National Forest

Parachute
Fire engines can't get to this fire high in the mountains, so firefighters are dropped in by parachute. This smoke jumper, along with nine others, will work to keep the fire from spreading.

Helmet
A hot gust of wind blows through her helmet's protective mask. She hears the crackle and roar of burning Ponderosa pines.

Chest Pack
If her parachute had failed, the spare one in this pack could have saved her life. In all, she carries about 110 pounds of equipment.

Work Clothes
Under her padded jumpsuit she wears fireproof clothes. When she hits the ground in 10 seconds, she'll step out of the jumpsuit. She must try to keep a cool head even though the smoky air is over 100 degrees.

Gear Bags
She packed enough supplies for three days. Her bags contain work gloves, a hard hat, clean socks and a T-shirt, a bottle of drinking water, and a toothbrush.

◄ *A person seems very small compared to the towering trees of Redwood National Forest.*

The wood from trees is another natural resource. Wood is used for making everything from houses to paper to pencils. But even though we need wood for so many uses, it's still important to leave some forest land natural and untouched. This way, people in the future will be able to enjoy the beauty of the forests too. And they will have enough trees to meet their needs for wood as well.

Agriculture and Water

Another important resource is California's rich farmland. Agriculture brings more than 16 billion dollars to the state each year. This is from fruit and vegetables, dairy products, cotton, cattle, nuts, and grain. The Central Valley and the Imperial Valley are the two main farming regions.

Trees, crops, animals, and people all depend on one of California's most important natural resources—water. People use fresh water for drinking, bathing, washing their clothes and dishes, and for many other needs. California is a very dry state, so people have to take care not to use too much water. Just as people must save the forests for others to use and enjoy in the future, they must also take care of the water and keep it clean and plentiful. ■

■ *Why are trees a resource to be used and protected?*

R E V I E W

1. **FOCUS** What natural resources are found in California?

2. **CONNECT** Why is the climate of California a natural resource?

3. **HISTORY** Why can you find seashells on some of the mountaintops of the Sierra Nevada?

4. **CRITICAL THINKING** In what ways do you think people might be a danger to California's forests?

5. **ACTIVITY** Bring to class an item that uses one of California's natural resources. Explain why you chose that item.

25

Geography of California

A Valley or a Dam?

M y heart weeps when I see giant redwoods that have stood since before the arrival of the Spanish explorers falling to the saws and axes of the lumber companies.

Naturalist John Muir

S hould San Francis- coans curtail [shorten] their Satur- day night bath to make sure that John Muir and his nature-loving friends can go for a pleasant walk in the woods? We think not.

S. F. Chronicle

▼ *Below, John Muir (on right) stands with President Theodore Roosevelt. Muir took many important leaders on tours of the Yosemite Valley. He wrote letters to newspapers to tell people about the need to save the nation's natural resources.*

Background

John Muir loved nature so much that in 1867 he took a 1,000-mile walking trip from Indiana to the Gulf of Mexico. Along the way he collected plants, made drawings of them, and described them in his notebooks. Muir's nature studies also took him on trips through North and South America, Australia, and Africa.

But Muir is most widely known for his work in California's Yosemite Valley. His studies showed that all living things depend on each other to live. He believed that harming one form of life could someday harm all living things. Muir saw that the Yosemite Valley was in danger. Lumber companies were cutting down trees like redwoods and giant sequoias that had stood for hundreds of years.

Muir started a project to set aside Yosemite as a protected area. As a result, in 1890 Yosemite became one of the country's first national parks.

Conflict Over the Land

Not everyone shared Muir's views about the best use of land and resources. In 1900, the city of San Francisco asked the United States government to build a dam in the Hetch Hetchy Valley of Yosemite. The big concrete dam would trap the waters of the Tuolumne River. That would cause water to build up behind the dam, creating a reservoir. San Francisco wanted the water that the reservoir would hold. The growing city feared it could not survive without the new water supply from the Hetch Hetchy Valley.

Muir, of course, was strongly against the plan. The dammed-up water would flood the valley, destroying the land and trees that provide homes for millions of animals and birds. He suggested that the city find some other source of water. In 1908 the citizens of San Francisco voted in favor of the dam. The national government also said yes to the plan. San Francisco got the water it needed to grow. But a beautiful natural resource disappeared forever.

▲ Today the Hetch Hetchy Valley is flooded with the waters of the Tuolumne River, above.

Decision Point

1. What was the argument in favor of building the dam?
2. What was the argument against building the dam?
3. If you had been a San Francisco citizen in 1908, what information would you have wanted to vote wisely on the issue?
4. Imagine that your community today were running out of water. It needed to destroy a nearby natural resource to find a new water supply. What action would you want to take as a citizen?

Should the Hetch Hetchy dam be built?

New water supply for San Francisco allows city to grow.

Dam floods valley, destroying major area of natural beauty.

Build the dam.

Look for a different water source for San Francisco.

▲ The O'Shaughnessy Dam was finished in 1923.

27

Chapter Review

Reviewing Key Terms

border (p.6)
climate (p.14)
continent (p. 5)
geography (p.13)
globe (p.5)

human resources (p.22)
mineral (p.22)
mountain range (p.16)
natural resources (p.22)
region (p.13)

A. Choose the key term that best completes each sentence.

1. Because it is round, a _____ cannot show all the lands and oceans of the world at the same time.
2. Part of the _____ between the United States and Mexico follows the natural line of the Rio Grande.
3. The Central Valley is a _____ of rich farmland and vineyards.
4. Flat deserts, high mountains, and rocky coasts are some examples of California's _____.
5. Borax is a _____ mined from the earth in Death Valley.
6. A _____ is a long row of mountains.

B. Write the key term that describes each group of words below:

1. North America, Europe, Africa
2. cool and damp, warm and sunny, hot and dry
3. scientists, farmers, children
4. oil, wood, sunshine

Exploring Concepts

A. Copy this chart on a separate paper. Add a new column in which you write the answers to the questions about California.

Information About California	
Location	Where is California located?
Region	What regions does it have?
Climate	What is its weather like?
Natural Resources	What are some of its natural resources?
Human Resources	What are some of its human resources?

B. Write one or two sentences to answer each question below. Use details from this chapter to support your answers.

1. What information do maps and globes give you about the earth?
2. What two large countries share a border with the United States?
3. What makes each of California's four geographic regions a special place?
4. How have fiery forces within the ground changed California?
5. What natural resources does California need to grow crops?

Reviewing Skills

1. Read the paragraph below. Which sentence gives the main idea of the paragraph? Which sentences give details that support the main idea?

   The plants and animals of California's desert region have special ways of getting the water they need. A type of bush, called the mesquite bush, has roots almost 40 feet long, which it uses to find water deep underground. The kangaroo rat uses its large nose to gain back moisture from its own breath. Other desert animals get water from the plants they eat.

2. Look at the United States vegetation map on page 330 of the Atlas. This map shows the kinds of vegetation, or plant life, that grow in different areas of the United States. Use the map and the map legend to answer the following questions: How many regions are shown on the map? How do you know? What color stands for the grassland region? What color stands for the forest region?

3. One of the vegetation regions is called the tundra. What kind of book would tell you what the word *tundra* means? Where could you look to find out more about the plants of this region?

Using Critical Thinking

1. Why do you think it is important for people to take care of California's natural resources?

2. Each year thousands of people visit California. Explain why someone might want to visit your area.

3. Which of California's natural resources might other states use?

4. The space shuttle lands at Edwards Air Force Base in the California desert. Why do you think the desert is a good place for the shuttle to land?

Preparing for Citizenship

1. WRITING ACTIVITY Make a postcard of a place in California that you would like to visit. On the front, draw a picture of the place. On the back, write three sentences describing the area. Beside this message, write the name and address of a person who might like to receive your postcard.

2. ART ACTIVITY Build a clay model of California. First trace a map of California onto a piece of poster board. Use this outline map as a base for your model. Show the physical features of California's geography. Include mountains, deserts, lakes, and rivers. Look at the map of California on page 329 of the Atlas for the information you need.

3. COLLABORATIVE LEARNING Work as a class to make a map quiz game. Use the maps of the United States on pages 322-327 of the Atlas. Each person in the class should write two questions about the maps. Include questions such as the following: What states are on the West Coast of the United States? How many states share a border with California? What is the capital of Montana? Choose one person to ask the questions. Players can use the map to answer the questions.

Chapter 2
The First Californians

The lives of the earliest Californians were closely connected to the natural world. Their ceremonies revolved around the seasons, the sky, and the earth. Today, scientists learn about these early people by studying the objects they used.

A woman brought gifts such as baskets from her family when she married. Baskets were valued objects, and some were used during ceremonies.

Many ceremonies were first performed thousands of years ago. Some Indian leaders wore feather hats and capes during these ceremonies.

14,000 YEARS AGO	12,000 YEARS AGO	10,000 YEARS AGO	8,000 YEARS AGO

9,000 YEARS AGO Hunting families live in southeastern California.

14,000 YEARS AGO

The 1,200-year-old painting below gives clues about what life for the early Californians might have been like.

The 300-year-old Mojave clay figure at right shows a baby in a woven cradle.

6,000 YEARS AGO	4,000 YEARS AGO	2,000 YEARS AGO	TODAY

6,000 YEARS AGO California Indians use milling stones to grind seeds to eat.

1769

Discovering the First Californians

Key Terms

- strait
- archaeologist
- tribe

► *A museum scientist examines Ice Age bones for an exhibit at La Brea Pits.*

D awn breaks over the land. The night shadows begin to disappear from the grassy valley, and sunlight spreads across a wide lake. From out of a thick clump of trees steps a huge animal. What could it be? It looks like a brown elephant with woolly hair and enormous tusks. Its long trunk swings back and forth as it lumbers toward the lake to drink. The animal is a mammoth. Close by it, a herd of deer grazes peacefully.

Suddenly, a low snarl breaks the stillness. A saber-toothed tiger has come to hunt. Its long teeth gleam in the morning light. The mammoth lifts its huge head and trumpets a warning. The tiger leaps from its cover and races toward the deer. They spring away from the tiger and dart to safety.

Animals like these lived in southern California about 40,000 years ago. But no people lived in California then.

The First People Arrive

Today it is hard to imagine California without people. But for millions of years only animals lived in North America. Then, about 12,000 years ago, some hunters arrived in what is now California. The timeline on the next pages shows how long ago that was. Those early hunters were descendants, or later relatives, of people who had come to North America by land from Asia.

You could not make this trip by land today. Asia and North America are now separated by a part of the Pacific

Early hunters in California used spears like this one.

What natural features are pictured on the map below?

Ocean called the Bering Strait. A **strait** is a narrow passage of water connecting two larger bodies of water. During the Ice Age, a period of time between two million and 12,000 years ago, the Bering Strait did not exist. Instead, a grassy plain connected the two continents. People and animals could cross this plain from Asia to North America on foot.

The people who came across the land bridge from Asia hunted giant moose, antelope, and even mammoths. They depended on these animals for food. As the animals roamed from place to place in Asia, the hunters and their families followed them. When some of the animals wandered across the land bridge to North America, some of the hunters moved too.

Slowly these hunters made their way southward across North America. They finally reached many different areas of the continent, as the map on this page shows. Among these people were the first Californians. They settled in all of California's regions—in northern mountains, in its river valleys, along the coast, and in drier areas of the southwest. ■

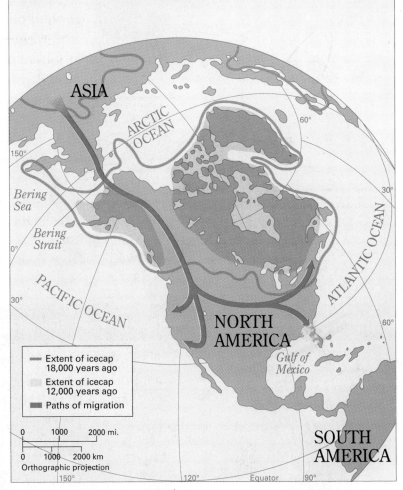

People Move to North America

ASIA

ARCTIC OCEAN

60°

150°

Bering Sea

Bering Strait

0°

PACIFIC OCEAN

30°

30°

NORTH AMERICA

ATLANTIC OCEAN

60°

Gulf of Mexico

SOUTH AMERICA

— Extent of icecap 18,000 years ago

Extent of icecap 12,000 years ago

■ Paths of migration

0   1000   2000 mi.

0   1000   2000 km

Orthographic projection

150°   120°   Equator   90°

■ *Why did people from Asia cross into North America?*

33

Scientists Find Clues to Early Life

➤ *The figure of the hunting woman was carved from whale bone. She was made by a descendant of the first people to come to North America.*

There are no written records of what life was like for these early people of North America. But there are many clues to how they lived. Scientists called **archaeologists** *(ahr kee AHL uh jihsts)* look for clues that will help them understand how people once lived. Archaeologists carefully dig and sift through layers of earth. They search for objects made and used by people who lived long ago. These objects may include bits of pottery, beads, or spear points. Then archaeologists try to decide how early people used these objects. A stone with one chipped edge might have been used to cut meat or scrape animal skins. A stone bowl might have been used to grind seeds and nuts or to hold food. A shell necklace might tell what people wore and what they valued.

Like detectives, archaeologists try to solve mysteries. In 1970, an archaeologist named Stuart Streuver led an important dig in Illinois. Workers there found large, dark, round marks on the surface of the earth. Streuver had studied marks like these before. He knew that the marks showed where wooden posts

➤ *For hundreds of years hunters from the anorthern part of Alaska have used knives like this one to cut and scrape meat.*

12,000 years ago | **10,000 years ago** | **8,000 years ago**

15,000-12,000 years ago
Asian hunting groups cross a bridge of land into Alaska. They become the first people in North America and begin to travel southward.

9,000 years ago
The early hunters appear in California. They make and use sharp stone tools and spear points.

7,000 years ago
Wandering tribes begin to collect plants and seeds. They now no longer depend on hunting alone to obtain their food.

had once stood to hold up the walls of early Indian houses. But he had never seen marks this big before. Streuver told the workers about the importance of their find.

> **D**o you realize that you have just discovered the earliest permanent homes in North America? Earlier dwellings have been found, but the post holes were very small, indicating that they were for temporary shelters. These guys, back in 5,000 B.C. [about 7,000 years ago] were cutting down tree trunks measuring eight to ten inches in diameter for those posts. Nobody in his right mind would spend that kind of labor for a temporary shelter. These buildings were meant to last for years!

This discovery helped Streuver understand that these early Indians had given up their life of roaming from one hunting ground to another and had settled in one place.

At times archaeologists are stumped by the clues they find. In the southeastern California desert, they are puzzled by some large circles where rocks are cleared from the ground. Some archaeologists think that the circles were used for religious events. Others think the sites were camping places for early hunters. If more clues are found, the mystery of these circles may someday be explained. ■

People Live in Tribes

Archaeologists have studied places where early people lived to learn about their lives. The first people in California lived in villages along the coast or by rivers and streams.

6,000 years ago	4,000 years ago	2,000 years ago	Today

2,000 years ago
Indian peoples gather in permanent settlements. They make tools for special purposes from animal bones and horns.

500 years ago
Yurok and other tribes build sweathouses in their communities. Indians relax in steam-filled houses. Rituals and leisure time are important parts of their cultures. Christopher Colombus discovers the islands of the Caribbean and calls them "the Indies" The island people are called Indians by the European explorers.

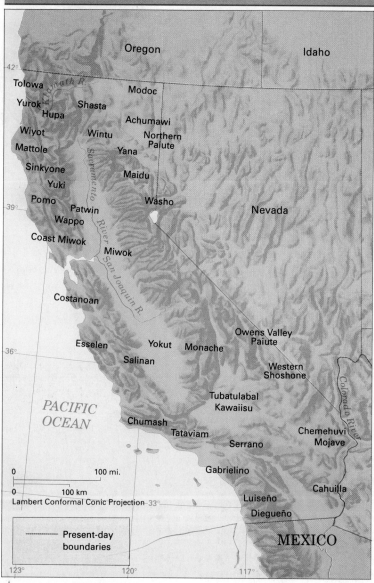

California Indian Tribes

Early villages had a few hundred or as many as a thousand people in them. As villages grew, there were not always enough animals or plants to supply them with food. So some people moved away and started new villages where they could find more food. Women and men often married others from nearby villages that were part of the same tribe. A group of people who live in the same area and are related to each other are called a **tribe**. The Yurok tribe, for example, lived in 50 villages scattered along the Klamath River and the Pacific coast. Members of a tribe also speak the same language and have similar religious beliefs.

By 1492, more than 100 tribes lived all over California, from the northern mountains to the southern deserts. The map on this page shows where some of the tribes were living in California at that time. The European explorers who came to the Americas then thought that they were in India. So they called the people they met Indians. These people are now sometimes known as American Indians. ■

▲ *Which tribes lived close to where you live now?*

■ *What is a tribe?*

R E V I E W

1. **FOCUS** How do archaeologists know about the first people who came to California?

2. **CONNECT** Compare the tribal map on this page with the map of California's regions in Chapter 1. In what region did the Pomo and Cahuilla (kuh WEE yuh) tribes live? What natural resources were available to each tribe?

3. **SOCIAL SYSTEMS** Most people today live in groups, but these are seldom called tribes. What are some groups of people that you are a part of?

4. **CRITICAL THINKING** Predict what archaeologists might think 1,000 years from now when they look at objects people used in the 1990s.

5. **WRITING ACTIVITY** Imagine you are an early Californian. Write a journal entry describing why you are clearing all the rocks from a large circle of desert ground.

LESSON 2

Living with the Land

*T*he New People made by Coyote found that the land was fair and that there was plenty of food. People learned to live by watching to see how the animals lived. From the Crane they learned to spear and eat fish. From Trout they learned how to swim. Deer taught the New People how to run fast. Ants taught them that much could be done by working together. Indian women watched the birds build their nests, and from this they learned how to weave baskets.

From all the creatures, great and small, the people learned how to live in the New Land. The people looked at the Sun and gave thanks for its light and warmth and for making things grow. They danced to give thanks for the world they lived in.

Helen Bauer, *California Indian Days*

THINKING FOCUS

Why did California Indians trade with other tribes?

Key Terms

* legend
* trade
* community

Indian children listened to their parents and grandparents tell stories like the one above. These stories, or legends, told of early events and important people in a tribe's history. A **legend** is a story handed down from adults to children over many years. It explains the beliefs of a people and the way they view their world. Many legends tell about how people and nature work together.

You will learn about how early people living in California used the natural resources of their regions. Each tribe's way of life depended on the plants, animals, and geography of the region where the tribe lived.

South American Indians used the natural resources in their lands to make this shield.

37

The First Californians

The Yurok: Salmon Fishers

In the northwestern corner of California, the Klamath River rushes from the mountains to the ocean. The redwood trees there once towered over the villages of the Yurok. The region provided rich natural resources for this tribe. The Yurok dug clams and caught fish from the sea. They also gathered berries and acorns for food. Another important source of food for the Yurok was salmon.

Each spring thousands of salmon raced up the Klamath River from the ocean. The first person to see them yelled out the news. Then everyone prepared for days of hard work. The Yurok used spears and weirs *(weerz)* to catch the salmon. A weir is a woven stick fence. The Yurok placed the weirs across the river to stop the salmon from leaping upstream. When many salmon had collected behind the weirs, the men speared the fish. Then the women cleaned the salmon, dried them in the sun, and stored them in baskets. After their work, the Yurok danced to give thanks for the salmon.

When the catch was finished, the Yurok traveled along the coast in redwood canoes and traded some of the salmon to other tribes. To **trade** is to give something to another person in return for something of theirs. The Yurok traded their dried salmon for dentalium *(den TAY lee uhm)* shells. Because the shells were hard to find, the Yurok valued them highly. Beads made from these shells served as money. A person owning several strings of dentalium shell beads was considered wealthy among the Yurok. The Yurok traded the beads and the salmon for soapstone bowls or tools they could not make from the resources in their region. Other California tribes also used these shells as money.

This lesson will tell a story about a string of shell beads. It begins with a Yurok girl who traded the beads for a flute. Many trades later, the beads

Redwood trees grow along the northwestern coast of California. The Yurok cut planks from the redwoods to build their houses. They also dug out redwood logs to make large canoes.

These dentalium shells were found along the northwestern coast of California. Many tribes used the shells as money. They carved the shells and strung them as beads. The longest strings of beads were most valuable.

came into the hands of a Chumash chief. The story will continue through the lesson as you learn about the trading life of various tribes in early California. ■

■ *What were the important natural resources for the Yurok?*

The Chumash: Master Boat Builders

The Chumash lived in villages along the California coast, near where Santa Barbara is today. The Chumash depended on the ocean, but not for salmon. They caught crabs and dug clams to eat. Otters swam near the coast, and the Chumash hunted them for their skins. They traded the otter skins to other tribes for tools or food.

Chumash villages were of different sizes. Some had as many as a thousand people. Each large village chose a leader, or chief. Several smaller villages might choose one chief to serve all of them together. A group of people living together under the same leader is called a **community**. The chief oversaw all that went on in the community. Outsiders had to ask permission from the chief when they wanted to hunt on the community's land. The chief was usually a man who had inherited, or taken over, the position from his father. But among the Chumash, if a chief had no sons, a daughter might serve as the next leader of her community when the chief died.

The Chumash had one resource that most other tribes did not have. On some of their lands, thick tar seeped up from out of the ground. The Chumash used the tar to seal the insides of baskets to make them waterproof. They also used tar to seal the cracks between the boards of large wood canoes.

The Chumash were the finest boat builders among California Indians. They called their canoes tomols *(TOH mohlz)*. There is a picture of one on this page. The Chumash gathered pieces of redwood they found washed up along the shore. Then they split the wood into boards to build the canoes. The Chumash paddled across the choppy Santa Barbara

▼ *The Chumash built canoes from redwood planks that they bound together with milkweed string. The seams between the planks were sealed with tar. Each canoe had at least one double–bladed redwood paddle. The canoes were decorated with colorful painting that reflected tribal legends.*

The First Californians

Channel to some islands about 30 miles away. There they traded otter skins for the island peoples' stone tools.

One day the Chumash chief who owned the shell beads heard that six Mojave *(moh HAH vee)* had come to his village to trade. The chief hurried to greet them, bringing the shell beads with him. He hoped to trade with the Mojave for something new and different. ■

■ *How did the Chumash use the natural resources where they lived?*

The Mojave: Desert Farmers

The Chumash chief knew that the Mojave lived far from the ocean, in a region very different from his own. He had heard stories of this hot, sandy land to the southeast. Scrubby pines and cactus plants grew along the trails and around the Mojave villages. The Mojave built large, rectangular houses with mud-covered grass roofs. The mud and grass kept the houses cool in the summer heat.

Although their region was very dry, the Mojave did have a source of water. The Colorado River flowed through some of their lands and was a very important resource. Every spring the river flooded its banks, leaving a fine layer of mud on the surrounding land. In this rich topsoil, the Mojave grew squash, melons, pumpkins, and corn. They were one of the four California tribes that raised crops along a river. If it did not rain enough in a certain spring and the river did not flood, the Mojave called for help from one of their people—a rainmaker. This person gathered the community together. He asked the sky spirits to send rain so that the crops would grow. The rainmaker sang prayers and danced.

The Mojave did not depend only on their crops. They fished from the wide river and hunted small game like rab-

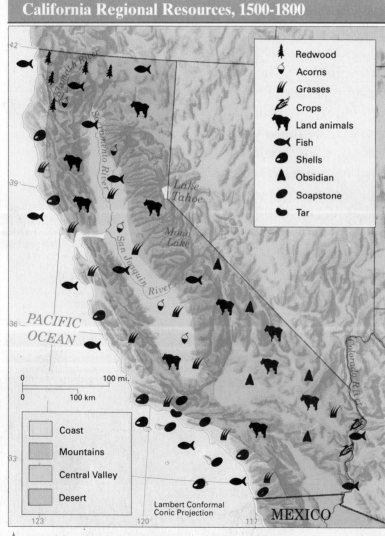

California Regional Resources, 1500-1800

Redwood
Acorns
Grasses
Crops
Land animals
Fish
Shells
Obsidian
Soapstone
Tar

PACIFIC OCEAN

Lake Tahoe
Mono Lake
Klamath River
Sacramento River
San Joaquin River
Colorado River
MEXICO

0   100 mi.
0   100 km

Coast
Mountains
Central Valley
Desert

Lambert Conformal Conic Projection

▲ *Which of the resources of the Chumash are unlikely to be found in the desert region?*

◄ *A farmer from the Hopi tribe in Arizona raises corn much like that grown by the Mojave.*

bits, mountain sheep, raccoons, and skunks. The Mojave also traded with other tribes for items they could not make from their desert resources, such as wooden bowls, horn spoons, and dentalium shell beads.

The Chumash chief met the traders and found that they had brought many foods from their desert lands. The traders carried dried yellow squash, corn, and pumpkins that they had grown. The chief traded the shell beads for two baskets of dried pumpkin, a delicious food that the Chumash could not obtain from their own lands.

The Mojave traders traveled on foot more than 150 miles to get back to their land in the southeastern desert. Along the way they stopped and traded with other tribes. The dentalium shell beads that had traveled from the northwestern corner of California, along the coast to the Chumash chief, finally found their way into the hands of a southern tribe living close to the Mojave land. The beads had moved from tribe to tribe, passing through regions that offered different resources. ■

■ *How did the Mojave differ from other California tribes?*

R E V I E W

1. **FOCUS** Why did California Indians trade with other tribes?

2. **CONNECT** How do you think archaeologists today know that the Yurok, the Chumash, and the Mojave traded with each other?

3. **CRITICAL THINKING** Look at the Resources Map on page 40. How did the California Indians use the food and nonfood resources pictured on this map?

4. **GEOGRAPHY** Use the map on page 328 of the Atlas to trace the route of the string of dentalium shell beads. Name some modern cities along the route.

5. **ACTIVITY** Make up a legend about how the Chumash learned to build canoes. Use animals from the region as main characters. Then tell your legend to the class.

Organizing Information

Here's Why

In this chapter you have learned how three Indian tribes used the natural resources found in their regions. Organizing this information on a chart will help you to remember the new facts you have learned.

Here's How

Look at the chart to the right. Three tribes are listed under the heading "Tribe." The next column has the heading "Food They Ate." The different foods each of the tribes ate are listed in that column. Look at the chart to answer these questions: Which tribe included vegetables in their diet? Which tribes had clams in their diet?

Try It

You can make your own charts to help you organize, compare, and remember information. Start by copying the chart above. Be sure to make each box large enough for all of the information. Now add three more columns with the headings "Ways They Traveled," "Trade: What They Gave," and "Trade: What They Received."

Now look back at pages 37-41. As you read, collect facts and include them in the appropriate columns on the chart. Then answer these questions:

Tribe	Food They Ate
Yurok	Clams, salmon and other fish, berries, acorns
Chumash	Crabs, clams
Mojave	Squash, pumpkins, melons, corn, fish, small animals

1. How did each tribe travel?
2. What did each tribe trade with the other tribes for items they wanted?
3. Which is the best title for your chart?
   a. How California Indians Lived
   b. Three Indian Tribes
   c. Ways of Living

Apply It

Imagine that you are planning a trip to another state. List three states you might like to visit in a column headed "State." Then include two more columns with these headings: "Climate" and "Places to Visit." You can find this information in the Atlas or in a travel guide. Give your chart a title. Based on what you have learned, which state would you most like to visit?

L E S S O N   3

Life in an Indian Village

A group of young children has gathered around a circle drawn in the hard earth. They are playing a game with a stone-tipped pole and two hoops. A child named Wokna twists the pole nervously in his hands. Then he raises it over his shoulder like a spear, ready to throw. Two children are standing on opposite sides of the circle, holding the hoops. At the same moment, they roll the hoops toward each other. Wokna watches the hoops about to pass in the middle of the circle. Not yet . . . not yet . . . NOW! He throws the pole with all his strength. The pole sails cleanly through both hoops at once. The other children give a loud cheer. Wokna smiles as he places a pebble on a stone to keep the score.

THINKING FOCUS

How did children learn from adults in a Miwok community?

Key Terms

- ceremony
- tradition

◄ *Miwok children played a hoop game like the one played at this Mojave village.*

Everyday Activities

The hoop and pole game prepared children to hunt with spears when they were older. Indian children learned many skills by playing games or by helping adults.

Look at the Miwok village pictured on the next page as you read about the people who lived there over 200 years ago. This village of Gualacomne (*gwah luh COHM nay*) was on the east bank of the Sacramento River. It was southeast of the Yurok territory and about 400 miles northwest of the Mojave lands. Oak woods bordered the river valley. Almost 200 people lived there in round-topped houses made of earth. These were scattered around a large community house, or roundhouse, and a sweatlodge.

Some Miwok had special jobs. One man made arrow points from a shiny, black stone called obsidian (*ahb SID ee uhn*). Miwok boys learned how to chip obsidian into sharp points by watching this man work. Other men spent much of their time spearing fish, making basket fish traps, or making bows. Boys learned these skills too. They also learned to make their own arrows from stalks of dry grass.

Miwok girls learned special skills as they helped their mothers. They gathered berries and nuts in the meadows and woods. Mothers taught their daughters which plants were good to eat and which were poisonous. The picture on the next page shows women along the shore rinsing baskets of acorn meal. They are washing the meal to remove its bitter taste. Other women near them are weaving baskets from grasses and reeds they gathered near the river. They use the baskets for gathering, cooking, and storing food. Older girls helped their mothers by caring for the younger children. They gave the little ones dolls that

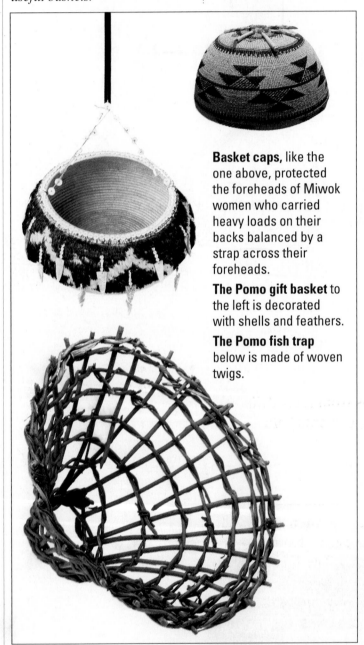

▼ *California Indians made many types of beautiful and useful baskets.*

Basket caps, like the one above, protected the foreheads of Miwok women who carried heavy loads on their backs balanced by a strap across their foreheads.

The Pomo gift basket to the left is decorated with shells and feathers.

The Pomo fish trap below is made of woven twigs.

were made from grasses or sticks.

Miwok children learned many skills from their daily activities. They also learned from special events held throughout the year. ■

Part of the Community

Ceremonies taught children much about their tribe and its way of life. A **ceremony** is a planned event that marks a special occasion like a wedding or holiday. The Miwok's northern neighbors, the Maidu (*MAY doo*), sang the song below during the fall. In a special ceremony, the Maidu asked the tribal spirits to bless the acorn harvest.

> The acorns come down from heaven.
> I plant the short acorns in the valley.
> I plant the long acorns in the valley.
> I sprout, I, the black acorn, sprout, I sprout.
>
> Maidu song recorded about 100 years ago

▲ What natural resources are the Miwok people in this picture using?

■ How would Mojave village activities differ from those of the Miwok?

45

The First Californians

Acorns

In the fall, oak trees shower acorns on the forest floor. All the Miwok helped collect acorns because they were such an important food for the tribe. They followed these steps to prepare acorns for a family meal.

Miwok families scooped acorns from the ground with these baskets. In one hour, a family of four people could collect over 250 pounds of acorns.

After cracking open the shell, the Miwok took out the acorn's meat. They pounded the meat between two rocks to make a paste called "chemuck." Then women placed the chemuck in a large basket and rinsed it with water to remove its bitter taste.

To cook the chemuck, the Miwok added hot stones and water to the basket. They had to stir the mixture quickly so that the rocks didn't burn holes in the basket. Finally, a family would eat out of one basket using shells or pieces of antlers as spoons. The chemuck was often eaten with pine nuts or juniper berries.

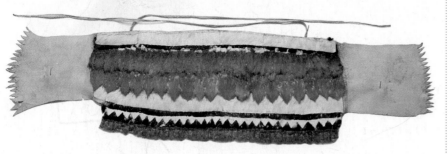

Like the Maidu, the whole Miwok community joined together to celebrate a good acorn harvest, a birth, or a marriage. During these gatherings children learned the traditions of their community. A **tradition** is a way of doing things that is handed down by older people to younger ones. Ways of dressing or of holding ceremonies are examples of traditions. People also keep their traditions by sharing songs, legends, and beliefs.

Several times each year the Miwok performed religious ceremonies that they hoped would bring them good supplies of food. The community gathered in a large roundhouse like the one pictured on page 45. There they watched dancers act out these ceremonies on a dirt floor covered with willow branches. Dancers wore colorful bird-feather headbands. The Indians used bird feathers in their ceremonies because they believed that birds had special powers. The dancers shook rattles made from pieces of dry wood split halfway down the center. The two halves clapped together as the dancers shook them. Other people stomped on hollow foot drums to beat a rhythm for the dancers. The drums were made by setting flat wooden planks over holes in the ground.

For many hundreds of years, the California Indians kept the traditions of their communities. They could not know how much their lives would soon change. ■

Across Time & Space

Today many Miwok live in communities called rancherias (rahn chai REE uhs). The Tuolumne (too AHL uh nee) Rancheria is a small group of Miwok families who live modern lives while keeping many of their traditions. The community still uses sweathouses and a dance house. But the Miwok have also built a modern tribal council building and a medical-dental clinic.

■ *How do the traditions and ceremonies of the Indians show their closeness to the natural world?*

R E V I E W

1. **FOCUS** How did children learn from adults in a Miwok community?
2. **CONNECT** If archaeologists were to uncover a Miwok village like the one pictured on page 45, what might they find?
3. **CULTURE** Describe the steps California Indians used to prepare acorns to eat.
4. **CRITICAL THINKING** Think of a ceremony your family attends or one of your family's own traditions. Describe this ceremony or tradition and compare it to those of your classmates' families.
5. **ACTIVITY** Look at the picture of the baskets on page 44. Choose one and draw a picture showing how the Miwok would have used that basket.

How Coyote Put Fish in Clear Lake

Anne B. Fisher

Where did the stars come from? What causes earthquakes? Indian legends answer these questions and many others about people and nature. These tales have been told for thousands of years. As you read the Pomo story of Coyote and the grasshoppers, ask yourself, "What parts of nature does this legend explain?"

Like the Miwok people you read about in Lesson 3, the Pomo tribe lived in northwestern California.

drought (drowt) a long period with no rain

Once long ago a terrible drought came over the land. Indians danced and danced for the Keeper of Rain, but nothing happened. Medicine Men sang chants for rain, but no rain came.

Lakes dried up. Creeks dried up. Rivers dried up.

Hawks flew with beaks open in the hot sun, their throats aching with thirst.

Blue-jays scolded from the tops of sun-scorched trees because there was no water.

Frog's throats were too dry to croak.

Then came more trouble! A great swarm of noisy brown grasshoppers arrived. So many grasshoppers came in a great cloud that they shut off the sun and the sky was dark. They rubbed their wings and feet together and made a "Zing-Zizz" that frightened Indian babies.

Grasshoppers "Zing-Zizzed" all over the land and ate up grass so the Indians couldn't collect seeds to grind into mush which they called *too*.

Indian babies cried for food. Indian fathers and mothers went hunting for game and nuts and berries. But the berries and nuts had dried up. Deer had gone away. There were no fishes because lakes and rivers were all dry.

Coyote was roaming the land, hunting for food and just one tiny sip of water for his hot, dry throat.

"If this dryness keeps up and Sun is so hot," said he, "my whiskers will wither and blow away and my tail will get singed and I'll look a fright."

When he saw the skinny, starving Indians and their hungry babies he forgot about his own troubles. Coyote loved Pomo Indians and their children.

"There must be something to do about dry times—to bring food," he thought. "Great Spirit wouldn't want us all to be thirsty and hungry."

He sat on his haunches one day and looked high into the sky. He looked so high that his neck stretched out six inches longer than it usually was.

Coyote asked Great Spirit: "Please, won't you send us on earth a drink and some food?" And he waited for Great Spirit to whisper the answer back into his big yellow ear.

"Eat grasshoppers," Great Spirit told him. "They're very good to eat, even if they do make brown spots of juice on the grass and keep zizzing all the time."

"Ugh!" Coyote complained, "Grasshoppers don't sound like a good meal to me!"

"Grasshoppers are juicy," Great Spirit whispered back. "You can't tell by just looking at a thing how good it tastes. I sent grasshoppers to earth. I never send anything that cannot be useful one way or another. Eat them and see!"

Coyote shook his head. Grasshoppers looked very hard and bony to him. "They'll scratch all the way down," he grumbled.

"Stop thinking about your own stomach!" Great spirit said "You love the Indians. They are hungry and thirsty. You want to help them, don't you?"

Coyote had to admit that the cries of Pomo children kept him awake nights and made his heart ache.

"Then eat grasshoppers for *them*, if not for yourself," Great Spirit told Coyote. "Miracles happen when beings do things they don't want to do—for the sake of others."

Just then Coyote heard the pitiful cry of an Indian boy who was thirsty and hungry.

He took a great breath and held his long nose with one paw, while he grabbed for those zizzing grasshoppers with the other.

Quick, down went those scratchy grasshoppers into his gullet. Coyote gulped a great gulp and swallowed them whole.

singed (sihnjd) burned

gullet throat

They weren't so bad after they were down and they did make his empty stomach feel better, but they scratched and tickled his insides.

"Take more grasshoppers!" Great Spirit urged. "The more you eat the more seeds will grow for Indian mush."

Coyote made a face, took a great breath, and grabbed pawful after pawful of grasshoppers and swallowed them whole until his stomach felt tight.

The grasshoppers did a lot of wiggling inside him. He looked around and found a few more grasshoppers. He thought of Indian children and their hunger for mush—but he just couldn't eat any more grasshoppers.

"I've done the best I can for Indians by eating grasshoppers so that grasshoppers can't keep eating seeds," he told Great Spirit. "I just can't swallow one more."

Great Spirit whispered back to him. "You have done well, Coyote. Never mind the few zizzers that are left. Look over your shoulder now at the dry spot where Clear Lake used to be."

Coyote was so full of grasshoppers that it was hard to move the least bit. But he wiggled and he groaned and twisted. Finally he managed to look over his left shoulder.

There—in the middle of the dry hole that had once been a lake—was a damp spot, a little bubbling spring!

"Now, go and dig at that spring," Great Spirit told him. "As you dig, more water will come—enough for all Pomo Indians."

"But I can't move!" Coyote complained. "I'm too full of grasshoppers. They're scratching my stomach."

"Thinking of your stomach again!" Great Spirit said sadly. "You don't love Pomos as much as I thought you did—or you would bestir yourself to bring them water and food."

Just then Coyote heard an Indian baby, Kulot, cry out for food and water.

He thought about that hungry Kulot and forgot his heavy stomach full of grasshoppers. He kept thinking how many people would be helped if he could get to the spring and dig.

So, he slid along on his stomach. He pushed hard with his legs. He strained every muscle in his back and slowly inched nearer and nearer to the little spring.

Whenever Coyote thought of himself, he couldn't move. But when he thought of the poor Indians, he could move

bestir move

faster. New strength came to him as if there were a mysterious spring bubbling up inside his own body.

"That's how miracles happen," Great Spirit whispered. "I knew you had a big heart, Coyote—a heart big enough to forget yourself for others."

Coyote was cheered on. He wiggled. He squirmed. He pulled. He pushed with all his might toward the spring.

Finally at sundown, after much wiggling and pushing and squirming, Coyote reached the spring. Feebly, he began to dig.

feebly weakly

As he dug with his front paws, strength came into them so he could dig more. Soon water flowed fast in a great stream and he took a drink.

He wanted to run to the Indians and tell them, "I've found *water*!" But his stomach was heavy and he was tired from all the work he had done.

"I must—I *must* go tell the Indians," he groaned "Poor Pomos need water." He pulled and tugged, but his legs wobbled so he just couldn't run. He could take only one or two steps before he sank down exhausted.

"I see your heartache for the Indians. I will tell them and send them to the water," Great Spirit whispered."You have done your part well, Coyote."

Soon Indians came to the water—Indian boys and girls and men, and women carrying babies. They all drank and felt better. The ache left Coyote's heart.

When the Indians had gone back to their tule huts and all was quiet, Great Spirit came close to Coyote.

tule (TOO lee) reed

"Now, for the magic," he whispered. "Watch what happens to those few grasshoppers you couldn't eat."

Coyote kept very still and watched. He saw the grasshoppers come to the little shining lake he had dug so Indians could drink. The grasshoppers flew over the lake with a zizzing sound. They saw their reflection in the water. With a quick dart they all jumped into the lake and turned into beautiful shining fishes!

Further Reading

Earth Namer: A California Indian Myth. Margery Bernstein and Jane Kobrin. This is a Maidu Indian story about the creation of the world.

The People Shall Continue. Simon J. Ortiz. This tale follows the history of the Native American people from the beginning of time to today.

Chapter Review

Reviewing Key Terms

archaeologist (p. 34)   strait (p. 33)
ceremony (p. 45)   trade (p. 38)
community (p. 39)   tradition (p. 47)
legend (p. 37)   tribe (p. 36)

A. Write the key term that belongs with each definition below:
1. a narrow passage of water that connects two larger bodies of water
2. a story handed down from adults to children over many years
3. a planned event that marks a special occasion
4. a way of doing things that is handed down by adults to children
5. a group of people who are related to each other, live in the same area, and share the same language and religion
6. a group of people living under the same leader

B. Choose the key term that best completes each sentence.
1. To an _____, buried objects are clues about how people lived in the past.
2. The Chumash children listened to the _____ about how their people had learned to make canoes.
3. The California Indians often _____d shells for things they needed.
4. Today, Asia and North America are separated by the Bering _____.

Exploring Concepts

A. Complete the cluster diagram at the right on a separate piece of paper. Add two more details about how each tribe used the natural resources of their region.

B. Support each statement below with two details from this chapter.
1. Hunting was a way of life for California's first people.
2. Archaeologists use clues from the past to help them understand how early people lived.
3. The first Indians of California lived in tribes.
4. Although Indian tribes lived apart, they had contact with each other.
5. The Indians passed down their way of life to others in their family and tribe.

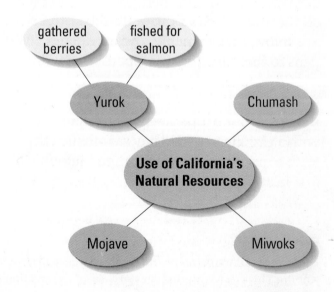

Reviewing Skills

1. Copy the table at the right on a separate paper. Head the third column "Houses." Fill in your table with information from this chapter. Then answer these questions: What two tribes lived in California's coastal region? Which tribe built houses made of wood?
2. Does the chapter tell what kind of houses the Chumash built? Where could you look for this information?
3. Reread the first paragraph of the legend on page 37. Which sentence tells the main idea of the paragraph? What details do the other sentences give to support the main idea?

Tribe	Region	
Yurok		
Chumash		
Mojave		
Miwok		

Using Critical Thinking

1. Each early Indian tribe in California had a different way of life. If you were an Indian of that time, in which tribe would you want to live? Why?
2. Members of Indian tribes depended on each other to live. How do family members depend on each other today?
3. "Nature is everything." What does that statement mean to you? What might it have meant to the first Californians?

Preparing for Citizenship

1. ART ACTIVITY Use an empty shoe box to make a diorama of California during the Ice Age. In your diorama, show what the land looked like 12,000 years ago and the kinds of animals that lived then. Lesson 1 in this chapter gives information about the mammoth and the saber-toothed tiger. Look in an encyclopedia to find out what each animal might have looked like.
2. INTERVIEWING Interview an older member of your family about one of your family's traditions. First have your family member describe the tradition. Then ask him or her questions such as when the tradition started, who started it, why it is important to your family, and how it has changed from year to year. Share what you find out from your interview with the class.
3. COLLABORATIVE LEARNING Make a Book of Days that illustrates holidays or other special events that members of the class celebrate with family and friends. First make a list of the celebrations you want to include in your book. Then work in small groups to illustrate each celebration. Include the dates of each event on your drawings, and write a paragraph for each drawing explaining how and why the celebration takes place. Collect all the drawings and put them in a notebook. Have one person make a cover for the book.

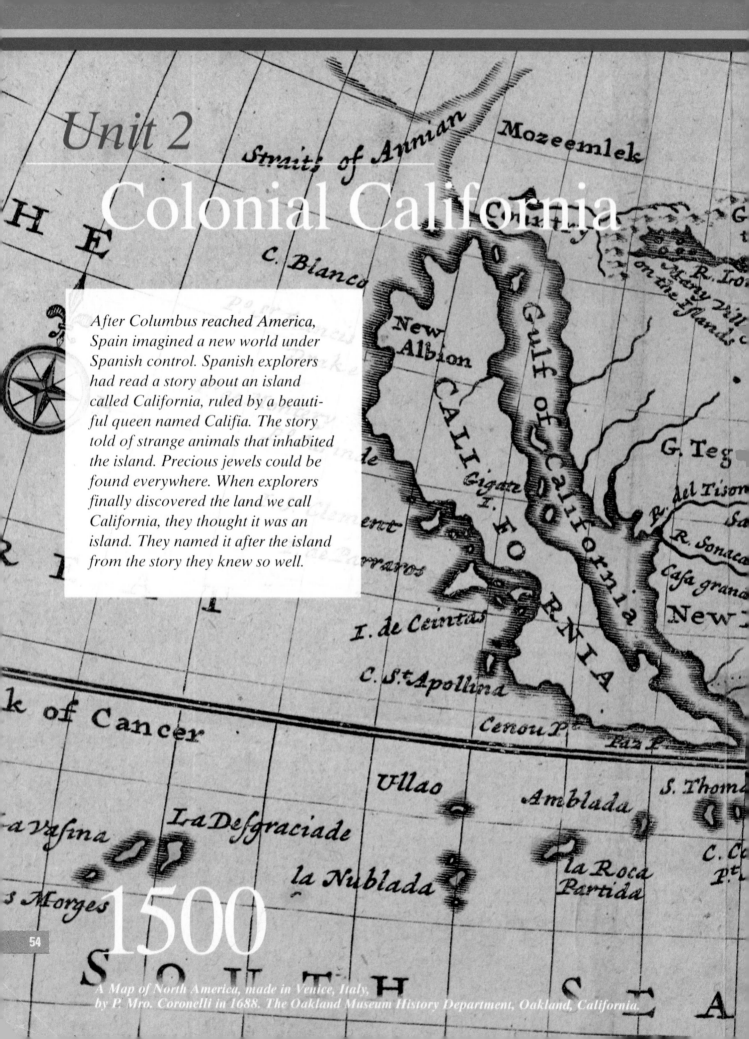

Unit 2
Colonial California

After Columbus reached America, Spain imagined a new world under Spanish control. Spanish explorers had read a story about an island called California, ruled by a beautiful queen named Califia. The story told of strange animals that inhabited the island. Precious jewels could be found everywhere. When explorers finally discovered the land we call California, they thought it was an island. They named it after the island from the story they knew so well.

1500

54

A Map of North America, made in Venice, Italy, by P. Mro. Coronelli in 1688. The Oakland Museum History Department, Oakland, California.

Sioux Lake

Nadouessis

Esana:

acsi:
res

que

Village
pes L.

Eko:
ros L.

Quirira

ato

ta Ke

Missouri R.

Many

Villages

Mexico

Cinaloa

Compo

rrientes
t Antonio

Zacatula

Orenta R.

Zamaroa R.

la Maligne

S. Lewis

R. de las Nassas

S. Sebastian
S. Iago
tello

Catalutla

Acapulco

P. Escondido
P. Angeles

Guatimala
S. Salvador
St Michel

North R.

Culiacan

MEXICO
or NEW

SPAIN

Nemepigon
Lake

Mino ny

UpperLake

Missilimakinac

Villages

Puants R.

Kikapous

Orentas
Itinese

Itinese

Mississipi R.

R. Rouge

R. de la Mobile
S. Lewis

S. Bernard B.

GULF of MEXICO

Panuco

R. Mexico

Tuspa
la Vera Cruz
Xiopa

Sn Sancto

P. Royal

C. Herita Mari

Viners I.

Monsoni

Sauteurs

Illinois

Huron
Lake

Savage
vil.

Oubach R.

R. des Cone.

haquei

English F.

CANADA

Toronto
Bay

L. S.

Errie L.

S. Sancto R.

Penfacola

Palaxy B.

Bernard B.

C. St Antonio

C. Conduedo

Bay of

Campechy

Campe

Quebec

Trois
Rivers
Mon

Quataris R.

Front
ac L.

Clare

S. Maria de
Palaxy

St Au
gustin

Tortugos

Havana

C. Caroche

Merida

of Honduras

Trux illa

valladoli

Nicaragua L.

Iroquois B
N
Y

Pen
filva

Mary
Lan

VIRGINI

Carolina
Charles
Town

Lookut

Alton He
St Matheo

Bahar

Bah

Andros

CUBA

Camanis

Camaron

Iamaica
P. Royal

NOR

Dios

Portobel
Sembla
Calid.

1850

55

Chapter 3

Spanish Explorers and Settlers

The California Indians lived peacefully on their land for thousands of years. Then, all of a sudden, things changed. Spanish soldiers and priests came to California. With them they brought different beliefs and a different way of life.

In the 1600s, southwestern Indians made this picture showing the arrival of the Spanish. Indians had never seen horses before.

1500	1550	1600	1650

1519

1602 Sebastian Vizcaino sails along the California coast to find a good harbor.

Indians hold onto many of their traditions and beliefs even while living at the missions. This painting by Ludovich Choris shows Indians performing a special dance.

Bells rang many times each day at the Spanish missions. They signaled the start of different activities.

During the 1800s, different kinds of money were used in California. An Indian made this English coin part of a necklace.

1750

1800

1850

1769 Father Serra starts the first mission at San Diego.

1832

Early Explorers

THINKING FOCUS

Why did Spain want to explore the California coast?

Key Terms

- expedition
- colony

A Spanish banner flutters from a tall mast. The banner opens to show a gold cross circled by white and blue flames. A group of sailors waits at the rails of the ship. Their eyes are on their leader, Hernando Cortés *(kor TEHZ)*. He stands on a barrel on the deck and stares at the sea out past the harbor. A short beard and dark hair frame his face.

Albert Marrin's book *Aztecs and Spaniards* contains a speech that Captain Cortés gave to his crew. "I know in my heart that we shall take vast and wealthy lands. . . . I offer you great rewards, although they will be wrapped about with great hardships. If you do not abandon me, as I shall not abandon you, I shall make you the richest men who ever crossed the seas."

It is February 10, 1519. Cortés orders the anchors hauled and the sails set. His 11 ships leave the island of Cuba. They head toward the open sea and sail west. They are traveling to a land the Indians call *Mexico*.

The sailors' hopes are high. They believe that they will serve God, bring glory to themselves and the King of Spain, and become rich.

➤ *This painting, made by Miguel Gonzalez (mee GEHL gahn ZAHL ez) in 1698, shows Cortés entering the capital of the Aztecs. A Spanish priest with a dark hat is next to him.*

58

Chapter 3

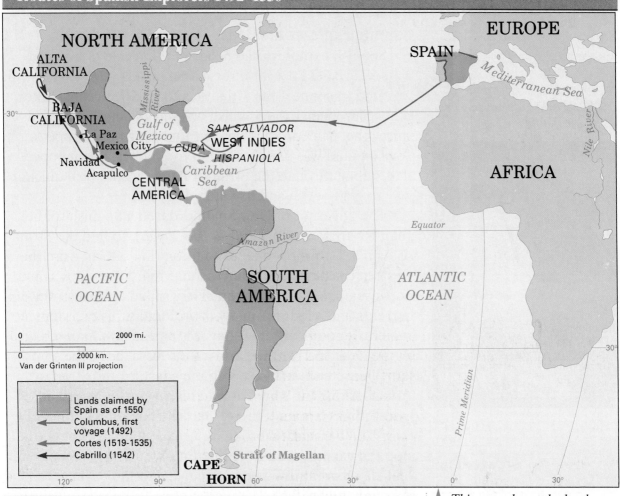

NORTH AMERICA

EUROPE

SPAIN

ALTA CALIFORNIA

Mississippi River

Mediterranean Sea

BAJA CALIFORNIA

Gulf of Mexico

SAN SALVADOR

La Paz

Mexico City

CUBA

WEST INDIES

Nile River

Navidad

HISPANIOLA

Acapulco

Caribbean Sea

AFRICA

CENTRAL AMERICA

Amazon River

Equator

PACIFIC OCEAN

SOUTH AMERICA

ATLANTIC OCEAN

0   2000 mi.

0   2000 km.

Van der Grinten III projection

Prime Meridian

Lands claimed by Spain as of 1550

Columbus, first voyage (1492)

Cortes (1519-1535)

Cabrillo (1542)

Strait of Magellan

CAPE HORN

This map shows the land claimed by Spain in North and South America during the 1500s. How were Cortés and Cabrillo helped by the voyages of Columbus?

Spain Starts a New Settlement

During the 1500s, Cortés was one of several Spanish explorers who sailed and marched to unknown lands. Ever since Columbus discovered the island of Hispañiola in 1492, Spanish explorers had made expeditions to North and South America. An **expedition** is a journey planned by a group of people for a clear reason.

Spain's main reason for sending expeditions to Mexico was to find lands rich with silver, gold, or other natural resources. Explorers had heard legends from the Aztec people who lived in Mexico. These stories moved the explorers to search for new lands. One legend told of the Seven Cities of Cibola (*see BOH lah*) that were said to lie far to the north of Mexico. The story told of cities so rich that the streets were paved with silver and gold.

Cortés found beautiful silver and gold treasures in the Aztec cities. The Spanish government started a colony in Mexico and ordered that all the riches found there had to be sent to Spain. A land controlled by another country is a **colony**. Spain called its colony New Spain.

59

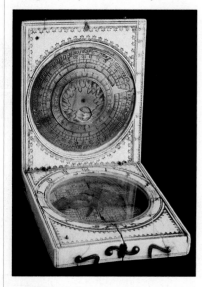

Spanish explorers of the 1500s used instruments like this compass to find their way.

Across Time & Space

Today the Panama Canal is a manmade Strait of Anián. The canal saves many ships from making the trip around the tip of South America. For more about the Panama Canal, see page 314 of the Minipedia.

■ *Why did Spanish explorers first come to North and South America?*

Cabrillo Explores the Coast

Spanish explorers had heard another tale of a narrow waterway called the Strait of Anián (*ah nee AHN*). The strait was said to connect the Atlantic and Pacific oceans. Like other Europeans, the Spanish wanted silk cloth, tea, and spices that came from Asia. But the trip from Europe to Asia by land was dangerous and took years. Spain hoped that sailing through the Strait of Anián would be a quicker way to get to Asia and its valuable goods.

The governor of New Spain ordered a Spanish soldier, Juan Rodríguez Cabrillo (*cah BREE yoh*), to find the Strait of Anián. Cabrillo led an expedition that set sail from the western coast of New Spain in June 1542. The ships sailed north searching for the strait. They sailed against strong currents and winds for many days. Finally, his two ships came to a good harbor. Today it is part of San Diego.

After exploring the harbor for several days, the ships left. They continued to search the coast for the Strait of Anián. Along the way, Cabrillo discovered some islands with Indians living on them. On the island of San Miguel (*mee GEHL*) Cabrillo broke his arm. But he did not let that stop the expedition. The ships continued as far north as present-day San Francisco. In January, Cabrillo's arm became infected and he died. The new captain followed Cabrillo's wish to explore the coast farther north. The sailors finally returned to New Spain without finding the Strait of Anián. But they were the first Europeans to visit the land the Spanish called California.

Galleons Sail for Riches

About 20 years after Cabrillo's expedition, traders from New Spain were making difficult voyages to southeast Asia. They crossed the Pacific Ocean to reach the Philippine Islands. The ships they used were called galleons. The traders loaded their galleons with silk, tea, and spices from the islands. Then they set out on a seven-month voyage back to New Spain. The galleons headed north from the Philippines to catch winds that carried them across the Pacific to the coast of California. They sailed south along that coast to a western harbor in New Spain. There the goods brought high prices from Spanish traders.

During these voyages sailors became sick and sometimes died. By the time traders reached California, they needed a settlement where they could get fresh water and food. But there were no settlements in California then. ■

Life on a Galleon

Heave ho! Crews of 60 to 100 sailors, some no more than 12 years old, worked on the Spanish galleons. Life was dangerous aboard these crowded ships. A sailor faced threats from storms, accidents, and even the food he ate.

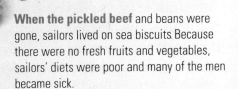

When the pickled beef and beans were gone, sailors lived on sea biscuits. Because there were no fresh fruits and vegetables, sailors' diets were poor and many of the men became sick.

After repairing sails sailors stood watch to protect the ship and its cargo of silk. Then the sailors went below to dry their clothes and get a few hours of rest.

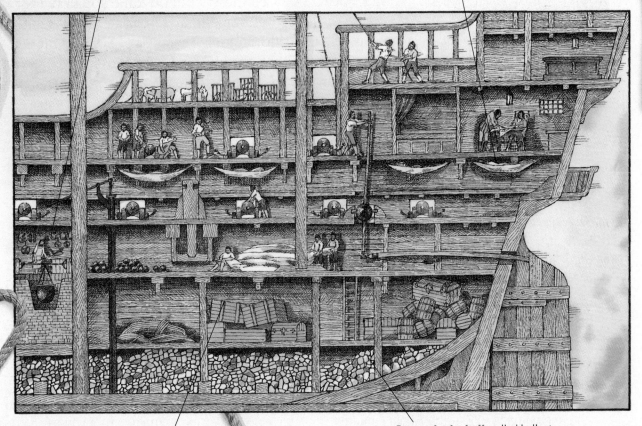

Rats and worms crawled into barrels of food in the hold. This section of the ship stored water, crates, ropes, sails, and even garbage. Younger crew members might be sent here for a punishment known as "holding."

Stones in the hull, called ballast, kept the galleon from turning over in rough seas. Dirty sea water collected here and had to be pumped out by the crew.

61

Drake Threatens New Spain

After 1570, England began to fight with Spain in the search to find the Strait of Anián and for the treasures Spain had found in Mexico. England's Queen Elizabeth I, sent the sea captain Francis Drake to attack Spanish ships and bring treasure back to England.

Drake raided Spanish galleons and settlements in New Spain. The Spanish called him The Dragon because of his quick attacks. From one galleon alone he took 26 tons of silver and 80 pounds of gold.

Pleased with the treasure Drake brought back to England, Elizabeth sent him on a round-the-world voyage. Drake battled fierce winds as he entered the Pacific Ocean through the Strait of Magellan. He raided Spanish galleons as he sailed north along the coast of South America.

➤ *Queen Elizabeth I showed her thanks to Drake by making him a knight.*

Finally, in 1579 Drake reached a fine harbor in northern California. He claimed the land around it for England. Then he sailed west across the Pacific to return to England.

This voyage threatened Spanish rule in the Pacific Ocean. Soon England was sending ships to the Pacific to trade in Asia. The Spanish had learned that they needed good harbors and settlements in California to protect their colonies from attack. ■

■ *Why did Spain feel threatened by Francis Drake?*

R E V I E W

1. **FOCUS** Why did Spain want to explore the California coast?

2. **CONNECT** Compare the map on page 59 with the one on page 328 of the Atlas. Find the name of the islands off the coast of California that Cabrillo discovered. What Indian tribe lived in the San Diego area at that time?

3. **ECONOMICS** Life was very hard for sailors on board Spanish galleons. Why did Spain keep sending ships to the Philippine Islands?

4. **CRITICAL THINKING** Why did England raid the Spanish galleons and not the Aztec villages?

5. **WRITING ACTIVITY** Imagine that you are a crew member on Cabrillo's voyage along the coast of California. Write two entries in your diary describing two things you see and do during the voyage.

Using Latitude and Longitude

Here's Why

Suppose you want to locate some of the places visited by the early Spanish explorers. You would use a globe or a map. The globes and maps you use today are marked with imaginary lines called lines of latitude and longitude. Learning how to use these lines will help you locate specific places more easily.

Here's How

You know that from a space shuttle, Earth looks like a round ball. Since globes are models of the earth, they are also shaped like balls, or spheres. The most northern point on the earth is the North Pole. It is found at the top of the globe. Find the North and South Poles on the two globes below. Where would the North and South Poles be found on a world map?

Now find the red line on the globe on the left. It is called the equator. The equator is an imaginary line that circles the earth from east to west. It divides the sphere-shaped earth into two half-spheres, or hemispheres. All the land and water north of the equator is called the Northern Hemisphere. All the land and water south of the equator is called the Southern Hemisphere.

Another imaginary line, called the prime meridian, runs from the North Pole to the South Pole. Find the prime meridian on the globe on the right. On the opposite side of the globe from the prime meridian is the International Date Line. Together, this line and the prime meridian make a circle around the earth that divides the earth into two more hemispheres. All the land and water that stretches west from the prime meridian to the International Date Line is known as the Western Hemisphere. What do you think the land and water east of the prime meridian is called?

The equator is a line of latitude, or a parallel. But it is not the only parallel. Find the equator on the globe on the next page. Then find the other parallels.

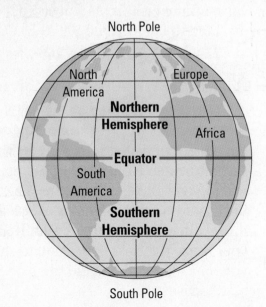

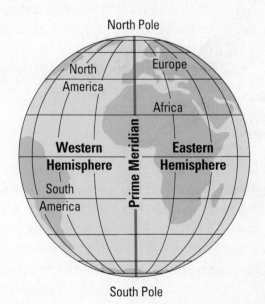

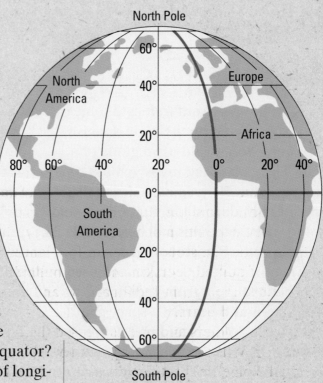

Parallels on globes and maps are numbered. The equator is labeled 0° (zero degrees latitude). The numbers of the other parallels show how far north or south of the equator they are. On the globe to the right, the first parallel north of the equator is 20°N (20 degrees north latitude). The first parallel south of the equator is 20°S (20 degrees south latitude). What other parallels on the globe to the right are north and south of the equator?

The prime meridian is a line of longitude, or a meridian. Find the other meridians on the globe above. They are numbered too. The prime meridian is labeled 0° (zero degrees longitude). On the globe above, the first meridian east of the prime meridian is 20°E (20 degrees east longitude). How is the first meridian west of the prime meridian labeled on the globe above?

You can locate any place on the earth by identifying its latitude and longitude. On the globe above, find the place where 20° north latitude meets 20° east longitude. On which continent is this place found? On which continent is the place at 20°S, 40°W located?

Try It

Maps also show lines of latitude and longitude. Use the world map on page 320 to answer these questions:

1. On his expedition around the world, Drake sailed from England across the Atlantic and around the tip of South America to California. Trace his route on the map. How many times did he cross the equator?
2. Was the colony of New Spain found in the Northern or the Southern Hemisphere?
3. In what two hemispheres would you find Spain? the Philippines?
4. Find the place at 40° north latitude and 100° east longitude. On which continent is this place located?
5. Find the place at 20°S, 140°E. On which continent is this place found?

Apply It

Use the world map on page 320 of the Atlas to plan a trip around the world. On a piece of paper, start a list by writing the latitude and longitude of the place where you will begin your trip. Then list the latitudes and longitudes of at least three other places you will visit. Read your list to the class. Ask them to show you on a map of the world the places you plan to visit .

L E S S O N 2

First European Settlers

About 200 years ago Spanish soldiers and priests began to settle California. Soldiers defended the expedition on horseback. They carried swords, pistols, and seven-foot lances. They wore jackets of quilted deerskin and used bullhide shields. These protected them from Indian arrows and the claws of mountain lions and bears.

Columns of soldiers and priests crossed the deserts and the mountains. Without maps, they cut new trails in a strange land. Sometimes food and water ran low. The soldiers could be defeated as easily by these conditions as by battles with Indians.

Spain Rediscovers Alta California

Spanish soldiers and priests did not march into California until nearly 227 years after explorers had claimed it for Spain. In fact, Spain had been more interested in finding a trade route than in settling the land. So Spain lost interest in

THINKING
F O C U S

Why did Spain want to settle Alta California?

Key Terms

- mission
- peninsula

◄ *A soldier sent on an expedition to Alta California in the 1700s looked like this. Horses carried many people and supplies for the expedition.*

California after explorers like Cabrillo failed to find the Strait of Anián. But in 1768, Spain learned that Russia wanted to build a colony in the region also. Then Spain acted quickly to settle the land it had claimed.

Don José de Galvez (*gahl VEHZ*), an official from New Spain, started an expedition. Galvez wanted to set up forts and missions near the harbors of San Diego and Monterey. **Missions** were settlements where priests from the Catholic Church taught their religious beliefs to the people nearby.

For 70 years, priests already had been teaching Christianity in the missions along the lower peninsula of California called the Baja (*BAH hah*). A **peninsula** is a finger of land that has water on three sides. Galvez hoped that setting up missions and forts in the upper region of California, called Alta California, would keep Russia and other countries from claiming the land.

Gaspar de Portolá (*pohr toh LAH*) was a governor of New Spain. He sent three expeditions that would start settlements in Alta California, beginning with San Diego. The first expedition left in three ships that sailed for San Diego from the Baja Peninsula in January 1769.

The two other expeditions set out for San Diego by land. Captain Fernando Rivera and Lieutenant Pedro Fages (*FAH hayz*) led one group. Portolá and Father Junípero (*hoo NEE peh roh*) Serra, a priest, headed the other. They

➤ *These gilded crosses are made from carved wood. They were made in Mexico in the 1700s. Crosses like these were brought with the padres to the new missions in California.*

▼ *The rocky coast of California provided few harbors for the explorers. Ships had no way of knowing the depth of the waters.*

traveled north along the Baja Peninsula carrying supplies on the backs of mules. Father Serra described the journey of 1769 in his diary:

After we passed one high mountain, another stood right in our way. We climbed up its slopes, hoping that from the summit we might be able to catch a glimpse of the ocean, only to be disappointed. From there we saw a shallow sort of valley, and then some hills and then a further chain of mountains just as high as the ones we had passed.

San Diego at Last

The journey was difficult for the other expeditions as well. The ships sailed close to the coast and were always in danger of hitting rocks. During the voyage, one ship sank with all its men and supplies, and four sailors on other ships died. Finally, two ships filled with sick sailors arrived in San Diego in April.

The land expedition led by Fages and Rivera arrived in San Diego in May of 1769. Several men had died. Many were sick from the long journey across the deserts and mountains of the Baja Peninsula. Portolá and Serra were the last to arrive in San Diego in early July. To celebrate their arrival, Father Serra built a large cross, a sign of Christianity. That spot would become the first California mission. Father Serra named the mission San Diego de Alcalá after a saint who had lived in Spain in the 1400s.

This 1776 map shows San Francisco Bay. Portolá was stopped by this huge body of water. He did not realize that it was San Francisco Bay.

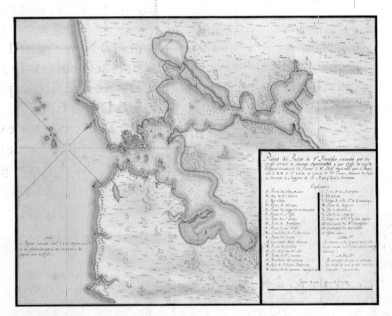

Portolá Discovers Monterey Bay

Portolá paused only long enough in San Diego to rest his men and mules. Then he continued north with 61 men to search for Monterey Bay. He passed by the bay without realizing that it was the place he was looking for. His expedition marched on. Days later, their food and supplies were running low. So Portolá and his men returned to the bay they had passed earlier. There they raised a cross and then returned to the mission at San Diego. The following spring Portolá traveled north again. This time he discovered that the bay he had passed before was indeed Monterey Bay. ■

■ *Why was the Portolá expedition important to Spain and to the Catholic Church?*

Spanish Explorers and Settlers

➤ *How did the land and sea slow the expeditions of Portolá and Anza?*

How Do We Know?

HISTORY *Most of our information about the Portolá expedition comes from the diaries that were kept by Pedro Fages, Portolá himself, and Father Serra. All of them describe the hardships of the journey from the Baja to Alta California.*

Explorers' Routes, 1769-1775

San Francisco
Monterey
Santa Barbara
San Diego
ALTA CALIFORNIA
SIERRA NEVADA
MOJAVE DESERT
Colorado River
Gila River
1774-1776
Tubac
ROCKY MOUNTAINS
Rio Grande
30°
1769
BAJA CALIFORNIA
Loreto
1769
La Paz
Gulf of California
SIERRA MADRE
120°
PACIFIC OCEAN
20°
Rio Grand de Santiago
Mexico City
110°

← Gaspar de Portolá
← Juan de Anza
← Supply ships sent for Portolá expedition
← California current

0   200 mi.
0   200 km
Lambert Azimuthal Equal Area Projection

Anza Takes Another Route

▼ *Linen cloth and beans were some of the supplies given to members of Anza's expedition.*

A young Spanish soldier named Juan Bautista (*bah TEE stuh*) de Anza heard how difficult the journey was from the Baja into Alta California. He wanted to open a new land route to San Diego and then on to Monterey Bay. The route would start in the Sonoran desert region of New Spain, where Arizona is today. With the offer of free land at Monterey, 30 families joined the expedition led by Anza. The expedition brought 695 horses and mules and 355 head of cattle. The settlers and their animals faced fierce desert storms as they crossed the unknown land.

> ometimes a solid wall of inky blackness made up of whirls and gulfs of dust roared down upon them. Then the Captain would call a halt. Fray [Father] Font prayed aloud and everyone softly repeated the prayer. . . . The children cried with fear, the burros brayed in terror and the horses closed their eyes and nostrils and bent their heads before the lashing whips of wind.
>
> Dorothy Erksine, *The Big Ride*, 1958

▲ *The Anza expedition spent much of the journey wandering in the desert looking for water.*

Finally in March 1776, the weary settlers reached Monterey. All had survived the difficult journey. They had covered 1,600 miles of vast deserts, rushing rivers, and rugged mountains. This land route from Sonora was as difficult as the route from the Baja. For this reason California remained set apart for many years. Its southern desert and mountains were difficult to cross on foot. Supplies still had to be sent by ship to San Diego and Monterey. ■

■ *Why did people decide to take the long journey with Captain Anza?*

R E V I E W

1. **FOCUS** Why did Spain want to settle Alta California?

2. **CONNECT** How was the Anza expedition different from the journey of the first hunters who came to California? Write the reasons why both groups came.

3. **GEOGRAPHY** How did geography affect the settlement of Alta California?

4. **CRITICAL THINKING** What were the advantages of the land route to Monterey? Would you have preferred to sail with the first expedition? Why?

5. **WRITING ACTIVITY** Write a script for a play about the Portolá expedition to San Diego.

69

Making a Timeline

Here's Why

In Lessons 1 and 2 you learned about the early explorers' expeditions and about the arrival of the first Spanish settlers in California. How will you remember the dates for all these events?

The timeline at the beginning of this chapter shows the years in which the events of the chapter occurred. A timeline helps you understand in what order events happened in history. Making your own timeline will help you organize and remember the dates of important events.

Here's How

First decide how many years your timeline will show. The timeline below begins with the year 1450 and ends with 1700. How many years does it show?

Then draw a line, and use a ruler to mark off equal sections. Decide how many years each section will stand for, and label the beginning of each section with the appropriate date. On the timeline below, each inch stands for 50 years. The first section begins with the date 1450. The next section begins 50 years later. Each smaller sections stands for 10 years.

Now you are ready to add the dates of important events to your timeline. Cortés set sail for New Spain in 1519. On the timeline below, this date is marked just before the line for 1520. Where is the mark for Columbus's voyage?

Try It

Now make your own timeline. Copy the timeline below. Then extend your timeline so that it ends with the year 1800. Make each inch stand for 50 years, and let smaller sections stand for 10 years. Add three more important dates from Lessons 1 and 2 to your timeline.

Apply It

Make a timeline of important events in your family's history. Choose the events you want to include, and find out when they happened. Decide how many years your timeline will show. Share your timeline with a friend or relative.

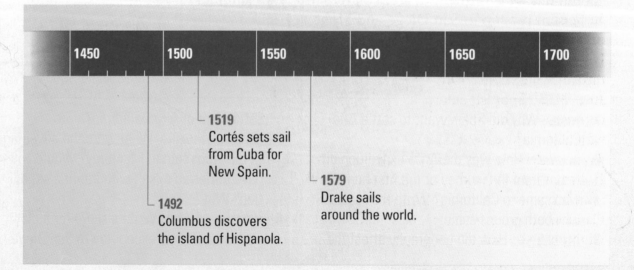

1450   1500   1550   1600   1650   1700

1519
Cortés sets sail from Cuba for New Spain.

1492
Columbus discovers the island of Hispanola.

1579
Drake sails around the world.

L E S S O N 3

Presidios, Missions, and Pueblos

Captain Gaspar de Portolá had made one land expedition to search for Monterey Bay in the fall of 1769. Even though he had not known the bay he passed was Monterey, he still raised a cross there. So in May 1770, Portolá and 12 soldiers left San Diego to search again for the bay. They followed the same route and came to the place where they had raised the cross. As the soldiers drew near, one of the men fell to his knees. The others gathered around him and stared at the cross in wonder. Meat, feathers, and shellfish were scattered beneath it. They saw arrows stuck in the ground and a string of sardines at its base. The Indians living nearby had left these things.

A week later, Father Junípero Serra arrived on the ship *San Antonio*. He came to start a second mission community. On June 3, the Spanish held a ceremony as the Indians watched quietly from the woods. Father Serra hung bells in the oak trees. As Captain Portolá threw a handful of earth into the air, he claimed the land for Spain. The soldiers fired guns and raised flags. Cannon boomed from the ship. The Indians ran from the frightening sounds of the Spanish celebration.

THINKING FOCUS

How did the missions, presidios, and pueblos help each other?

Key Terms

- padre
- presidio
- pueblo

◄ *Father Serra brought bells to each new mission he started in Alta California. The bells were used to welcome the Indians and to let them know when it was time to go to church.*

71

Spanish Explorers and Settlers

Father Serra Starts the Mission Chain

Father Serra looked at the cross and the soldiers in front of him. His dream of serving God in this new land was coming true. The Spanish government had chosen Father Serra to start more missions. Now his priests would bring the Spanish way of life to Alta California.

Indians Come to the Missions

Starting a mission was a way for Father Serra to bring the Indians into the Catholic Church. He believed that he was offering them something wonderful—religious faith. In return, they would leave their Indian way of life to live at the mission. Father Serra would also teach the Indians farming skills and trade crafts so that they would be able to support themselves.

The mission fascinated many Indians because it was so different from life in their villages. Some Indians were curious about this man in the long gown, who rang bells each morning and night. They had never seen animals like the cattle and sheep that wandered around the mission. The Indians accepted the new kinds of food and cloth-

➤ *Father Junípero Serra, was born on the island of Majorca (mah YAWR kah) off the coast of Spain. He came to Mexico and was then sent to California to start missions. He thought of Mission San Carlos Borromeo de Carmelo as his home.*

ing that the priests, or **padres** (*PAH drayz*), offered them. Many Indians joined the missions. They built churches and buildings, plowed fields, harvested crops, and took care of animals. The Indians' work allowed the missions to grow.

Father Serra lived by these words: "Always go forward. Never go back." He continued to push ahead. He asked officials in Mexico City for supplies to begin new missions. Father Serra started the missions close to fresh water for crops and near large tribes of Indians that he could bring into the Catholic faith. Over the next 13 years he started seven more missions.

Spain's plan to settle Alta California also included building forts and towns. Locate San Diego, Santa Barbara, Monterey, and San Francisco on the map on page 74. At all of these places the Spanish built forts, or **presidios**, to protect the coast from foreign troops. Food raised at the missions fed the soldiers living at the presidios. In return, the soldiers protected the missions. Towns, or **pueblos**, were also started near the missions for settlers from Mexico. A road called El Camino (*cah MEE noh*) Real (*ray AHL*) connected all of the presidios, missions, and pueblos. ■

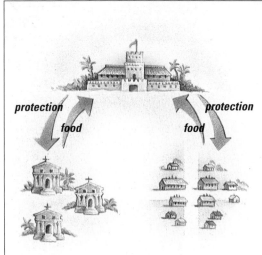

Food and Protection for Settlers

protection   food   food   protection

▲ *The mission and pueblo communities produced food for the presidios in exchange for protection. The pueblos did not grow in size until about 1830.*

■ *What did Father Serra have to do when he started a new mission?*

El Camino Real Connects the Missions

Walk along El Camino Real, or The Royal Road, from San Diego to Los Angeles as the padres did more than 200 years ago. Soldiers, Indians, padres, and other travelers use this road. You start your walk at the presidio at San Diego. There everything is safely inside four earthen walls. Small houses stand around a rectangular courtyard where the soldiers' children play. You see a soldier repairing one of the two cannon that protect the presidio from foreign ships entering the bay. Another soldier stands guard in front of the jail. Still other soldiers wearing deerskin jackets saddle their horses for a trip to a nearby mission. Their wives grind

▼ *Spanish cannon like this one protected presidios from attack.*

73

The Mission–Presidio Chain

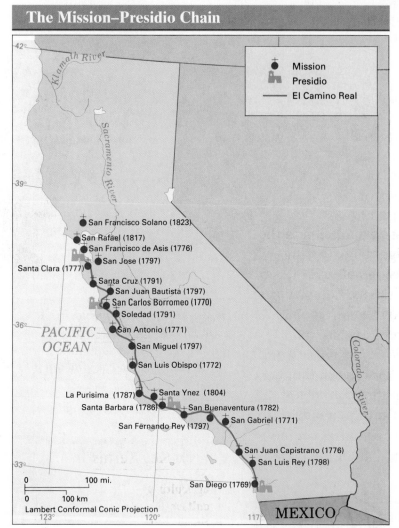

Legend:
- ✚● Mission
- 🏰 Presidio
- —— El Camino Real

Map labels (north to south):
- San Francisco Solano (1823)
- San Rafael (1817)
- San Francisco de Asis (1776)
- San Jose (1797)
- Santa Clara (1777)
- Santa Cruz (1791)
- San Juan Bautista (1797)
- San Carlos Borromeo (1770)
- Soledad (1791)
- San Antonio (1771)
- San Miguel (1797)
- San Luis Obispo (1772)
- La Purisima (1787)
- Santa Ynez (1804)
- Santa Barbara (1786)
- San Buenaventura (1782)
- San Fernando Rey (1797)
- San Gabriel (1771)
- San Juan Capistrano (1776)
- San Luis Rey (1798)
- San Diego (1769)

Rivers: Klamath River, Sacramento River, Colorado River

PACIFIC OCEAN

MEXICO

0   100 mi.
0   100 km
Lambert Conformal Conic Projection

▲ *Why were presidios located along the coast of California?*

■ *What was the purpose of El Camino Real?*

corn for the evening meal.

It will take about four days to walk to the pueblo of Los Angeles 140 miles away. Each night you will stop at a mission to sleep. After a full day's walk, with very tired feet, you reach Mission San Luis Rey. This mission was built in 1798, after the earlier missions built by Father Serra. You see that the mission has orchards and vineyards. It looks like a small farming village. The church and workshop buildings are the centers of most activities. You see several Indians mixing wet clay and straw to make adobe (*ah DOH bee*) bricks. Look at the pictures on page 99 to see how these bricks were made. The padre at the mission welcomes you. He offers you a warm meal and bed for the night.

It takes two and a half more days of walking before you reach the pueblo of Los Angeles. The pueblo had been settled by 12 families from Mexico. The Spanish government has given each family two lots of land, one to live on and one to garden. In return, the families give some of their crops to the presidios. The families graze their cattle and horses on land outside the pueblo. You find that the people at the pueblo are as friendly as the padres at the missions. They offer visitors a place to stay. You are glad to have a place to rest. ■

R E V I E W

1. **FOCUS** How did the missions, presidios, and pueblos help each other?
2. **CONNECT** Compare Father Serra's reasons for building missions to the reasons the Spanish government wanted settlements in Alta California.
3. **GEOGRAPHY** The missions were built near sources of fresh water. Look at the Mission and Presidio Map on this page and name four missions and their nearest rivers or lakes.
4. **CRITICAL THINKING** Why do you think Father Serra thought he was offering something wonderful to the Indians who lived at the missions?
5. **ACTIVITY** Use the map on this page as a resource. Then make your own map to trace the route of the walk along El Camino Real described on pages 73 and 74.

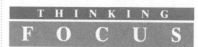

L E S S O N   4

Life on a Mission

If you were an Indian child living on a mission in the early 1800s, one of your jobs might be gathering olives. This small green fruit was one of several important crops raised at the missions. Lamps burned the oil made from crushing and pressing the olives. People also used the oil for medicine and in cooking.

Indian children took long poles with them as they went to gather olives from the trees. When they struck the branches of the trees with the poles, hard green olives showered down on them. Then the children scrambled to collect them into baskets.

Back in the mission courtyard, the children emptied their baskets into the mill. Olive mills were simple machines. The mill had a well lined with cement and a large grinding stone that fit inside it. A small, blindfolded mule walked around and around the mill, moving the large stone that crushed the olives. Then Indian women scooped up the crushed olives, stuffed them into sacks, and put them in a press. The press squeezed the sacks, and golden oil drained into large tubs. Finally, the oil was stored in covered jars.

THINKING FOCUS

What were the daily routines on a Spanish mission?

Key Terms

- agriculture
- culture
- revolt

◄ *Olives were one of many crops the Spanish brought to California. This is an olive press. A large block of wood is attached to the screw. Olives are dumped into the wooden box below. Then the block is screwed down to press the oil from the olives.*

75

Spanish Explorers and Settlers

A Daily Routine

Gathering olives was not the only farm work that went on at the missions. **Agriculture**, the raising of crops or animals, was an important activity on the missions. Their crops and animals supplied most of the food needed to feed the padres, the Indians, and the soldiers living nearby.

The padres taught the Indians Spanish methods of agriculture. They showed them how to care for cattle, sheep, and chickens and how to grow the new crops that had come from Spain. They also taught some Indians how to speak Spanish. One padre even taught the Indians at his mission to sing Christian songs for church services. The padres believed that the Indians needed to learn the Spanish culture to be good Christians. The way people live and what they believe is their **culture**.

The Spanish government had planned for the padres to turn the missions into pueblos at the end of ten years. By that time the Indians would be good Spanish citizens. But this never happened. The padres did not believe that the Indians were ready to live on their own in towns.

Work To Be Done

In 1812, Father Cabot of Mission San Antonio described how each day started for the Indians living there. "For their daily routine, the bell is rung at sunrise and after a meal of *atole* [wheat meal mush] . . . they assemble in the church." Father Cabot's report goes on to tell about how the Indians spent their days. The Indians did all of the physical work at the mission. In return, the Indians received their food, housing, Spanish clothing, and religious training. They farmed, constructed and repaired mission buildings, and practiced crafts like tanning leather. The padres supervised the Indians as they worked.

After breakfast and church services, everyone was given a job. Some Indian children gathered olives. Others chased birds from the fields. Adults weeded the gardens and picked fruit from the

▲ *The Spanish introduced new crops such as barley, oats, and wheat to California. Grapes grew wild in California, but they were also raised at the missions. The Spanish brought the first oranges to Los Angeles.*

➤ *A typical mission complex included the following:*
1. A central square with a courtyard, church, padres' rooms, workrooms, and storerooms
2. A tannery for making leather
3. Indian houses
4. An area for making adobe bricks, soap, and candles
5. Pasture land for cattle, sheep, and horses
6. Gardens, orchards, and vineyards.

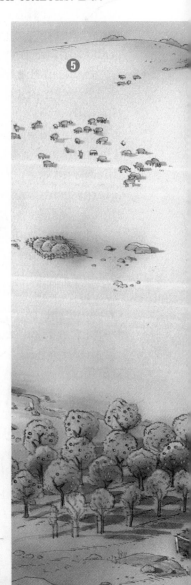

❺

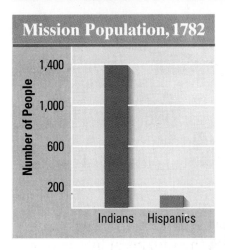

Mission Population, 1782

Number of People

1,400
1,000
600
200

Indians   Hispanics

orchards. Many cattle were raised at the missions. Older boys riding horses gathered the cattle that roamed the hillsides around the mission. Men slaughtered some of the cattle to get meat and leather. They scraped the hides for fat to make candles and soap. These would be sold to visiting traders.

At eleven in the morning, the Indian families gathered for more *atole*, served with meat, vegetables, and tortillas. After the meal, everyone rested and then returned to work. Children gathered firewood or cleaned straw from piles of wool. Indian women spun the wool and wove it into blankets and cloth. Late in the day, the Indians gathered for their evening meal. Then they would enter the mission church again for prayers. ■

◄ *The Indian population in 1782 was many times that of the Spanish population. It has been reported that only about 60 soldiers guarded all of the area between Monterey and San Diego at that time.*

■ *What were some of the animals and crops grown on the missions?*

Problems at the Missions

Although some Indians were content on the missions, many others were unhappy with this new way of life. By living at the missions the Indians gave up their own culture, the way of life they had known in their tribal villages. They could only leave the mission grounds with permission from the padres. They were not free to hunt or to pick berries

UNDERSTANDING CULTURE

You learn about culture from your parents, teachers, and friends. Culture includes religious beliefs as well as family and national customs. It also includes the foods people eat, the books they write, and the songs they sing. But the way people look, such as the color of their hair, eyes, or skin, is not a part of culture.

The padres sent to Alta California brought Spanish culture with them. They taught the Indians the Christian religion and how to grow crops and care for animals. They also brought foods such as tortillas and chocolate they had learned about from the Aztec culture of Mexico.

Sometimes geography can influence culture. For example, the people who live on the islands of Japan have depended on the ocean around them for food. Eating seafood is part of Japanese culture.

People start to learn their culture from the time they are young. If you learned the nursery rhyme "Jack and

Jill" when you were young, you were learning a part of the English culture. That rhyme came from English settlers who arrived in Virginia and New England 300 years ago. People all over the world sing songs that have been passed down for many years. In the United States people learn the song "Yankee Doodle." That song is a part of the culture of the United States.

The Spanish explorers brought their culture to the Indians they found living in Alta California. Some Indians accepted the new beliefs, the Spanish clothing, and ways of doing things. Others wanted to keep their own culture—one they had developed for themselves over thousands of years.

when they wanted. They no longer ate their traditional foods of wore their traditional clothing. Indians who had run away from the San Francisco mission were later asked to explain their reasons. One man said that he had left because he was beaten when he wept for a dead brother.

Mission Indians were not allowed to return to their tribes once they agreed to take part in mission life. Some ran away. But soldiers usually brought them back and sometimes whipped them. Others wanted to **revolt**. They wanted to rise up against their leaders, the Spanish padres and soldiers at the mission communities.

Sometimes Indians revolted violently. Six years after its founding, San Diego Mission was attacked by Indians. They set the mission on fire and killed one of the padres. In 1785 Toypurina, a 24-year-old Gabrielino woman, helped warriors of six villages to revolt against San Gabriel Mission. When she was arrested and questioned by the governor, she answered, "I hate the padres and all of you, for living here on my native soil, for trespassing upon the land of my forefathers."

The graph shows changes in the Indian population on one mission. Many Indians died of diseases brought by the Spanish. When crops failed, Indians didn't have enough to eat. Some became sick from the change in their diet on the missions. By the end of the mission period, the California Indian population was half the size that it had been when Father Serra raised his first cross at San Diego Mission.

By 1832 Father Serra's dream of a chain of missions had come true. But for the people who had lived in California for hundreds of years before the Spanish arrived, the growth of the missions was tragic. Thousands of Indian died, and by the end of the 1800s much of the Indian way of life had died also. ■

▼ *Detailed records of births, deaths, and baptisms were kept at each mission. Many of the deaths were caused by diseases like measles and small pox that the Spanish brought with them.*

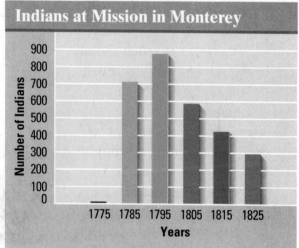

■ *Why did the Indians revolt against life on the missions?*

R E V I E W

1. **FOCUS** What were the daily routines on a Spanish mission?
2. **CONNECT** How did Indian culture change as Indians lived at the missions?
3. **ECONOMICS** What items did the missions produce? How were these products used by the padres and Indians?
4. **CRITICAL THINKING** What do you think would have happened if the Indians had not joined the missions?
5. **WRITING ACTIVITY** Make a list of reasons why an Indian might leave the mission. Then list reasons why an Indian might decide to stay at the mission.

Spanish Explorers and Settlers

California Place Names

Have you ever wondered where California's cities and towns got their unusual names? Did you ever ask yourself whether Tarzana, California, has something to do with the movie hero Tarzan? The answer is yes. Edgar Rice Burroughs, the writer who created Tarzan, founded the town. And did you know that Alcatraz is also the Spanish word for a pelican-like bird found on the San Francisco Bay island? You will now have a chance to learn more interesting facts about how California's places got their names.

Get Ready

You will need a map of the state and one of your city or town. See pages 328 and 329 for two maps you can use. You'll also need an encyclopedia and a dictionary. Look as well for books, pamphlets, and magazine articles about California place names. Then look in your library card catalog

► *The Spanish history of Los Angeles is revealed in many of the area's place names.*

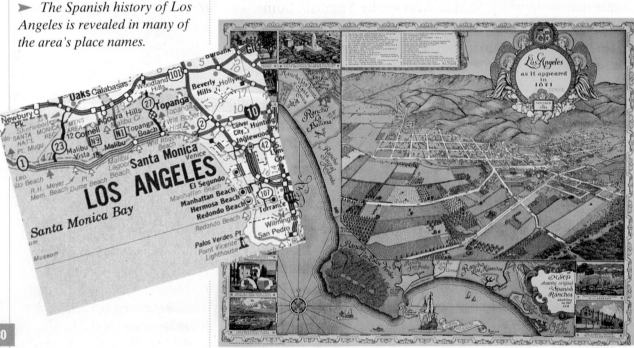

under "place names," or ask the librarian for help. (The librarian is a good person to get to know. He or she can be helpful to you throughout this project.)

Find Out

Next you'll need to find some place names you want to learn more about. These should not be hard to find. Just keep your eyes open next time you're in the car. Write down the names of the towns, rivers, parks, and mountains you pass. Then look at the maps you've gathered. Using these sources, make a list of at least 15 interesting place names you want to study.

Move Ahead

Now it's time to do some detective work. First, look in the books and other materials you gathered earlier. See if they give any information about the places in which you are interested. Look up the names in the dictionary and encyclopedia too. Next, visit or write the local historical society in the area you are studying. (Your librarian can help you find the numbers and addresses of these places.)

Often the name of a place gives you clues about the people who named it. These clues can help you narrow your search for information. For example, *Salinas* means "salt marshes" in Spanish. That tells you that it was named by people who spoke Spanish. Some places in California still have the names given by the Indians who lived there long ago. For example, *Yosemite* comes from the Indian word *uzamaite*, which may refer to grizzly bears. Many other names in California come from different Indian languages. With a little effort and practice, you can often spot these Indian and Spanish names.

Explore Some More

Start your own dictionary of place names and their histories using the names you've already studied. Expand your dictionary with new names and places. Include cities, towns, streets, parks, schools, and rivers. For each place, try to find out why a name was given. Whenever possible, use pictures to illustrate your places. Soon, your place-name dictionary will be full of interesting stories and information about your town and your state.

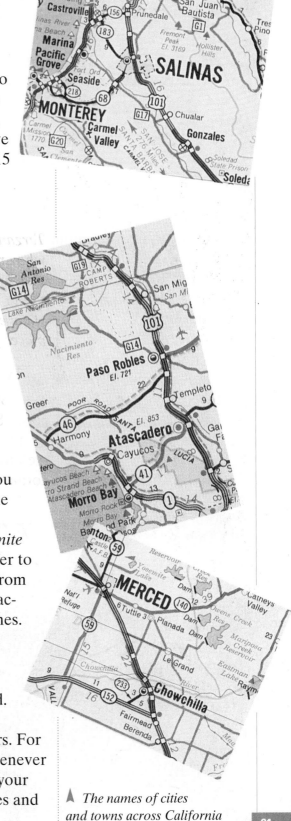

▲ *The names of cities and towns across California hold clues about their history.*

81

Chapter Review

Reviewing Key Terms

agriculture (p.76)
colony (p.59)
culture (p.76)
expedition (p.59)
mission (p.66)

padre (p.73)
peninsula (p.66)
presidio (p.73)
pueblo (p.73)
revolt (p.79)

A. Choose the key term that best completes each sentence.

1. In the 1760s, both Spain and Russia wanted to build a _____ in Alta California.
2. A finger of land surrounded by water on three sides is called a _____.
3. Twelve families from Mexico settled in the _____ of Los Angeles.
4. Some Indians wanted to _____ because they were unhappy on the missions.
5. _____ is the raising of crops or animals.
6. The padres wanted the Indians on the missions to learn the Spanish traditions and _____.

B. Write a sentence for each pair of words below:

1. expedition, Cabrillo
2. colony, New Spain
3. mission, Indians
4. presidio, soldiers
5. pueblo, settlers
6. padre, religion

Exploring Concepts

A. Complete the chart below on a separate piece of paper. For each of the explorers, tell the goal of his expedition and what he accomplished.

Explorer	Goal	Accomplishment
Cortés		
Cabrillo		
Portolá		
Anza		

B. Support each statement below with two details from this chapter.

1. Trade with Asia for spices, cloth, and tea was important to Spain.
2. An Indian legend led to many Spanish expeditions.
3. During the 1500s, England and Spain competed with each other.
4. In the 1760s, Russia's plan to build a colony in Alta California worried Spain.
5. Portolá's and Anza's expeditions to Alta California were dangerous trips.
6. Spanish missions in Alta California changed the Indians' way of life.
7. The California missions, pueblos, and presidios were connected by a road.
8. The mission Indians and the padres had different beliefs and traditions.

Reviewing Skills

1. Look at the world map on page 320. Name two countries found in the Northern Hemisphere and two countries found in the Eastern Hemisphere.
2. Use the world map again. Find the place at 60°N, 120°W. In what country is this place found?
3. Suppose you want to learn more about wheat, one of the crops the padres introduced to California. Would you find more information in an encyclopedia or in a dictionary?
4. The timeline on this page shows the dates for the founding of the California missions. Copy the timeline on a separate piece of paper. Then add the dates for the founding of three other missions. You can find these dates on the map on page 74.
5. Look at the United States climate map on page 330. How many climate regions does it show? Describe the climate near the area of the first mission.

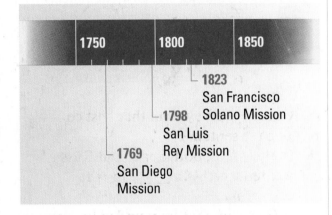

1750   1800   1850

1823
San Francisco
Solano Mission
1798
San Luis
Rey Mission
1769
San Diego
Mission

Using Critical Thinking

1. Why do you think the early explorers were men, and not women? What opportunities do women have today that they did not have long ago?
2. When two cultures come together each learns something from the other. What might the Indians and padres on the missions have learned from each other? How do we learn about other cultures today?
3. Think of the men and women who have led expeditions into space or under the ocean. What do these explorers have in common with Columbus, Cortés, and Cabrillo?
4. The California missions, pueblos, and presidios depended on one another for the things they needed. How do people in your community depend on one another today?

Preparing for Citizenship

1. **COLLECTING INFORMATION** Start a notebook in which you collect examples of Spanish culture in California today. You could include place names, foods, ceremonies, art, or buildings. Draw a picture of each example you find, and write a sentence to describe it.
2. **COLLABORATIVE LEARNING** Work as a class to make an illustrated timeline of the important events from this chapter.

Begin your timeline with the year 1450 and end with 1850. Decide which events you will include, and mark their dates on the timeline. Then work in small groups to illustrate each event and to write a paragraph that describes the event and tells why it was important. Attach the drawings to the appropriate dates on the timeline.

Chapter 4
Mexican California

New lands were offered to California's settlers, and the age of cattle ranching began. The new landowners worked hard to raise their herds. Although the people were now spread across California's countryside, they were linked by a strong Spanish culture.

Mexican citizens claimed huge pieces of land. To make a claim, a person drew a boundary map, or *diseño*, of the land.

Rancheros used tools like these in rodeos.

| 1800 | 1810 | 1820 |

1810

1810 On September 15, Miguel Hidalgo y Costilla launches the Mexican War for Independence.

August Ferran painted this picture showing daily work on a rancho. Here vaqueros are roping stray cattle.

Californians looked forward to the arrival of trading ships twice a year. The ships brought everything from Chinese feather fans to leather shoes.

1834 The Mexican government passes a land law that closes the missions in Alta California.

L E S S O N   1

Traders in California

THINKING FOCUS

Why was foreign trade important to the Californios?

Key Terms

- independence
- products
- barter

➤ *The painting to the right shows Monterey Bay in 1842. Foreign trading ships brought many products to the Californios. The tin teapot below might have come from New England and the child's saddle from Chile.*

Kaboom! A cannon blasts from the presidio, announcing that a trading ship has dropped its anchor in Monterey Bay. Men, women, and children race down to the shore on horseback and on foot. There they find people waiting for rides in rowboats that will carry them out to the ship. A young girl sits snugly between her mother and father in one of the rowboats. She hopes to get a new scarf from the ship's store.

Richard Henry Dana sailed on a Boston trading ship around 1834. He described the ship store in his book *Two Years Before the Mast:* "Our cargo was an assorted one; that is, it consisted of everything under the sun. We had . . . teas, coffee, sugars, spices, raisins, molasses, hardware, crockery-ware, tin-ware, cutlery, clothing of all kinds, boots and shoes. . . ." The trading ship has brought all these goods to the eager people of Monterey. The ship's store has so many brightly colored scarves that it will be hard to decide which one to buy.

War in Mexico Changes California

Trading ships like the one just described had not always come to California. Spain had stopped other countries from trading there. But in 1810, an important event changed Spain's control over trade in California.

The people from the part of New Spain that is now called Mexico had grown restless under Spanish rule. Spanish people who were born in Mexico could not hold the same jobs as the Spanish who came from Spain to rule them. The Mexican Spanish and the Indians of Mexico longed for **independence.** They wanted to rule themselves rather than be controlled by an outside government. In 1810, the people of Mexico decided to fight Spain for their independence.

Trading Ships Arrive

For the next 12 years the Mexican War for Independence raged throughout Mexico. The people of Alta California, who called themselves Californios, did not take part in the battles. In fact, the Californios didn't even learn that Mexico had won its independence from Spain until a year after the war ended. But the war brought many changes to the Californios too. Because of heavy war costs, the Spanish government could no longer afford to send supply ships to Alta California.

When Spain stopped sending supplies, other countries jumped at the chance to trade with the Californios. Russia, for example, built a fur-trading outpost called Fort Ross north of San Francisco. The Russians came to California to hunt fur seals and otters. They traded clothing and tools for food grown on the missions. Spain no longer had enough ships or soldiers to stop other countries from trading in California. Soon England and the United States began to send trading ships too. The Californios needed supplies and gratefully traded with the outsiders. When the war was over, the new Mexican rulers quickly encouraged foreign traders to come to California. ■

Compare this map of North America with the map on page 6. How does each map present its information?

Why did the Mexican people want to be independent of Spanish rule?

Mexican California

Hide and Tallow Trade Begins

About two dozen trading ships came to California each year through the 1840s. They carried many kinds of **products**, items that are made by nature, by people, or by machines. Most of the ships came from Boston to buy inexpensive leather for the shoe factories of New England. The ships sailed along the California coast. There the captains traded such products as boots, shoes, clothing, and spices for cattle skins, or hides, that were made into leather. When people trade goods without using money, they **barter** for those goods.

A single ship carried hundreds of pounds of hides. The Californios also bartered tallow— the purest part of cattle fat—for products from the trading ships. Tallow was used to make soap and candles.

When the ships were full of hides and tallow, they started their voyage back to Boston. They stopped in South America to sell tallow to candle and soap factories in Chile. Follow their voyage from San Diego on the chart of the hide and tallow trade on page 89. ■

■ *How did Californios use hides and tallow?*

UNDERSTANDING BARTER

*I*n times before people used paper money or coins, they bartered for what they needed. Four hundred years ago, Indians didn't have paper money or coins. Sometimes they used strings of shell beads as a form of money. But more often they would barter for things they needed. An Indian might trade an arrowhead for a grinding stone or a deerskin for a soapstone bowl. Barter is a way for people to trade for the things they need without using money.

Bartering is not buying. If you buy a pencil for 25 cents, you are not bartering for the pencil. But if you trade two baseball cards for a friend's sandwich, you are bartering. Of course, both you and your friend must agree on what makes a fair barter.

Sometimes people cannot agree on the value of their trade items. That may lead to an argument or conflict. Would you barter two Orel Hershiser baseball cards for a cheese sandwich? How about a cowhide for a tin teapot and a Chinese scarf?

The Californios you have read about in this lesson traded cattle hides for goods. They didn't need paper money or coins. They simply bartered the hides and tallow from the cattle they raised for goods brought into Monterey and San Diego by the New England trading ships.

❶ California

In San Diego a Californio slaughters a steer,

He stretches the steer hide to dry in the sun.

An Indian boils the tallow, then packs it in a bota.

A Boston trader barters with the Californio: the tallow for a shawl worth $2 and the hide for spices worth $2. The trader barters with many other Californios as well.

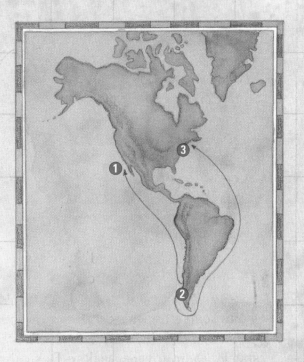

❷ Chile

The next morning the trading ship sets sail for South America. In Chile a local merchant meets the trading ship.

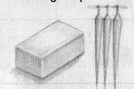

The merchant buys many botas of tallow for $3 a piece. One bota is enough to make 20 cakes of soap and 60 candles. He sells the candles for 10¢ a piece and sells each cake of soap for 15¢.

❸ New England

The trading ship sails around Cape Horn and north to Boston. There, the owner of a shoe factory buys the hide for $3.

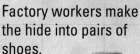

Factory workers make the hide into pairs of shoes.

Another trader buys the shoes for $4 per pair. This trader sails south, around Cape Horn and then north to San Diego. There, he barters with a Californio: a pair of shoes for 2 botas of tallow and 2 hides.

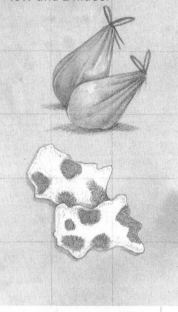

R E V I E W

1. **FOCUS** Why was foreign trade important to the Californios?
2. **CONNECT** Describe the similarities and differences you see between the Californios' hide and tallow trade and the trades Indians made for things they needed.
3. **GEOGRAPHY** Use the world map on pages 320–321 in the Atlas to find how many continents a trading ship would pass while sailing from Boston to San Diego.
4. **CRITICAL THINKING** Tell why this statement is true: The Californios and the foreign traders needed each other.
5. **ACTIVITY** Have you ever bartered for something? Draw a comic strip describing your experience.

L E S S O N   2

From Missions to Ranchos

THINKING FOCUS

How did the closing of the missions affect the Indians, the padres, and the new Mexican settlers?

Key Terms

- rancho
- land grant
- vaquero
- ranchero

◄ *Reatas are ropes of braided horsehair.*

It is a hot afternoon. Dry brown grass covers the wide valley for miles in every direction. A grove of oak trees gives the only shade in sight.

Four horseback riders—three men and a woman—appear in the distance, heading for the trees. One of the men holds an end of a coil of rope called a reata (*ree AH tuh*). He drops the coil onto the ground and rides until the rope is straight. He has finally measured the last section of land. When the riders reach the shade, the man hands the reata to the woman and examines a handmade map called a *diseño* (*dih SEHN yoh*).

"According to the *diseño*," he says to the woman, "this grove of trees marks the northwest corner of your ranch. We have measured three thousand reatas since we left the four large rocks in the southwest corner. This will be an enormous ranch, Señora."

"I hope to raise thousands of cattle and horses," the woman answers.

End of the Missions

Beginning in 1834, scenes like this were common near the pueblos and missions of California. Each alcalde (*ahl CAHL deh*), or mayor of the pueblo, helped many new landowners measure land for cattle ranches, or **ranchos.**

After the Mexican War for Independence, the new Mexican leaders wanted to get rid of everything connected with the old Spanish government. The new leaders ordered the Spanish missions closed in Alta California. Many Spanish padres went back to Mexico or Spain. A few stayed on to serve as church priests, but they no longer ran the mis-

sions. The Mexican government divided the mission lands and herds among mission Indians, Californios, and new Mexican settlers.

Mission lands were not divided equally. The Californios and new Mexican settlers received over eight million acres in government gifts of land called **land grants**. Californio and Mexican families got these land grants by preparing *diseños* and proving that they were Mexican citizens.

Hardship for the Indians

The new government also gave each Indian on a mission some land and cattle. But few Indians ever became landowners. Some returned to the mountains and deserts to try to live as their ancestors had. Others lost their land to dishonest settlers.

Many Indians found it hard to survive at this time. The Indians who had grown up on the missions did not know the old ways of their people. The padres had taught them to eat Spanish foods, to wear Spanish clothes, and to raise crops and animals. The Indians had come to depend on the food, clothing, and shelter that the missions provided. When they were forced to look for food in the mountains and deserts, they often could not find enough to eat.

Some Indians found work on the ranchos. Men and boys who had learned to ride horses on the missions worked as **vaqueros** (*vah KEH rohs*), or cowboys. Indian women worked as housekeepers for the new ranchers, the **rancheros.** They washed and mended clothes, cared for children, and cooked meals for the rancho families and Indian workers. Indians did not gain freedom when the missions closed. They simply gained new masters, the rancheros. ■

▲ *People have always changed the land where they lived. The Indians, the padres, and the new Mexican settlers each built different kinds of houses. Look at the pictures from left to right. Can you tell who built which house?*

Across Time & Space

After 1834, mission buildings were no longer cared for. Some were damaged by earthquakes. In the early 1900s, California citizens began to repair the mission buildings. Missions are now one of California's leading tourist attractions.

■ *What hardships did Indians face after the missions closed?*

Ranchos and Rancheros

The first land grants were offered to men who were already living in California. These men were mostly officers or soldiers at the presidios or friends and relatives of government officials. Later, other Mexican citizens applied for land grants too. Juana Briones de Mirande (*Meer AHN deh*) was one of only 26 women who received land grants in California. She owned a rancho near San Francisco for many years. Like women in Spain, Mexican and Californio women were allowed to own land separately from their husbands.

Most rancho lands were open grasslands rolling over miles of California hillsides. Why do you think there weren't many land grants in the northwestern and the southeastern regions of California?

The new rancheros raised cattle for the hide and tallow trade. The map on this page shows the area that the Mexican government divided into land grants for ranchos. In the picture you see a rancho landscape. A rancho often covered about 75 square miles of land. That is larger than the area covered by some cities and towns today. When Mission San Gabriel closed, its nearly 2,400 square miles of land became 24

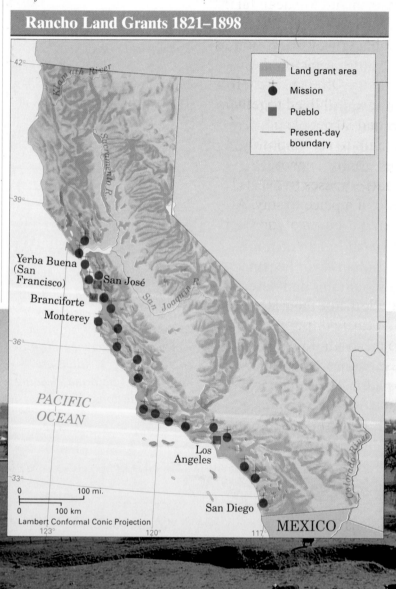

Rancho Land Grants 1821–1898

Land grant area
Mission
Pueblo
Present-day boundary

Klamath River
Sacramento R.
Yerba Buena (San Francisco)
San José
San Joaquin R.
Branciforte
Monterey
PACIFIC OCEAN
Los Angeles
Colorado River
San Diego
MEXICO

0   100 mi.
0   100 km
Lambert Conformal Conic Projection

ranchos. Thousands of cattle roamed the unfenced land, eating the wild grass that grew almost everywhere. Fifty cows could eat the grass on more than a square mile of land each year. That explains why ranchos were so large.

This painting by James Walker shows a rider and his horse on a rancho. Notice the silver decorations on the horse's bridle and on the man's clothes.

The rich rancheros kept the customs of well-to-do Spanish and Mexican families. They lived in large adobe, or clay brick, houses like the one pictured on page 91. Often a ranchero's grandparents, aunts, uncles, and children all lived together. These large households sometimes had 30 people in them. Such big households needed much help to run smoothly. Indian servants did the work at these large ranchos.

Rancheros often opened their large houses to guests. They welcomed any traveler in need of a place to stay. A few of the wealthiest rancheros even put bowls of money in their guest rooms for their visitors to use.

Hardships on the Ranchos

Not all rancheros were wealthy. Some of them struggled to make a living from small herds of cattle or poor grazing land. They lived in small adobe houses with dirt floors, few windows, and cowhide doors. These rancheros had to do more of the work on their ranchos themselves. And, of course, all rancheros lived miles from their neighbors. They often lived a day's ride on horseback from the nearest pueblo or neighboring ranch. ■

■ *Explain why most ranchos were very large.*

R E V I E W

1. **FOCUS** How did the closing of the missions affect the Indians, the padres, and the new Mexican settlers?

2. **CONNECT** Look at the picture on page 92 of this lesson. Tell how the Indians, the padres, and the rancheros all used the land they found in California.

3. **CULTURE** How did rancheros become wealthy?

4. **CRITICAL THINKING** How do you think rancheros learned about events on other ranchos or in other parts of the world?

5. **ACTIVITY** Pretend you are a Mexican citizen in 1834. You have received a land grant. Draw a diseño to show the boundaries of your land. Use symbols to stand for features like hills, rivers, and trees.

Mexican California

Identifying Causes and Effects

Here's Why

Events in history are often related in a chain of causes and effects. For example, closing the missions changed the lives of many people in California. This event caused other events to happen. Identifying cause-and-effect relationships will help you understand how events in history are connected.

Here's How

An event that leads to other events is a cause. The events that happen as a result of the cause are effects.

The diagram below shows that closing the missions was a cause. It led to other events. As a result of the closing of the missions, some Indians fled to the mountains and deserts. This event was an effect. What other effects are shown in the diagram?

Asking the right questions can help you to identify causes and effects. To identify the possible causes of an event, ask yourself, "Why did it happen?" For example, you might ask, "Why did most padres return to Mexico and Spain?" Then think of events that happened earlier. Do any of them explain why the padres returned? If so, they are causes. To discover the effects of an event, ask, "What happened as a result?"

Word clues can also help you to identify causes and effects. The word clues *because, since, for,* and *in order to* often signal that a cause will follow. The words *so, therefore,* and *as a result* are often clues that an effect will follow.

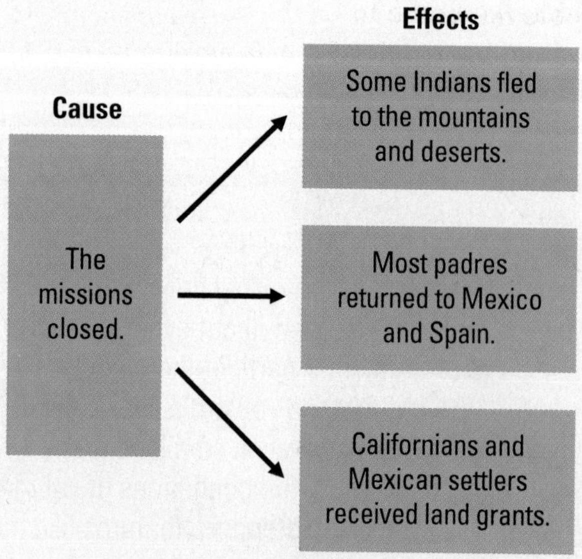

Try It

Make a chart with two headings: "Causes" and "Effects." Then read the examples below. Write the causes and effects in the appropriate columns on your chart. Remember to look for word clues and to ask, "Why did it happen?" and "What happened as a result?"

1. In 1810, the people of Mexico decided to fight Spain because they wanted their independence.
2. New England factory owners needed leather to make shoes, so they bought hides from the Californios.
3. The rancheros held rodeos in order to sort their cattle.

Apply It

Think of a story you have read. Then think of something the main character did. Ask yourself, "Why?" to discover the cause of the character's action. Ask, "What happened as a result?" to figure out the effects of the character's action.

Effects

Cause

The missions closed.

Some Indians fled to the mountains and deserts.

Most padres returned to Mexico and Spain.

Californians and Mexican settlers received land grants.

LESSON 3

Ranchos and Pueblos

A gate swings open and dozens of frightened, mooing calves crowd into the pen. The smell of cattle and clouds of dust fill the air. A vaquero whirls his reata above his head and ropes a calf. Two other vaqueros quickly bring the calf to the ground as a third uses a hot branding iron to burn the ranchero's brand onto the calf's hide. Then, as the rope is loosened, the calf scampers away to the safety of the herd.

Since dawn, the vaqueros have been sorting cattle driven in from the open range. The cattle have roamed freely for months. Cattle from different ranchos have mixed together, and new calves have been born. Now the vaqueros must sort the cattle by brand and group them into herds. They separate the new calves from their mothers and give them the brand of the rancho they belong to.

The alcalde has declared a two-day holiday for the roundup, or **rodeo.** Everyone from the pueblo has come to help with the work. After sorting and branding, hundreds of cattle must be slaughtered and skinned.

THINKING FOCUS

How did the pueblos depend on the ranchos?

Key Terms

- rodeo
- plaza
- town council

▼ *The Spanish brought the use of branding irons to California.*

95

Mexican California

► *This drawing by Carlos Nebel shows the kind of clothing worn by people living on a rancho.*

How Do We Know?

HISTORY *Some of the information about life on the ranchos and pueblos comes from the book* Life in California *by Alfred Robinson, written in 1846. Robinson was a sailor from a trading ship. He married a Californio woman and settled in San Diego.*

Rancho Life

Rodeos took place in January and April. During the rest of the year rancheros directed the Indian vaqueros and servants who worked on the ranchos. Step back in time to the 1840s to visit a rancho on an ordinary day.

An adobe house with a tile roof sits on a small hill. From the front porch you can see land and cattle in every direction. If you follow your nose, you will come to an outdoor kitchen where Indian women are busy preparing the noontime meal. A pot of spicy beef and vegetables fills the air with its delicious smell. Enter the house. You hear the sound of children's voices reciting a lesson. Since there are no schools nearby, a tutor comes to the rancho a few times each year for about a week to teach the ranchero's children. After class, the children go outside to ride horseback. Horses roam freely in great herds as the cattle do. Girls and boys can simply grab the nearest horse and use it for the day. Rancho children learn riding tricks even before they are 10 years old.

Look in the sheds across from the house. Here Indian men repair wagons and tools and Indian women weave wool cloth. As you walk by another shed you smell boiling tallow. Workers stir huge vats of boiling fat to make soap and candles. The rancheros depend upon their Indian servants and laborers to make their ranchos run smoothly. To learn more about the work of the Indian vaqueros, see A Moment in Time on the next page. ■

■ *Describe daily life on a rancho.*

A Vaquera at Work

2:00 P.M., October 3, 1830
A rodeo near the Rancho
Sal Si Puedes.

La Reata (Lariat)
She twirls the braised rawhide lariat and aims for the calf's neck. When she pulls the calf to the ground, other vaqueros will brand it MM.

Carne Seca (Dried Beef)
She carries half a piece of tough dried beef in her leather pouch. The other half she ate for lunch while in the saddle.

Chaparreras (Chaps)
Thorns tore into these leather coverings when the vaquera chased the calf through the thick underbrush.

Silla (Saddle)
The vaquera digs her knees into the saddle. Her father gave her this when she became the first woman on the rancho to work with the vaqueros.

Mustang
His hooves pound across the valley. The vaquera broke this wild horse herself, teaching him to stop, turn, and gallop.

Pueblo Life

▼ *This painting called* Horse Race *by Ernest Narjot shows how people from the pueblos gathered for special occasions. The racers are Indians, probably vaqueros from a nearby rancho.*

Though rancheros were many miles from the pueblos, they were still part of pueblo life. Each pueblo had a few hundred adobe houses grouped around a wide **plaza**, or town square. The town hall, a church, and ranchero houses faced the plaza. The rancheros stayed in these houses when they came to the pueblo to meet with hide and tallow traders and to record their brands with the alcalde.

Saddlers, blacksmiths, innkeepers, and laborers lived and worked in the pueblos. They depended on the business of the rancheros and traders for their living.

The citizens of the pueblo elected a **town council**. This was made up of a group of officials who met to talk about town affairs. The council chose an alcalde who acted both as mayor and as judge.

The pueblos were not only centers for government, but also for fiestas. A fiesta was a festival held after a rodeo or as a part of a wedding or religious holiday. During a fiesta everyone from the pueblo gathered in the plaza. They watched horse races and enjoyed outdoor feasts. Many young couples danced the fandango, a lively, whirling dance. The Californios held on to their Spanish traditions. But newcomers from outside California would soon change the Californio way of life. ■

➤ *The ranchero hat and rebozo (ruh BOH soh), or scarf, were common pieces of clothing worn by Californios for work and at fiestas.*

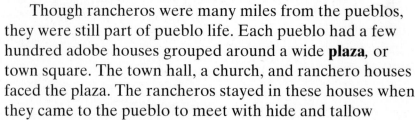

■ *What was the importance of the ranchos to the pueblos?*

R E V I E W

1. **FOCUS** How did the pueblos depend on the ranchos?
2. **CONNECT** Compare the work of a vaquero to the work of a sailor on a Spanish galleon. What similarities do you see?
3. **ECONOMICS** Describe the different jobs people performed on ranchos during the time of Mexican rule.
4. **CRITICAL THINKING** What might cause rancho herds to grow larger or smaller? How would these changes affect life on the ranchos and in the pueblos?
5. **WRITING ACTIVITY** Pretend you are a newspaper reporter living in a pueblo around 1840. Write three questions you would ask a ranchero and an alcalde.

Chapter 4

Giving Oral Directions

Here's Why

Suppose you are given directions for making the adobe bricks used to build the rancheros' houses. But the steps are out of order. It will be very hard for you to complete the task properly. Giving oral directions is an important skill that you can use in and out of school.

Here's How

Study the following rules for giving oral directions.
1. Tell the purpose of your directions.
2. Give one step at a time, in the right order. Use clue words such as *first, then,* and *next.*
3. Include enough details to make each step clear.
4. Speak clearly so that listeners can understand what you are saying.

When you are being given oral directions, listen carefully. Ask yourself, "Are the steps in the right order? Can I picture them in my mind?" Always ask questions if you do not understand.

Try It

The pictures and captions below show the steps for making adobe bricks. But the steps are out of order. Study the directions. Ask, "How can I put the steps in the right order? Can I add clue words or details to make the directions easier to understand?" When you have finished changing the directions, give them to the class orally. Have classmates answer these questions: Did the speaker speak clearly? Were the steps in the right order? Were they easy to understand?

Apply It

Choose a task, such as how to change a flat tire on a bike or how to take a picture with a camera. Prepare directions for doing the task. Then give your directions to classmates orally. Ask them to comment on the order of the steps. Have them tell if there were enough details so that they could picture the steps in their minds. Encourage them to ask questions about your directions.

Spread the bricks in the sun, and let them bake until they are hard.

Fill the wooden forms with the mixture of clay, water, and straw.

Mix clay and water with a little bit of straw.

When the bricks are dry, take them out of the forms.

Carlota

Scott O'Dell

This story shows traditions on a wealthy rancho and how they are about to change.

    Carlota de Zubarán lives on her family's rancho with her younger sister Yris, her father Don Saturnino, her grandmother Doña Dolores, and their servant Rosario. Her father has arranged the marriage of Yris and Don Roberto, the son of their neighbor, Don César. Doña Dolores is against the marriage. She and Don Saturnino are discussing the problem in this scene. As you read, ask yourself, "How might Carlota feel as she listens to her father and her grandmother argue about the marriage?"

*I*t rains," he said.

"To good purpose," Grandmother said.

"What is the purpose? We do not require floods and torrents."

"The marriage," Doña Dolores answered. "It gives time to make changes. Roberto can marry Carlota instead of Yris."

"Don César and I have thought of the marriage. We have talked about it for five years."

"It is not proper that the younger daughter marry first."

"Don César and I have given thought to everything. This as well. It is not what is proper, but what is best for Yris and Carlota."

My grandmother puffed away calmly. She shifted her feet, looking for Rosario's back, but Rosario had not returned. He was outside, under the *portale*, feeding the big eagle that belonged to my father.

"Carlota and Don Roberto," Father said scornfully, pulling at his pointed beard. "Have you asked their permission?"

"Permission," Doña Dolores replied, "as you well know, is not required."

"It would be prudent, nonetheless," Don Saturnino said, keeping his temper. "Carlota is not Yris. She is a true de Zubarán."

"The difference is great," my grandmother said. "This I

portale (pohr TAHL ay) a covered porch

prudent wise and practical

admit. You have seen to that. You have raised Carlota as a vaquero. She thinks of nothing but horses. Gray horses. Bay horses. White horses. Spotted horses. Palominos. Horses! She will not walk fifty steps. Instead, she will get on a horse and ride the distance."

What she said was true. I *had* been raised as a vaquero. I had been taught to do everything a horseman could do. My father had even named me after his son, Carlos, who had been killed by the Piutes.

"Yris is a girl of the *sala*, good at needlework and the viola," Doña Dolores said. "She is not suited to Don Roberto."

"Neither is Carlota," my father said. "Nobody is suited to Don Roberto. That he is Don César's only son is a misfortune."

"The hairy worm," my grandmother said. "It is your fault. You might have found one of the Bandinis for her. Or even a Yorba. All else failing, one of the numerous Palomareses."

Doña Dolores bounced up from the chair and hobbled to the window and gazed out at the rain falling. I saw her cross herself and I knew that she was praying for the rain to last forever. I walked to the door, leaving them to continue their talk, which would grow very fierce before it ended.

It did not trouble me. I had no intention of marrying Don Roberto, with his fat cheeks and fat little hands. And whatever Doña Dolores threatened — she sometimes said during these fights that she, and she alone, was the owner of the forty-seven-thousand-acre Rancho de los Dos Hermanos — but whatever she threatened, my father would never consent to such a marriage.

Furthermore, he would try to keep me at his side, as long as ever he could. And I did not mind the thought. I liked to ride with the vaqueros. I liked to go with my father and do the things he did. The truth was, as my grandmother often said, I thought little of anything except horses, all kinds and colors of horses. Nothing pleased me more than to be in my cordovan saddle with the big silver spurs on my heels.

Piutes (py YOOTS) a California Indian tribe

girl of the **sala** (SAH lah) a girl of the drawing room; a well-trained and well-mannered girl

viola a large violin

Bandinis, *Yorba*, *Palomareses* families that live near the de Zubaráns

Further Reading

To Touch the Sky. Augusta Fink. This is the story of Cristobal, a Californio boy, and his Indian friend, Mactutu.

Chapter Review

Reviewing Key Terms

barter (p.88)
independence (p.87)
land grant (p.91)
plaza (p.98)
products (p.88)
ranchero (p.91)
rancho (p.90)
rodeo (p.95)
town council (p.98)
vaquero (p.91)

A. Write the key term for each definition below:
1. a ranch
2. a cowboy
3. a town square
4. a rancher
5. a cattle roundup
6. a government gift of land
7. to trade without using money

B. Choose the key term that best completes each sentence.
1. Ships sailed to California carrying spices, shoes, and other _____.
2. The people of Mexico fought for _____ from the Spanish government.
3. Some Indians worked herding cattle and housekeeping on the new _____s.
4. After the war, the Mexican settlers received _____s from the new Mexican government.
5. The members of the _____ were elected by the citizens of the pueblo.
6. The Californios _____ed hides for the goods brought by the trading ships.

Exploring Concepts

A. Complete the chart at the right on a separate paper by listing two effects caused by each event in column one.

B. Support each statement below with two details from this chapter.
1. The people of Mexico wanted to be independent from Spain.
2. Closing the missions brought change to the padres and the mission Indians.
3. The Californios depended on trade with other countries.
4. The new Mexican government divided the mission lands into land grants.

Event (cause)	Effect 1	Effect 2
Mexican War for Independence		
Closing of the missions		
Beginning of the ranchos		

5. Many rancheros kept the traditions of Spanish and Mexican families.
6. The pueblos and ranchos depended on one another.
7. Many Indians worked on the ranchos.

Reviewing Skills

1. Read this sentence: Rancheros branded their cattle so they could tell which cattle belonged to them. Does the word *so* signal a cause or an effect?
2. The directions below are for a chili sauce, but the steps are out of order. Put the steps in the right order, and add word clues to make the directions easier to follow. Write the directions on a separate piece of paper.

   A. *Cook on low heat for about one hour.*
   B. *Put all the ingredients in a big pot.*
   C. *You will need 12 tomatoes, 3 onions, 3 green peppers, 1 red chili pepper, 3 tablespoons sugar, 2 cups vinegar, salt, and pepper.*

   D. *Chop the tomatoes, onions, green peppers, and chili pepper into small pieces.*

3. In the early 1800s, Russia traded with the Californios. Today Russia is part of the Soviet Union. Find the Soviet Union on the world map on page 320. In which two hemispheres is it found?
4. If you want to locate places in California and Mexico on the same map, would you use a world map or a map of North America?

Using Critical Thinking

1. How would life be different today if people bartered for what they needed instead of using money?
2. Most people want to work at jobs where they can earn a living and feel a sense of accomplishment. If you had lived on a rancho or in a pueblo, what job would you have liked? Why?
3. Few Indians became landowners. If the Indians had received land grants, how might their lives have been different?

Preparing for Citizenship

1. **ART ACTIVITY** Make a brand that you can use to mark the items you own. Use any combination of letters, numbers, or shapes you like.
2. **GROUP ACTIVITY** Work in a small group to plan a Barter Day for your class. Ask your classmates to bring in small inexpensive items that they would be willing to trade. In your group decide what kinds of items can be bartered and how the trades will be made. Make a list of rules to make sure the trades are fair. Then present your plan to the rest of the class.
3. **COLLABORATIVE LEARNING** As a class project, make a mural that shows what daily life was like on a rancho and in a pueblo. Work in two teams—a rancho team and a pueblo team. Find information in this chapter that will help you illustrate the setting, people, and activities of the rancho and the pueblo. Everyone on each team should help to plan and draw the pictures. When the mural is completed, have a spokesperson from each team explain the group's illustration.

Unit 3

Newcomers Change California

It was a time of change and a time for decisions. California was free of Spanish rule. Soon, newcomers would arrive in search of gold, in search of dreams. Ernest Narjot, who painted this picture, was one of those newcomers. He came from France seeking gold. He came with thousands of others from all over the world. These people and their ideas would change the face of California forever.

1820

Placer Mining at Foster's Bar
by Ernest Narjot, 1851. Bancroft Library

1870

Chapter 5
Newcomers from the United States

It was the 1820s, and the United States was beginning to notice California. This growing interest led a handful of hardy travelers to make the journey to the West. By the end of the 1840s, the path to California was well worn. Thousands of people from around the world were making their way to California.

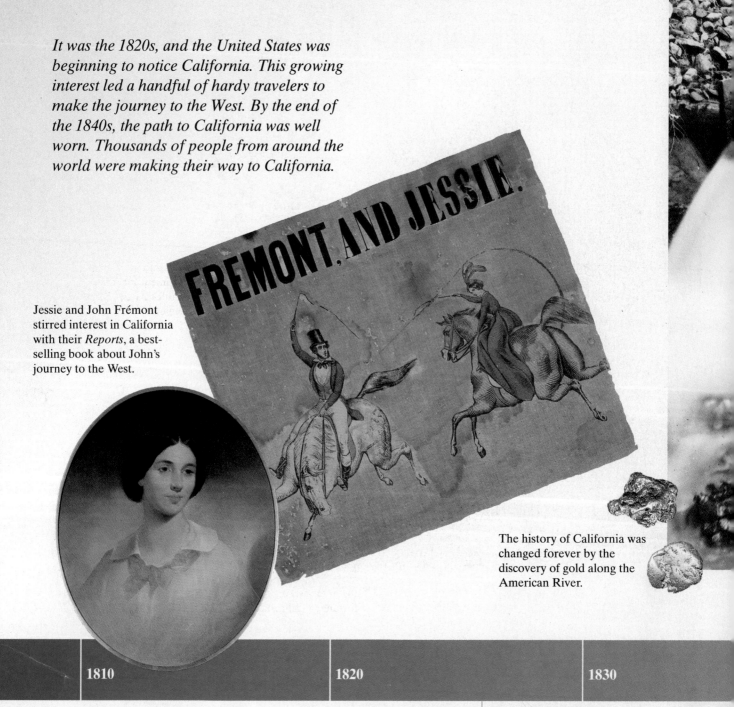

Jessie and John Frémont stirred interest in California with their *Reports*, a best-selling book about John's journey to the West.

The history of California was changed forever by the discovery of gold along the American River.

1810	1820	1830

1820

1826 Jedediah Smith becomes the first person from the United States to journey overland to California.

The banjo was basic equipment for many a California-bound traveler.

1849 Two miners work together, seeking their fortune in California.

1840   1850   1860

1839 John Sutter arrives in California. He later builds a saw mill where gold is first discovered.

1856

LESSON 1

Pioneers in California

Why were pioneers from the United States attracted to California?

Key Terms

- pioneer
- frontier

The howling winds battered the weary bodies of Jedediah Smith and his two friends. High in this mountain wilderness, hundreds of miles from any camp or town, the rugged men faced hunger, cold, and death.

Just days before, Smith and his men had been enjoying the peaceful beauty of the San Joaquin Valley. There, Smith's crew had found thousands of the beaver they had been looking for. They trapped hundreds of the animals, whose valuable skins they would later sell. Trapping was so successful that Smith decided to journey to his camp at the Great Salt Lake to find more trappers. But to get there, he had to cross these mountains.

Smith and his men pushed onward through the eight-foot-deep snow. Each step was a struggle, but slowly they moved forward. When their food ran out, the men ate the meat of their horses. At last, Smith's crew crossed over the mountains and headed down the other side. They had made it! Smith and his men had become the first people from the United States to cross the mighty Sierra Nevada.

Growing Interest in California

Smith's journey took place in 1826. At this time, trading ships from Boston, New York, and other cities were visiting California's ports often. But Smith and a handful of other adventurers were interested in more than just a short stop at California's coast. They wanted to explore California itself.

The First by Land

Smith's job was trapping beaver. But by the mid-1820s, these furry animals were becoming harder to find in the United States. Smith decided to go to

► *Among the few familiar sights on Smith's journey were animals like this coyote (ky OH tee).*

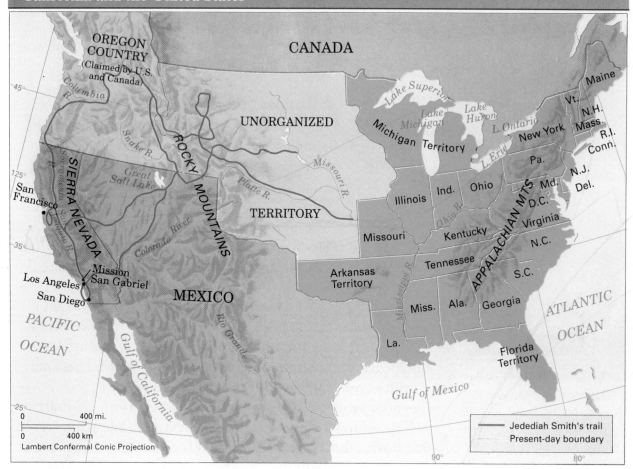

California and the United States

OREGON COUNTRY (Claimed by U.S. and Canada)

CANADA

UNORGANIZED

Columbia R.

Snake R.

ROCKY MOUNTAINS

Great Salt Lake

SIERRA NEVADA

San Francisco

Sacramento R.

San Joaquin R.

Colorado River

Platte R.

Missouri R.

TERRITORY

Michigan Territory

Lake Superior

Lake Michigan

Lake Huron

L. Ontario

L. Erie

Maine

Vt.

N.H.

Mass.

R.I.

Conn.

New York

Pa.

N.J.

Del.

Md.

D.C.

Ohio R.

Illinois

Ind.

Ohio

Missouri

Kentucky

Virginia

N.C.

APPALACHIAN MTS.

Mission San Gabriel

Los Angeles

San Diego

MEXICO

Rio Grande

Gulf of California

Arkansas Territory

Mississippi R.

Tennessee

Miss.

Ala.

Georgia

S.C.

La.

Florida Territory

ATLANTIC OCEAN

PACIFIC OCEAN

Gulf of Mexico

0   400 mi.

0   400 km

Lambert Conformal Conic Projection

— Jedediah Smith's trail
-·- Present-day boundary

45°   125°   35°   25°   90°   80°

California in search of beaver and adventure.

Getting to California would be a great challenge. At that time, no one from the United States had ever journeyed so far west by land. In front of Smith stretched a rugged region that was unknown even to his Indian guides. But when he crossed the blazing Mojave Desert, Smith became the first person from the United States to go overland to California.

Mexican officials were not pleased to see Smith. They wanted the United States to trade at California's ports. They also feared that the United States might want to take over California. The Mexican officials thought that Smith was a spy from the United States, so they ordered him to leave. Smith fled from the officials and headed north into the San Joaquin Valley, trapping beaver as he went. Finally, he turned east and made his historic crossing of the Sierra Nevada.

To the United States, Smith was a **pioneer**. This means that he journeyed into a new land and showed the way for others to follow. But to Mexican officials in California, Smith was not just a pioneer. They thought his visit showed

▲ *Why do you think no one from the United States had traveled overland to California?*

▲ *Pioneers came to California to find adventure and wealth. Smith, for example, came looking for valuable beaver furs.*

Newcomers from the United States

Harvey Dunn showed the rugged overland route to California in his painting Jedediah Smith in the Badlands.

■ *Why did the Mexican government welcome Abel Stearns and not Jedediah Smith?*

that the United States was interested in California. This outside interest in their land was not welcome.

A Business Pioneer

The Mexican government had a more friendly feeling toward Abel Stearns, another pioneer from the United States. In 1828 Stearns sailed to California from his home state of Massachusetts to open a trading business in Los Angeles. Like Jedediah Smith, Stearns saw the opportunity to find wealth in California. But unlike Smith, Stearns had respect for the Mexican government. He shared his knowledge of business with the Californios to help them improve their trading methods. At the same time, Stearns was so successful in his business that he became the wealthiest man in Los Angeles.

Stearns chose to become a Mexican citizen. He married a Californio woman and learned the Spanish language. Mexican officals gave Stearns a large land grant because he respected and worked with their government. The Mexican officials could see that Stearns was not a threat to their control of California. ■

More Arrivals in California

Smith and Stearns led the way to California. During the next 20 years, hundreds of settlers would follow them. They were eager to explore the land beyond the edge of the settled part of the country. This land was called the **frontier**.

Sutter's Fort

One of these settlers was John August Sutter. In 1834 Sutter had come to the United States from Switzerland to find his fortune. But after two failures in business, he decided to go to California to start a new life.

Like Abel Stearns, Sutter agreed to become a Mexican citizen. In return, the Mexican government gave Sutter 30,000 acres of land in the Sacramento Valley. Today this land is part of the city of Sacramento.

With the help of hundreds of Indians, Sutter built a huge settlement on this land. The village had a fort, workshops, and farms. He called it New Helvetia *(hel VEE shuh)*, or New Switzerland. As Sutter's settlement grew, it became an important stopping place for other explorers and settlers from the United States.

The Donner Party

By the 1840s the first wagon trains had set out for California. But only the strongest of the settlers could complete the dangerous journey across the Sierra Nevada.

In 1846 a group of 87 settlers led by the Donner family got into terrible trouble on their way to California. The group tried to take a short cut from the trail they were following. Instead of saving time, the Donner Party became hopelessly lost. When they finally reached the Sierra Nevada in the month of October, snow had already blocked their path.

The Donner Party was stuck for the winter at what is now Donner Lake. So much snow fell that they could not hunt for food. As their food supply ran out, members of the party began to starve. In December, several of the men set out on foot to find help. Finally, a rescue party from Sutter's Fort reached Donner Lake. The Donner Party had been trapped in the snow for seven months. Only 47 people were still alive.

Stories like that of the Donner Party discouraged many people from coming to California. Still, hundreds of others set out for the West Coast every month. The number of settlers from the United States in California was growing. ■

How Do We Know?

HISTORY *One of the surviving children in the Donner Party, Eliza P. Donner Houghton, grew up to write a book about the journey. She wrote* Expedition of the Donner Party and Its Tragic Fate *in 1911.*

◄ *The story of the Donner Party reminded the country of the great danger of the journey to California.*

■ *What does the experience of the Donner Party tell you about traveling to California in the early 1840s?*

R E V I E W

1. **FOCUS** Why were pioneers from the United States attracted to California?

2. **CONNECT** Find an example of other pioneers in California from your earlier reading.

3. **ECONOMICS** Why did the Mexican government want ships from the United States to visit California, but not explorers?

4. **CRITICAL THINKING** Do you think the Mexican government had reason to fear the arrival of people from the United States? Explain your answer.

5. **WRITING ACTIVITY** Imagine you are a settler going to California in 1846. Write a paragraph explaining why you are moving to California.

Measuring Distances on a Map

Here's Why

Look at the size of the state of California on different maps in the Atlas. On the world map on page 320, California appears to be small. On the United States maps and the California maps, it appears to be larger.

Of course, the size of the state doesn't actually change. California appears to be different sizes because maps are drawn to different scales. For example, on one map an inch might stand for 50 miles, but on another map an inch could equal 1,000 miles.

Suppose you want to find out how far a pioneer family had to travel to get from Iowa to California on the Oregon trail. To figure out the distance between two places, you need to use a map scale.

Here's How

Look at Map A below. It shows the overland trails followed by early pioneers from the United States. Now find the map scale. A map scale is a straight line with distances marked on it. Each section stands for a certain number of miles. On Map A, each section on the scale stands for 50 miles.

You can use the map scale to measure the distance between Sacramento and Carson City. Line up the edge of a piece of paper with the dots that show

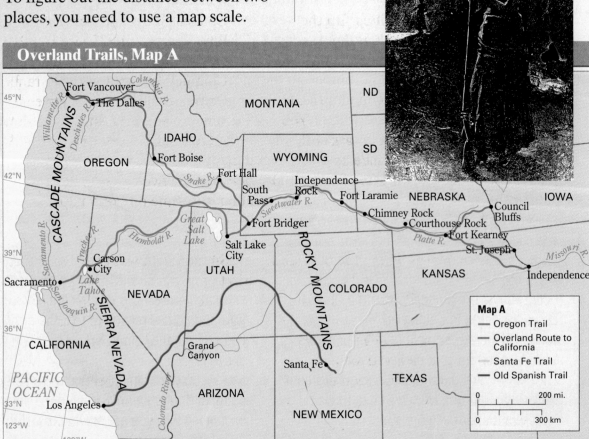

Overland Trails, Map A

Fort Vancouver
The Dalles
Columbia R.
Willamette R.
Deschutes R.
CASCADE MOUNTAINS
MONTANA
ND
IDAHO
OREGON
Fort Boise
WYOMING
SD
Snake R.
Fort Hall
42°N
South Pass
Independence Rock
Sweetwater R.
Fort Laramie
NEBRASKA
IOWA
Chimney Rock
Council Bluffs
Fort Bridger
Courthouse Rock
Great Salt Lake
Fort Kearney
Humboldt R.
Platte R.
St. Joseph
Missouri R.
Salt Lake City
Sacramento R.
Trucke R.
ROCKY MOUNTAINS
39°N
Carson City
UTAH
KANSAS
Independence
Sacramento
Lake Tahoe
NEVADA
COLORADO
San Joaquin R.
SIERRA NEVADA
36°N
CALIFORNIA
Grand Canyon
PACIFIC OCEAN
Santa Fe
Colorado River
ARIZONA
TEXAS
33°N
Los Angeles
NEW MEXICO
123°W
120°W

Map A
— Oregon Trail
— Overland Route to California
— Santa Fe Trail
— Old Spanish Trail

0   200 mi.
0   300 km

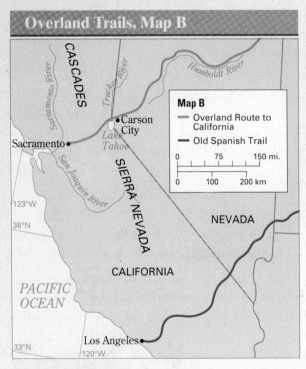

Overland Trails, Map B

CASCADES

Trukee River

Humboldt River

Sacramento River

•Carson City

Sacramento•

Lake Tahoe

San Joaquin River

SIERRA NEVADA

NEVADA

123°W

36°N

CALIFORNIA

PACIFIC OCEAN

33°N

Los Angeles•

120°W

Map B
— Overland Route to California
— Old Spanish Trail

0   75   150 mi.

0   100   200 km

the locations of the two cities. On the paper, make a pencil mark at the dot for Sacramento and another pencil mark at the dot for Carson City.

Now put the paper on the map scale. Place the first pencil mark on the 0. You will see that the second dot marks off about 100 miles. The distance between Sacramento and Carson City is about 100 miles.

Compare Map A with Map B above. Map B was drawn to a different scale. It shows only the places where the overland trails reached California. Find Sacramento and Carson City on Map B. The distance between the two cities looks longer on Map B than it does on Map A. But use the map scales on each map to figure out the distance between the two cities. You will find that both maps show that Sacramento and Carson City are about 100 miles apart.

Do not be fooled by the size of a map. Distances between places may look longer on one map than they do on another because maps are drawn to different scales. Always use the map scale to find the distance between places.

Try It

Pioneer Catherine Haun and her husband left Clinton, Iowa on April 24, 1849, and arrived in Sacramento six months later. They followed the Oregon Trail, stopping along the way at Council Bluffs and at some of the other places named on Map A.

Use the map scale to measure the distances between each of the two places listed below.
1. Council Bluffs and Fort Kearney
2. Fort Kearney and Courthouse Rock
3. Courthouse Rock and Fort Laramie
4. Chimney Rock and Fort Laramie

Compare the distance between Sacramento and Los Angeles as shown on the two maps. Use the map scales on each map to measure the distance between the two cities. Is the distance about the same on both maps?

Apply It

Suppose you want to plan a family trip to one of the national parks in California. Use the map of California on page 329 of the Atlas. How many miles does each section on the scale stand for? Figure out how many miles you would have to travel from your town to Sequoia National Park. How many miles would you travel from Sequoia National Park to Lassen Volcanic National Park?

113

Patty Reed's Doll

Rachel Laurgaard

The Sutter's Fort Historical Museum has a wooden doll that belonged to a girl named Patty Reed in 1846. In this story, Patty's doll tells the adventures of the Donner Party on their journey from Illinois to California. Here you join the frightened pioneers as they climb the frozen Sierra Nevada in a dangerous snowstorm. As you read, ask yourself, "What were these pioneers feeling as they tried to cross the mountains?"

In Lesson 1 you learned about the Donner Party. These early pioneers faced many hardships as they crossed the Western frontier.

As we traveled up toward Truckee Lake, snow began to fall. When the clouds lifted from the summits of the mountains and the folks saw that they were covered with white, I could tell that they were frightened.

"Oh, it will be awful if we are snowed in," Patty said to Puss.

"We won't be. Papa will be coming any day now to meet us," her sister answered confidently.

Along the edge of Truckee Lake the mules plodded through soft, deep snow.

"Why, there's a cabin," Patty called out. The mule and Indian we were clinging to proved to be the best trail breakers, so we were somewhat ahead of the rest.

marooned stuck or stranded

"It was built by a party that got marooned up here a few years ago, they told me," Mr. Stanton said. "We are close to the summit—only three miles or so."

We struggled on under a full moon, until the Indians made it known to Mr. Stanton that the snow had covered the trail and they were lost. We turned back and, arriving at the cabin we had passed, we found the Breen family already in possession.

in possession staying in the cabin

However, they weren't much better off than the rest of us, crowded in the remaining wagons. Rain poured down in the night and leaked through the cabin roof of pine boughs just as it did through the tattered canvas of the wagon tops.

boughs (bowz) branches

114

"The rain will melt the snow, won't it?" Patty's mother asked.

"It may not be rain up on the pass," Mr. Stanton answered in a worried tone. "When it rains lower down, it snows up above, they say."

He was right. Floundering through the drifts next day, we were able to advance only a mile or two before nightfall. Wet and cold from plunging into the deep snow, the folks gathered around a blazing log fire that night in frightened consultation.

"We'll have to abandon the wagons, there's no doubt of that," someone said. "If we strap our provisions to the backs of the oxen, we may be able to pack through."

"It will be slow going with all the children," someone else said. "Every grownup will have to carry a child. The snow's much too deep for the little ones to make it alone."

The next day they tried to carry out this plan. The oxen were not very co-operative. The children laughed to see them wallowing in the snow. But it was no laughing matter to the men who were trying to salvage enough food to get their families safely across the mountains.

It was late afternoon when we started, and Patty and I were in the lead, with Salvador and the donkey making a road for the struggling line of people behind us. In some places the snow was waist deep and, carrying children and driving unruly oxen, they were able to move only at a snail's pace. Finally the snow got so deep that the mule we were clinging to kept falling head first into the gullies filled with snow. Patty was taken off, and Mr. Stanton and the Indians tried to ride ahead and find the road, while the rest waited behind.

By the time they returned, the wet, discouraged families were huddled around a roaring campfire in a dead pine tree filled with pitch. The oxen had rubbed off their packs against trees, and everyone was too exhausted to struggle on.

Mr. Stanton tried to persuade them that they must. They could get through, he thought, if it didn't snow any more.

consultation discussion

provisions supplies and food

salvage save

pitch thick sap that burns easily

Further Reading

The Secret Valley. Clyde Robert Bulla. This is the story of the adventures of the Davis family, who come to California in 1849 from Missouri.

L E S S O N   2

Mexico Defeated

THINKING
F O C U S

How did the United States gain control of California from Mexico?

Key Terms

- rebel
- nation
- treaty

W hat could that be? It wasn't even morning yet! General Mariano Vallejo *(vuh YEH hoh)* jumped from his bed to see what the noise was outside his home. From his window, he saw about 30 rough-looking men gathered in the road outside. Through the dim light of the dawn he could see that they were settlers from the United States. They looked as if they were ready for trouble.

By this time, Vallejo's wife, Francisca Benicia, was awake. She knew that these men were after her husband, who was in charge of the old Mexican military base at Sonoma. She urged her husband to try to escape. No, Vallejo said. He would go meet the men face to face. Bravely, he went to the front door and opened it.

Revolt and War

It was the spring of 1846, and there were about 2,000 settlers from the United States in California. Tensions were mounting between the settlers and the Californios. Many Californios did not want these new settlers in California unless the settlers would agree to live by the Californios' rules. The settlers were not going to leave without a fight. Each side had made angry threats against the other. So when Vallejo saw the group of rough-looking settlers outside his home, he was not sure what to expect.

Bear Flag Revolt

Vallejo learned that the men at his door were taking over the military base. What's more, they were taking him prisoner. But Vallejo saw that there was little to fear from these settlers. For one thing, they did not even bother to take away his sword. And Sonoma, the military base they were capturing, had few weapons and no soldiers. It was even infested with fleas. So Vallejo decided to go along with the rebels. People who fight against the government are **rebels.** Vallejo invited the rebels into his house and offered them refreshments.

After Vallejo's warm welcome, the rebels got down to their task. At Sonoma they raised a flag that displayed a grizzly bear and the words "California Republic." The rebels said that they were creating a new **nation.** They were setting up a new government that would rule California the way they wanted. The rebels announced that their California Republic was at war with Mexico. But so far, it had been a very peaceful "war." In fact, the rebels and Vallejo had been quite friendly with each other.

As the story of what happened at Sonoma spread, others were not in such a friendly mood. Mexican officials were angry and prepared to fight back. Settlers in the area rushed to defend the California Republic at Sonoma. Without waiting for official orders, a United States Army officer named John C. Frémont took charge of the rebels. He ordered them to hold Vallejo under tight guard.

Before long, 300 settlers had joined the rebels. This was a large force in California at that time. In fact, it is possible that the Bear Flaggers could have defeated the Mexican government in California. But they never got the chance. Before the Bear Flag Revolt began, the United States government in Washington, D.C., had declared war on Mexico.

▼ *California's state flag is based on the flag made by the Bear Flag rebels.*

Across Time & Space

The original California Republic flag, made by Bear Flagger William C. Todd, was hand-drawn on unbleached cotton. The star in the upper left corner and the grizzly bear next to it were dyed with blackberry juice. In 1911 California chose to use Todd's flag as the model for the present state flag of California.

◄ *The Bear Flag rebels announced that they were forming a new nation. This nation would share their ideas and beliefs.*

117

Newcomers from the United States

News of the war did not reach the rebels until July 9, 1846. On that day the United States Army rode into Sonoma and took over the battle to defeat the Mexican government.

War in California

In the 1840s many people in the United States believed that their nation should rule all the land between the East and West coasts. Mexico owned much of this land. So the United States decided to go to war with Mexico to try to win this land.

Most of the Mexican War was fought in Texas and Mexico. But two major battles took place in California, at San Pasqual and San Pedro. In these battles, Californio soldiers fought brilliantly. Stephen W. Kearny, a general in the United States Army, admired their horseback-riding skills.

UNDERSTANDING NATIONS

At the time of the Bear Flag Revolt, California was part of the nation of Mexico. But the Bear Flag rebels did not feel that they were a part of Mexico. They were not happy with the Mexican government that ruled California. So the rebels decided that they would create a new nation based on their own beliefs.

What Makes a Nation

A nation is a group of people who live in a certain place, united under a single government. That government makes rules for the nation and helps provide for its citizens' needs.

You live in the nation called the United States. Your government protects you and your fellow citizens by providing for the nation's defense. Your government also arranges important services for its citizens. For example, it gives loans for building housing and for education.

Common Beliefs and Values

But a nation is more than just a group of people joined under one government. The people of a nation share their own special history and traditions. In the United States, for example, we celebrate independence from England on the Fourth of July. And each year, we celebrate the memory of our nation's leaders on holidays like Presidents' Day and Martin Luther King, Jr. Day. School children across the nation start the day by singing "The Star Spangled Banner" or reciting "The Pledge of Allegiance." By sharing these traditions, we feel that we're a part of something important.

The making of a nation does not happen quickly. The feelings and beliefs shared by a nation's people take time to grow and deepen. California's Bear Flag rebels did not have the time to build these feelings and beliefs. So their nation, the California Republic, soon faded away.

He said that the Californios were "the very best riders in all the world." The Mexican army, however, did not have enough soldiers to fight in California for long. In January 1847 the armies from the United States chased the last Californio soldiers out of Los Angeles. The retreating soldiers ran into Frémont and his troops at Cahuenga Pass. There they surrendered without a fight. From that day on Frémont called himself the "Conqueror of California," even though he had done none of the fighting. ■

■ *The 300 Bear Flag rebels might have been able to conquer California by themselves. What does this say about California in the 1840s?*

California Captured

The United States had captured California in 1847, but the fighting in the Mexican War lasted until the winter of 1848. Finally, Mexico and the United States agreed to stop their fighting. On February 2, 1848 the two nations signed a treaty in the Mexican village of Guadalupe *(gwah duh LOO peh)* Hidalgo. A **treaty** is an official agreement between two or more nations.

The treaty that the United States and Mexico signed is known as the Treaty of Guadalupe Hidalgo. As part of this treaty, Mexico agreed to give a large area of land to the United States. This land, which is known as the Mexican Cession *(SEHSH uhn)*, is shown on the map. The treaty cut the size of Mexico almost in half. It also made California the property of the United States, though it did not make California a state.

▼ *After the war, the borders of the United States stretched from coast to coast.*

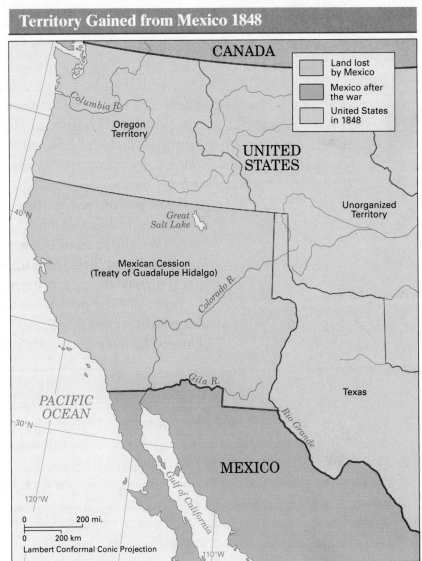

Territory Gained from Mexico 1848

The Change of Power

Some Californios were not happy that California now belonged to the United States. A few of these angry Californios made plans to fight the

United States so that they could win back their land. But nothing ever came of these plans.

Most Californios accepted the Treaty of Guadalupe Hidalgo because they thought that it would protect them. The treaty promised that Californios who had owned land in California before the war would be allowed to keep it. The treaty also made the Californios citizens of the United States. As citizens, the Californios would have the same rights as other United States citizens.

The fact that California now belonged to the United States did not upset most Californios. At first, United States officials did little to change life in California. They kept the old form of government the Californios had used before the war. They even allowed many Californio alcaldes to keep their old jobs. This meant that control of government in many towns was still in the Californios' hands.

Most people in California noticed few changes in their daily lives. Indians and Californios continued to live as they had. Also, the lives of the few settlers from the United States changed little. Many of these settlers looked forward to a return to the peaceful life they had known before.

Little did the people of California know of the events that would soon take place. Soon, their land would be changed forever. ■

With the Treaty of Guadalupe Hidalgo, the United States and Mexico agreed to end the war.

■ *Why might some settlers from the United States have wanted California to stay as it was before the war?*

R E V I E W

1. **FOCUS** How did the United States gain control of California from Mexico?

2. **CONNECT** Find another example of a revolt in California from your earlier reading.

3. **GEOGRAPHY** Why do you think the Bear Flag rebels did not know for a long time that the United States and Mexico were at war?

4. **CRITICAL THINKING** What do you think the Bear Flag rebels hoped to achieve by creating their new nation?

5. **ACTIVITY** By comparing the maps on pages 119 and 324, find the states that are located on land of the Mexican Cession.

Chapter 5

LESSON 3

The Rush for Gold

The January morning began like many others. James W. Marshall walked down to the American River to check on the sawmill he was building for John Sutter.

At the water's edge, a flash of light caught Marshall's eye. Then he saw another flash and another. Curious, Marshall stopped to look at the dozens of bright sparkles twinkling in the shallow water. He plunged his hand into the icy stream and scooped up a handful of sand. In the sand were several shiny yellow flakes. Could it be?

Marshall stared hard at the glittering sand. He did not know whether to believe his eyes. But the longer he studied the yellow flakes sparkling in his hand, the more certain he became. Finally, Marshall could no longer keep his startling discovery to himself. "I have found it!" he shouted out loud. At that moment in 1848, gold was discovered in California. And the gold rush began.

THINKING FOCUS

What was the gold rush, and what did it mean to the United States and the world?

Key Terms

- gold rush
- forty-niners
- isthmus

◄ *James W. Marshall stands in front of Sutter's Mill, where he made the discovery that started the California gold rush. The piece of gold that he found on that day in 1848 is shown below.*

The Rush Is On

Marshall decided to show the gold to his boss, John Sutter. If there was more gold to be found, Marshall explained, the two men would be rich. Sure enough, when Marshall and Sutter returned to the sawmill, they found many more flakes and nuggets. Suddenly, their excitement was interrupted by a loud cry of *"Oro! Oro! Oro!"* Another worker

121

Newcomers from the United States

at the mill, shouting in Spanish, had found gold too. Marshall's discovery was no longer a secret.

Within six weeks, all of the workers at Sutter's Fort had left to hunt for gold. The discovery of gold would soon bring amazing changes to the rest of California as well.

Rumors of Riches

In San Francisco, rumors of gold near Sutter's Fort began to swirl around town. As it became clear that the rumors were at least partly true, Californians scrambled to the gold fields in huge numbers. So many left for the mines that on May 17, 1848, a newspaper called the *San Francisco Californian* gave this report:

> The merchants and mechanics are closing doors, the lawyers and alcaldes leaving their desks, the farmers neglecting their crops, and whole families forsaking [leaving] their homes, all suffering from the effects of this fever.

By late 1848, the gold rumors had spread to the eastern United States. In December, President James K. Polk gave a speech in which he talked about California's gold. Newspapers from around the world carried the story.

Gold Fever!

The year 1849 marked the beginning of the **gold rush**. This was the large flow of miners who traveled to California to find gold. Driven by dreams of great riches, thousands of people, most of them young men, packed their trunks for

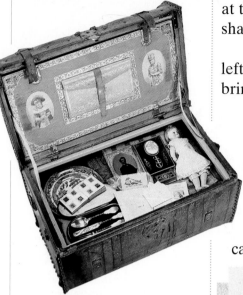

▲ *When word of gold spread, people from around the world packed their trunks and headed for California.*

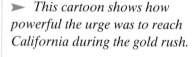
➤ *This cartoon shows how powerful the urge was to reach California during the gold rush.*

California. By mid-January of that year, one out of every five men in Plymouth, Massachusetts, had left home to search for gold. The story was the same in cities and towns around the world. These daring gold-seekers were called **forty-niners** because they began their journey to search for gold in 1849. ■

■ What does the cartoon on page 122 say about many of California's forty-niners?

◄ In the 1840s pioneers traveled in large groups of covered wagons. They traveled about 15 or 20 miles a day.

By Land and Sea

Before the forty-niners could find their fortunes in the gold fields of California, they had to get there. The journey to California was a challenge because traveling by land or sea was still very difficult.

The Overland Journey

The least costly way to get to California was the overland route. Unlike the Donner Party and other early travelers, most forty-niners could choose from many good trails. Still, these trails presented dangers such as flooded rivers, burning deserts, and steep mountain passes. Many travelers did not prepare well for the six-month trip. They brought too much clothing and too many supplies. These heavy loads wore out the animals that pulled their wagons.

Finding fresh water was another problem. At the beginning of a stretch of dry desert, one traveler left a message for those who followed: "Expect to find the worst desert you ever saw and then find it worse than you expected. Take water, be sure to take enough." When forty-niners did find water, it was often unsafe to drink. Many died of diseases caught from unsafe water.

How Do We Know?

HISTORY *Newspaper articles and advertisements helped spread gold fever across the nation and the world. Many of these newspapers have been saved in libraries and museums, where they can still be read today.*

123

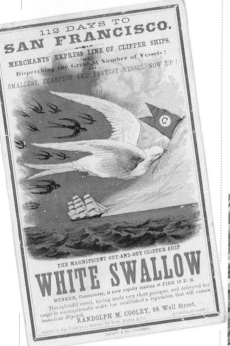

Sea Travel

Forty-niners also traveled to California by sea. The ships sailed from the eastern United States, went around South America, and then north to San Francisco. The ships were crowded. Passengers often spent the six-month journey bored and seasick. The waters of Cape Horn on the southern tip of South America were often stormy and frightening. The verses from "On the Banks of the Sacramento," a song of the time, told the story:

*A*round Cape Stiff in seventy days,
Around Cape Stiff is a mighty long ways.
When we was tacking 'round Cape Horn,
I'd often wished I'd never been born.

So blow, blow, blow, for Californio,
There's plenty of gold so I've been told
On the banks of the Sacramento.

The Panama Route

The fastest way to California was by steamship to Central America. From there forty-niners crossed the 75-mile-wide Isthmus *(IHS muhs)* of Panama. An **isthmus** is a narrow strip of land that connects two larger sections. After crossing the isthmus, forty-niners boarded steamships that ran up the coast of Mexico to California. The whole trip might take a month if a traveler could get a ticket. When tickets were available, they were costly. Also, the food was bad. One passenger wrote, "The pork is rusty, the beef rotten, the duff [bread dough] half-cooked and the beans contain two bugs to a bean."

The hardships of travel to California were many. But the adventurers who made the long journey had high hopes of finding gold. So the flood of forty-niners seemed to grow each day. ■

▲ *Hundreds of ships made the trip around Cape Horn during the gold rush. Sometimes, the ships were leaky and the captains poorly qualified to make the voyage.*

■ *What were the advantages and disadvantages of traveling through the Isthmus of Panama?*

R E V I E W

1. **FOCUS** What was the gold rush, and what did it mean to the United States and the world?

2. **CONNECT** What advantage did the forty-niners who traveled overland have over earlier travelers like the Donner Party?

3. **ECONOMICS** How do you think the gold rush changed cities and towns like Plymouth, Massachusetts?

4. **CRITICAL THINKING** Forty-niners were said to have gold fever. Why do you think the word "fever" was used?

5. **ACTIVITY** Based on the cartoon on page 122, draw a picture of your own gold rush traveling machine.

LESSON 4

Gold Mining

"Gold Mine Found!" "New Gold Mine!" "The Gold Mine Again!" Every day, newspapers screamed the latest gold rush news. What was everyone so excited about?

Gold—some people say that the shiny metal has always made people act a little bit crazy. Gold is beautiful to look at. It is also worth a great deal of money. Today an ounce of gold might be worth 400 dollars or more. During the gold rush, gold was worth 16 dollars an ounce. At the time, that was a lot of money.

For most forty-niners, finding an ounce of gold took a day of hard work. But in the busy mining towns, forty-niners found that their 16 dollars did not buy much. One man reported paying 43 dollars just for breakfast for two. There was so little food in California that restaurants could charge whatever they wanted. In addition to this, clothes and supplies cost a lot of money.

Of course, a few miners found much more than an ounce of gold a day. But most were not so lucky. A great many struggled just to find a few pennies' worth of gold.

THINKING FOCUS

What was it like to be a gold miner in gold rush California?

Key Terms

- claim
- technology

▲ *Forty-niners eagerly weighed the gold they mined to see how rich they had become.*

Finding a Mine

The first thing a miner had to do was to find some land to mine. When a miner declared that an area belonged to him or her, that land was called a miner's **claim**. Forty-niners looked for their claims along the many rivers flowing

125

Newcomers from the United States

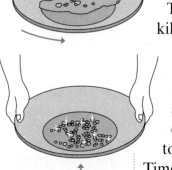

Pans like these were used to separate gold from sand.

■ *Why did miners have to stake their claims?*

down from the Sierra Nevada. Gold had been collecting in these streams for thousands of years. As rain and melted snow rushed down the mountainsides, water washed away bits of gold layered in the rock. The heavy gold then settled in the sand of the rivers fed by the rushing water.

Most of the mining land was owned by Indians. But this did not stop the miners from setting up their claims. The miners chased the Indians away. Some miners even killed Indians to get their land.

If there were many miners in an area, a claim might be only a few feet wide. If there were few miners, claims might cover hundreds of feet. To keep others away, miners placed stakes around their claims. They called this "staking a claim." But some miners still tried to steal, or "jump," other miners' claims. A Moment in Time on the next page tells more about the forty-niners. ■

Mining for Gold

Once the miner found and staked a claim, it was time for some hard work. Unlike James Marshall, most miners could not simply pick up gold from the ground.

The Panning Method

The earliest and simplest method of gold mining was panning. To pan, a miner filled a flat-bottomed pan with dirt and water from the riverbed. The miner then swirled the water around. The heavy gold would separate from the sand and dirt. When the gold settled to the bottom of the pan, the miner could collect it.

The Rocker

The rocker was another early piece of mining equipment. Forty-niners could mine much more earth with a rocker than they could with a simple pan.

To use a rocker, miners often worked in pairs. First, the miners dumped dirt into a small tray. One miner then poured water over the dirt while the other moved the rocker back and forth.

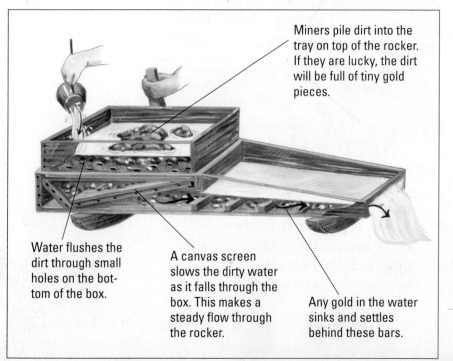

Miners pile dirt into the tray on top of the rocker. If they are lucky, the dirt will be full of tiny gold pieces.

Water flushes the dirt through small holes on the bottom of the box.

A canvas screen slows the dirty water as it falls through the box. This makes a steady flow through the rocker.

Any gold in the water sinks and settles behind these bars.

Forty-niner

2:30 P.M., August 15, 1850
A mountain stream near Sacramento

Blistered Hand

Swinging his pick since dawn has raised new blisters on this miner's rough hands. He was a bookkeeper from Maine, and all this stooping and digging is harder work than he thought it would be.

Wild Grapes

He found these grapes as he moved downstream to get away from other miners. His food is rarely exciting — flapjacks and bacon every day.

Backpack

He bought this pack in San Francisco for 50 dollars — 10 times what it would have cost back East. Strapped to the top are the first letters he's received from home.

Nugget

"Yahoo! Now that's more like it!" This is the biggest nugget he's ever seen. He'll build a lean-to right here, set up camp, and stake his claim.

Goldmining Pan

He has been working on his twenty-sixth panful of dirt since this morning. The cloudy water just cleared. Until now, he has only seen flakes of gold at the bottom of the pan.

Boots

His cold toes are pressed against soaking wet leather. These boots haven't been dry in weeks.

▲ *After much of the gold had been mined from the riverbeds, miniers used hydraulic mining to unearth more gold.*

The water washed through the dirt and out of the box. Wooden bars on the bottom of the rocker trapped the gold as the water flowed through.

Large-Scale Mining

By the mid-1850s, most of the gold had been mined from the rivers. Miners were no longer finding much gold with pans and rockers. So they began to use new **technology** to reach their goal. This means that they found better methods, equipment, and ways to use science. Part of this technology included the use of huge hoses to spray water against riverbanks and mountainsides. The powerful streams of water tore away tons of sand, dirt, and gravel. This new method, called hydraulic mining, allowed miners to get at gold buried deeper in the ground.

This new technology was harmful to the earth. The huge piles of gravel left over from hydraulic mining blocked the flow of rivers. The blocked rivers often overflowed onto farmland. Fish and wildlife also suffered. This hurt the Indians too, because they needed the fish in the rivers and the nearby wildlife for food. ■

■ *What was one reason miners began to use more complicated machines for mining?*

Living in the Mines

California's miners spent a great deal of energy looking for gold. Some forty-niners really did strike it rich. Others caught a lifelong case of gold fever. They spent the rest of

Chapter 5

their lives chasing rumors of gold all across North America. But for most miners, the dreams that brought them to California quickly faded. What money they did make was soon swallowed up by the high prices.

A Difficult Life

The failure of many miners was made worse by the hard life at the mines. In an 1852 letter, Mary Ballou spoke for many forty-niners. Ballou wrote, "I would not advise any Lady to come out here and suffer the toil and fatigue that I have suffered for the sake of a little gold, neither do I advise any one to come."

A miner named Charles Bennett wrote to a friend about the lack of food in his mining camp. Like hundreds of others, Bennett became ill from not eating well and had to leave the gold fields. He told his friend that the best way to find riches was to grow food for the hungry miners.

▼ *Whole families made the hard journey to California to search for gold.*

Miners Beyond the Mines

Because of problems like these, most forty-niners had left the mines by the mid-1850s. Some went back to their old homes. Many stayed in California and worked on farms or ranches or in stores and businesses. They settled new towns and raised families. With their skills and energy, these former miners played an important role in the growth of California in the late 1800s. The years ahead would be every bit as exciting as the crazy days of the gold rush. ■

■ *Besides the gold they found, what did the forty-niners contribute to California?*

R E V I E W

1. **FOCUS** What was it like to be a gold miner in gold rush California?
2. **CONNECT** Where else have you read about Indians losing their land to newcomers to California?
3. **ECONOMICS** What is one reason that the rocker allowed miners to mine more earth than they could with a pan?
4. **CRITICAL THINKING** Why do you think so many people came to California even though few became wealthy?
5. **WRITING ACTIVITY** Imagine that you are a miner. Write a letter home to your family telling about your life in the gold fields.

Chapter Review

Reviewing Key Terms

claim (p.125)
forty-niners (p.123)
frontier (p.110)
gold rush (p.122)
isthmus (p.124)

nation (p.117)
pioneer (p.109)
rebel (p.117)
technology (p.128)
treaty (p.119)

A. Choose the key term that best completes each sentence.
1. The Bear Flaggers were _____s who wanted to form their own nation.
2. When the United States and Mexico signed a _____, the land of California became part of the United States.
3. A _____ is a group of people joined together under one government.
4. As gold became harder to find, miners used new _____ to help them uncover gold buried deep in the ground.

B. Write a sentence for each pair of words below:
1. pioneer, frontier
2. claim, miner
3. forty-niners, gold rush
4. isthmus, Panama
5. Mexican War, treaty

Exploring Concepts

A. Complete the chart at the right on a separate paper. Use information from this chapter.

B. Write one or two sentences to answer each question below. Use details from this chapter to support your answers.

Group That Came	Examples of People Who Came	Year They Came	Reasons They Came
First pioneers			
Settlers			
Gold miners			

1. How was Jedediah Smith's journey across the Sierra Nevada important to later United States pioneers?
2. What hardships did settlers face on their way to California?
3. Why were Mexican officials worried when settlers from the United States began to arrive in California?
4. What disagreements did United States settlers and the Californios have?
5. How did the Treaty of Guadalupe Hidalgo affect the lands controlled by the United States and Mexico?
6. How did the discovery of gold in California affect people in the rest of the country?
7. What different methods did miners use to find gold?

Reviewing Skills

1. Why is a map scale useful?
2. Imagine that you are a gold miner and want to travel from Salt Lake City, Utah to Sacramento, California. Use the map on page 112 to find how many miles you would travel.
3. Now look at the map of California on page 324. Is the real distance between Salt Lake City and Sacramento the same on this map? Why does the distance look different on the two maps?
4. Actual roads do not often follow a straight line between two places. If you were traveling by car, which map would help you choose the shortest route between two places, a subway map, a population map, or a road map?
5. Suppose a forty-niner from the East Coast asked you how to get to California by traveling across the Isthmus of Panama. Prepare directions on how to get from the East Coast to California by the Panama route. Use information in Lesson 3 and be sure to follow the rules for giving oral directions. Then give your directions to the class. Ask them to trace your route on a map.

Using Critical Thinking

1. For the early pioneers, the overland journey to California was long and dangerous. How have modern ways of transportation made the trip easier?
2. In the 1840s the western part of the United States was the frontier of the country. Now much of the West has been explored. What new frontiers are people exploring today?
3. Many governments have gone to war over the rights to own land. Why do you think the United States government wanted to own all the land between the East and West Coasts?

Preparing For Citizenship

1. **ART ACTIVITY** For those with "gold fever," traveling to California was a challenge. Make a poster advertising a trip to California by a land or a sea route. Use words and pictures to show the advantages of the method of travel you choose.
2. **WRITING ACTIVITY** Imagine that you and your family are making the journey westward over the Oregon Trail. Write three diary entries that describe some of the adventures you experience.
3. **GROUP ACTIVITY** Songs often tell stories. Work with a partner to write a song that tells the story of the pioneers, the Bear Flaggers, or the gold miners of California. You may write your own melody or use a favorite tune. Tape-record or perform your song for the rest of the class.
4. **COLLABORATIVE LEARNING** Jedediah Smith, Abel Stearns, and John Sutter traveled to California for a better life. Divide the class into three teams to perform three different skits about these pioneers. Each team should choose students to write the skit, act the parts, design the costumes, and direct the performance. In your skits, show how each man struggled to reach California and to survive there.

Chapter 6

California Becomes a State

The gold rush and the flood of forty-niners forever changed California. The thousands of newcomers struggled to build a new California that would better serve their needs. Meanwhile, the Californios saw their place in this changing land fading away.

California's new government moved several times before finally settling in Sacramento.

Not all forty-niners made their money mining gold. These men entertained others by playing their violins.

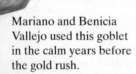

Mariano and Benicia Vallejo used this goblet in the calm years before the gold rush.

1845	1850	1855

1849

1856 San Francisco citizens form a group to stop the city's continuing crime problem.

SAN FRANCISCO.

1864 San Francisco grows quickly in the years following the gold rush, becoming California's first great city.

| 1860 | 1865 | 1870 |

1862 Many rancho land grants are still being challenged in court.

1870

LESSON 1

After the Gold Rush

THINKING FOCUS

In what ways did the gold rush change California?

Key Terms

- delegate
- convention

▼ *During the gold rush, thousands of forty-niners camped on the outskirts of San Francisco.*

Ouch! Walter Colton's eyes filled with tears as the barber's dull razor tugged at his rough whiskers. After a few more painful scrapes of the barber's blade, Colton wished he had left his beard unshaven. But it was too late. As Colton later wrote, "By then one side is partly off and you try the agony again." So Colton let the barber finish. But the biggest shock came when the barber told Colton the price of the shave—four dollars! Four dollars? That was more than some miners made in a week of hard work digging for gold.

Colton had just returned to San Francisco after several weeks in the gold fields. He had been looking forward to a nice shave. But the experience was pure torture. Why, the barber hadn't even sharpened the razor properly. He had just scraped it along his dusty bootleg and started shaving. The barber seemed too busy to care what Colton thought.

A Flood of Miners

Though his prices were high and his service was poor, Colton's barber had plenty of customers. The number of people living in San Francisco had grown quickly. In 1847

there were 500 people in the city. By 1850 there were up to 35,000 residents. San Francisco was overflowing with forty-niners. And each day, hundreds more arrived.

A Different San Francisco

San Francisco was more than crowded. It was bursting at the seams. In his 1963 novel *By the Great Horn Spoon!* the writer Sid Fleischman describes this busy scene through the eyes of a young traveler named Jack:

> The wharf seemed a mile long and the noisiest place on earth. Jack was dazzled by what he saw—tattooed islanders and East India sailors and silent Chinese with pigtails dangling behind them like black chains. There were Mexicans moving about to the jingle of their heavy silver spurs and Chileans in long serapes [wool capes]. There were mule skinners and businessmen, and there were miners in jackboots and red flannel shirts, with the mud of the diggings still in their beards.

San Francisco was a busy city. But it was not always a pleasant place to be. The many new buildings were poorly built. When it rained, the streets became seas of mud so deep that horses sometimes drowned in them. People threw sacks of beans, bags of flour, old stoves, and rotting beef into the streets to make a sort of sidewalk. The city's few police officers could not control all the people. Many people were worried about the lack of order in the growing city.

◄ *The 1851 photograph shows a very different Montgomery Street from the one shown in the 1847 illustration above. How has it changed?*

California Becomes a State

135

Water washed away the gold from rocks in the Sierra Nevada. Why were mining towns built on the rivers below the mountains?

Major Mining Towns of the California Gold Rush

Oregon

Nevada

PACIFIC OCEAN

San Francisco

Monterey

Sacramento R.

Feather R.

Yuba R.

American River

Poker Flat

Downieville

Nevada City

Marysville

Grass Valley

Auburn

Coloma

Placerville

Lake Tahoe

Sacramento

Sonoma

Cosumnes R.

Mokelumne R.

Calaveras R.

Stanislaus R.

Tuolumne R.

Merced R.

Stockton

Whiskey Flat

Angels Camp

Columbia

Sonora

Jamestown

Mariposa

San Joaquin River

• Gold rush towns
• Other important towns and cities

0   100 mi.

0   100 km

Lambert Conformal Conic Projection

What effect did the forty-niners have on California's cities and towns?

New Mining Towns

San Francisco wasn't California's only growing city. Sacramento and Stockton also welcomed hundreds of forty-niners. The miners picked up supplies in these cities, then set out for the gold fields on foot, on mules, or in carts. After arriving in the mining region, the miners built ramshackle mining towns. They gave the towns colorful names like Rattlesnake Diggings and Git Up And Git. Many of these towns disappeared as soon as the gold ran out or when better diggings turned up somewhere else. But some of the other towns, like Placerville and Downieville, still exist today.

In the early days of the gold rush, life in the mining towns was usually peaceful. Miners worked hard and spent their spare time dreaming of their faraway homes. But within a few months, the riverbanks became crowded with forty-niners. Most of them did not find the gold they wanted. Some of the unlucky miners decided it was easier to steal gold than to dig for it. Claim jumping also became a common problem. As the stealing increased, so did the fighting among the miners. Soon life in the mining towns became dangerous. ■

A Changing Government

From the days of Jedediah Smith, the Californios had worried about newcomers from the United States. But the gold rush made the Californios even more concerned. The graph on page 137 shows how quickly the number of forty-niners grew. Worse, many miners from the United States treated the Californios badly. These Americanos, as the

Californios called them, acted as if California were all theirs. When the Californios tried to mine gold, Americanos forced them from their mining claims. The Californios felt unwelcome in their own land.

Many Americans also felt uncomfortable in California. They were unhappy about conditions in the cities and towns. The newcomers wanted California to become a state, with a government like the states they had come from. If California became a state, citizens could vote for their leaders. They could choose leaders who would work to improve the conditions in California.

General Bennett Riley was the United States official in charge of California in 1849. He decided to call an election so the Californios and Americans could choose delegates. The **delegates** would speak and act for the citizens who chose them. Riley then called a meeting for the new delegates. At this **convention** delegates would decide California's future. ■

Families like the Lugo family lived peacefully before the gold rush. The chart below shows how quickly California grew.

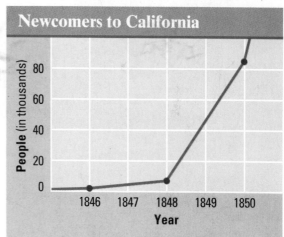

Newcomers to California

Summarize the concerns of the Californios and the newcomers from the United States.

R E V I E W

1. **FOCUS** In what ways did the gold rush change California?
2. **CONNECT** From your earlier reading, find an example of conflict between Californios and settlers from the United States.
3. **GEOGRAPHY** Look at the map on page 136. Why do you think so many forty-niners passed through the cities of San Francisco, Sacramento, and Stockton?
4. **CRITICAL THINKING** If you were a Californio, would you trust the Americans to treat you fairly at the convention? Explain your answer.
5. **WRITING ACTIVITY** Write a news story about life in San Francisco during the gold rush. Include interviews with Californios and newcomers.

Your Family History

During the gold rush, people came to California from around the world. Was one of these settlers from your family? Most Californians do not have ancestors who were forty-niners. But they do have stories about the first family member who came to California.

Get Ready

You can explore your family history by talking to family members and others in your community. You will need a notebook and a pen, or a tape recorder. It will also help if you can make photocopies of pictures and papers you find.

Find Out

Begin by talking with your parents. Take notes or record their answers. You can ask questions such as:

1. What countries did their parents and grandparents come from, and when did they first arrive?
2. How did they earn a living when they first arrived?
3. What are some interesting stories about your ancestors?
4. What was happening in history at the time?

You may ask other relatives and family friends the same questions. You may even write letters to relatives you can't interview in person. Be sure to ask these people if they have any family pictures, birth certificates, wedding announcements, and other papers you can use or copy.

Another place to visit is your local library. There you might find books that tell you what your family name means. The library might even have a town history that tells about some of your ancestors. Ask your librarian to help you look, and make copies of what you find.

Move Ahead

Now it's time to sort out the information you've collected. Look at your notes or listen to your recordings, and write down what seems important or interesting to you.

Now look at the pictures you have collected. Which tell the most about your family story?

Write a family history based on the information you've gathered. You can write the story using your own words. You can also use the words of the people you interviewed to tell the tale.

Next make a scrapbook from what you've written and from the pictures that go with it. If you could not get photocopies of family photographs, draw pictures that show how you imagine your ancestors looked.

Explore Some More

You've got a good start on your family history, so don't stop now! You and your family make new history every day, and you can record this new history as it happens. For example, save ticket stubs from ball games and concerts, letters from friends, awards from clubs or sports teams—anything that tells about who you are and what you've done. Keep these items in your notebook. Write down the date and a short explanation about what each object means. Do the same thing for other people in your family. Over time you'll build a rich source of history that you can share with your relatives. And your family's history will live on.

What do the details in the photographs on these pages tell you about these families?

139

California Becomes a State

Seeing Population Changes

Here's Why

Thousands of Indians died from disease when they moved to the missions. How did the Indian population change when the missions closed? How did it change when more new groups of people came to California? You can use a line graph to see what happened over time to the number of Indians in California. A line graph shows facts in a way that is easy to read and understand.

Here's How

The graph on this page tells you how many Indians lived in California in different years. The numbers along the left of the graph stand for thousands of people. The numbers along the bottom of the graph show dates. To see how many Indians lived in California in 1840, find 1840 on the bottom. Follow the 1840 line up until you come to a dot on the line graph. At the left you see the number 250. There were 250,000 Indians in California in 1840.

Now find the dot on the line graph for the year 1850. Look at the number to the left. What was the 1850 Indian population?

You can also use the line graph to see how the Indian population changed between 1840 and 1900. The red line slants down, which means the number of Indians was smaller. What would it show you if the red line slanted up? What would it mean if it went straight across?

Try It

Look at the graph on page 137. What dates are shown? What do the numbers at the left represent? What facts does this graph give you about the population of newcomers to California? How did the population change from 1846 to 1848? How did it change from 1848 to 1850? What happened in California between 1848 and 1850 to change the population?

Apply It

Look in a newspaper or magazine for a line graph. What is the graph's title? What numbers are along the left of the graph? What numbers are along the bottom? What facts do the slanting lines give? What changes do the lines show?

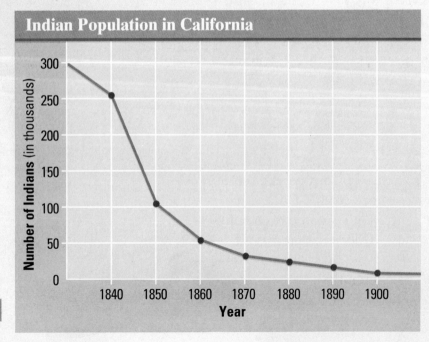

Indian Population in California

Number of Indians (in thousands): 0, 50, 100, 150, 200, 250, 300

Year: 1840, 1850, 1860, 1870, 1880, 1890, 1900

LESSON 2

The Thirty-first State

Dressed in their traditional clothes, the Californio delegates walked proudly into Colton Hall. All eight sat down at a single table, to show that they were united. But beneath their proud looks, the Californios were worried.

It was September 3, 1849, the first day of California's convention. The Californios were afraid that the American delegates might insult them. After all, there were forty Americanos compared to their eight. One of the Californio delegates, Mariano Vallejo, had been taken prisoner during the Bear Flag Revolt by Robert Semple, an Americano delegate. How would Semple and the other Americanos treat Vallejo today? Along with their concerns, six of the Californios did not speak any English. Would their ideas about the future of California, their home, be understood or even listened to?

The Californios probably did not know it, but the American delegates were worried too. Half of them were less than 35 years old. They had never taken part in an important convention before. The Americans wanted to make California a state. But they knew that they would need the Californios' help. Would the Californios work together with them?

THINKING
FOCUS

How did the constitutional convention change California?

Key Terms

- constitution
- slavery

The Convention Begins

To show their friendliness to the Californios, the Americans asked Vallejo to walk with Semple to the front of Colton Hall. Seeing the two men together made both sides realize that they could forget their differences and work together. The tension was broken. Now the delegates could begin the important work of the convention.

One major issue the delegates had to decide was how big California would be. In 1849 California did not have

California Becomes a State

official borders. To the west, the ocean formed a natural border. To the south was Mexico, and to the north was the Oregon Territory. These borders were clear. But the delegates still had to decide on an eastern border.

A Natural Border

The delegates had different ideas about where California's eastern border should be. Some of the delegates wanted California to cover most of the land the United States had won from Mexico in the Mexican War. Much of this land had been part of California before the war. The map shows how large an area this was. But most of the delegates realized that if California was this large, it would be hard to govern. They wanted a border that would make the state smaller and easier to control.

These delegates chose to place the border along the Sierra Nevada and the Colorado River. They saw that the mighty mountains and the wide river formed a natural border. This is where California's eastern border is today.

Two Californias

Some Californio delegates wanted to split California into two sections. One section would cover the northern part of California, above San Luis Obispo. The other section would cover the southern part, where many Californios lived. There the Californios would not be outnumbered by Americanos, who lived mostly in the north. Most delegates, however, did not want to cut California in two. So they agreed that it should remain one large area. The map on page 328 shows California's borders as they are today.

If California had been divided in two, which half would you live in today?

Suggested Borders for California

UNITED STATES

Great Salt Lake

California

Colorado R.

Gila R.

PACIFIC OCEAN

40°N

30°N

120°W

110°W

Gulf of California

Rio Grande

MEXICO

Mexican Cession

Californios' proposed Mexican boundary

American–proposed California boundary

Present–day California boundary

0   100   200 mi.

0 100 200 km
Lambert Conformal Conic Projection

Voting Rights

The delegates also talked about who would be allowed to vote in California. Many American delegates wanted to keep Indians from voting. But the Californios disagreed. One of their delegates, Manuel Dominguez, had both Spanish and Indian roots. He would not be allowed to vote if the Americanos had their way. A Californio delegate, Pablo de la Guerra, spoke of the great history of California's Indians. He said, "They were a proud and gifted race, capable of forming a government for themselves." The American delegates still would not change their minds. But they did agree that they could not keep one of the delegates from voting. So they came up with a plan to allow Dominguez to vote. Most other Indians, though, had to wait almost 75 years before they could vote in California.

Indians were not the only group denied voting rights. Blacks, women, and Chinese were also left out. In 1870 black men received the vote. Women had to wait until 1911. Most Chinese could not vote until 1943. ■

◄ *Manuel Dominguez, a Californio delegate, was part Indian. Many delegates wanted to keep Dominguez and other Indians from voting.*

■ *Why did the Californios and the Americans differ on the topics of borders and voting rights?*

▼ *California's constitution tells how the people of California are to be governed, or ruled.*

The Task Is Finished

The delegates discussed many topics at the month-long convention. They decided what rights the citizens would have and how the government would work. Everything they decided was written into an official agreement called a constitution. The **constitution** listed the rules and government duties for the new state. Among many other things, California's constitution stated who could vote. It also stated that married women could own land. In 1849 no other state had given women this right. But the delegates hoped to get more women to move to California. They wanted this because so few women lived there.

On October 12, 1849 the delegates signed California's constitution. Even the Californios seemed pleased. They had not won on every issue. But they

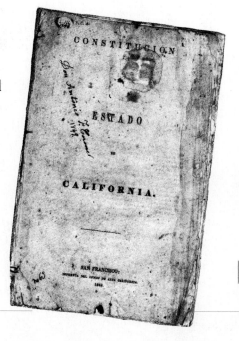

had been treated with respect. The other citizens of California seemed pleased too. A month later they voted to accept the constitution.

Congress Accepts California

The people of California had approved the constitution. But before California could become a state, the United States Congress also had to approve the constitution. That task would not be so easy.

Slavery was a major issue in the United States in 1850. **Slavery** is a system that allows one person to own another. In the southern states, slaves were black people owned by white people. Farmers used slaves to pick cotton and tobacco. But many people in the North were bitterly against slavery.

There was no disagreement on slavery in California. Every delegate at the convention agreed that California should not allow slavery. But this created a problem for Congress. Since 1812 Congress had kept the number of states for slavery the same as the number against slavery. If California became a state, there would be one more state against slavery, so the balance would be upset. Some people in Congress did not want this to happen.

It took nearly a year for Congress to decide what to do. People in California began wondering if Congress would ever accept their constitution. At last, Congress reached an agreement. On September 9, 1850 President Millard Fillmore officially made California the thirty-first state.

On October 13, a ship sailed into San Francisco Bay.

▼ *The streets of San Francisco filled with happy citizens when news of California's statehood arrived.*

Above the ship waved a banner reading "California Admitted." As word spread, the city celebrated. In her book *A Frontier Lady*, Sarah Royce recalled how "the roar of cannon rolled over the waters, and met answering roars from fort and ships. Everybody was laughing." Soon, all California was celebrating along with San Francisco.

Biddy Mason Is Freed

How much difference could a constitution make in people's lives? For Biddy Mason, California's constitution made a huge difference.

Biddy Mason was a slave from Mississippi. In 1852 her owner, Robert Smith, brought her to California. Although California did not allow slavery, Smith continued to treat Mason as a slave. He did not free her or pay her for her work.

◄ *Biddy Mason helped many people in Los Angeles. She was known for her generosity.*

Three years later, Smith decided to return to Mississippi. But someone told the sheriff that Smith was keeping Mason as a slave. The sheriff took Mason away from Smith. Later a judge set her free.

Biddy Mason moved to Los Angeles. She worked long hours as a housemaid and nurse, and saved as much as she could. Because women could own property, Mason bought a house. She shared her money with the poor, and gave land for churches and nursing schools. She is remembered today for her work to improve the education of black children.

Biddy Mason's remarkable story shows how the constitution helped citizens of the new state. But as you will see, the constitution did not solve all of California's problems. ■

■ *What good and bad opinions might Biddy Mason have had about California's constitution?*

R E V I E W

1. **FOCUS** How did the constitutional convention change California?
2. **CONNECT** From your earlier reading, find an example of unfair treatment of Indians.
3. **GEOGRAPHY** The delegates thought that a smaller California would be easier to govern. Why might a smaller area be easier to govern than a larger one?
4. **CRITICAL THINKING** Why do you think the delegates chose not to allow women, blacks, Indians, or Chinese to vote?
5. **WRITING ACTIVITY** Imagine that your school is having a convention to talk about changes in how the school is run. Write a list of topics you would like to talk about at this convention.

LESSON 3

Law and Order

THINKING FOCUS

How did Californians try to keep peace and order in their new state?

Key Terms

- vigilante
- justice
- law

➤ *The legend of Joaquin caused great fear among the people of California. Finally, the state offered a reward for the bandit's capture.*

Joaquin! Just the whisper of his name sent chills down the spines of Californians. It was the winter of 1852–1853, and the legend of Joaquin Murieta and his gang was spreading quickly across California. In the cities and towns, fearful citizens shared stories of murder, stolen cattle, and stagecoach robberies. Joaquin! they gasped. No one felt safe. Joaquin seemed to be everywhere at once. In fact, he was often accused of committing crimes in different places at the same time. Who was this Mexican bandit? Was he a real person?

The people of California were not taking any chances. They hired a man named Captain Harry Love to find Joaquin. Love searched for three months across the countryside of California without success. Finally, in the last week of July, he and his men cornered a group of Mexicans at Panoche *(puh NOH chee)* Pass, in what is now San Benito County. A gunfight followed, and two of the Mexican bandits were killed.

Captain Love returned to tell the people his story. He claimed that one of the dead men was the bandit Joaquin.

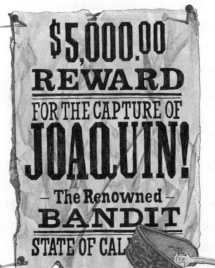

He said this even though he had little proof that the man was Joaquin. The frightened citizens of California did not seem to care about proof. They wanted to believe that Captain Love had killed Joaquin. They cheered when they heard the news of the Mexican bandit's death. And Captain Love collected his reward of 5,000 dollars.

Crime in California

Most stories about Joaquin were probably untrue. But his legend shows how fearful Californians had become. They could see that being a state would not solve all their problems. California was as disorderly as before. San Francisco was especially wild. James King, a popular newspaper reporter, often wrote about crime in San Francisco. In one story, King attacked a city official named James Casey. Casey became so upset that he killed King.

Citizens Take Action

When word spread that Casey had killed King, many citizens got angry. Some decided that they could not wait for a judge to punish Casey. So they went to the jail where the police had taken him. The angry citizens forced their way past the police and took Casey. Then they hanged him.

These citizens were **vigilantes** *(vihj uh LAN teez)*. These are people who capture and punish others without having the right to do so. The vigilantes' group became very popular in San Francisco. More than 6,000 people joined the group. In three months the vigilantes hanged three more people and forced many others to leave the city. Citizens in other California towns formed their own groups like the one in San Francisco.

The vigilantes took James Casey away from the police to punish him. Many citizens in San Francisco supported the vigilantes and joined their group.

Vigilantes Go Too Far

The vigilantes were worried about crime. But they did not care about **justice**. This means that they did not care about treating people fairly or respecting other people's rights. They punished people without letting them tell their side of the story. They ignored what the police and judges said. They only did what they wanted. By doing this, the vigilantes broke the **law**, which is the set of rules that all people must obey. But so many citizens supported the vigilantes that even the police could not stop them. ■

■ *Why do you think so many citizens joined the vigilantes, even though the vigilantes broke the law?*

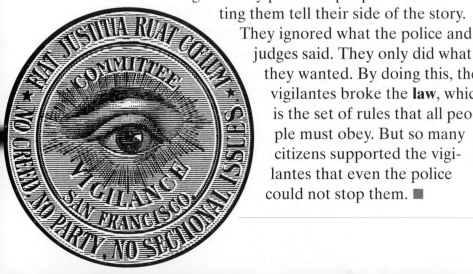

California Becomes a State

Mining Town Trouble

Law and order was also a problem in California's many mining towns. Stealing and fighting were common in these busy, crowded camps. Police or sheriffs often lived a day's horseback ride away. Miners did not want to spend time guarding prisoners while they waited for the sheriff. The miners wanted to dig for gold, so they often took care of problems themselves. Because they were in a hurry, they quickly punished people they thought had committed a crime. Like the vigilantes, the miners ignored justice.

UNDERSTANDING JUSTICE

The vigilantes in California were trying to protect themselves and their belongings. They took strong action to catch and punish people who they believed had broken the law. But in doing this, the vigilantes treated many citizens unfairly. The vigilantes ignored justice.

Our Justice System

In the United States, we have a special way to decide fairly who has broken the law. It is called the justice system. At the head of this system is the Supreme Court. Sandra Day O'Connor, seen here, is a member of that court.

The justice system would not be fair if a person who was robbed decided who was guilty. That is why a judge or a group of people called a jury decides who is guilty. During the trial the victim and the suspect tell their sides of the story. Then the judge or jury decides whether the suspect committed the crime. If the person is guilty, then he or she is punished.

Our justice system helps make sure that there is justice, or fair treatment, for everyone. People who steal, for example, are punished. That's because taking something that belongs to another person is unfair. But it is also unfair to punish people for crimes they did not do. (Have you ever been blamed for something your brother or sister did?) So our justice system gives suspects a chance to tell their stories to someone who will be fair.

Vigilantes Ignore Justice

California's vigilantes thought that they were helping to stop crime. But they ignored the justice system. They did not give suspects the chance to tell their stories to a fair judge. As a result, many people in California did not receive justice. And many people were punished unjustly.

That's the way it happened in the mining town of Old Dry Diggings. One January day in 1849, a group of 200 miners captured three men who they thought had committed robbery and murder. Two of the suspects were from France and the other was from Chile. None of the three could speak English, so they had no chance to tell the angry miners their side of the story. But that did not stop the miners from deciding to hang the three suspects. In fact, when one of the miners begged the others to treat the suspects fairly, the mob threatened to kill him too.

The Miners Hang the Men

The three suspects were hanged. They died without knowing why they were being punished. When others learned about the hanging at Old Dry Diggings, the town became known as Hangtown.

The miners of Old Dry Diggings were a lot like the vigilantes in California's cities. The miners did not follow justice or obey the law. They did not care about treating people fairly. They took the law into their own hands so that they could go back to their claims and dig for more gold. They refused to wait for the police to come to their town to arrest the suspects in a crime.

Both the vigilantes and the miners thought that they were helping to make California a better and safer place to live. But their type of thinking did not make California a better or safer place for everyone. Many people, such as the Californios, suffered greatly when other citizens took the law into their own hands. ■

▲ *Miners often solved crime problems quickly so that they could go back to digging for gold.*

■ *The three men who were hanged at Hangtown did not speak or understand English. Why is this important?*

R E V I E W

1. **FOCUS** How did Californians try to keep peace and order in their new state?
2. **CONNECT** Based on your earlier reading, explain why crime was a problem in the mining towns.
3. **CIVIC VALUES** Instead of punishing people themselves, how might the vigilantes have

fought crime in California?

4. **CRITICAL THINKING** When vigilantes forced many criminals to leave San Francisco, they broke the law. Do you think the vigilantes were right or wrong when they did this?
5. **WRITING ACTIVITY** Write a speech about why it is important to obey the law.

California Becomes a State

Jamoka Jack

Sid Fleischman

The story of Jamoka Jack comes from By the Great Horn Spoon *by Sid Fleischman. The tale tells of the adventures of a boy named Jack Flagg and his butler Praiseworthy. They leave Boston to try their luck in the gold fields of California. As you read this story, ask yourself, "What was life like in Hangtown when Jack and Praiseworthy arrived there?"*

You read in Lesson 3 about how the town of Old Dry Diggings was renamed Hangtown. This story shows what life was like in this mining town.

skewer stick through

jackboots heavy boots that extend above the knee

The stagecoach climbed as if it were part mountain goat. It lurched, it halted, it bucked, it leaped and it clung. At times there was a sheer drop to one side of the trail. Far below, the pine trees looked to Jack like sharp green lances waiting to skewer them if they slipped. He only looked once in a while.

They were almost at the diggings, he told himself—he'd been telling himself that for days. But at last, the stagecoach arrived, bringing a cloud of summer dust all the way from Sacramento City.

"Hangtown, gents!" the driver snapped, with a final crack of his whip. "Looks mighty quiet today. Don't see nobody standin' under a pine limb with his boots off the ground."

A dog greeted them at the end of the street and barked them all the way up to the Empire Hotel. The passengers got out. There was road dust in Jack's eyebrows, in his ears and down his neck. Now that they had arrived he had gold fever so bad that he didn't see how he could wait another five minutes to get his shovel in the ground.

Hangtown!

Everywhere he looked there were men in jackboots and colored shirts. There wasn't a woman to be seen. The miners were coming-and-going or standing-and-talking or sitting-and-whittling. Blue freight wagons were being unloaded. Blindfolded mules were being loaded. The store shacks on both sides of the street were raised on wood pilings, like short legs, and looked as if they had just walked to town.

Jack shouldered the shovel and Praiseworthy shouldered the pick. On the roof of the stage the driver was throwing down trunks and hand luggage.

"What's the best hotel in town?" asked Praiseworthy.

"The Empire."

Praiseworthy glanced at Jack. "Unless I miss my guess there's only one hotel in town—the Empire."

It was exactly one hour and five minutes before Jack saw the diggings. First Praiseworthy registered at the hotel. They washed. Immediately Praiseworthy wrote a letter to Dr. Buckbee, advising him that Cut-Eye Higgins was in Hangtown, but that the map had fallen into the hands of a gang of highwaymen.

"Can we go now?" said Jack, fidgeting. He had polished his horn spoon so much he could see his nose in it.

"Go where?"

"The diggings."

"Oh, the diggings will still be there after lunch, Master Jack."

Praiseworthy's patience was a marvel—and an exasperation. They had come more than 15,000 miles and now they had to stop to eat. Jack didn't care if they passed up eating for a week. A month, even. He wondered if he could ever grow up to be as easygoing as Praiseworthy.

But once they sat down in the hotel restaurant Jack discovered he was so hungry that he ordered bear steak. The only other item on the menu was sowbelly-and-beans, and Jack figured you had to be starving to order that.

"You and the boy want bread with your grub?" asked the waiter. He was a big fellow in floppy boots.

"Why not?" answered Praiseworthy.

"It's a dollar a slice."

The butler slowly arched an eyebrow.

"Two dollars with butter on it."

Praiseworthy peered at Jack, and then smiled. "Hang the cost, sir. We're celebrating our arrival. Bread and butter, if you please!"

The bear steak was greasy and stringy, but something to write home about. Jack forced it down. After they left the restaurant Praiseworthy bought a pair of buckskin pouches at the general merchandise store and emptied the gold dust

highwaymen men who rob travelers on a highway

exasperation a cause for anger

151

out of his glove. The index finger was springing a leak. Jack liked the new leather smell of the pouch. He tucked it under his belt, next to the horn spoon, and was beginning to feel like a miner. Then, with tin washbasins under their arms and the pick and shovel across their shoulders, they set out for the diggings.

The day was hot and sweaty. When they reached running water they saw miners crouched everywhere along the banks. They were washing gold out of the dirt in everything from wooden bowls to frying pans.

"Anybody digging here" asked Praiseworthy when they came to a bare spot.

"Shore is," came the answer. "That's Buffalo John's claim."

The butler and the boy moved on upstream. Here and there miners were shoveling dirt into long wooden troughs, set in running water, to catch the flakes of gold.

"Anybody digging here?" asked Praiseworthy.

"Yup," came the answer. "That's Jimmie-from-Town's claim."

On and on they went, looking for a place to dig. They passed miners in blue shirts and red shirts and checked shirts and some in no shirts at all. Picks assaulted the earth and shovels flew. Weathered tents were staked to the hillsides and the smell of boiling coffee drifted through the air. After they had walked a mile and a half Jack began to think they would never find a patch of ground that wasn't spoken for.

Suddenly a pistol shot cracked the mountain air. Praiseworthy's washbasin rang like a bell and leaped from his arm and went clattering away.

"You there!" a voice from behind bellowed.

Praiseworthy turned. His eyes narrowed slowly. "Are you talking to me sir?"

"Talkin' and shootin'. What you doin' with my washpan under your arm?"

Jack stared at the man. He had a thick, tangled beard and his ears were bent over under the weight of his slouch hat.

"Needless to say, you're mistaken," Praiseworthy answered. "Until this moment I've had the good fortune never to set eyes on you or your washpan, sir."

"We don't take kindly to thievery in these parts," growled the miner, stepping forward. "A man steals around here, we lop off his ears. That's miners' law."

troughs (trawfs) containers used as strainers

slouch hat a soft hat with a broad brim

"Do you have any laws against shooting at strangers?"

"Nope."

Jack couldn't imagine Praiseworthy with his ears lopped off. He took a grip on the handle of the shovel as the miner came closer. His heart beat a little faster and he waited for a signal from Praiseworthy.

The miner belted his pistol and picked up the washpan. He crimped an eye and looked it over.

"It's mine, all right."

"You're either near-sighted or a scoundrel," said Praiseworthy.

Jack was ready to fight, if not for their lives—at least for Praiseworthy's ears. Just then, a flash of tin in the sunlight, from a pile of wet rocks, caught Jack's eye. He dropped the shovel and went for it.

"Is this your pan?" Jack said.

The miner's bushy eyebrows shot up like birds taking wing. "It is at that, ain't it?" Then he laughed as if the joke were on him. "I'd forget my boots if I didn't have 'em on."

Praiseworthy peered at the man. Apparently, shooting at strangers by mistake didn't amount to anything in the diggings. The miner hardly gave it another thought.

crimped wrinkled up

scoundrel an evil person

Further Reading

The Golden Venture. Jane Flory. This is the story of a young girl who stows away in her father's wagon when he travels to California to look for gold.

The Bandit of Mok Hill. Evelyn Sibley Lampman. An orphan boy from San Francisco joins a friendly family in the gold fields. This book takes a realistic look at life in the gold rush days.

Coarse Gold Gulch. Marion Garthwaite. Two children from Vermont come to California to search for their father. The children have exciting adventures with Californios, Indians, and Chinese immigrants.

California Gold Rush: Search for Treasure. Catherine Chambers.

Reading California's State Seal

Here's Why

The delegates who wrote California's constitution approved the design of the state seal in 1849. This seal of California is on all official papers of the state today. Looking closely, you will see that the seal is a picture with many parts. Each part is a symbol that stands for an idea about California. To read the seal's message, you need to know how to understand the meanings of symbols.

Here's How

A symbol is one thing that stands for another thing or for an idea. For example, the U.S. flag is a symbol of the United States of America. Its parts are also symbols. The stripes represent the original colonies. The stars stand for the states.

Parts of the California seal stand for some important ideas about the state. Some of these parts and what they mean are pointed out below.

Try It

Explain more symbols on the seal. What idea about California does the miner represent? What do the wheat and the grapes represent? Count the stars at the top. What do they stand for? The Greek word *eureka* is the state motto. It means "I have found it!" What idea about California does it stand for?

Apply It

Create a seal for your school. Include symbols of what students do there. What important ideas do you want to show?

Ships stand for commerce.

Goddess Minerva stands for wisdom.

Mountains stand for the Sierra Nevada.

Grizzly bear stands for fierceness.

EUREKA

THE GREAT SEAL OF THE STATE OF CALIFORNIA

L E S S O N   4

Californios Lose Their Land

P ablo de la Guerra rose to his feet and prepared to give his speech. In front of him sat the members of California's senate, part of the state government. De la Guerra was a senate member and an important Californio leader. Lately, he had been hearing many terrible stories about the problems of his people. It was the spring of 1856, and de la Guerra realized it was time to speak out about the sad fate of the Californios:

> I have seen old men of sixty and seventy years of age weeping because they have been cast out of their ancestral [family] home. They have been humiliated and insulted. They have been refused the privilege of cutting their own firewood.

De la Guerra was angry because many Californios were losing their ranchos. This land had belonged to the Californios from the days of Mexican rule. The Californios had feared losing their land since the beginning of the gold rush. And now their fears were coming true.

THINKING FOCUS

How did the Californios lose their land?

Key Terms

- squatter
- commission

◄ *The rancho was the center of the Californios' world. It was where they worked, raised families, and met friends.*

155

California Becomes a State

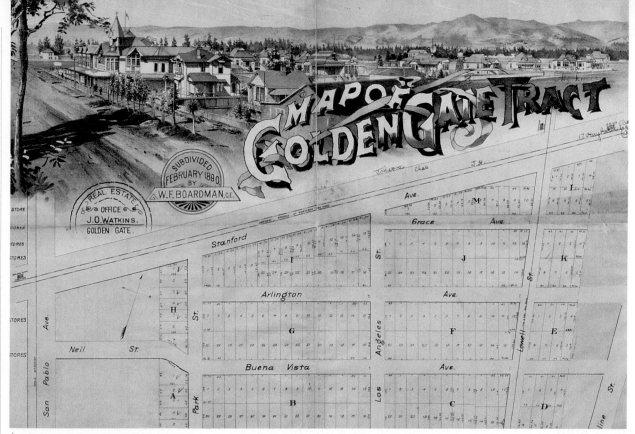

▲ *Rancho San Antonio once covered the land that is now Oakland, Berkeley, and Alameda. By the late 1800s, this land was being broken up into thousands of small pieces.*

Across Time & Space

Many Californios lost their ranchos to squatters, but the names of the ranchos live on in modern California. Cities and towns like Rancho Palos Verdes, Rancho Mirage, and Rancho Sante Fe remind us of the days when the rancheros owned huge patches of land that spread for miles.

A Threat to the Ranchos

To the Californios, ranchos of 40,000 acres did not seem unusual. But when settlers from the United States saw these great ranchos, they became angry. They saw that there was enough land on a single rancho for hundreds of farms. They thought it was unfair for one person to own so much land. Worse, the rancheros grew few crops on their land. The settlers felt that it was wasteful to use so much good land just for cattle.

Some Americans decided simply to move onto the ranchos and start their own farms. These people were called **squatters**, and they were breaking the law. There were so many squatters that the rancheros could not keep them off their ranchos. Even the police and courts could not stop all the squatters. Some rancheros gave up and sold their ranchos. That way, they at least got some money for the land. But other rancheros did not want to sell the land that their family had owned for many years.

Often squatters were not satisfied to have just a ranchero's land. On some ranchos, squatters took the ranchero's cattle and cut down the ranchero's trees. Little by little, the squatters took over the whole rancho. This happened to the Peralta family in 1852 on their Rancho San Antonio. The Peraltas had owned San Antonio since the 1820s. But one day squatters stopped the Peraltas from entering their own home. The Peraltas had no choice but to move. They could not fight all the squatters on their rancho.

The Government Acts

Squatters were not the only threat to the rancheros. Soon after the squatters began moving onto the ranchos, the United States Congress passed the Land Act of 1851. This act created a commission to decide whether the rancheros were the proper owners of their ranchos. A **commission** is a group chosen to do a certain job. If the rancheros could not convince the commission that they were the rightful owners, they would lose their ranchos. ■

■ *Why were the Californios unable to stop the squatters from taking their land?*

Bad News for Rancheros

It was not easy for rancheros to prove that they owned their land. For one thing, many did not understand English. They had to hire lawyers to tell them what to do.

In spite of the problems the rancheros faced, the Land Commission usually ruled in their favor. But the commission took up to 17 years or more to settle each case. For most rancheros, this ruling came too late. Over the years, many rancheros spent all of their money paying lawyers. They finally had to sell their land in order to survive. So in the end, most rancheros lost their homes.

California had many laws to protect the rights of the Californio rancheros. But these laws were not enough. The Californios could not fight the large numbers of people who wanted their land. Slowly, the great ranchos that had been at the center of the Californios' world disappeared. As they disappeared, the old Californio way of life came to an end. The Californios would now have to make their living on land that belonged to others. ■

▼ *In the early 1800s there was a handful of ranchos in the Los Angeles area. Today this land is home to 13 million people.*

■ *How did the Land Commission both help and hurt the Californios?*

R E V I E W

1. **FOCUS** How did the Californios lose their land?
2. **CONNECT** From your earlier reading, explain how the ranchos were "at the center of the Californios' world."
3. **CIVIC VALUES** In what ways did the law and the government fail to protect the Californio rancheros?
4. **CRITICAL THINKING** In what ways do you think the rancho squatters were like the vigilantes and the miners?
5. **ACTIVITY** Hold a debate to discuss whether it was fair or unfair for the rancheros to own their huge ranchos when many settlers had little land.

Chapter Review

Reviewing Key Terms

commission (p. 157) law (p. 147)
constitution (p. 143) slavery (p. 144)
convention (p. 137) squatter (p. 156)
delegate (p. 137) vigilante (p. 147)
justice (p. 147)

A. Write the key term for each definition:
1. a rule that all citizens must obey
2. a person who captures and punishes others without the authority to do so
3. fair treatment of everyone, using the same rules and laws
4. a group chosen to do a certain task
5. one who settles on someone else's land

B. Choose the key term that best completes each sentence.
1. Each citizen voted for a _____ who would speak for his or her concerns.
2. Until the _____, California did not have official borders.
3. California's _____ said that married women would have the right to own their own property.
4. Every delegate agreed that there should be no _____ in California.
5. Many Californios lost their land even though _____s were passed to protect them.

Exploring Concepts

A. Complete the cluster diagram below on a separate paper by adding words to describe two more problems that are discussed in this chapter. Give two examples of each problem shown in the diagram.

B. Read this statement: During the gold rush, the population of California's towns grew rapidly. Write two reasons why this rapid population growth was good. Write two reasons why the rapid growth was bad.

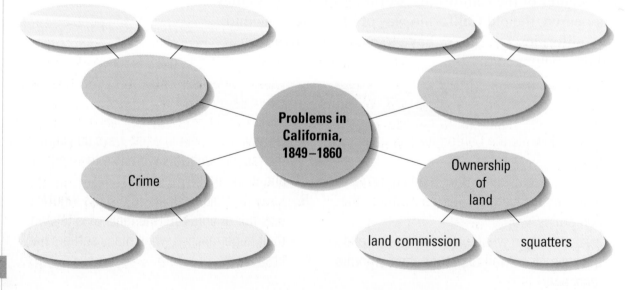

Problems in California, 1849–1860

Crime

Ownership of land

land commission

squatters

Reviewing Skills

1. Look at the line graph at the right. What did coffee cost before the gold rush? What did it cost in 1850?
2. The Statue of Liberty is a symbol that stands for an idea. What is that idea? Name another United States symbol.
3. Make a timeline to show when people got voting rights in California. Begin with the year 1850 and end with 1950. Mark off sections for every 10 years, and write in the dates. Let smaller sections stand for five years. Then add the dates that show when white men, women, black men, Indians, and Chinese people got voting rights.
4. What kinds of books might tell you more details of Biddy Mason's story?

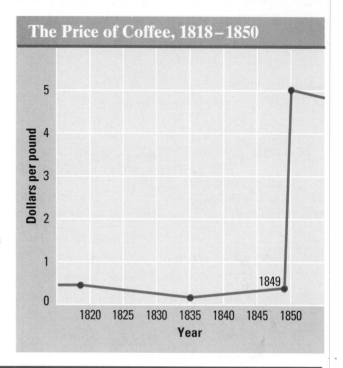

The Price of Coffee, 1818–1850

Using Critical Thinking

1. James King criticized James Casey. Casey was so angry that he shot and killed James King. Do you think it was wrong for San Francisco's vigilantes to punish Casey without holding a trial? Explain your answer.

2. Although the Californios and Americans had many differences, they worked together to write California's constitution. How could different groups work together today to make a community better for everyone?

Preparing for Citizenship

1. **WRITING ACTIVITY** Pretend you are a newspaper reporter at the California convention of 1849. Decide whom you want to interview and what you would like to know about that person. Write a newspaper article including details that answer the questions *who, what, when, where,* and *why.*

2. **ART ACTIVITY** Draw a picture of a gold rush scene in San Francisco or in some other California city. Include details such as the kinds of people in the city and the types of buildings and businesses.

3. **COLLABORATIVE LEARNING** The seal of California uses words and pictures to give a message about the state. Work as a class to design and draw a modern seal for California. First meet in small groups to brainstorm a list of symbols that tell something about the state today. As a class, decide which ideas each group will illustrate. Outline the seal on a large sheet of paper. Then add each group's illustration to the seal. Also include on the seal any words the class thinks are important.

Growth and Development

As the gold rush ended, Californians set out in new directions. They put their plows to the earth, and they built links with the rest of the country. The railroad became the most important link and a symbol for the strength and energy of the growing state.

1850

Union Pacific workers building the railroad between California and Nebraska. Photograph courtesy of The Oakland Museum History Department.

1920

Chapter 7

The Transcontinental Railroad

California had become a state, but Californians still felt separated from the rest of the country. During the 1850s and 1860s, the state reached out to build closer links with the East. The strongest of these links would be the railroad.

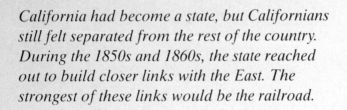

A crew of workers struggled to find a way to build a railroad through the mountains.

Stagecoaches like this improved the speed and comfort of the cross-country journey to California.

1850	1854	1858

1850

1869 Many people see that the best way to connect California to the other states is by railroad.

	1862		1866		1870

1861 The Civil War begins. California sides with the Northern states, or the Union.

1863 Construction on a railroad between California and the other states begins.

1869

L E S S O N 1

Linking California to the East

Why did Californians in the 1850s and early 1860s feel cut off from the other states?

Key Terms

- communication
- transportation
- transcontinental

► *The Pony Express, with its dashing, daring riders, delivered news and mail to California quickly.*

William Campbell rode like the wind, his pony slicing through the icy air. In a frozen leather pouch he carried a message all of California was waiting to hear. It was Abraham Lincoln's first speech as President of the United States.

Starting at Fort Kearney, Nebraska, Campbell and his fellow Pony Express riders would take Lincoln's message on a 1,600-mile journey to Sacramento. It was March, a dangerous time to cross the frozen Sierra Nevada. But the citizens of California would not wait. They did not like being the last to know the nation's news. "Where is Lincoln's message?" they asked.

Halfway across the country, a cold and tired Campbell neared the Pony Express station. He raised a horn to his lips and let out a loud blast. The next rider, hearing the sound, quickly saddled up his pony. When Campbell raced into the station moments later, the second rider grabbed the pouch from Campbell's hand and set off at a gallop. The message reached Sacramento in seven days, faster than any message had ever traveled before. Soon all of California had read Lincoln's speech.

California Feels Cut Off

Even though the Pony Express had set a record, Lincoln had already been President for nearly two weeks before Californians read his speech. The people knew that other important events were taking place in the East. Lincoln's speech had told of the growing differences between the North and South over slavery. But **communication**, the sending of news and messages, was slow. Problems in communication made Californians feel cut off from the rest of the country.

A Long, Hard Trip

Californians had good reason to feel as if they were cut off from the other states. In fact, two-week mail delivery was lightning fast compared to the speed of **transportation**, the movement of people and goods. As the map shows, transportation by covered wagon over rugged plains, blazing deserts, and steep mountains might take four to six months. Sailing around South America took up to six months or more. Using the short cut across the Isthmus of Panama saved travelers time, but the journey still took about a month.

Transportation problems raised the cost of food and other goods. In the 1850s much of California's food, clothing, tools, and other items came from the East. Californians had to pay high prices for these goods because transportation was so expensive.

Travel Time to California

NORTH AMERICA

San Francisco · Sioux City · Council Bluffs · New York · Boston

St. Joseph

Charleston

Gulf of Mexico

PACIFIC OCEAN

ATLANTIC OCEAN

ISTHMUS OF PANAMA

SOUTH AMERICA

0   120°   2000 mi.

0   2000 km
Hammer Interrupted
Equal Area Projection

—— Cape Horn route: from six to eight months
—— Panama route: about one month
—— Overland route: from four to six months

CAPE HORN

▲ *Which route is the shortest distance? Why do you think this route did not take the shortest time?*

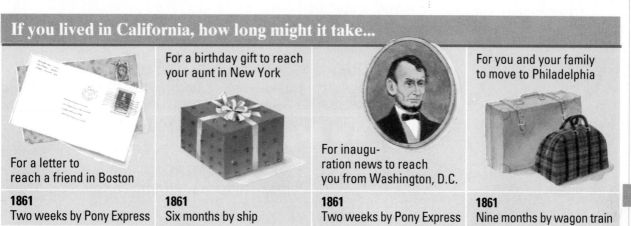

If you lived in California, how long might it take...

For a letter to reach a friend in Boston	For a birthday gift to reach your aunt in New York	For inauguration news to reach you from Washington, D.C.	For you and your family to move to Philadelphia
1861 Two weeks by Pony Express	**1861** Six months by ship	**1861** Two weeks by Pony Express	**1861** Nine months by wagon train
Today Two days by US Mail	**Today** Seven days by US Mail	**Today** Instantly by TV or radio	**Today** Six hours by plane

Efforts at Reaching Out

People began looking for better links with the states in the East. One company used camels to carry goods across the hot, dry land beyond the Sierra Nevada. But the camels got sore feet from cactus plants on the trails. Drivers grew angry with the smelly "humpbacked brutes" and quit.

Other ideas worked better. In 1858, for example, John Butterfield started the Butterfield Stage Line, which carried mail, packages, and people. Butterfield's stages gave important service to California, making hundreds of trips between California and the Mississippi River. Even so, the Butterfield Stage took 24 days to make its trip.

Another idea that helped California was the telegraph. In 1861 workers finished setting up wires across the country, even though buffaloes sometimes knocked down the poles. The diagrams show how the telegraph worked. It could send messages across the country in minutes. The telegraph was so fast that it soon put the Pony Express out of business.

Still, people wanted more. They dreamed of building a **transcontinental** railroad, which would make it possible to travel from coast to coast in just a few days. This railroad would solve California's transportation problems. But it would cost millions of dollars. Who would pay for it?

How would its tracks cross the steep Sierra Nevada? No one could answer these questions. So for California, the transcontinental railroad remained a dream. ■

■ *Even with the Butterfield Stage and the telegraph, Californians were still not satisfied. Why not?*

An operator uses Morse code and a telegraph machine to send messages. The dots and dashes are made by pressing a lever.

The telegraph machine turns the dots and dashes into electrical signals. The signals travel instantly over a wire.

Electricity makes clicking noises—dots and dashes—in the telegraph machine. An operator hears the clicks on the other end and writes out the letters that form the message.

Civil War Begins

In the summer of 1861, this dream was interrupted by important news from Fort Sumter, South Carolina, and Bull Run, Virginia. The Civil War had begun. The Southern

Union States During the Civil War

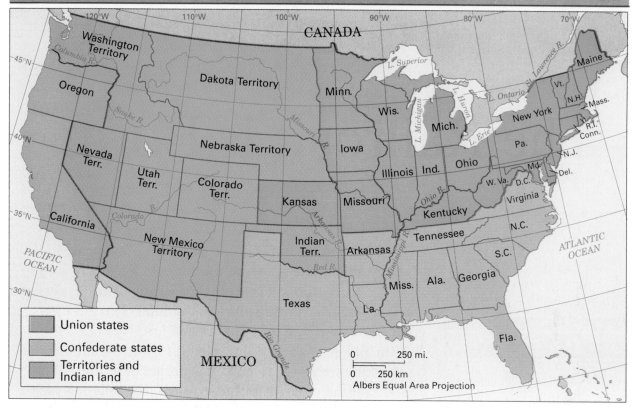

Union States During the Civil War map

- Union states
- Confederate states
- Territories and Indian land

0 — 250 mi.
0 — 250 km
Albers Equal Area Projection

states had broken off from the United States because of disagreements over slavery. They formed a new country called the Confederate States of America. The remaining states called themselves the Union. The Union was fighting to keep all the states together in one country.

California decided to side with the Union in the Civil War. During the war, California became more cut off than ever from the East. The Union and Confederate armies needed all the food and supplies the Eastern states could produce. So the flow of goods to California slowed to a trickle. More than ever, the people of California needed better ties with the rest of the nation. Maybe this was the time to make the dream of a transcontinental railroad come true. ▪

▲ *What other state besides California might have felt cut off from the rest of the country?*

▪ *What effect did the Civil War have on California?*

REVIEW

1. **FOCUS** Why did Californians in the 1850s and early 1860s feel cut off from the other states?
2. **CONNECT** Find an example from Chapter 6 of how the disagreement over slavery had affected California in the past.
3. **ECONOMICS** Why were many goods so expensive in California?
4. **CRITICAL THINKING** What steps might Califor-

nians have taken to lower their costs for food and other goods?

5. **ACTIVITY** Using the map on page 324, figure the number of miles between the center of Nebraska and Sacramento. How many miles per day would the Pony Express have to travel to cover this distance in seven days?

The Transcontinental Railroad

LESSON 2

The Railroad Is Born

What problems did Theodore Judah and the Big Four have to solve before they could build the transcontinental railroad?

Key Terms

- survey
- invest

➤ *These are the mountains that Judah was hoping to build a railroad over. Does it surprise you that some people thought he was crazy?*

Theodore Judah stood on a mountain peak, looking at the scene before him. At his feet, a rocky cliff dropped sharply into a valley 1,000 feet below. It was as if the mountains had put up a great stone stop sign in his path.

But Judah was not about to stop for the mountains. He was looking for a way to make his dream of a transcontinental railroad come true. Judah knew that building such a railroad meant crossing over the Sierra Nevada. So here he was, trying to find a way to lay railroad tracks from the top of this cliff down to the valley below. As you can imagine, it would not be easy for Judah to follow his dream.

Following a Dream

Making Judah's dream come true would be a challenge. But Judah would not give up. His wife, Anna Judah, wrote in a letter about how hard Judah worked at his goal.

Everything he did from the time he went to California to the day of his death was for the great continental Pacific Railway. Time, money, brains, strength, body and soul were absorbed. It was the burden of his thought day and night, largely of his conversation, till it used to be said, "Judah's Pacific Railroad crazy."

—Anna Judah, 1889

At times, Anna Judah was one of the few people who believed in her husband's ideas. But Judah was not concerned that he did not have a lot of people behind him. "We must keep the ball rolling," he would tell his wife.

Finding a Route

Judah knew that before others believed in him, he would have to show them that his dream could work. He would have to prove that a railroad could cross the Sierra Nevada.

To find an answer to this difficult problem, Judah and his assistant, Daniel Strong, climbed deep into the Sierra Nevada. Judah and Strong stopped often to **survey**, or measure, the height of the mountains.

After weeks of searching, the men found the railroad route they were looking for. By following this route, Judah figured, the tracks would not rise too steeply or cross too many deep valleys. Judah and Strong were so excited by their discovery that they did not notice the coming of a winter storm. A sudden blizzard forced them from their camp in the middle of the night. Fighting snow and darkness, Judah and Strong barely made it to safety.

How Do We Know?

HISTORY *Theodore and Anna Judah traveled to many places. Wherever they went, Anna wrote letters to her family and friends. Many of these letters described her husband's thoughts, words, and work. Anna Judah's letters give valuable information about the man who helped build the first transcontinental railroad.*

▲ *This is the compass Theodore Judah used to help him survey the mountains. Below is a map Judah made of his idea for a route through the mountains. Judah drew this map by hand.*

Map of the designated Route of the Central Pacific R.R. of California section from the City of Sacramento

The Transcontinental Railroad

Over the years, the Big Four would build a fortune of 200 million dollars from Judah's company.

■ *Many people thought Theodore Judah was crazy. Why did people feel this way about Judah?*

▼ *This map shows where the new railroad companies planned to lay tracks.*

Looking for Money

Now Judah had a route for his railroad, but he had no money to build it. To raise this money, he founded a company called the Central Pacific Railroad Company.

One night Judah met with four business people in Sacramento. These men saw Judah's railroad as a chance to become wealthy. They agreed to **invest** in the company. This means that they gave money, hoping to get more money back in the future. Their decision to invest was wise. They earned so much money by investing in the company that they became known as the Big Four.

Judah then went to Washington, D.C., to ask the Union government for help. His timing was perfect. The Union wanted to help California so that the state would stay on the Union side in the Civil War. So in July 1862, Congress agreed to help Judah's company build a railroad from California to the East. Congress also decided to help another railroad company build from the East toward California. This company was the Union Pacific. ■

Pushing Judah Out

Building on the railroad began at Sacramento in 1863. But within months, Judah and the Big Four began to have disagreements. Judah wanted to build the railroad carefully,

Proposed Transcontinental Railroad

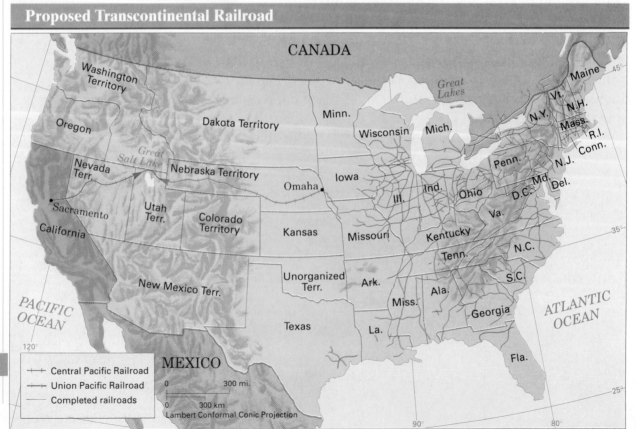

CANADA

Washington Territory

Oregon

Great Salt Lake

Nevada Terr.

Sacramento

California

Utah Terr.

New Mexico Terr.

PACIFIC OCEAN

120°

Dakota Territory

Nebraska Territory

Omaha

Colorado Territory

Minn.

Wisconsin

Iowa

Kansas

Unorganized Terr.

Texas

MEXICO

Mich.

Ill.

Missouri

Ark.

Miss.

La.

Ind.

Ohio

Kentucky

Tenn.

Ala.

Georgia

Great Lakes

Maine 45°

Vt. N.H.

N.Y.

Mass.

R.I.

Penn.

Conn.

N.J.

D.C. Md. Del.

Va.

N.C.

S.C.

ATLANTIC OCEAN

Fla.

35°

25°

Central Pacific Railroad
Union Pacific Railroad
Completed railroads

0   300 mi.
0   300 km
Lambert Conformal Conic Projection

90°   80°

BREAKING GROUND AT SACRAMENTO JAN. 8, 1863 FOR FIRST TRANSCONTINENTAL RAILROAD

whatever the cost. The Big Four said that they did not have the money to build so carefully. They wanted the railroad to be built their way if it was to be built at all.

The disagreements grew worse and worse. The Big Four began to hold secret meetings without Judah. They were tired of Judah's complaints, so they decided to force him out of the company. But Judah was not about to let the Big Four keep him from his lifelong dream. He was going to fight back.

In the fall of 1863, the Judahs left San Francisco and set sail for New York. There Judah hoped to find people who would help him buy the Central Pacific back from the Big Four. But during their trip across the Isthmus of Panama, Theodore Judah caught yellow fever. On November 2, he died. Judah was only 37 years old.

The Company Grows

Without Judah, the Big Four quickly turned the Central Pacific Railroad Company into a huge business. Within a few years, these men were among the most powerful and wealthy people in California. Not everyone liked the Big Four, however. To many Californians, the Big Four were heartless men who would do almost anything to make more money. As their power grew, the Big Four became more and more unpopular in California. ■

This painting shows Judah with the Big Four. These men were Leland Stanford, Collis P. Huntington, Charles Crocker, and Mark Hopkins.

Across Time & Space

Today passengers coming out of the train station in Sacramento see a large monument in memory of Theodore Judah. The monument is made of stone from the Sierra Nevada.

■ *Based on what you know about Theodore Judah, do you think he would have found some way to buy back the Central Pacific from the Big Four?*

R E V I E W

1. **FOCUS** What problems did Theodore Judah and the Big Four have to solve before they could build the transcontinental railroad?

2. **CONNECT** Based on what you read in Lesson 1, why do you think many people did not take Judah's railroad plan seriously?

3. **ECONOMICS** Why did the Big Four decide to invest in Judah's railroad company?

4. **CRITICAL THINKING** In a few sentences, state the reasons for the disagreement between Judah and the Big Four.

5. **WRITING ACTIVITY** Imagine that you are Theodore Judah. Write a speech telling people why a railroad would be good for the state and why they should invest money in your railroad company.

Reading a Time Zone Map

Here's Why

The earth rotates from west to east. As the earth rotates, sunlight hits different places at different times. Each day, sunlight hits the East Coast of the United States three hours earlier than it hits the West Coast.

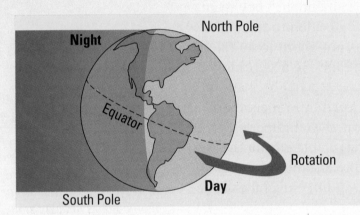

In the 1800s, each community set its own clocks by the sun. Clocks in different places did not agree. This system was confusing, and problems arose. When the transcontinental railroad was finished in 1869, the trains needed to run on a set time schedule. Finally, in 1883 the United States was divided into four time zones. The clocks in one zone all said the same time. This system solved the railroad's time-schedule problem. By understanding time zones on a map, you can figure out what time it is in different parts of the country.

Here's How

There are four time zones in the mainland of the United States. They are the Eastern, Central, Mountain, and Pacific Time Zones. Alaska and Hawaii also have time zones. Look at the map on page 331 of the Atlas. It shows which states are in each of the time zones. The clock in the Eastern Time Zone says 7:00. The clock in the Central Time Zone says 6:00. It is one hour earlier. As you go west from the Eastern Time Zone, subtract one hour for the Central Time Zone, one more hour for Mountain Time, and another hour for Pacific Time. There is a difference of three hours between the East and West Coasts.

Try It

Look at the time zone map on page 331 and answer the questions below:

1. Name one state in each time zone.
2. Name three states that are in more than one time zone.
3. Name the time zone that is just to the east of the Mountain Time Zone.
4. When it is 7:00 A.M. in Iowa, what time is it in Vermont? Louisiana? Colorado? Nevada? New York?
5. As you go east from Sacramento, does the time get earlier or later?

Apply It

Using the Atlas, plan a trip to six U.S. towns or cities. Begin in Los Angeles and end up in Washington, D.C. Be sure to include places that are located in each time zone. Trace your route on the map on page 324. If it is 4:00 P.M. when you arrive in Washington, D.C., what time is it in each of the other cities?

L E S S O N   3

Building the Railroad

This is war! Union Pacific work crews set off a blast of explosives right in front of Central Pacific workers, blowing up their track. Central Pacific crews fight back by rolling boulders onto the rails of the rival crew. Back and forth the battle goes.

It is 1869, and the Central Pacific and Union Pacific are in a bitter race. Each company receives valuable land from the United States government for each mile of track it builds. As the railroad nears its finish, there are few miles left to build. Who will lay these tracks and get the land? This is what the crews are fighting to decide.

T H I N K I N G
F O C U S

What were some of the challenges that the builders of the Central Pacific Railroad faced?

Key Terms

- construction
- engineering
- laborers

◄ *This picture shows some of the fighting that went on between the Central Pacific and Union Pacific crews.*

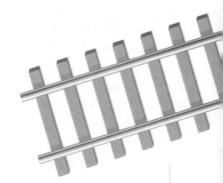

Laying the Tracks

The battles between the railroad crews were terrible. But the Central Pacific workers were already used to struggling for every inch of track. **Construction**, or the work of building, was hard in the rugged and cold Sierra Nevada.

173

The Transcontinental Railroad

Tunneling Through the Sierra

How could a train get through the mountains? The Central Pacific Railroad found a way. Workers slowly chipped and blasted through solid rock to make tunnels hundreds of feet long. Crews often worked all day to cut away just eight inches of rock.

pick

Workers chipped at the rock with picks. On their shoulders they wore wooden yokes like the one below to carry away buckets full of rock and dirt.

wooden yoke

Chinese laborers completed the most dangerous and difficult work. They worked 12 hours each day, 6 days a week. The Chinese laborers lived in tents, even in the bitter cold. Some lived in tunnels dug beneath the deep snow.

vertical tunnel into the center of the mountain

Kaboom! Tunnel workers blasted into the rock with black powder. A crew dug from each end of the tunnel. To speed up the digging, workers blasted a shaft from the top of the mountain. This allowed other crews to dig out the middle of the tunnel.

timber supports

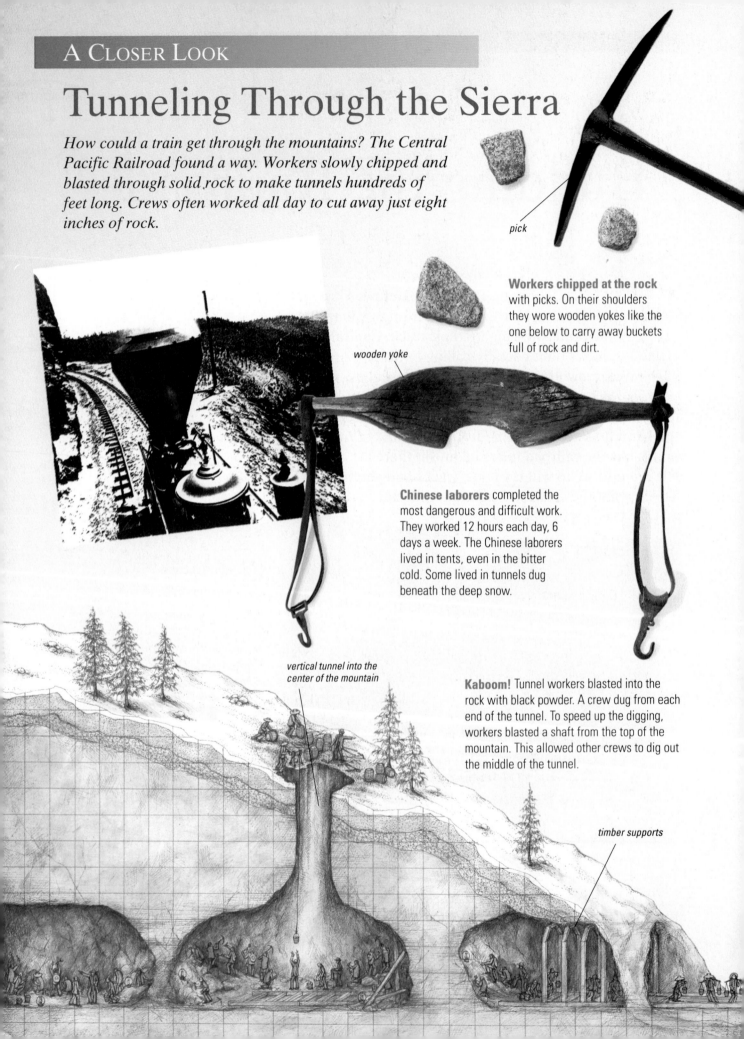

Winter made construction even more dangerous. Temperatures often dropped far below freezing. Forty-foot drifts of snow covered the mountains. Some workers had to spend the winter working in tunnels beneath the deep snow. ■

■ *Think of the pictures you have seen of the Sierra Nevada. Why would it be hard to build a railroad over these mountains?*

Looking for Workers

Construction in the Sierra Nevada was a huge job. But careful engineering solved many problems. **Engineering** is the use of scientific knowledge and rules to build something. The Big Four also needed thousands of **laborers,** or workers, to finish their part of the railroad. These laborers were not always easy to find or keep.

Labor Problems

The early railroad construction was done by laborers from California. But soon after the work began, news of silver in nearby Nevada spread among the work crews. So many laborers left for the silver mines that construction nearly stopped. Work went so slowly that in the first two years, crews laid only 50 miles of track. The Big Four knew that if they did not find more laborers, they would never finish the railroad.

Chinese to the Rescue

Charles Crocker, one of the Big Four, had an idea. Why not hire some of the many Chinese in California to work on the railroad? The Big Four were so pleased with how well the Chinese laborers worked that they hired as many as they could find. They even sent people across the ocean to China to find more workers for the railroad. Before long, most of the laborers on the Central Pacific were Chinese.

The Chinese workers proved their value again and again. They were the workers who took on the most dangerous and difficult jobs. Sadly, the Chinese were also the ones who froze to death in the bitter mountain cold. Many more Chinese workers died in snow slides or in the explosions used to blast away rocks. Without the skill and sacrifice of these Chinese laborers, the Central Pacific may never have made it across the Sierra Nevada. ■

▼ *The Chinese were given many of the hardest and most dangerous jobs in building the railroad.*

■ *How did the Chinese railroad workers help the Central Pacific railroad to finish its job?*

175

The Transcontinental Railroad

The Great Finish

In 1868, Central Pacific laborers finished their work in the Sierra Nevada. They had reached the flatter lands beyond the mountains at last. Free from the steep rocks and snow, workers laid track at an amazing pace. A reporter from the *Chicago Tribune* described the laying of track:

> The process was continuing as rapidly as a man could walk. Behind the car followed a man dropping spikes, another setting the ties well under the ends of the rails, and thirty or forty others driving in the spikes and stamping the earth under the ties. The moment that one car was emptied of its iron, a number of men seized it and threw it off the track and into the ditch and the second followed on with its load.

Central Pacific engineering and work crews kept up their fast pace. Once they laid a record 10 miles of track in a single day. Before long they had reached the Promontory Mountains in Utah. But here work slowed as the Central Pacific and Union Pacific crews carried on their bitter battle. The finish of the railroad waited while the two sides fought.

Finally, the two sides agreed to join tracks at a place called Promontory Point. By May 10, the two sets of rails rested only a few feet apart. Soon a golden spike would connect the rails. Train whistles would join the voices that for years had sung songs cheering for the railroad.

▼ *The transcontinental railroad connected California and the rest of the United States. With the railroad came the beginning of the end for the wagon train.*

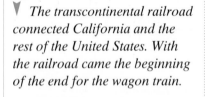

THE GREAT
OVERLAND RAIL ROUTE
VIA
CENTRAL PACIFIC
RAIL ROAD,
Connecting at TERMINUS
WITH THE
UNION PACIFIC
RAIL ROAD,
And at OMAHA
With all Roads Leading to
Chicago,   St. Louis,
Cincinnati,   Louisville,
New York,
And other Cities of the Eastern and Southern States.

CHAS. CROCKER, Gen'l Sup't.
T. H. GOODMAN, Gen'l Pass. Agent.

*T*he cars will soon be on the track,
the locomotive screaming;
Across the continent and back, the trains
will soon be steaming;
With Fremont as our engineer, and Dayton by his side,
We'll jump into the railroad cars and all take a ride.
Huzza for the railroad, huzza for the railroad,
The great Pacific Railroad on which we all will ride.

"Huzza for the Railroad," 1856

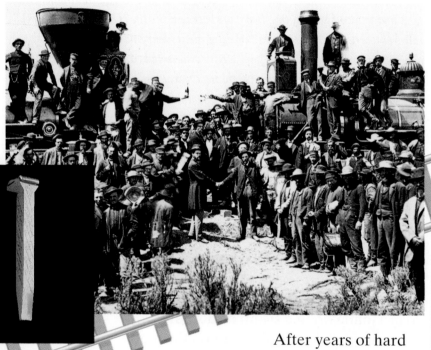

After years of hard work and grand dreams, the job was finished. The two coasts of the United States were at last linked by the iron rails of the transcontinental railroad. For California, the new railroad was a dream come true. ■

◄ *When the railroad was finished, the crews celebrated the driving of the golden spike. Notice which group of people is missing from this picture.*

■ *Why were work crews able to lay the track so quickly in Nevada and Utah?*

R E V I E W

1. **FOCUS** What were some of the challenges that the builders of the Central Pacific Railroad faced?
2. **CONNECT** From your earlier reading, find an example of the dangers of the Sierra Nevada.
3. **ECONOMICS** How do you think the new transcontinental railroad will change other businesses that carry people and goods across the country?

4. **CRITICAL THINKING** Why do you think the Chinese laborers were left out of the "last spike" picture?
5. **WRITING ACTIVITY** Imagine that you are on the first train to cross the Sierra Nevada. Write a short story about your journey.

The Transcontinental Railroad

The New Railroad

John Henry

The sound of John Henry's hammer rings in many traditional folk tales and work songs. All the stories are based on the life of a real man, a black railroad worker in the 1870s. In this song, John Henry with his hammer races against a steam-powered drill. John Henry's story tells us about the early days of the railroads in this country. As you read, ask yourself, "How would it feel to tunnel through a mountain using only a hammer?"

The transcontinental railroad, which Chinese laborers helped to complete, brought many changes to California and the rest of the country. This song and this poem offer two very different views of the first railroads.

John Henry was a little baby,
Sittin' on his gran'ma's knee,
Oh, he lift up a hammer and a little chunk of steel,
Said, "This hammer's gonna be the death of me. Lord, Lord.
Yes, this hammer's gonna be the death of me."

The captain says to John Henry,
Gonna bring a steam drill 'round,
Gonna take that drill out on the road,
Gonna drive that steel on down. Lord, Lord.
Gonna drive that steel on down.

John Henry drove through fourteen feet,
The steam drill only drove nine;
But he drove so hard that he broke his poor heart,
And he laid down his hammer and he died. Lord, Lord.
Yes, he laid down his hammer and he died.

They took John Henry to the graveyard
And they buried him deep in sand.
Now ev'ry train that comes a-chuggin' round
Says, "Here lies a steel-drivin' man." Lord, Lord.
Says, "Here lies a steel-drivin' man."

The Flower-Fed Buffaloes

Vachel Lindsay

Enormous herds of buffaloes once lived on the Great Plains, but they were hunted to near-extinction by 1874. From train windows, railroad travelers often shot buffaloes for sport. The homelands of many Indians, like the Blackfeet and the Pawnee, were also changed by the coming of the railroads and the growth of the United States. As you read Vachel Lindsay's poem, ask yourself, "How does the poet feel about the railroads and the disappearance of the buffaloes?"

The flower-fed buffaloes of the spring
In the days of long ago,
Ranged where the locomotives sing
And the prairie flowers lie low:—
The tossing, blooming, perfumed grass
Is swept away by the wheat,
Wheels and wheels and wheels spin by
In the spring that still is sweet.
But the flower-fed buffaloes of the spring
Left us, long ago.
They gore no more, they bellow no more,
They trundle around the hills no more:—
With the Blackfeet, lying low,
With the Pawnees, lying low,
Lying low.

trundle move with a rolling motion

Further Reading

Land of the Iron Dragon. Alida E. Young. This book tells the story of Lim Yan-Sung, a Chinese immigrant boy who joins the transcontinental railroad crews.

Chapter Review

Reviewing Key Terms

communication (p.165) laborers (p.175)
construction (p.173) survey (p.169)
engineering (p.175) transcontinental (p.166)
invest (p.170) transportation (p.165)

Choose the key term that best completes each sentence below. Then write one or two sentences to explain why you chose that word.

1. Before the railroad, one type of _____ people used to travel to California was the covered wagon.
2. The Big Four decided to _____ in the Central Pacific Railroad because they hoped to become rich.
3. Thousands of people worked to lay tracks for the _____ of the railroad.
4. People in California did not hear news about the Civil War for weeks because _____ between the East and West Coasts was slow.
5. It was necessary to _____ the Sierra Nevada before the best route for the transcontinental railroad was found.
6. The most dangerous work on the railroad was done by Chinese _____.
7. Theodore Judah wanted a _____ railroad that would connect California to the eastern states.
8. Figuring out how to lay tracks through the steep, rugged mountains was a problem of _____.

Exploring Concepts

A. The chart below shows three different early methods of linking California with other states. Copy the chart on a separate piece of paper. Then complete the chart by answering the questions in the headings across the top. Use information from the chapter in your answers.

B. Write one or two sentences to answer each question below. Use details from this chapter to support your answers.
1. Why did the Union Pacific and Central Pacific work crews fight?
2. What became of Theodore Judah's dream after he died?

Method	What was it?	What did it carry?	How long did it take?
Pony Express	Riders on ponies		
Butterfield Stage Line	Stagecoaches		
Telegraph			

Reviewing Skills

1. Look at the map on page 331 of the Atlas . Use the map to figure out what time it is in Anchorage, Alaska and in Honolulu, Hawaii when it is 6:00 P.M. in Los Angeles, California.
2. Rosa lives in Miami, Florida in the Eastern Time Zone. It is 9:00 A.M. in that city. She wants to call friends in Dallas, Texas; Denver, Colorado; and Portland, Oregon. On a separate piece of paper, write the times for the empty clocks below. How much longer must Rosa wait until it is 9:00 A.M. in Dallas? in Denver? in Portland?
3. Using the map on page 324, figure the number of miles people would travel to get from St. Louis to Sacramento.
4. We know something about Anna Judah because she wrote letters that describe her thoughts and feelings. Where could you look for information about other women who were important in California history?

Pacific	Mountain	Central	Eastern
(clock)	(clock)	(clock)	(clock showing 9:00)

Using Critical Thinking

1. The transcontinental railroad improved travel between California and the other states. How do you think the transcontinental railroad changed the lives of people in California?
2. Food and other products that are brought from another place usually cost more than food and products that are grown or made at home. Why? Who would be paid the extra money?
3. Thomas Edison, the great inventor, said, "Genius is one percent inspiration and 99 percent perspiration." He meant that you must work hard in order to make a good idea work. How does this saying fit the life of Theodore Judah? How does it fit your own life or the life of someone you know? Give examples to support your ideas.

Preparing for Citizenship

1. ART ACTIVITY Pretend you have written a book called *Chinese Laborers and the Railroad*. Design a cover for this book. On the front, write and illustrate the title. On the back of the cover, write a paragraph about one of the most interesting parts of your story.
2. COLLABORATIVE LEARNING On a television or radio talk show, the host asks guests questions about their lives. As a class project, present a talk show. Choose one student to be the host. Choose other students to be the guests. The guests are Theodore Judah, the Big Four business owners, Anna Judah, and some railroad laborers. Other students can make up the audience. Each student in the audience should prepare a question for one of the guests.

Chapter 8

Agriculture Advances

As California grew, people began to discover a new richness beyond the gold mines. They found that richness in the soil. Farming provided new opportunities and new challenges.

Many miners turned to farming to seek their fortunes. Californians began to grow dozens of different kinds of grains, fruits, and vegetables.

1850	1860	1870

1870 Wheat is California's most important crop.

1850

The growth of agriculture meant a greater need for labor. Thousands of newcomers to California worked the fields and orchards.

Riverside, with its valuable orange groves, grew quickly. The rest of southern California was growing too.

1880

1890

1900

1888 The refrigerated railroad car helps farmers ship crops across the country.

1900

LESSON 1

Farming Takes Hold

THINKING FOCUS

How did California's agriculture change in the years following the gold rush?

Key Terms

- production
- experiment
- refrigeration

▼ *California's farmers connected many small plows to make one giant gang plow.*

A s you look into the distance, the horizon itself appears to be moving. A great machine, which seems nearly a mile long, chews up the rich soil in huge chunks. The machine draws closer, and the earth trembles beneath your feet. Dust fills the air in a thick cloud. A rising wave of sound swells around you as your ears fill with "the click of buckles, the creak of straining leather, the subdued [quiet] clash of machinery, the cracking of whips, the deep breathing of nearly four hundred horses, the abrupt [sharp] commands and cries of the drivers, and, last of all, the prolonged, soothing murmur of the thick brown earth."

Writer Frank Norris described these sights and sounds in his 1901 novel *The Octopus*. These giant machines, pictured below, were called gang plows. They were widely used on California's farmland in the second half of the 1800s. At this time, California's farmers needed all the help they could get in farming the land. As the state grew in the years following the gold rush, so did its need for food. And so did the task facing its farmers.

Changes in Land Use

Giant gang plows were new to California, but farming was not. Long before the 1850s, Indians grew corn and beans on riverbanks. The Spanish grew fruits, vegetables, and grains on the missions. Mexican rancheros raised cows for meat, hides, and tallow.

During the gold rush, people found that they could make money selling food to the many new people pouring into California. The Chinese were among the first to realize this. Next to their mining claims, Chinese miners planted small vegetable gardens. They often found that they could make more money selling vegetables than digging for gold.

Chinese Gardeners

Many Chinese left mining to become full-time farmers. Each day they picked ripe vegetables from their gardens. They loaded the vegetables into baskets, which hung from poles balanced on their shoulders. Then the Chinese gardeners went from house to house selling their vegetables.

Chinese gardeners, with their small farms, helped meet California's growing demand for food. By doing so, they filled an important role during a time of fast growth in the new state. ■

■ Explain why there was such a need for the food that Chinese gardeners grew.

The Growth of Wheat

In the 1850s Californians proved that they could grow enough food for the state's growing number of people. Among the many new settlers in the state were thousands of farmers. They were eager to plow the land. By the 1860s food from California's farms began to feed the rest of the country as well as the world.

Wheat was the favorite crop for these new farmers. Many settled in California's Central Valley, an area that was perfect for wheat farming. There a farmer could plow the land easily because it was flat and had few rocks or trees to get in the way. The rich soil, wet from winter rains, fed the wheat. The dry summer heat helped it ripen. California's

◄ *In the late 1800s golden fields of wheat spread across California's Central Valley.*

■ *Give three reasons why the Central Valley was perfect for wheat farming.*

▼ *Luther Burbank used his love and knowledge of plants to create improved flowers, grains, and trees, as well as fruits and vegetables.*

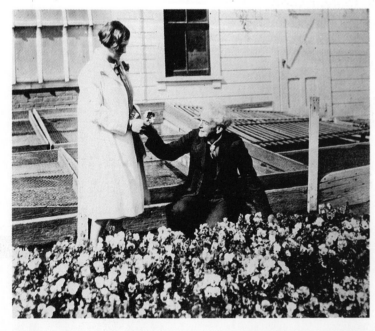

wheat was so good that it became known around the world. Italians used it for their pasta, and the French used it for their famous breads.

Wheat farmers were very successful. They made so much money from selling the wheat that they called their farms bonanza farms. On these great farms, giant gang plows turned over the rich earth. Each year Californians grew even more wheat. Writer Charles Nordhoff, in his 1874 book *California for Travellers and Settlers*, gave this description of the Central Valley:

> *W*heat, wheat, wheat, and nothing but wheat is what you see on your journey as far as the eye can reach over the plain in every direction. Fields of two, three, and four thousand acres make but small farms; here is a man who "has in" 20,000 acres; here one with 40,000 acres and another with some still more preposterous [incredible] amount—all in wheat.

Wheat farming was good for many farmers. But in time it proved to be harmful to the soil. Growing the same crop year after year drained minerals from the soil. This caused wheat **production**, or the total amount grown, to drop. By the 1890s farmers had to find new crops to plant. ■

The Move to New Crops

Many farmers started to grow fruits and vegetables. All across California these new crops were becoming as successful as wheat had been in the years before. The map on the following page shows how new crops helped to make California agriculture grow. Much of this success was due to the work of a scientist named Luther Burbank.

Luther Burbank's Contributions

Burbank moved to California in 1875 to follow his life's work as a plant scientist. He performed **experiments** to study and to learn more about the seeds of different plants. These tests helped him understand how to develop new kinds of plants. His goal

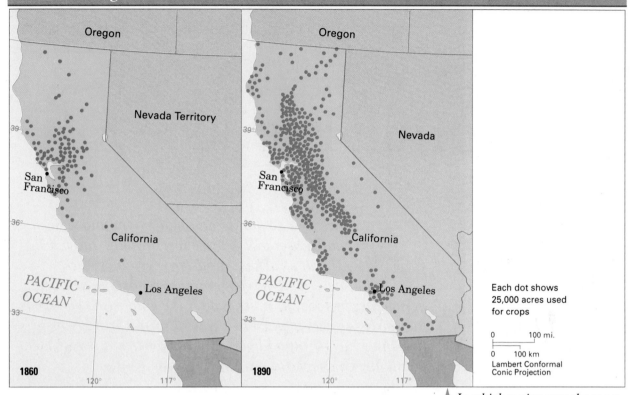

Growth of Agriculture in California 1860-1890

1860

1890

Each dot shows 25,000 acres used for crops

0   100 mi.
0   100 km
Lambert Conformal Conic Projection

was to grow fruits and vegetables that would taste better and stay fresh longer. Burbank became famous around the world for the many types of crops he developed on his experimental farm in Santa Rosa. Even today farmers grow fruits and vegetables developed by Burbank. To learn more about crops grown in California, see Exploring Produce.

A Growing Reputation

In the 1870s the fame of California's farms spread. Railroads carried the state's crops across the country. Much of the food was canned to keep it from spoiling during the long journey. Then in 1888 the railroads began using boxcars with **refrigeration**. These cars used ice to keep food cold and fresh, so it did not need to be canned. Thanks to refrigerated railroad cars, people from across the country could enjoy fresh California fruits and vegetables. ◼

▲ *In which region was the most land turned into farmland between 1860 and 1890?*

◼ *Give two important reasons for the growth of California fruit and vegetable farming.*

R E V I E W

1. **FOCUS** How did California's agriculture change in the years following the gold rush?

2. **CONNECT** How have large farms and ranches played an important part in the history of California?

3. **GEOGRAPHY** How did California's geography affect the state's agriculture?

4. **CRITICAL THINKING** Wheat farming was good for farmers but harmful to the soil. Which do you think is more important? Explain your answer.

5. **ACTIVITY** Make a list of the different foods you eat during the week. How might this list change if there were no refrigeration?

Agriculture Advances

California Produce

A twenty-one pound onion, a 131-pound squash, and a beet that is three feet around! Tall tales? Not at all. These monster vegetables were described in a government report on California agriculture in 1853, four years after the gold rush. The seeds that early farmers planted helped California grow. Now let's find out which fruits and vegetables grow here today. Later, you'll have a chance to taste them.

Get Ready

You'll need to bring a notebook and a pen or pencil. You might also bring along a large envelope for collecting labels from crates, the wooden boxes used to transport fruits and vegetables.

Find Out

If you live in a city, plan a visit to your neighborhood supermarkets or produce (PROH doos) markets. Produce is fruits and vegetables. Also look for open-air farmers' markets, like the one held in San Francisco's Civic Center Plaza. If you live outside the city, plan a visit to nearby markets or fruit stands—or talk with farmers about what they grow.

At the market, see how many types of produce you can name without looking at the signs or labels. Now look at the signs or talk to the grocer to discover which fruits and vegetables were grown in California. Next, find out what part of California they are grown in. Make notes on what the items look like and in which towns or counties they are grown. Ask the grocer if you may peel off crate labels to take with you.

▲ California farmers grow more than 200 kinds of fruits and vegetables. How many can you name?

Move Ahead

Work with your classmates to make a California produce booklet. Write up your notes and then share them with others. Make a list of the different types of fruits and vegetables the class has learned about. Now choose one fruit or vegetable you've studied. On a left-hand page, write down all the facts you know about it. Then bring in a recipe that uses that fruit or vegetable. Some examples might be recipes for apple pie, broccoli soup, or carrot salad.

Write the recipe down on the right-hand page. Illustrate the pages of your cookbook with crate labels, magazine pictures, and your own drawings of fruits and vegetables.

Of course, no recipe is complete without a taste test. Try out one of the recipes at home and share it with your family and friends.

▲ *Labels can help you find out where in California different produce is grown.*

Explore Some More

Some produce is harvested year-round. Other produce can only be found in the stores during certain times of the year. California almonds, for example, are in season in September, while cherries arrive in May. So on your next trip to the market, you may find fruits and vegetables you didn't see last time. Keep an eye out for new produce to add to your notebook and to your recipe collection. Find out when your favorite fruits and vegetables are in season by using reference books or by asking farmers, your grocer, or someone in your family.

LESSON 2

Growth in Southern California

What are two important reasons for the growth of southern California?

Key Terms

- industry
- competition
- boom

➤ *Posters like this were placed all across the United States and even in Europe.*

"Oranges for health; California for wealth." Advertisements like this made people from all over the country want to come and live in sunny southern California.

The poster you see here is one of those advertisements. It promises plenty of rich land, bursting with fruit and covered with sunshine. The container overflowing with fruit, vegetables, and grain is called a cornucopia. To people in the rest of the United States, southern California must have seemed like a huge cornucopia.

The poster also announces over 43 million acres of land for sale. Railroad companies in California owned much of this land, and they wanted farmers to buy some of it. New residents would mean new customers for their railroad. To get farmers to come to California, railroads decorated their trains with streamers and ribbons. They offered free food and drink to those who would go west.

Advertisements and offers like these worked. As the *Los Angeles Times* noted in 1887, "All the world is interested in California." During the 1880s, as many as five thousand people a week spilled into southern California. The land that had escaped the frenzy of the gold rush now faced a rush of its own.

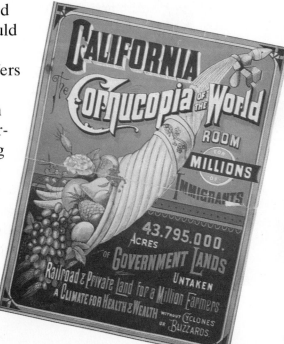

Southern California's Oranges

Many people came to southern California just to grow oranges. They believed that the fruit that had made southern California famous could make them successful too.

Oranges had a long history in California. The Spanish grew them on the missions in the 1700s. Those oranges were dry, seedy, and sour, but people ate them anyway.

Until the late 1800s the orange crop in California had not been very important. The orange **industry**—the business of growing and selling oranges—remained small. Then in 1873 the orange industry took a big turn. In that year, Luther Tibbets made the 65-mile trip to Los Angeles from his home in Riverside. At the post office, two small orange trees were waiting for Tibbets. The trees grew a special orange called the navel orange. They had been grown in Brazil, a country in South America.

Under the care of Eliza Tibbets, Luther's wife, the trees grew well. The oranges tasted delicious—they were juicy, seedless, and sweet. The trees became so valuable that the Tibbetses had to place a barbed-wire fence around them to stop theft. Soon other farmers were growing navel oranges. By 1900 millions of orange trees dotted the land. ■

Across Time & Space

Before the late 1800s most people ate oranges only as a special treat. As the orange industry in California grew, advertisements persuaded people to eat more oranges. Today oranges and orange juice are part of the daily diet of millions of people.

■ *Give one possible reason for the success of the navel orange besides its good flavor.*

▲ *The railroad helped California's farmers get their oranges and other crops to Eastern cities quickly.*

Railroads and Growth

Oranges were one reason for southern California's growth. The railroads were another.

In the 1870s the Southern Pacific, which used to be called the Central Pacific, was California's only railroad. Its rates were high, but people had to pay what the railroad charged. There was no other railroad they could use.

191

The Journey of a California Orange

Oranges used to be expensive and hard to find in many cities in the United States. Then in the 1870s, delicious new varieties of the fruit came to California. Railroads began carrying the oranges all across the nation.

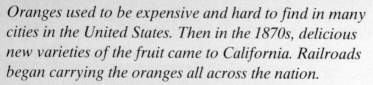

Pack them in! As a number of orange trees in California grew quickly, so did the orange industry. Whole train-loads of oranges were heading East by 1886.

Keep them cold! In 1888, railroad companies began to build refrigerated cars. These kept the oranges fresh longer. Every 24 hours, trains stopped at icehouses to repack the cars with ice.

192

Move them out! Soon, California oranges were arriving regularly in cities as far away as Baltimore. Today, people can enjoy fresh-squeezed orange juice every day from coast to coast.

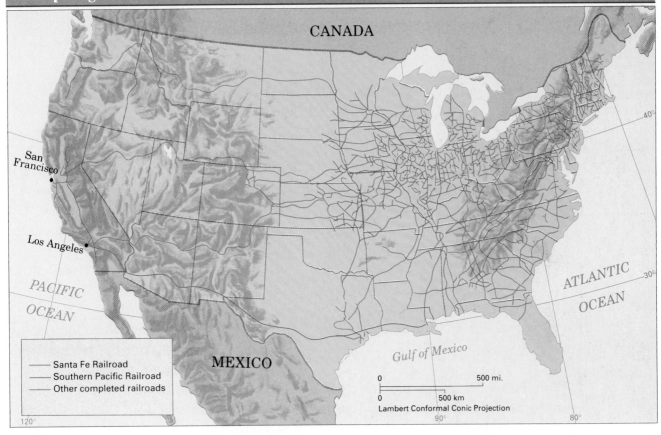

CANADA

San Francisco

Los Angeles

PACIFIC OCEAN

MEXICO

Gulf of Mexico

ATLANTIC OCEAN

— Santa Fe Railroad
— Southern Pacific Railroad
— Other completed railroads

0   500 mi.
0   500 km
Lambert Conformal Conic Projection

Then in 1885 a railroad called the Santa Fe began running in California. The Santa Fe and Southern Pacific each wanted riders to ride their railroad and not the other. This means that they were in **competition** with each other. Hoping to attract more customers, the railroads lowered their prices. One cut its transcontinental fare from 125 dollars to 100 dollars. The other dropped its fare to 50 dollars, then to 25 dollars. For a few days the fare dropped to just 1 dollar.

This competition caused a period of fast growth, which is called a **boom**. In 1887 alone, two hundred thousand people traveled to southern California. Thousands stayed. Some bought land and planted oranges or other crops. Others took jobs in growing cities like Los Angeles. Southern California was in a boom, just as the northern part of the state had been 30 years before. ■

▲ *Do you think that the Santa Fe will compete with the Southern Pacific in other parts of California besides the southern part?*

■ *Give two reasons why railroad competition might have helped southern California grow.*

R E V I E W

1. **FOCUS** What are two important reasons for the growth of southern California?
2. **CONNECT** Why had northern California grown more quickly than southern California?
3. **ECONOMICS** Give at least two reasons why the railroad companies wanted people to move to California.
4. **CRITICAL THINKING** What would you expect railroad advertisements to show about life in California? Explain your answer.
5. **ACTIVITY** Create a poster to attract people to come and live in your city or town.

193

Agriculture Advances

Drawing Conclusions

Here's Why

When you read, you should try to do more than just remember facts and ideas. You can also think about these facts to develop new ideas of your own. This process is called drawing conclusions. By drawing conclusions, you can understand more about what you read. For example, you can better understand the changes that were made in California agriculture.

Here's How

You learn new information about different topics from the books you read. To draw conclusions, you explore these new ideas by connecting them to what you already know about the topic. The diagram below shows how to draw a conclusion about the climate in which oranges grow best. What have you read about where oranges grow? What do you know about California's climate? What conclusion can you draw about the climate that is best for oranges? Combine what you read with what you already know and draw your own conclusion.

Try It

Read each of the statements below to learn more about farming in California. Think about what you already know about each topic. Then draw a conclusion about each statement.

1. Navel orange trees from Brazil grew well when they were planted in southern California.
2. Many more oranges were shipped to the East Coast after the refrigerated boxcar was developed.
3. Farmers had to spray orange trees with chemicals.
4. California's Central Valley was perfect for wheat farming.
5. Many Chinese forty-niners decided to grow vegetables rather than mine for gold.
6. Few farmers wanted to grow the dry, sour, and seedy oranges like the ones from the missions.

Apply It

Suppose you want to grow a flower or a vegetable in an outdoor garden. Read the seed packet about the conditions that are best for growing this plant. The amount of sunlight and water the plant needs are important. What do you already know about the climate of your area? What conclusion can you draw about how well this plant will grow?

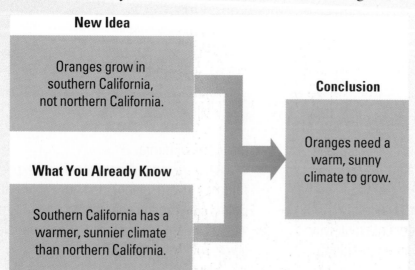

New Idea

Oranges grow in southern California, not northern California.

What You Already Know

Southern California has a warmer, sunnier climate than northern California.

Conclusion

Oranges need a warm, sunny climate to grow.

L E S S O N   3

Problems Facing Agriculture

S ome called it Starvation Valley because life on the land was a race against hunger. New settlers struggled to farm in this valley located in the Tulare *(too LAIR ee)* Basin of the southern Central Valley. Each season brought new hardships upon the settlers. Floods, frost, lack of rain, and sandstorms battered their fields and ruined their crops.

But one group of hard-working farmers was not bothered by these difficulties. They called their piece of Starvation Valley Mussel Slough *(sloo)*. These farmers believed that by working with each other they could meet the difficult challenges of nature.

Their task was a big one. The farmers of Mussel Slough worked hard to survive on the harsh land. Slowly, their efforts began to pay off. Seeds sprouted and continued to grow. The farmers began to have hope that this time Starvation Valley would not live up to its name. It looked as though they were going to win their struggle to establish new farms at Mussel Slough.

T H I N K I N G
F O C U S

What were some of the challenges that faced California's farmers in the second half of the 1800s?

Key Terms

- irrigation
- levee
- migrant laborer
- tenant

◄ *Like the farm workers shown here, the farmers of Mussel Slough had to struggle to make their crops grow.*

195

Agriculture Advances

Water Problems

In much of the nation, farmers rely on summer rains to help their crops grow. But there is little summer rain in many parts of California, including the Tulare Basin. The farmers of Mussel Slough had to dig trenches to a nearby river to bring water to their fields.

The network of trenches that the farmers built is called an **irrigation** system. Even today, most of California's farms depend on water from such systems. But building an irrigation system is expensive. Few farmers can afford to build their own. So many farmers, like those of Mussel Slough, join together to share the cost.

Other farmers may buy land that has already been irrigated. In 1881, for example, George Chaffey built an irrigation system in southern California on 2,500 acres of land he called Etiwanda. He then sold pieces of this land to farmers. Those who bought land also bought the right to use water from the system. Soon other people, such as Harriet Russell Strong of the San Gabriel Valley, were building communities like Chaffey's.

Increase in the Amount of Irrigated Land

1870
60,000 acres

1880
350,000 acres

1889
1,000,000 acres

1899
1,500,000 acres

▲ In 30 years the amount of irrigated land in California increased by almost 30 times.

➤ Water from an irrigation system can turn poor land into valuable farmland.

Too Much Water

Water created a different problem for some farmers. Along the Sacramento River, for example, farms often lost

crops to spring floods. To stop flooding, farmers built high ridges called **levees** along the riverbanks. The first levee was built in the 1850s, but it took 50 years for the levees to completely control flooding. Fortunately for the farmers, the state and federal governments paid much of the cost. ■

■ *Explain two ways that water can create problems for farmers.*

Land Problems

Californians had found that they could work well with nature to make their farms productive. But they found it a little more difficult to work with each other.

In the 1870s a few people owned most of the land in California. The Southern Pacific owned one of every ten acres in the state. The railroad decided to make money from its land by selling some to farmers. That is how the farmers at Mussel Slough got their farms. The railroad agreed to sell the land at five dollars an acre, and even let the farmers use the land before the sale was completed. The farmers thought that the land would soon be theirs. They went ahead and built their irrigation system and planted crops.

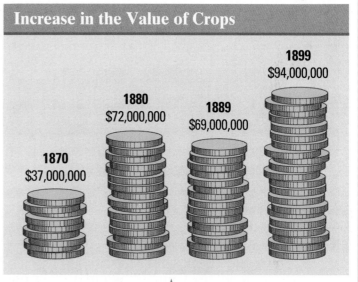

Increase in the Value of Crops

1870
$37,000,000

1880
$72,000,000

1889
$69,000,000

1899
$94,000,000

▲ *Irrigation helped increase the value of crops. This made farmland more valuable.*

The Southern Pacific then realized that the farmers' work had increased the value of the land. So the railroad decided to break its promise to the farmers. It found two men who agreed to pay 25 dollars an acre for the land. When these men tried to move onto the land, the Mussel Slough farmers fought back. In the battle that followed, the two men and five farmers were killed.

To many who heard the story of what happened at Mussel Slough, the railroad was clearly wrong. Still, the railroad was able to drive the farmers off the land. A character from Frank Norris's book *The Octopus* explains the problem:

> *I* wish I could have talked to you and your friends before you went into that . . . fight. I could have told you how little chance you had. When will you people realize that you can't buck against the railroad? Why, Magnus, it's like me going out in a paper boat and shooting peas at a battleship.

Based on the selection you just read, do you think the book The Octopus *is for or against the railroad? Explain your answer.*

The public did not support the railroad's actions at Mussel Slough. But there was little they could do to fight against the railroad's power. ■

Patterns for the Future

What happened at Mussel Slough was much like events that took place elsewhere in the state in the late 1800s. Although there were small farms in California, a large portion of the land remained in the hands of wealthy people or companies like the Southern Pacific Railroad.

UNDERSTANDING MIGRANT LABOR

Since the gold rush, migrant labor has been a key to the success of California agriculture. Owners of the bonanza wheat farms, for example, needed help each year to harvest their crop. They hired thousands of Chinese migrant laborers. The work was hard and lasted for only a few weeks a year on each farm. When the work on one farm was done, the Chinese had to move to other farms to find work. Often they found no work at all.

Not all farms used migrant labor. The need for migrant laborers depended on the type of crops and the size of the farm. Many family farms were small enough that the family itself could provide all the labor. They lived on their farms year-round, sometimes with a few full-time workers.

Many People Contribute

Migrant laborers have come to California from around the world, including Mexico, China, Japan, and the Philippines. People from many nations have played important parts in the history of migrant labor.

As more people have come to California from different nations, the number of migrant laborers has grown. Because of the large supply of laborers in California, landowners have been able to pay low wages. If the laborers complained, there was always someone who would do the work for low pay.

In some ways, little has changed in California agriculture. Many of California's farms are still very large, and migrant laborers provide most of the labor. But migrant laborers have come a long way in improving their jobs. By working together, migrant laborers have made many gains in pay and in living and working conditions.

Small family farms have always been rare in California. Large farms owned by big businesses, like the one shown below, control much of California agriculture.

Most of the work on these large farms was performed by crews of workers called **migrant laborers.** These workers traveled to farms and picked the fields of ripe crops. When they were done, migrant laborers moved on to look for work on other farms that had crops ready to be picked.

Besides the migrant laborers, there were other farmers called **tenant** farmers. These farmers paid rent to use land that belonged to someone else. Tenant farmers usually stayed on the same land year after year.

Farm ownership in the 1800s followed a pattern that you can still see throughout California. Many farms are owned by large companies. These huge farms produce a tremendous amount of food. They help feed people all across the United States and around the world. As it was years ago, much of the labor on these farms is done by migrant laborers. In many ways, California agriculture has changed very little in the last one hundred years. ■

■ *Why is much of the work on California's farms done by migrant laborers?*

R E V I E W

1. **FOCUS** What were some of the challenges that faced California's farmers in the second half of the 1800s?
2. **CONNECT** From your earlier reading, find an example of a disagreement over the use of California's farmland.
3. **GEOGRAPHY** Why do you think farmers of today still must depend on irrigation systems to grow their crops?
4. **CRITICAL THINKING** In what ways would California be different today if the pattern of large farms had been broken in the 1800s?
5. **WRITING ACTIVITY** Pretend you are a reporter covering the events at Mussel Slough. Interview some townspeople. Write down their reactions and feelings toward the railroad.

Chapter Review

Reviewing Key Terms

boom (p.193)
competition (p.193)
experiment (p.186)
industry (p.191)
irrigation (p.196)
levee (p.197)
migrant laborer (p.199)
production (p.186)
refrigeration (p.187)
tenant (p.199)

A. Write a sentence for each key term below. Include details that give clues to the meaning of the term.
1. boom
2. experiment
3. levee
4. production
5. tenant

B. Choose the key term that best completes each sentence.
1. Crops of fruits and vegetables that can spoil are kept fresh by _____.
2. A _____ moves from farm to farm to pick crops when they are ripe.
3. The _____ between California's two railroad companies resulted in lower ticket prices for passengers.
4. The orange _____ in California was changed when two little trees arrived.
5. To water their crops, many California farmers use an _____ system.

Exploring Concepts

A. Complete the chart below on a separate piece of paper. In the left column, list five more problems that farmers in California faced. In the right column, describe how these problems were solved.

Problems	Solutions
Oranges from the missions were dry, seedy, and sour.	Luther Tibbets brought the navel orange to California. Navel oranges are juicy, seedless, and sweet.

B. Support each statement below with two details from this chapter.
1. After the gold rush, the farming industry in California became very successful.
2. During the 1880s, railroad companies encouraged farmers to move to California.
3. Farmers in California were helped by railroads in the state.
4. Farmers in California were hurt by the railroad.
5. Water has been a problem for farmers in California.
6. The large farms in California need many laborers during the harvest and other important times.
7. The move to fruit and vegetable crops helped California agriculture grow in the late 1800s.

Reviewing Skills

1. Draw a conclusion from the pair of statements below. Use what you have learned in the chapter to help draw your conclusion.
a. The Southern Pacific was the only railroad in California, and its prices were high.
b. When the Santa Fe Railroad started running in California, people began buying fewer tickets from the Southen Pacific Railroad.

2. Many Chinese stopped mining and became full-time farmers. Why do you think they did this?
3. By the 1890s, many farmers in California had to begin growing new crops of fruits and vegetables. What was the cause of this event?
4. Suppose you want to find out more about Luther Burbank and the experiments he did on plants. In what kinds of books will you look?

Using Critical Thinking

1. Luther Burbank developed new fruits and vegetables. Some of this produce tasted better than the kinds that had been grown before. What other improvements do you think farmers might have wanted?

2. "An orange is a slice of California sunshine." Why is this slogan a good advertisement for the California orange industry? Why would it make people want to buy oranges?

Preparing for Citizenship

1. **ART ACTIVITY** Imagine you are a farmer who grows vegetables. It has not rained for months, and your plants are dying. You need to get water from the river to your dry land. Draw a diagram of an irrigation system that will bring water to save your crop. Make sure that all the plants in your field get water.

2. **COLLECTING INFORMATION** Look and listen in the world around you for advertisements for different kinds of food products. In a notebook, write a list of advertisements you see on television, on billboards, or in buses and subways.

    Cut out advertisements from magazines and newspapers and paste them in the notebook. Think about how each advertisement makes you want to eat the food it shows.

3. **COLLABORATIVE LEARNING** Set up a classroom debate between the farmers of Mussel Slough and workers for the Southern Pacific Railroad.

    The class should divide into two teams. The team of farmers should meet to list reasons why they don't want to pay 25 dollars an acre to own the land they have been farming. The team of railroad workers should list reasons why they raised the price from 5 dollars an acre. Each team should use information from the chapter to support its arguments.

    Each team should choose two members to speak during the debate. These students will give their team's arguments and reply to the arguments of the other team.

Chapter 9
The Mixing of Peoples

Starting with the gold rush, California earned the reputation as a land of dreams. People from around the world came to California for new opportunities. But life was harder than people thought it would be. The new Californians faced the challenges and helped build a better, richer state.

These people from Scandinavia enjoyed a picnic in their new California home.

1850	1860	1870	1880

1850

1882 The Chinese population in California begins to drop as the United States Congress makes it harder for Chinese to move here.

Japanese people formed a group in Los Angeles to help each other start new lives in California.

These two labels give hints of Irish and Italian culture in California. The Irish and Italians were two of California's largest groups of newcomers.

SHAMROCK BRAND
VALENCIAS
PACKED BY
PLACENTIA MUTUAL ORANGE ASS'N.
PLACENTIA ORANGE COUNTY CALIFORNIA GROWN

PASTORE
DOUBLE GALLON
(Doppio Gallone)
100% Pure
OLIVE OIL
(Ollo Degli Italiani)
PACKED BY
PASTORE OLIVE COMPANY
SELMA, CALIFORNIA
Net Contents 2 Gallons

| 1890 | 1900 | 1910 | 1920 |

1920

LESSON 1

The New Californians

Who are immigrants, and why did they come to California?

Key Term

- immigrant

▼ *Immigrant farmers in California often raised crops they knew from their old countries. Armenians introduced figs to the state.*

Franco Torrano sits with a pen in his hand and a sheet of paper in front of him. He is writing a letter to his father, who still lives in the small Italian town of Verbicaro (*vur bih KAH roh*). Franco dips his pen in the inkwell as his brothers, Carmelo and Pietro, tell him what to write.

Until Franco came to live with them in San Francisco, Carmelo and Pietro did not send many letters home to Italy. They did not know how to write, so they had to pay someone to write letters for them. Their father complained about not getting enough news from his sons in California. So Pietro suggested that young Franco go to school to learn to write. Then Franco could move to California to help his brothers send more letters home.

The letter that Franco is writing today will not please their father. When Carmelo and Pietro came to California in 1906, they agreed to stay only four years. But the shoe repair shop that they opened in San Francisco has been doing so well that they want to stay in California. Now they are writing to tell their father that San Francisco will be their new home.

Why California?

The Torranos were **immigrants**. These are people who move to another country so that they can make a new home there. Often people become immigrants to look for better jobs. Or they may be seeking safety from wars or violence in their old countries.

As California grew in the 1800s, it attracted thousands of immigrants from around the world. Thanks to the gold rush, people everywhere thought of California as a place to find wealth. Many had also heard of the warm sunshine and rich farmland of the Central Valley. So, many immigrants believed that California was the place where they could make their dreams of a better life come true. ■

Immigrants from Europe

Many immigrants came to the United States from European countries such as Ireland, Germany, Portugal, France, and Sweden. To find out where these countries are, see the Atlas, pages 320–321. Often the immigrants settled in East Coast cities like New York or Boston.

Hagop and Garabed Seropian, for example, came to the United States from Armenia. Armenia was a country in southeast Europe that is now part of the Soviet Union. At first the Seropians made their new home in Massachusetts. Then a doctor told Hagop that California's sunny weather would be better for his health than the cold of New England. In 1881, the Seropians became the first Armenians to move to California.

Other immigrants came to California because they had been unhappy in the eastern United States. There, the immigrants' languages and traditions made them seem different from the other people. Immigrants were often treated cruelly by people who did not understand their cultures. The few jobs they could find usually paid very little. So immigrants had to live in poorer neighborhoods called ghettos (*GEH tohz*). Life was so hard in the East Coast cities that thousands of immigrants left for California. Here they hoped to find the life they had been looking for when they first came to the United States. ■

Immigrants from Asia

While thousands of immigrants were coming to California from Europe, others were crossing the Pacific Ocean from Asia. For these Asian immigrants, life in California would be a huge change. Most of them knew nothing about life in this country. Unlike many Europeans, they had not lived in an East Coast city first. So, when Asians entered California, they found unfamiliar people and cultures.

■ *What is one reason immigrants saw California as a land of wealth?*

▼ *In the eastern United States, the living conditions for many European immigrants were very unpleasant.*

■ *What hardships did many European immigrants find when they first settled in the cities of the eastern United States?*

A Mix of Cultures

Chinese Shopkeeper

11:32 A.M., August 14, 1872
A dock in San Francisco

Hat

This is the only Western-style clothing that he wears. The shopkeeper has tucked his long braid, or queue, underneath his hat.

Silk Jacket

A ship from China docked in the fog. The shopkeeper has studied each face appearing at the ship's rail to spot his wife. In honor of her arrival, the man has worn his best silk jacket.

Pocket Watch

After leaving his first job on the railroad, the shopkeeper bought this gold watch. He checks it nervously as he waits for his wife, whom he has not seen in seven years.

Fresh Fruit

The shopkeeper has brought some juicy peaches from his fruit market as a welcoming gift. He knows that his wife will have eaten little or no fresh food since she left China two months ago.

A Letter from Home

He received this letter from his wife after he sent the money for her voyage to California. The letter tells him when she will arrive in San Francisco.

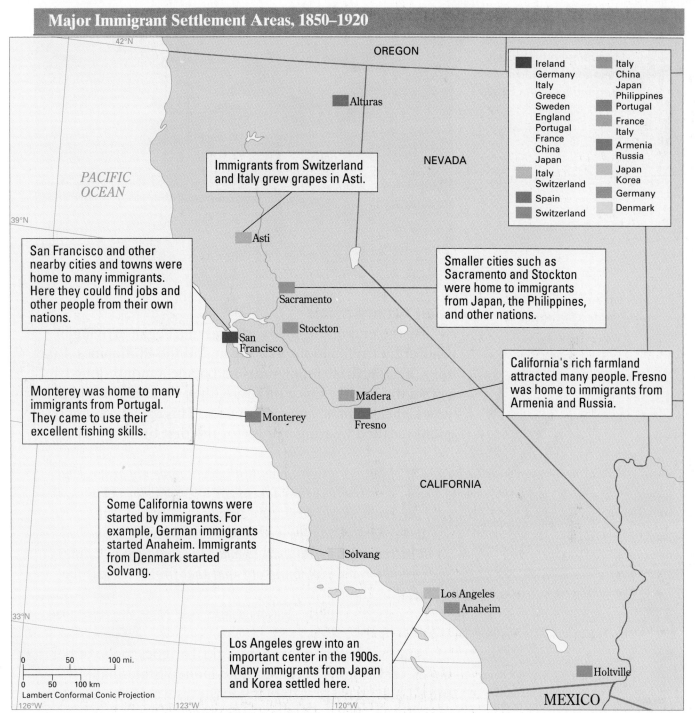

Major Immigrant Settlement Areas, 1850–1920

OREGON

Alturas

PACIFIC
OCEAN

NEVADA

Immigrants from Switzerland and Italy grew grapes in Asti.

Asti

San Francisco and other nearby cities and towns were home to many immigrants. Here they could find jobs and other people from their own nations.

Sacramento

Stockton

San Francisco

Smaller cities such as Sacramento and Stockton were home to immigrants from Japan, the Philippines, and other nations.

Monterey was home to many immigrants from Portugal. They came to use their excellent fishing skills.

Monterey

Madera

Fresno

California's rich farmland attracted many people. Fresno was home to immigrants from Armenia and Russia.

CALIFORNIA

Some California towns were started by immigrants. For example, German immigrants started Anaheim. Immigrants from Denmark started Solvang.

Solvang

Los Angeles
Anaheim

Los Angeles grew into an important center in the 1900s. Many immigrants from Japan and Korea settled here.

Holtville

MEXICO

Ireland	Italy
Germany	China
Italy	Japan
Greece	Philippines
Sweden	Portugal
England	France
Portugal	Italy
France	Armenia
China	Russia
Japan	Japan
Italy	Korea
Switzerland	Germany
Spain	Denmark
Switzerland	

0   50   100 mi.
0   50   100 km
Lambert Conformal Conic Projection

Early Asian Arrivals

The first Asian immigrants were from China. Many of them were drawn to California by stories of the gold rush. In fact, the Chinese called California *Gam Saan*, or Gold Mountain. The brave workers who helped to build the transcontinental railroad were another important group of Chinese immigrants. Like many other immigrant groups, the Chinese did not plan to stay in California forever. Most wanted only to save some money and then return home. To learn more about the lives of the Chinese immigrants, see A Moment in Time, page 206.

Immigrants often settled in communities with other immigrants from their nation. This map shows a few of the areas where they settled in California.

207

A Mix of Cultures

➤ *Asian immigrants quickly made new homes for themselves and their families in the United States.*

▼ *Japanese immigrant laborers wore sandals like these.*

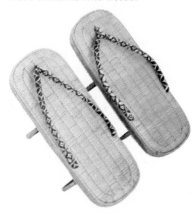

■ *What was one difference between the immigrants from Europe and those from Asia?*

Later Asian Arrivals

By the end of the 1800s, immigrants began arriving in California from nations like Japan and the Philippines. Like the Chinese, these immigrants had made a month-long trip across the Pacific. Once on shore, they entered a world of new sights, sounds, and experiences. This Japanese immigrant recalled wearing a dress for the first time:

> I t felt very tight. I couldn't even move my arms. That was the first time I had ever worn Western clothes, so I thought they were supposed to be like that. . . . Later, Mrs. S. taught me to sew my own clothes. She had a pattern that we all used to make the same dress in different materials. So I found out that that first dress was too small.
>
> Evelyn Nakano Glenn, *Issei, Nisei, War Bride,* 1986

Another Japanese woman, Yuki Torigoe, spoke of her hopes very simply: "I came to the United States happily since I had heard that the United States was a good country." But for many immigrants, life in California was not exactly what they expected it to be. ■

R E V I E W

1. **FOCUS** Who are immigrants, and why did they come to California?

2. **CONNECT** From earlier chapters find some examples of other immigrants who had come to California.

3. **GEOGRAPHY** Why might European immigrants have settled in East Coast cities when they first came to the United States?

4. **CRITICAL THINKING** What do you think immigrants from China expected to find in California? Explain your answer.

5. **ACTIVITY** Using the map on page 320, compare the distances between California and Europe and between California and Asia.

LESSON 2

Conflicts Between Cultures

T he Chinese man held his breath, bracing himself for the insult. In China, a man's queue (*kyoo*), the long braid that hung from the back of his head, was an important tradition. The Chinese were taught that pulling a man's queue was a sign of great disrespect. But to cut it off, as these people were about to do—just the thought of it made his face burn with shame.

Scenes like this actually took place in San Francisco in the 1870s. The people who were about to cut off the Chinese man's queue were following a law called the "pigtail ordinance." This law said that if a Chinese man was found guilty of a crime, his queue could be cut off.

To the Chinese, the law seemed unfair. Why, they wondered, should we have our hair cut off when others do not? Do we not deserve the same treatment as other people?

THINKING FOCUS

How have immigrants been treated in California, and how have they responded?

Key Terms

- discrimination
- reservation

◄ *Chinese men were proud of their long queues.*

Unfair Treatment

The Chinese were treated unfairly partly because people did not understand their ways. The Chinese did not dress, talk, or wear their hair as other Californians did.

209

Because the Chinese seemed different, other people singled them out for cruel treatment. Mistreating a group of people just because of their appearance is a kind of **discrimination**. Sadly, California's past includes many examples of this and other kinds of discrimination.

When settlers from the United States began arriving in California, over 100,000 Indians lived in the area. The settlers did not respect the Indian way of life. They took Indian lands, chased the Indians away, and even killed them. The United States government did set aside small areas of land called **reservations** for Indians to live on. But Indians often could not find enough food on their reservations. By the early 1900s, hunger, disease, and violence had wiped out most of California's Indians.

One who did survive was Ishi, a member of the Yahi tribe. During the gold rush, many Yahi were killed by miners. Each year, more Yahi died. By 1911, when a hungry and frightened Ishi wandered into the town of Oroville, he was the last Yahi in the world.

The people who found Ishi took good care of him. In return, Ishi helped researchers learn about his people. But Ishi never gave away his real name. This he would share only with other Yahi. So the researchers named him Ishi, the Yahi word for "man." ■

During the gold rush, Ishi's people had been chased into the mountains. By 1911, only Ishi survived.

■ *Explain why the number of Indians in California started to fall in the mid-1800s.*

➤ *The laws passed by the United States government caused the Chinese population in California to drop. Compare this graph with the population graph in the Minipedia, page 311.*

More Discrimination

The Indians suffered terribly from discrimination. Asians faced strong discrimination too. Like the Indians, Asians were often the victims of violent attacks. The

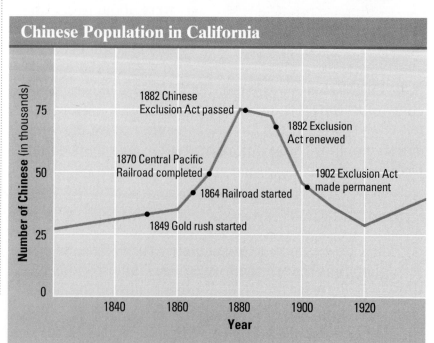

Chinese Population in California

1882 Chinese Exclusion Act passed

1892 Exclusion Act renewed

1870 Central Pacific Railroad completed

1902 Exclusion Act made permanent

1864 Railroad started

1849 Gold rush started

Number of Chinese (in thousands)

75

50

25

0

1840   1860   1880   1900   1920

Year

United States government even passed laws against Asian immigrants. As the graph on page 210 shows, these laws helped keep many Asians out of the country completely.

Starting in 1910, Asians who wanted to enter California had to stop at Angel Island in San Francisco Bay. Here, government officials quizzed immigrants about their reasons for coming to California. Questioning went on for days, weeks, sometimes even a year or more. During this time, immigrants were kept like prisoners in crowded buildings. Many Asian immigrants were never allowed into California.

Many Chinese passed the time on Angel Island by carving poems into the walls of the bare wooden buildings. One such poem appears on the following page.

◄ *As fewer Chinese moved to California, the Chinese population grew older. The few Chinese children in California were treasured.*

UNDERSTANDING DISCRIMINATION

Immigrants have often been mistreated in California. They have been mistreated not because they did something wrong, but just because they spoke a certain language or came from a certain country.

Discrimination is cruel and mean. But it is more than that. Two people who have had a car accident may say mean things to each other. But this is not discrimination. The people are angry only at each other, and only because of the accident. If they had not had an accident, they would not have argued.

With discrimination, all people in a certain group are treated unfairly, no matter what they do or say. For example, in some towns all girls are kept from playing certain sports. They are kept off the teams simply because they are girls.

For California's immigrants, discrimination has been a real threat to survival. Immigrant groups have struggled hard to win the fair treatment all people deserve. For many groups, the struggle continues today.

211

A Mix of Cultures

I nstead of remaining a citizen of China,
　　I willingly became an ox.
I intended to come to America
　　to earn a living.
The Western-styled buildings are lofty;
　　but I have not the luck to live in them.
How was anyone to know that my
　　dwelling place would be a prison?

Translated by Him Mark Lai and Genny Lim in *Island* by Him
Mark Lai, Genny Lim, and Judy Yung, 1986

■ *What were two ways that Asians in California suffered from discrimination?*

➤ *Chinese girls attended school in their own neighborhood in San Francisco.*

▼ *Italians in California used a type of boat they knew from Italy. The felucca (fuh LOO kuh) helped the Italians build successful fishing businesses in their new land.*

Angel Island's walls bear many poems like this. These poems tell of the hope and anger of the thousands of immigrants who stayed at Angel Island. ■

Trying to Survive

In spite of hardships, immigrants held on to the dreams that had drawn them to California. They looked for ways to survive until they could make their dreams real.

Often, immigrants settled together so they could help each other feel more at home. In his 1975 novel *Dragonwings*, Laurence Yep tells of a Chinese boy named Moon Shadow and his arrival in San Francisco's Chinese neighborhood: "Suddenly I felt as if I had come home," Moon Shadow says. "The houses and the stores had all the right colors and shapes, for they had been built . . . by the Tang [Chinese] people. It looked much like the streets in Canton, the city in the Middle Kingdom [China] from which I had sailed. The roofs of the buildings here were tiled and arched, and the walls, windows, and doorways were in gold or red or green."

Europeans who had lived in East Coast cities already knew a little about life in this country when they arrived in California. Some had learned English. They seemed to blend in more than the Asians did. So they did not suffer as much discrimination as the Asians. Still, finding their way in California was a struggle for the Europeans too. Some of them succeeded by using knowledge from their old countries. For example, Italians used feluccas to help them become leaders in the fishing industry. Immigrants from Portugal formed groups to help each other get settled. Also, Irish immigrants joined together to improve their working conditions.

For Japanese immigrants, starting families was important for survival in California. But in the early 1900s, the United States was allowing few Japanese women into the country unless they had family here. So Japanese men in California set up marriages with women in Japan. They did this by trading pictures with the women. Once the wedding was arranged, the women, called "picture brides," were allowed into California.

Through all their hardships, California's immigrants helped each other and followed their dreams. They made the state a richer place for everyone. ■

▼ *"Picture bride" marriages were not always easy for the women or the men. But they helped the Japanese people put down deep roots in the United States.*

■ *Give one reason why European immigrants faced less discrimination than Asians.*

R E V I E W

1. **FOCUS** How have immigrants been treated in California, and how have they responded?

2. **CONNECT** Find an example of discrimination in Lesson 1 of this chapter.

3. **CIVIC VALUES, RIGHTS, AND RESPONSIBILITIES** In what way was the "pigtail ordinance" a kind of discrimination against the Chinese?

4. **CRITICAL THINKING** Why do you think immigrants continued to come to California in spite of discrimination?

5. **WRITING ACTIVITY** Write a journal entry describing how you would feel if you faced any of the kinds of discrimination described in this chapter.

213

LESSON 3

Contributing to California

How have California's immigrants contributed to the state?

Key Terms

- landmark
- ethnic group

➤ *Ghirardelli's chocolate products brought him great success. They also added to the flavor of California.*

Domingo Ghirardelli (*gihr uhr DEH lee*) came to California from Italy to look for gold. Like many of his fellow forty-niners, he was greatly disappointed. After a month in the gold fields, Ghirardelli still had not found the fortune he was seeking. He could see that his hopes of finding wealth in California might fail unless he came up with a new plan.

Ghirardelli used his head and found the answer to his problem. Seeing that many miners had a taste for fancy foods, he started making fine chocolate and hard candies. He sold his treats throughout California's mining region. By 1851, his business had grown so much that he built a large factory, which still stands today in San Francisco. Ghirardelli's factory gave jobs to many Italian immigrants. It helped Ghirardelli achieve his dream of a better life in the United States. It also added to the richness of the growing state.

Colorful California

Ghirardelli was just one immigrant who helped change California into a state of many nations. You can see reminders of these different nations in many of the state's **landmarks**, or important places. In cities like Los Angeles, San Diego, and Sacramento, the reminders are everywhere.

On the next page, you can take A Closer Look at immigrant contributions to the city of San Francisco.

Not all immigrants' contributions are in the cities, though. Many of California's farms and ranches have been built with the help of immigrants. Most of today's migrant workers are immigrants.

Think of the names of the foods you eat and of the street you live on. Many of these names have come from one of California's ethnic groups. An **ethnic group** is a group of people who come from the same nation or share the same culture. ■

Gifts of Ideas

Most Californians have contributed quietly to their communities. Although they have given much to California, few people remember their names today. Some people, however, have won fame for their achievements.

Maria Amparo Ruiz de Burton

Maria Amparo Ruiz de Burton was not an immigrant, but she did belong to one of California's important ethnic groups, the Californios. In 1885, she wrote a book called *The Squatter and the Don.* In her book, Ruiz de Burton wrote about the loss of the Californios' ranchos: "It makes me heartsick to think how unjustly the native Californians have been treated. I assure you, sir, that not one American in a million knows of this outrage."

Ruiz de Burton became a writer because she wanted people to know what had happened to the Californios. But at the time, it was unusual for a Californio woman to be a writer. Ruiz de Burton wrote her book using a false name.

■ *Must a person be famous to contribute to his or her community? Why or why not?*

Across Time & Space

In recent times, thousands of immigrants have come to California from countries in Southeast Asia, such as Vietnam and Laos. These immigrants left their countries to escape the effects of war there.

◄ *In her book* The Squatter and the Don, *Ruiz de Burton wrote about the end of the Californio way of life. That way of life is captured in this picture of the fandango, a favorite Californio dance.*

215

A Mix of Cultures

Immigrants Bring New Ideas

Newcomers from around the world have made important contributions to San Francisco life. Many of the city's wonderful sights, sounds, smells, and tastes were brought here by immigrants.

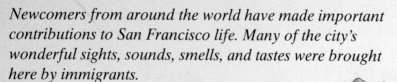

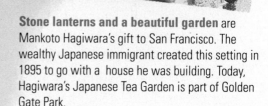

Stone lanterns and a beautiful garden are Mankoto Hagiwara's gift to San Francisco. The wealthy Japanese immigrant created this setting in 1895 to go with a house he was building. Today, Hagiwara's Japanese Tea Garden is part of Golden Gate Park.

A secret ingredient helped Isidore Boudin's business grow in 1849. Each loaf of the French Bakery's famous sourdough bread began with a piece of dough from an earlier loaf.

Failure led to success for Germany's Levi Strauss. His first effort at making tents for forty-niners failed. Strauss decided to dye his leftover cloth blue and make pants. But the pockets tore when miners stuffed them with gold or tools. So Strauss strengthened the seams with copper pins, or rivets.

The hilly streets of San Francisco helped Andrew Hallidie dream up his invention. When he arrived from England in 1894, he felt sorry for the city's horses, who often slipped on the steep streets. Hallidie developed a system of cars powered by underground cables that pulled them up the hills. The cable car system he invented still carries passengers today.

She used the name C. Royal. This was the only way to get her book printed. Because of Ruiz de Burton's efforts, people today remember her words and her real name.

Ng Poon Chew believed that newspapers, like his Chung Sai Yat Po, *were "the people's tongue." Ng used his paper to help Chinese people share their ideas and concerns.*

Ng Poon Chew

Ng Poon Chew (*nn poon CHEE oo*) was another person who wanted to share his ideas. After coming to California from China at the age of 15, Ng worked as a housekeeper and learned English. In 1884, he went to San Francisco to study. There Ng met other Chinese and had many discussions about the problems of Chinese immigrants.

Ng wanted to help other Chinese people share their thoughts. He believed that newspapers provided a valuable way for people to spread their ideas. In 1889, he started a newspaper for Chinese readers. He called it the *Chung Sai Yat Po*, or *Chinese American Daily Paper*.

Ng used the paper to fight for the rights of the Chinese. Because of his efforts, he was often invited to other cities in the United States to give talks about discrimination against the Chinese. Ng crossed the country 86 times spreading his ideas. Ng spoke not only for himself and California's Chinese immigrants. He spoke for thousands of people who shared the dream of a better life in a new land. ■

■ *What ideas did Maria Amparo Ruiz de Burton and Ng Poon Chew contribute to California?*

R E V I E W

1. **FOCUS** How have California's immigrants contributed to the state?
2. **CONNECT** What contributions have immigrants made outside of California's cities?
3. **CULTURE** What did Maria Amparo Ruiz de Burton hope to achieve by writing her book?
4. **CRITICAL THINKING** In what ways can people contribute to the culture of their community?
5. **ACTIVITY** Draw a map of your community. Then mark places on the map where you can find reminders of different ethnic groups.

A Mix of Cultures

Using the Card Catalog

Here's Why

Suppose you want to find out more about one of the immigrant groups you read about in this chapter. You go to the library to get some books. Which of the thousands of books in your library can help you? To find books with information about your topic, you can go to the library card catalog. Knowing how to use the card catalog will help you to find the books you need.

Here's How

The card catalog in the library is a cabinet that has many small drawers. The drawers are filled with cards. On the front of each drawer you will see one or more letters. These letters tell which cards are in the drawer. The cards are arranged in the drawer in alphabetical order beginning with the letters shown on the front.

Each book in the library has at least three cards. It has a title card, an author card, and one or more subject cards.

The title card has the title of the book at the top. Title cards are filed alphabetically by the first letter of the first word in the title. (If the title begins with *A, An,* or *The,* look under the first letter of the second word.) Suppose you want to find a book called *The Japanese Americans*, by Harry L. Kitano. Look in the drawer labeled *J*, for *Japanese*. The card will look like the front card below.

If you want a book that you know was written by Harry L. Kitano, but you don't know the title of the book, look for the author card. An author card looks like the back card below. What information does this card have at the top? Author cards are arranged alphabetically in the drawers of the card catalog. They are filed by the first letter of the author's last name. In which catalog drawer would you look for books written by Harry Kitano?

973.'
04956   Kitano, Harry L.
          The Japanese Americans

          "The Peoples of North America" series
          Chelsea House Publishers, NY 1988
          92 pp. Revised Edition

The Japanese Americans

973.'
04956   Kitano, Harry L.
          The Japanese Americans

          "The Peoples of North America" series
          Chelsea House Publishers, NY 1988
          92 pp. Revised Edition

If you want to find books on a certain subject, look at subject cards. Subject cards in the catalog are filed alphabetically by the first letter of the name of the subject. Suppose you are interested in the subject *immigrants*. This word begins with the letter *I*. Look at the subject card below. Notice that the subject is printed at the top of the card in capital letters. The author's name is below that. On the next line is the title.

IMMIGRANTS

973.'
04956

Kitano, Harry L.
The Japanese Americans

"The Peoples of North America" series
Chelsea House Publishers, NY 1988
92 pp. Revised Edition

Suppose you look in the card catalog and find a card for a book you want. You know that the book is in the library. How do you find it on the shelves? Letters or call numbers appear on the left side of most cards. They tell the section of the library and the shelf where you can find the book. The call number matches a number on the spine of the book.

Try It

Try your skill at using the card catalog by answering these questions.

1. Which kind of catalog cards would help you to find books about Angel Island? In which drawer will you find these cards?
2. Which kind of card would help you to find a book by Jenny Ling? In which drawer will you find this card?
3. Which kind of card would help you to find the book *The Squatter and the Don*? What letter or letters would be on the front of the drawer in which you would look for this card?
4. How do you use the numbers on the left of most cards?

Apply It

Many immigrants came to California from Chile. Suppose you want to learn more about this country. Find three books about Chile in the card catalog. Copy the title, author, and call number for each book. Then find the books on the shelves.

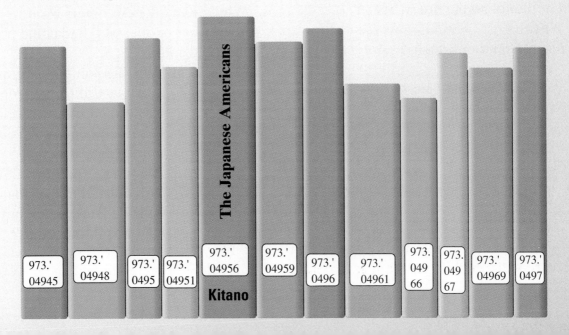

973.'
04945

973.'
04948

973.'
0495

973.'
04951

973.'
04956

The Japanese Americans

Kitano

973.'
04959

973.'
0496

973.'
04961

973.
049
66

973.
049
67

973.'
04969

973.'
0497

Chapter Review

Reviewing Key Terms

discrimination (p.210)   landmark (p.214)
ethnic group (p.215)   reservation (p.210)
immigrant (p.204)

A. Write a sentence for each pair of words below, using both words in the pair. Then write sentences telling how the words in each pair are related.

1. discrimination, unfair
2. immigrant, change
3. landmark, state
4. ethnic group, culture
5. reservation, land

B. Choose the key terms that best complete the sentences with blanks in the following paragraph.

Many _____ from Europe and Asia traveled to California in search of better lives. Thousands of immigrants came from many countries. They brought with them the languages and cultures of their old countries. Because they seemed different from other people, the newcomers suffered from _____. The Indians in California also suffered from discrimination. Their land was taken over by new settlers, so the Indians were sent to live on _____s. In spite of many hardships and challenges, people from each different _____ have contributed to California. You can see reminders of these contributions in many important _____s in the state.

Exploring Concepts

A. Complete this chart on a separate paper with information from the chapter.

B. Write one or two sentences to answer each of the following questions.

1. Why did many immigrants see California as a land of dreams?

Immigrant Group	Where did they come from?	Why did they come?	How were they treated?	What did they contribute?
Asian immigrants				
European immigrants				

2. What countries did some of California's Asian immigrants come from?
3. In what ways were the Asian and European immigrants alike?
4. Why did many newcomers want to live near other people who had come from their old country?
5. Why did some immigrants move to California from Eastern cities?
6. What happened to Asian immigrants at Angel Island in San Francisco?
7. What did Maria Amparo Ruiz de Burton do, and why was it important?

Reviewing Skills

1. Look at the library catalog card at the right. What type of card is it? In which drawer would you find this card?
2. Suppose you need information about the Chinese community in a California city. Which type of card will help you find a book with this information? What do you think the word at the top of the card would be? What drawer would you look in for this card?
3. Look at the time zone map on page 331 of the Atlas. Suppose that it is 12 noon in the Central Time Zone. What time is it in each of the other three time zones on the mainland of the United States?

> **IMMIGRANTS**
>
> 973.' di Franco, Phillip
> 0451   The Italian Americans
>
> "The Peoples of North America" series
> Chelsea House Publishers, NY 1988
> 93 pp.

4. If you were interested in learning more about Ghirardelli's chocolate factory, where could you go for information? What kind of books would you look in? To whom could you write a letter?

Using Critical Thinking

1. Discrimination hurts everyone involved in it. How does it hurt not only the people being treated unfairly, but also the people who are treating them that way?
2. The United States has been called a "melting pot" of different people. Explain what you think "melting pot" means. How might immigrants in California have been part of the United States melting pot?
3. Your culture is as much a part of you as the culture of each immigrant was a part of him or her. How can people of different cultures learn to live together more peacefully?

Preparing for Citizenship

COLLABORATIVE LEARNING Ng Poon Chew, a Chinese immigrant, believed that newspapers give people a way to share their ideas. As a class project, start a monthly newspaper for the students in your grade. Everyone in the class should contribute to the project. Form separate groups to perform each of these tasks: (1) thinking of story ideas, (2) writing articles, (3) drawing illustrations, (4) printing the paper, (5) putting the pages of the paper together, and (6) handing out the paper to students in your grade.

The newspaper should contain articles about students and events in your school and in the community. Each issue should feature at least one article about a person who has been a good citizen. You may also want to include articles about people whose families are recent immigrants to California.

Begin by choosing one person from each group to make up the staff in charge of the newspaper. Ask your teacher to provide any advice you might need.

221

Unit 5

Modern California

At the end of the 1800s, there were no freeways. Californians still traveled by horse and carriage. Telephones, electric lights, and movies were a mystery to most people. But in the early 1900s, Californians leaped into modern times. New inventions, new industries, and most of all, new people, made the modern California that you know today.

1890

Junction of Interstate 980, Interstate 880, and Highway 24, Oakland. Copyright Steve Proehl.

2050

Chapter 10

Building a Better California

"We can do anything." Californians seemed to live these words in 1900. It appeared that they could do anything, be anything, and build anything. Californians faced problems with a sense of adventure and courage. Progress, they thought, had no limits. For a long time, they were right.

This car, called the Pioneer, is thought to be the first "horseless carriage" made in California.

1890	1900	1910

1911 Women get the right to vote in California.

1895

1929 Pilot Louise Thaden won the National Women's Air Derby. It was the first cross-country air race for women.

San Pedro Harbor is built, allowing ships to come to Los Angeles. This increases trade and helps industries to grow.

1920

1930

1940

1927 The first movie with sound, called a "talkie," is made in Hollywood.

1940

LESSON 1

Growth of Industry

THINKING
FOCUS

How did four big events help California's southern coast grow in the early 1900s?

Key Terms

- aqueduct
- canal

➤ *Charlie Woods's gusher, one of the world's largest, sprayed oil for miles. The well pumped more than 9 million barrels of oil over 18 months.*

Poor Charlie Woods. Here he was on another lonely evening, drilling for oil at another spot in the middle of nowhere. Somebody had named this place "Lake View." But the only view was of a dirt road stretching across the flat land of the San Joaquin Valley. The Union Oil Company had lost interest in this site, and the workers had too. Charlie and his crew would drill a little deeper tonight, down to about 2,200 feet. But for what? As a foreman for Union Oil, Woods had watched over the drilling of well after well. But the earth just seemed to laugh at him. It coughed up only rock and dust. His crew called him "Dry Hole Charlie." But as dawn came the next morning, March 15, 1910, Charlie got a new nickname.

First there was a rumble, then a tremble. The drilling platform began to sway, and the workers ran for their lives. Then they stood back and watched in wonder as a huge hole opened in the ground. From deep within the earth, a gusher of oil as wide as a house shot into the air.

Woods danced with joy in the thick, black rainfall of oil. From then on, they'd call him "Gusher Charlie."

Oil Booms in California

By the time Charlie hit his gusher, drillers had been discovering oil up and down the California coast since the late 1800s. The biggest oil strikes were in the Los Angeles area, Santa Barbara County, and the San Joaquin Valley along the Kern River.

The Californians of the early 1900s were not the first to use oil. Long ago, the Chumash Indians had used it for sealing their canoes. Californios had used oil to make the roofs of their adobe houses. But with the new machines and industries of the early 1900s came a far greater need for oil. Oil was so valuable that people called it "black gold."

New Uses of "Black Gold"

The raw oil that comes from the ground makes many types of fuel. One type is diesel fuel. Before oil was used, trains ran on burning coal. This left a trail of dirty black smoke behind them. Diesel fuel was much cleaner and easier for trains to use. Many new machines, like tractors, also ran on diesel fuel. As oil became more plentiful, tractors began to replace the horses and plows that farmers had used for so long. But the biggest user of oil was the automobile. The new horseless carriage, as it was called, ran on gasoline, another type of fuel.

The oil boom was one of the biggest changes to come to California since the Spanish explorer Juan Rodriguez Cabrillo landed on the southern coast. With the boom came new growth, money, industries, and people. ■

▲ *In 1909 Earl Gilmore loaded a big barrel of gasoline onto a horse-drawn cart and began selling fuel for 10 cents a gallon. The world's first gas station was open for business.*

■ *Why did oil become so valuable in California?*

Growth Brings Water Problems

If you wanted adventure in the early 1900s, you headed for California's southern coast. The region had been bursting with activity ever since the land boom of the 1800s. Agriculture was growing, and so were industries such as fruit packing, canning, and shipping. New railroad lines connected the many towns of the long southern coast, and newcomers came on each train. Many of them were coming to join the excitement of the oil boom. The center of all this activity was Los Angeles.

Thirsty Los Angeles

By 1905, Los Angeles was a city of 200,000 people, with fancy homes, hotels, and beaches. But this growing city had a growing problem. It was running out of water. Los Angeles was built on the desert. The nearby Los Angeles River did not have enough water for all the people. So city officials came up with a surprising idea. They would bring another river to the city.

The river that Los Angeles wanted was in the Owens Valley. This was nearly 250 miles away, across empty desert and tall mountains. Could the water be brought from so far away? Yes, said William Mulholland. Mulholland was head of the city's water department. He took on the job of building a giant water pipe, called an **aqueduct** *(AK wih duhct),* to bring the water of the Owens River to Los Angeles. This project is explained in A Closer Look at the Los Angeles Aqueduct on the next page. It was one of the biggest engineering projects in the country's history. Many people thought the aqueduct could not be built. But under Mulholland's leadership it was finished in 1913. Now that it had enough water, Los Angeles was ready to grow. ■

■ *What problems did Los Angeles face in meeting its water needs?*

➤ *Spring Street, Los Angeles, was lined with trolleys, shops, hotels, and automobiles in 1900.*

The L.A. Aqueduct

Los Angeles needed water. And city officials weren't going to let anything or anyone get in their way. They came up with a secret plan to take the water from the Owens River, 250 miles away.

In the early 1900s, Los Angeles began quietly buying up land around the Owens River, so the city could control the flow of water. When the farmers in the Owens Valley found out they were going to lose their water, they fought to stop the plan, but they lost.

William Mulholland led a team of 100,000 workers, using modern tractors and 20-mule teams to build the giant pipe. They tunneled through the Sierra Nevada and worked in desert temperatures of over 100 degrees.

Water gushed into the aqueduct on November 5, 1913. But the troubles had just begun. Twice, angry farmers dynamited holes in the aqueduct. They took control of a pumping station to try to force Los Angeles to share the water.

SIERRA NEVADA

SAN JOAQUIN VALLEY

San Francisco

Owens River

Los Angeles Aqueduct

MOJAVE DESERT

SAN FERNANDO VALLEY

PACIFIC OCEAN

The farmers' efforts failed. The aqueduct survived. The water allowed Los Angeles to grow. The San Fernando Valley, outside Los Angeles, became a major farming region.

New Projects Boost Trade

While Mulholland was building the aqueduct, two other engineering projects were going on that would change the future of Los Angeles. One was the building of San Pedro Harbor. A harbor is a protected body of water that is deep enough for ships to dock in. As you can see from the map, San Francisco has a curved coastline. This gives it a perfect natural harbor. But the Los Angeles coast was nearly straight. Its waters were not deep enough for a harbor. So Los Angeles had to dig a harbor. The work on the project began in 1899 and was finished in 1914. San Pedro Harbor made Los Angeles a major port.

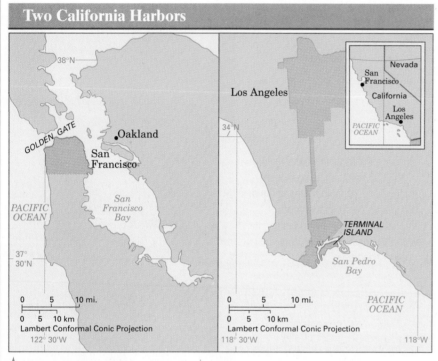

Two California Harbors

▲ *In what ways do you think the geography of San Francisco made it grow more quickly than Los Angeles?*

■ *How did the construction of San Pedro Harbor and the Panama Canal help Los Angeles?*

A New Route to the East

At the same time, a new transportation link for Los Angeles was opening up in the Isthmus of Panama. There the United States had just finished building a 51-mile-long **canal**. This is a manmade waterway for ships. The Panama Canal was cut right through the isthmus to connect the Pacific and Atlantic Oceans. To learn more about the Panama Canal turn to the Minipedia, page 314.

When the canal opened in 1914, Los Angeles and other California cities cheered. Now, ships loaded with California goods could reach the East Coast in just one month. ■

R E V I E W

1. **FOCUS** How did four big events help California's southern coast grow in the early 1900s?

2. **CONNECT** What changes helped the southern coast grow in the late 1800s?

3. **HISTORY** What were the good and bad effects of the aqueduct?

4. **CRITICAL THINKING** How might the new Panama Canal have changed the railroad companies' business?

5. **ACTIVITY** Make an advertisement for Los Angeles in 1915. Draw pictures to show some reasons why people should come to the city.

Making a Bar Graph

Here's Why

Water is even more valuable in California today than it was when William Mulholland built the Los Angeles Aqueduct. Every day, each Californian uses about 70 gallons of water for drinking, cooking, bathing, and cleaning. All together the people of Los Angeles use over one billion gallons of water daily—60 times as many gallons as the people of Sacramento.

Bar graphs are a good way to present facts like these. Bar graphs make information easy to read. They can also help you compare facts about different items.

Here's How

Look at the bar graph below. At the bottom of the graph are names of cities. The numbers on the left stand for millions of gallons of water. As you move up the left side of the graph, each line you cross means ten million more gallons.

The bars show how many gallons of water each city uses in a day. Find the top of the bar for Fresno. Now look across to the left. The top of the bar reaches almost all the way to 60 million gallons. Fresno uses about 59 million gallons of water a day.

Suppose you want to add the daily water use for Sacramento to the bar graph. At the bottom of the graph next to Fresno, you would write Sacramento. From the chart below, you know that Sacramento uses 23 million gallons of water daily. You would draw the bar for Sacramento so that the top of the bar reached just above the line for 20 million.

Daily Household Water Use

City	Gallons of Water
Anaheim	13 million
Fresno	59 million
Sacramento	23 million
Ventura	4 million

Try It

Now make your own bar graph of water use in California. Start by copying the bar graph on this page. Then add the information for Sacramento and Ventura listed in the chart. Use your bar graph to answer these questions: Which city uses the least amount of water? Which city uses more water, Anaheim or Ventura?

Apply It

Make a bar graph that shows how many students in your class have blue eyes, how many have brown eyes, and how many have green eyes.

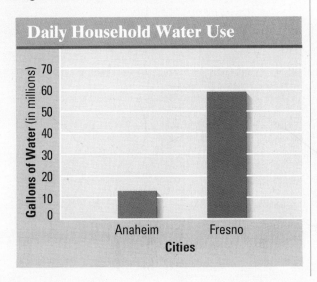

Daily Household Water Use

L E S S O N   2

Progress for People

THINKING
F O C U S

What problems did Californians try to solve in the early 1900s?

Key Terms

- bribe
- Progressives

➤ *The earthquake of 1906 was not nearly as destructive as the fire that followed it. One family had set a fancy table with the silver spoon and the china plates and teacup shown here. But the fire's heat turned them into melted ruins.*

ost people were still asleep. After all, it was only about five o'clock in the morning. But something was waking the animals. All over the city, dogs began to whine and bark. Horses stamped and snorted. The animals sensed something the sleeping citizens of San Francisco did not.

Walking his beat in the grey light, police officer Jesse Cook saw it coming. First, a sound like thunder swelled around him. Then the street began to move up and down. "It was as if the waves of the ocean were coming towards me, billowing as they came," Cook recalled. The city of San Francisco was riding a wave of earth and rock. Earthquake!

Across the city, roofs caved in, chimneys fell, and stoves overturned. Church bells rang and rang as the city rocked. Fires broke out everywhere. But the earthquake had snapped the city's water pipes. Since they were without water, firefighters could only watch sadly as San Francisco burned. The earthquake of April 18, 1906, lasted less than a minute. But the fires burned for three days. In the end, about 3,000 people were killed and 28,000 buildings were destroyed—including City Hall.

◄ *The people of San Francisco amazed the rest of the country by quickly rebuilding their city.*

San Francisco Cleans Up

People said the city would never be rebuilt. They were wrong. Even before the smoke cleared, the people of San Francisco began to put their city back together. Money, food, and workers poured in from all over the country. William Randolph Hearst asked the readers of his newspaper, the *San Francisco Examiner*, to give every nickel they could. President Theodore Roosevelt sent army troops and government money. The city's mayor, Eugene Schmitz, moved quickly to set up the rebuilding.

Rebuilding the Government

These were Schmitz's finest days as mayor. But they didn't last for long. For years, Schmitz's city government had been controlled by a few powerful business leaders. These men ran the big gas, telephone, and railroad companies. They gave bribes to the mayor and other city officials. A **bribe** is money given to someone to persuade him or her to act dishonestly. City officials took thousands of dollars in bribes. In return, they let companies like the Southern Pacific Railroad charge high prices. This hurt many California businesses that couldn't pay such costs.

So as the citizens of San Francisco rebuilt their City Hall, they decided to rebuild their city government too. A group of citizens worked to stop companies from giving bribes. Many business people and city officials were brought to trial. Mayor Schmitz was kicked out of office. ■

Across Time & Space

On October 17, 1989, the San Francisco area received another powerful jolt. California's second largest earthquake of the 1900s struck at 5:04 p.m., killing more than 60 people. As in the 1906 quake, San Franciscans moved quickly to repair billions of dollars' worth of damage. To learn more about earthquakes and how they work, turn to the Minipedia, page 312.

■ *Why was the city government of San Francisco in need of rebuilding?*

California Builds a Better Government

The big industries that grew up in the early 1900s brought great progress to California. But in San Francisco and throughout the state, some businesses had grown much too powerful. The Southern Pacific became the most hated company of all. It held power over newspapers, transportation, other businesses, and the state government. Finally, one man rose to fight the railroad. His name was Hiram Johnson. He was a lawyer who had helped get Mayor Schmitz out of office.

Johnson was a member of the Progressives. The **Progressives** were a group of people across the United States who wanted to make the government and society better. Progressives worked to pass laws that would stop businesses from controlling the government. In 1910, Johnson ran for governor. He promised to "kick the Southern Pacific Railroad out of politics."

Johnson's promise made him very popular, and he won the election. As the new governor, he kept his word. He set up new rules that kept railroad prices low and stopped the bribing. The great giant, Southern Pacific, had been beaten. ■

➤ Hiram Johnson traveled 20,000 miles by car over bad roads during his successful run for governor. At the time trains were the easiest form of transportation. But Johnson was an enemy of the Southern Pacific and refused to ride the railroads.

■ What kind of progress did the Progressives try to bring about?

Women Bring Change

Cleaning up government was mostly the work of men. Women were kept out of government. They did not even have the right to vote. Still, women became a strong force for progress in California.

All around them, women saw families suffering. Men, women, and even children worked long hours in places like the canneries of southern California and the laundries of San Francisco. The pay was so low that families went hungry. Housing was crowded and rundown. Often food was not safe to eat.

Because women had no power in government, they could not change these conditions. But they had another weapon. They could write. In magazines, newspapers, and books, women called for better treatment of workers and families. Charlotte Perkins Gilman was one woman who spoke out strongly for change. She loved children and worked hard to make their lives better. In a 1908 poem, she wrote about the child's cry for help:

> Give me the good ye know,
>   That I, the Child, may grow!
>   Light, for the whole day long,
> Food that is pure and strong,
> Housing and clothing fair,
> Clear water and clean air,
> Teaching from day to day,
> And room—for a child to play!

The writings of Gilman and other women urged the government to make laws that would protect workers and families. Women helped bring about new schools and housing, safer food, and higher pay for laborers. One of the biggest victories was in 1911, when the Progressives passed a law that gave California women the right to vote. ■

Across Time & Space

In the early 1900s, working conditions were bad not only in California, but throughout the United States. Young girls and boys worked in clothing factories, coal mines, and farms. All over the country, Progressives fought to get children out of these jobs and into school.

■ *How did women bring change to California when they had no say in government?*

◄ *In the early 1900s young children worked long hours at hard labor in canneries like the one pictured here.*

REVIEW

1. **FOCUS** What problems did Californians try to solve in the early 1900s?
2. **CONNECT** What good and what problems were created by growing industries?
3. **CULTURE** What problems did Charlotte Perkins Gilman attack in her poem?
4. **CRITICAL THINKING** Why do you think it is wrong for a person to bribe someone?
5. **WRITING ACTIVITY** Pretend you're a reporter in San Francisco in 1906. Write an article describing the earthquake and the fire that spread through the city afterward.

The Great Earthquake

Eleanor Deering Mathews

In Lesson 2, you learned about the Great Earthquake of 1906. Here is what happened to one family.

Inside an old trunk in his attic, Edgar Mathews Sliney found a diary that his mother had kept when she was nine years old. In this diary she described events of the 1906 earthquake. Read this account to find out how peoples' lives were changed as a result of this disaster.

*I*n the year of 1906, on Wednesday, April 18, at 17 minutes past 5 in the morning, the great earthquake shock came.

When everybody was asleep they were awakened by a terrible falling of chimneys; the bricks from the chimneys fell and knocked down ours and other people's front steps. It lasted for 47 seconds. Then, as soon as it was over, Papa told us to get up and dress as quick as possible so we could get out and talk with the other people.

While we were dressing, a few shocks came but none like the first one. It was worse in San Francisco than any other place. As soon as we were dressed, we were out in front, and we could hardly get out because our brick steps were just covered with bricks and different parts of the wooden steps that had fallen.

When we got across the street, a lady told us that she got out of the house as soon as she saw the chimney fall and knock our steps down.

There were piles of people out in the street, with their wrappers and bed slippers on looking at the different chimneys that had fallen, and some of us were walking around the block to see the other houses.

On our way around, we passed one house that had the whole front ready to fall off. Some of the houses were not touched on the outside, but many of the ornaments were

wrappers loose robes

ornaments decorations

broken inside. . . .

In a little while Mamma told us to go in and get something to eat. We couldn't cook hardly anything, because the gas went so very slow, and we couldn't cook on the range because the chimney was off, so we didn't have much breakfast.

Of course we didn't want to stay in the house, so we went outside. In a little while we decided to go to the Alta Plaza, a little park about two blocks away. Mamma went in and put up some lunch, so we could eat it at the park. In a little while we started off with the Thompsons and the Mullinses. We had some blankets which we spread out on the lawn, so we wouldn't get wet. We strung daisy chains some of the time, and every few minutes we went to see the fire, which was way over in the Mission district. It looked very near to us and it looked as if the whole city was afire. It started by the people over in the Mission getting up early and starting a fire in the stove, and when the earthquake came it set fire to the house.

Another fire started in Hayes Valley and grew larger and larger until it met with the other fire.

We asked some of the men that were coming from downtown how the fire was. Some said it was going toward the waterfront. The smoke of the fire was gray and red, and every time we looked up, it looked larger.

In a little while we had our lunch, and pretty soon a dog came along and ate our can of sardines.

Late in the afternoon we came back to the house and had some supper, which was only a few crackers and a cup of milk, and a leftover dish of peas.

The Thompsons were going to stay in the park all night, so we wanted to. We started off with two coats apiece, and some steamer blankets and a mattress, and a basket of provisions.

We found that the Thompsons had a very nice place in the bushes to sleep, so we took a place right near to them. The Mullinses and some more of our friends were there too. Some of the people had tents to sleep in.

In the morning about half-past 5, we packed up and started home.

All day Thursday people were going past with piles on their backs. Some were dragging their trunks behind them, others had canary cages and dogs with them, and it all was

canary a green or
yellow songbird

237

a very funny sight.

. . .Papa and I went over to see Mrs. Thompson and asked her if the fire had crossed Van Ness. Somebody said that it had, so Papa came back and told us to get our things ready and start.

I took my bird, Ole, in one hand, and his seed can in the other and started off. Hester had her hands full, and Mamma did too. Papa was behind us with his back loaded with bedding, and the mattress.

. . .We landed a little way from the Presidio, with all our things.

A little while later, Hester and Papa came up with the trunk, which was on a coaster. Pretty soon a soldier told us we had to go in the Presidio. Mamma and I came back to the house to get a few more things. And I tell you, I hated to think that our house might go up in smoke and flames. . . .

When we got back to where we had put our things, we began moving them into the Presidio. The cinders from the fire were falling in every direction, but not so bad, where we were.

. . .Pretty soon we saw Papa and Mr. Kauser coming with some bundles. Mr. Kauser had bought a whole box of fig bars. The man was going to charge him $5, but put it down to two and a half. The man was also going to charge him a dollar for a bottle of milk but put it down to 30¢. Very soon we had our supper and went to sleep.

In the night I was awakened by a horse that was loose. He was coming very near us, so we got up and went outside the stone wall. Hester fell down on a rock, because she was in such a hurry to get out.

Mr. Kauser chased the horse and made her run all the more, so Papa went up and made her more tame. Pretty soon she went away, and there was another horse that was tied near us, but he did not disturb us any. In the morning some men that owned the horse we chased could not find her anywhere, so she must have disappeared during the night.

In a little while, I went up to see where the Thompsons and Mullinses were. I saw their blankets, but no sign of them, but later on some people told us that they had gone to Alameda.

Pretty soon we started home with our things, and found that the fire had only crossed Van Ness on Bush Street and

coaster a small tray on wheels

238

was under control. It was also coming toward the water-front. The water was turned off so that the firemen could use it all for the fire. We had to drink water out of bottles, because there wasn't any water to wash cups in. The hydrants still had water in them, but it had to be boiled before drinking, so afterwards we had enough water to wash and wash the dishes in.

Friday we made a little stove in the street, out of bricks, and some people had their real stoves to cook on.

We didn't use napkins at the table, because they would be so dirty that when they were washed they wouldn't get clean, so we had one napkin we passed around the table. . . .

After a while Papa came home and we went in. We finally got in bed and had our clothes on. In the morning Papa went to the Presidio to hunt for friends. He couldn't find any, but there were some people who were burnt out and hadn't saved a thing, so Papa gave them our rug and mattress and some blankets and my small pillow.

After lunch he found a lady crying, and he asked her what was the matter. She said her husband was in the Presidio and she was waiting for him. She said they were burnt out and didn't save much. Papa said that she and her husband could have a room in our house. So pretty soon the doorbell rang and they gave us a note which Papa had given them saying that they could have Hester's room, if it was not taken.

Mr. and Mrs. Wood (that is their name) went and got their things and pretty soon returned to the house.

The street cooking went on in the same way, but every day the food tasted better. The pots and pans got so dirty that I don't believe anybody could get them clean.

© *San Francisco Chronicle* Reprinted by permission

Further Reading

The Story of the San Francisco Earthquake . R. Conrad Stein.

Recognizing Fact and Opinion

Here's Why

Progressives, like Ellen Gates Starr in the picture below, wrote many articles about the dangers of child labor. The Progressives tried to persuade lawmakers to protect children. Sometimes they reported the facts. At other times they gave their opinions.

When someone is trying to persuade you to do or think something, it is important for you to recognize the difference between fact and opinion.

Here's How

A fact is a statement that is true. It can be checked or tested. An opinion is a statement that one person believes to be true. An opinion cannot be checked.

Read the two sentences below.

1. In 1900, 16-year-old boys worked in the Pennsylvania coal mines.
2. I think that 16-year-old children are too young to work.

The first sentence states a fact. You can check the statement by looking in an almanac. The second sentence states an opinion. It tells what one person believes to be true.

Words like *I think, I believe, agree, disagree, should,* and *most* can be clues to an opinion. In the second sentence above, the words *I think* are a clue. They show that this statement is what one person believes to be true. Other people may disagree.

Try It

Read the sentences below. Decide whether each statement is a fact or an opinion. To help you decide, ask yourself if the statement can be checked, and look for word clues.

1. In one Philadelphia wool mill, a child earned only three dollars a week.
2. Children under 16 should go to school instead of working in the factories.
3. Reporters found six-year-old children working in the canneries.
4. I agree that 15 hours of work a day can ruin a child's health.
5. In the coal mines, the most dangerous job was leaning over the coal chutes to separate the coal from the other rocks.

Apply It

Look in a newspaper. Find two sentences that state facts and two sentences that state opinions. Bring your sentences to class. Have a classmate decide which statements are facts and which statements are opinions.

L E S S O N   3

New Challenges

Do you have a nickel? Then let's go to the movies! It's 1915, and for only five cents you can go to a nickelodeon, one of the world's first movie theaters. People buzz with excitement as they fill the fancy new hall. Children wiggle impatiently in their chairs. Before them is a stage with blue velvet curtains. Off to the side, a piano player is pounding out a bouncy tune. Finally, the curtains part, and the show begins.

What's this? No sound? That's right, these movies are silent. The piano player sets the mood, playing happy music during the happy parts and sad music during the sad parts. But people are here to have fun, so the plot is mostly happy. In fact, it's mostly silly. A policeman falls into a flour barrel. Somebody gets a pie in the face. A lady crashes through a hole in the floor. Somebody else gets a pie in the face. A robber falls into a black, sooty chimney. And another guy gets a pie in the face. Everybody gets pies in their faces! And in the audience, all the people have smiles on their faces.

THINKING FOCUS

What events helped and hurt California from 1917 to 1940?

Key Terms

- tourism
- Dust Bowl
- Great Depression
- New Deal

◄ *In the early 1900s audiences flocked to see the new moving pictures. Nickelodeons like Los Angeles's International Theater, pictured here, sprang up across the country.*

241

Building a Better California

The camera pictured below was used in Hollywood during the 1940s. It was just one of many cameras that has filmed the magic of Hollywood during the movie industry's long history.

Wartime and Peacetime Growth

The audiences of the early 1900s loved these silly stunts. They helped people keep their minds off their troubles. In 1917 the United States entered World War I. The war, which was fought in Europe, brought hard times for many Americans. Families lost fathers, brothers, and sons in battle. But the war also brought growth. California industries produced food for the troops, cotton for uniforms, oil for war machines, and ships for the Navy.

The Movie Boom

World War I even helped the movie business. Many people went to the movies to enjoy themselves and forget about the war. In California, movie-making was becoming a big industry. The warmth and beauty of southern California attracted many young filmmakers. New film studios were built in the growing city of Hollywood. After World War I ended in 1918, Hollywood grew even more. In the late 1920s silent movies were replaced by "talkies," movies with sound. These new films brought more money and jobs to Hollywood. Movie stars grew rich and famous.

The films also drew new visitors to the state. They came to tour the studios and to see the stars. **Tourism**, or travel for pleasure, was becoming a big industry. The tourism and movie industries, along with the oil and agriculture industries, kept California growing in the 1920s. But more hard times were just around the corner. ■

■ *In what ways did California grow during World I and afterward?*

➤ *Early movie sets bustled with activity as people learned the tricks of the new industry. Buster Keaton, seated in the car, was one of the funniest and most popular of the silent film stars.*

Depression and the California Dream

You couldn't get away from the dust. It whipped your skin, stung your eyes, and filled your mouth and lungs. You could see a dust storm coming for miles across the flat plains, looking like the clouds of a thunderstorm.

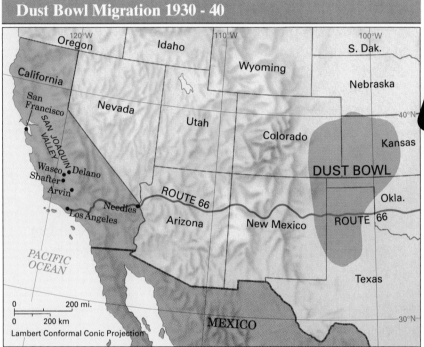

Dust Bowl Migration 1930 - 40

◄ *Families from Dust Bowl states such as Arkansas and Oklahoma followed Route 66 across New Mexico and Arizona and into California.*

Storms like these tore through the region shown on the map above. The area became known as the Dust Bowl. The **Dust Bowl** was a 50-million-acre region in the middle of the United States where dust storms raged during the 1920s and 1930s. A major cause of the Dust Bowl was drought, which is a long period of time without rain. Drought left the soil very dry. Winds blew the dry soil into giant curtains of dust. These dust storms destroyed many farms.

The Great Depression Hurts Workers

The Dust Bowl happened at the same time as another terrible event in history—the Great Depression. The **Great Depression** was a time when many workers all over the country lost their jobs. People were left without money to pay their bills or feed their families. Because of the Great Depression and the Dust Bowl, many people lost their homes, their farms, and their businesses. Some lost so much that they just wanted to get away and start a new life somewhere else. California seemed to be a good place to do that.

In the movies, California looked like a place with rich

243

HISTORY *Dorothea Lange photographed the hardship of the Depression and the heroic struggles of families to survive. Lange's famous pictures of the Dust Bowl farmers have left us an unforgettable record of this heartbreaking period in history.*

and beautiful people who had happy lives. Attracted by this picture of California, families loaded their cars with everything they owned and headed west. Overloaded cars streamed down Route 66, the main highway to California.

The families poured into California farming towns. They had heard there were jobs working on the farms. Men, women, and children went to work in the fields. Most earned as little as 90 cents a day. In her book *Blue Willow*, Doris Gates tells the story of Janey Larkin, the daughter of Dust Bowl farmers who flee to California. Janey's home in the story is like the real-life houses of this time.

*I*t was exactly like the inside of a chicken coop, and not much larger. In one corner was an iron bedstead with more rust than paint on it. The mattress, which spent most of its time traveling on the top of the Larkin car, had been dumped onto it…. Across the room was a small stove as rusty as the bed. Two chairs placed facing each other were doing duty just now as a rest for the washtub. A wobbly table was the only other piece of furniture.

Camps with dozens of homes like Janey's were set up along rivers near the farms. There was little food, and often there were no bathrooms. Families moved from place to place, following the crops. They picked cotton in one season and potatoes or sugar beets in the next. Children got schooling when they could.

Life in California was far from life in the movies. But it was better than starving. The families kept coming. ■

■ *How did the Dust Bowl and the Great Depression affect California?*

➤ *Dorothea Lange took this photograph of a homeless family on the road in 1938. Some families got so hungry that they had to sell their cars to get money for food. Then they were forced to walk from town to town, looking for work.*

Help for the Needy

During the early 1930s, the nation's hope was running low. People were jobless, hungry, and suffering. So when Franklin Delano Roosevelt became President in 1933, he promised "a new deal" for the country. The **New Deal** was the name given to the set of programs Roosevelt created to bring hope to the nation and lift it out of the Great Depression. The New Deal put thousands of people to work building roads, canals, and parks throughout the United States.

Building a Bridge

By the time President Roosevelt announced his New Deal, California had already begun to put people back to work. High over the icy waters of San Francisco Bay, a huge structure was taking shape. It was the magnificent Golden Gate Bridge.

The bridge took thousands of people four years to build. When finished it was nearly two miles long. The work was hard and dangerous, but people who hadn't worked in years were grateful for the job.

As one crew member said, the bridge workers knew they were "building the greatest structure in the world." The Golden Gate Bridge was finished in 1937. It stood as a sign of the strength that would pull the country out of the Great Depression. ■

▲ Workers on the Golden Gate Bridge battled high winds and fog, often with only a net between them and the ice-cold water. Eleven workers died during the project.

■ *How did the New Deal help California?*

R E V I E W

1. **FOCUS** What events helped and hurt California from 1917 to 1940?

2. **CONNECT** How do you think the oil and technology boom of the early 1900s helped boost tourism?

3. **HISTORY** Give two reasons why California attracted Dust Bowl farmers.

4. **CRITICAL THINKING** Why was it important to lift people's spirits during the Great Depression?

5. **WRITING ACTIVITY** Imagine you are a child of a migrant family during the Dust Bowl. Write an entry in your diary describing how you feel about leaving the Dust Bowl and starting a new home in California.

245

Chapter Review

Reviewing Key Terms

aqueduct (p.228)
bribe (p.237)
canal (p.230)
Dust Bowl (p.243)

Great Depression
(p.243)
New Deal (p.245)
Progressives (p.238)
tourism (p.242)

A. Choose the key term that best completes each sentence.

1. During the _____, companies closed and workers lost their jobs.
2. _____ worked to create a better government and society.
3. High winds and a lack of rain created a _____ in Oklahoma and Kansas.

4. _____ and the movie industry bring many visitors to California.
5. To overcome the country's problems, President Franklin Delano Roosevelt started a program called the _____.
6. The Los Angeles _____ is a giant water pipe that carries water to the city.

B. Write a sentence for each pair of words below:

1. Progressives, bribes
2. canal, Panama
3. aqueduct, Owens River

Exploring Concepts

A. Complete the chart below on another paper with information from the chapter.

B. Support each statement below with two details from this chapter.

1. The oil boom changed the lives of many Californians.

Place	Problem	Cause	Solution
Los Angeles	The city needed water.		
San Francisco	The city government was dishonest.		
United States	Many workers lost their jobs.		

2. People from the Owens Valley and the city of Los Angeles had a disagreement about water.
3. Good transportation by sea was important for Los Angeles.
4. After the 1906 earthquake, the people of San Francisco had to rebuild their government as well as their city.
5. Progressives in California helped workers get the protection they needed.
6. The Great Depression was a time of suffering for many people.
7. The New Deal helped lift the country out of the Great Depression.

Reviewing Skills

1. The chart at the right shows how many barrels of oil were produced in 1910 by five different states. Use this information to make a bar graph. Then answer these questions: What do the bars on your graph stand for? Why do you think a bar graph is a good way of organizing information?
2. Read the two sentences below. Which sentence states a fact and which sentence states an opinion?
   a. I think Hiram Johnson did a good job as mayor of San Francisco.
   b. The Panama Canal opened a short cut between the Atlantic and Pacific oceans.
3. Suppose you want to read more about President Franklin D. Roosevelt. What kinds of books would you look in for more information?
4. What kind of library card would help you find another book by Doris Gates?

Oil Production, 1910	
State	**Barrels of Oil**
California	73 million
Illinois	33 million
Oklahoma	52 million
Texas	9 million
West Virginia	12 million

Using Critical Thinking

1. Imagine that the Los Angeles Aqueduct had not been built. How do you think life today might be different for the city of Los Angeles and the people of the Owens River Valley?
2. Citizens like Charlotte Perkins Gilman persuaded lawmakers to make changes by writing articles in newspapers and magazines. What other ways do citizens of the United States have of changing their government?
3. The New Deal programs brought many improvements to the state of California. What new improvements would you like to see in California today?

Preparing for Citizenship

1. **WRITING ACTIVITY** Write a letter to a community official about a problem in your city or town. Describe the problem and give a solution. Try to persuade the official to change the situation you write about.
2. **GROUP ACTIVITY** Imagine that you could plan your own city. Work as a group to draw a map of your city. Decide what human and natural resources the city will need and how the city will be linked to the rest of the country. Use map symbols and a legend, and give your city a name. Then describe your city to the rest of the class.
3. **COLLABORATIVE LEARNING** As a class, plan a movie about the journey of a farm family from the Dust Bowl to California. Work in small groups to plan scenes that describe the homes they left behind, their trip to California, and the work camp where they settle. In your movie, tell how the family's life has been changed.

Chapter 11

World War II and Beyond

During the 1930s and 1940s, people lived through depression and war. When World War II finally ended, people were ready for a better life. New industries had taken root in California, bringing progress and change to the state. So people came to California, the state of beauty, sunshine, new industries, and new inventions.

Following the war, people settled down to raise families. The many children raised during the 1950s enjoyed childhoods that were very different from those of their parents.

1950 Freeways join the many new communities in California, bringing change to the way people live.

1940	1945	1950

1945 World War II ends.

1940

Most homes in the United States had televisions by the 1960s. TV changed family life and gave a new boost to Hollywood.

This magazine ad shows a shiny new DeSoto. Large comfortable cars became an important part of life in California suburbs.

8 out of 10 owners say, "De Soto is the most satisfactory car I ever owned"

DeSoto

1955

1960

1965

1955 Walt Disney's first theme park opens in Anaheim.

1965

L E S S O N 1

California in Wartime

How did World War II change life in California?

Key Terms

- manufacturing
- shipyard

➤ *A Japanese American child sits on an old suitcase waiting to be sent to an internment camp.*

> **W**e sacrificed the new car, the lovely gas range, the refrigerator, the vacuum cleaner, the rugs, sofa and the rest of the household furnishings. Dad had a wonderful collection of rare and tropical fish . . . Little by little our home was broken up and all the fancy dreams we planned for you had to be altered [changed].

Ellen Kiskiyama wrote these words to her son, Arthur, in 1942, when he was just a baby. She wrote them so that when Arthur was older he could read about the terrible thing that had happened to his family.

It all started on December 7, 1941. On the radio the Kiskiyamas heard the awful news. Japanese planes had just bombed a United States military base at Pearl Harbor, Hawaii. The United States declared war on Japan. Ellen Kiskiyama, a Japanese American, was frightened. What would happen to her and her family? Their non-Japanese friends told them not to worry. After all, the Kiskiyamas were American citizens, and they had done nothing wrong.

But the young mother had good reason to be afraid. The family was ordered to report to a government station. They had to sell everything they owned. Then the Kiskiyamas were moved to a place in Wyoming called an internment camp. Like thousands of Japanese Americans on the West Coast, they were to be kept in internment camps until the end of the war.

War in the Pacific Causes Fear

Japan's surprise attack on Pearl Harbor killed 3,700 people. Bombs destroyed 18 ships and 170 airplanes. The next day the United States declared war on Japan and entered into World War II. Americans across the country were angered and frightened by the attack. But Californians were especially concerned.

California is directly across the Pacific Ocean from Japan. Some people expected Japanese planes to fly over Los Angeles at any moment. There was a great fear that Japanese Americans on the West Coast might help Japan invade the country. So California officials begged the United States government to set up internment camps.

From 1942 until the Japanese lost the war in 1945, more than 100,000 Japanese Americans were held in the camps. The camps were built in the deserts of California, Arizona, and Utah, and in other areas far away from the coast. People lived in buildings of concrete, steel, or scrap wood. Barbed wire and soldiers with guns surrounded the camps. The internment camps were dusty, crowded, and grim.

Many Japanese Americans wondered why they were there. They had no desire to help Japan invade the West Coast. In fact, Japanese Americans remained very loyal to the United States in World War II. It took many years for the country to realize its terrible mistake in building the internment camps. But at the time, the country worried only about defending its coast. ■

▼ *The news of Pearl Harbor shook the nation. Across the country, people joined in the war effort.*

■ *Why did World War II cause so much fear in California?*

War Brings New Jobs and People

To fight the war, the United States needed food for soldiers and oil for planes and tanks. As it had done in World War I, California played a big part in providing these important supplies. But World War II brought much more business to California. A huge manufacturing industry grew in the state. **Manufacturing** is the process of turning materials into finished products. For example, planes and ships are manufactured from steel. To learn more about California's manufacturing industry, see the Minipedia, page 310.

251

World War II and Beyond

The war effort depended on women to help manufacture weapons and machinery. The woman below is using a torch to join metal pieces together.

The country badly needed ships to fight sea battles and to carry soldiers and supplies. Without enough ships, the war would be lost. President Roosevelt needed a way to manufacture them, and fast.

The President called on Henry Kaiser. Even though he had never built a ship before, Kaiser was known for getting things done. He had engineered many big projects, like the huge Hoover Dam, that people had thought would be impossible.

Kaiser answered the President's call by building Liberty Ships at his four **shipyards** in Richmond, on the San Francisco Bay. At these shipyards, Kaiser workers manufactured nearly 700 ships during the war. A Liberty Ship weighed 10,000 tons, but building one was like putting together a toy. Each part of the ship had a number. Workers connected one numbered part to the next. Kaiser shipyards could finish a Liberty Ship in three-and-a-half days. Before the war, the same job had taken up to a year.

Opportunities for Women

War industries grew very quickly in California. Airplane factories and shipyards employed up to 600,000 people. Suddenly, California needed workers. Before the war, most factory jobs were held by men, usually white men. But so many men were off fighting the war that companies had to offer these jobs to women.

Before World War II, not many women worked. Most stayed home to care for their families. But now they joined the war effort. Some women went overseas to serve in the military. They drove jeeps, handled supplies, and worked in hospitals. Others stayed home and took jobs in factories and shipyards. Women did jobs like riveting, using heavy

This is a model of the Liberty Ships built by Henry Kaiser. The giant ships carried war supplies around the world. To provide enough steel for the huge ships, he created Kaiser Steel Company in Fontana.

UNITED STATES MARITIME COMMISSION
LIBERTY SHIP
BUILT AND ENGINEERED UNDER THE DIRECTION OF
ADMIRAL E. S. LAND AND ADMIRAL H. L. VICKERY
BY THE
OREGON SHIPBUILDING CORPORATION
PORTLAND, OREGON
THE PERMANENTE METALS CORPORATION
RICHMOND, CALIFORNIA

tools to join the steel plates of ships.

World War II changed the lives of many women. Marguerite Hoffman took a job at Douglas Aircraft in Los Angeles. "You know," she said, "I learned to stand up for myself working with men all those years at Douglas."

Opportunities for Black Americans

Companies needed workers so badly that they had to make another big change. They began hiring black Americans. Until the war, many companies had refused to hire any blacks. But during 1942, when the shipyards started hiring black workers, about 10,000 blacks a month poured into California from the southern and eastern United States. These people formed new communities in places like Oakland near San Francisco and San Pedro near Los Angeles.

World War II was a difficult time in the country's history. But for most Californians the war brought a feeling of pride. It united people in helping the country. The war also brought an end to the Great Depression by creating new jobs. It made manufacturing a major California industry. ■

Across Time & Space

World War II was fought all over the globe. The United States was at war not only with Japan, but also with Germany and Italy. Today, however, these countries are all on friendly terms.

■ *Why did factories hire new groups of workers during World War II?*

REVIEW

1. **FOCUS** How did World War II change life in California?
2. **CONNECT** Name two ways that the war brought relief from the Great Depression.
3. **HISTORY** How did the war change the lives of women in California?
4. **CRITICAL THINKING** How do you think Kaiser's manufacturing system improved shipbuilding?
5. **WRITING ACTIVITY** Imagine you had to give up your home and everything you own and move to the desert. Write a letter to a friend describing your experience.

Conducting an Interview

Here's Why

Some of your relatives and neighbors were alive during World War II. Perhaps one of them worked in a factory making a product for the war. You can interview them to learn about World War II.

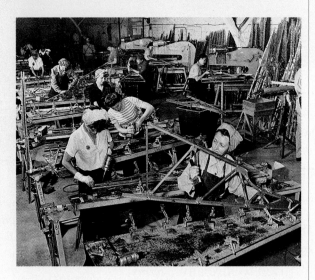

Here's How

You may have seen an interview on television. An interview is a kind of conversation between two people. The interviewer asks questions, and the other person answers them.

In an interview, you must ask the right questions to get the information you want. Here are some guides to follow when you plan an interview.

1. Decide what you want to know.
2. Make up questions. Ask *Who? What? Where? When? Why?* and *How?* Do not ask questions that can be answered with *yes* or *no*.
3. Begin by telling the person the reason for your interview.
4. Ask your questions clearly. Listen carefully to the answers.
5. Take notes on the answers. Don't write every word. Write only enough to help you remember what the person said.
6. If you don't understand an answer, ask more questions about it.
7. Thank the person.
8. Review your notes. Write a summary of the most important information.

Try It

Work with a partner. Take turns interviewing each other about a favorite activity. Make up questions and follow the guides for interviewing.

Apply It

Interview an older relative or neighbor about his or her experiences during World War II. Use questions like these:
1. Where did you live during the war?
2. How did the war change your life?
3. What interesting experiences did you have?

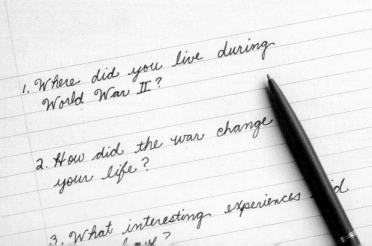

1. Where did you live during World War II?

2. How did the war change your life?

3. What interesting experiences d

LESSON 2

New Uses of Science and Technology

Could it be done? Could a person travel at supersonic speed—that is, faster than the speed of sound? When a British pilot tried it in 1947, his plane was blown apart. Now Chuck Yeager (*YAY gur*), a test pilot at Edwards Air Force Base in California, was going to risk his life to answer the question.

In early October 1947, Yeager took his first flight in the X-1, a new top-secret navy jet. In his 1985 autobiography, *Yeager,* he describes the experience:

> The X-1 glides like a bird. I'm flying in total silence, aware only of the sound of my own breathing through the oxygen mask, and my ship is graceful, responsive, and beautiful to handle. It's a fabulous ride that I wish would never end.

One week later, on October 14, Yeager was strapped into the cockpit of the X-1. As he fired up each of the four engines, a 20-foot sheet of flame shot from the plane. The X-1 climbed to 45,000 feet. Strangely, the faster Yeager went, the smoother the ride got. Suddenly the needle of the speedometer went off the dial at about 700 miles per hour. Nothing happened.

Yeager could hardly believe he had done it. The X-1 was flying at supersonic speed. Yeager was flying faster and higher than any pilot in history. Far below him a tremendous BOOM! rocked the desert. It was a sonic boom, a shock wave that is made when an object reaches the speed of sound. This was the first sonic boom ever heard. The X-1 "zoomed me into the history books," Yeager wrote.

THINKING FOCUS

How did new technology benefit California from 1945 to 1965?

Key Terms

- aviation
- aerospace

Chuck Yeager spent many years at Edwards Air Force Base testing new aircraft.

Science Breaks Barriers

The war was over. All the old war planes had gone to the junkyards. But a new age of aviation was just beginning. **Aviation**, the building and flying of airplanes, became a giant industry in California after World War II.

One of the reasons for the growth in aviation was the invention of jet aircraft. The government chose Edwards Air Force Base as a main testing station for its new jets. The base was way out in the California desert, where the tests could be done in an open space and in secret.

California had all the resources needed to make aviation grow. It had many fine colleges with scientists from all over the world. These scientists helped create better airplane designs and more powerful engines. California also had manufacturing industries that had grown up during World War II. Airplane manufacturers now began making jets instead of the old warplanes. Other companies made engine parts and steel.

The new jets, like the one Yeager flew, could reach the very edge of the sky. But people wanted to go beyond that edge and into the darkness of space. This desire led to the development of rocket technology. As rockets were being designed and tested, California's aviation industry got a new name. **Aerospace** was the new word that included spacecraft as well as airplanes. California's aerospace industry is described in A Closer Look at Aerospace, below.

A CLOSER LOOK

Aerospace History

From airplanes to spaceships, California has been a pioneer in aerospace engineering. The three aircraft below come from three different periods in the state's aerospace history.

Propeller planes reached for the sky. In the 1920s, T. Claude Ryan of San Diego built the *Spirit of St. Louis.* Its pilot, Charles Lindbergh, became the first person to fly across the Atlantic Ocean.

Diving to New Depths

While test pilots explored the sky, Francis P. Shepard was exploring the deep sea. He spent nearly 30 years in the waters off the coast of San Diego trying to figure out what the bottom of the ocean looked like. His research showed great valleys, volcanoes, canyons, and mountains under the ocean.

Shepard knew that the ocean floor must be very beautiful, but he couldn't see it. His ideas about the land beneath the sea came from instruments, measurements, and guesswork. Divers had gone down as far as they could. Shepard wanted to go farther.

In 1964, he got his wish. Shepard became the first American to explore the ocean floor in a deep-sea submarine. This "Diving Saucer" was developed by famous explorer Jacques Cousteau. It took Shepard 800 feet down into the ocean. On his way to the bottom from the saucer's window he saw rainbow-colored plants and fish. Then he finally saw the mysterious land that he had spent most of his life studying. In his notes he described the view: "It is so completely out of this world that it is breathtaking." ■

▼ *Schools of fish, brightly colored sponges, and a rocky landscape were just some of the sights Shepard saw when he explored the ocean's floor.*

■ *In what ways did aviation and science grow and change in California after World War II?*

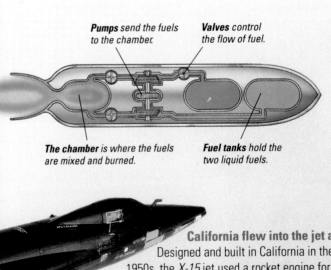

Pumps send the fuels to the chamber.

Valves control the flow of fuel.

The chamber is where the fuels are mixed and burned.

Fuel tanks hold the two liquid fuels.

California flew into the jet age.
Designed and built in California in the 1950s, the *X-15* jet used a rocket engine for extra power and distance. In a rocket engine, two liquid fuels mix and burn. At high temperatures, gases escape rapidly and the jet shoots forward.

The space age arrived in the 1960s.
The California Institute of Technology helped develop rockets that carried U.S. astronauts to the moon. In the 1970s, scientists developed *Voyager 2*, which sent back photos of Saturn's rings and Neptune's icy moons in the 1980s.

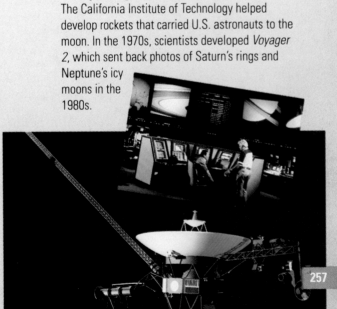

People and Machines Boost Agriculture

Ever since machines were invented, people have worried that technology would replace human beings. But in California agriculture, people and machines worked together in a new period of growth after World War II.

The human part of California farming had changed very little since the days of the Chinese gardeners and the Dust Bowl families. Farms needed a steady flow of migrant laborers to plant, care for, and pick their crops. For years most of these laborers had come from Mexico. They traveled with the seasons on the route shown on the map below.

▼ *Use this map to explain how climate affected the route of the migrant workers.*

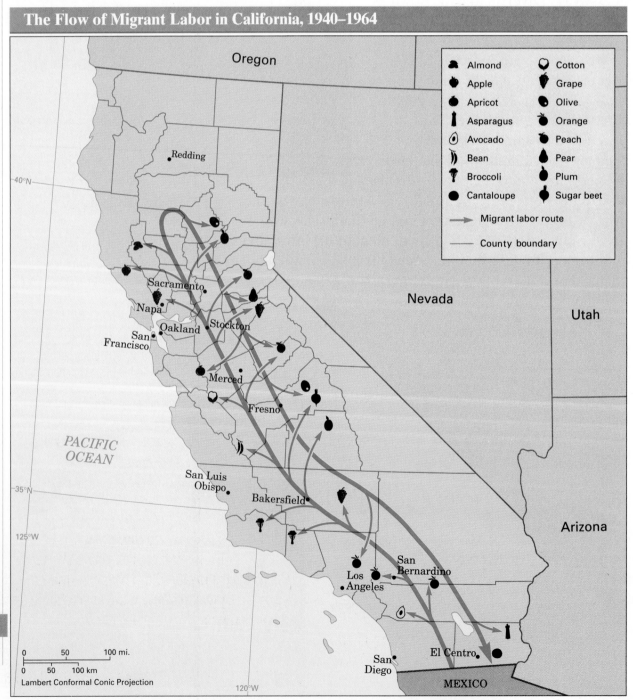

The Flow of Migrant Labor in California, 1940–1964

Oregon

Nevada

Utah

Arizona

PACIFIC OCEAN

MEXICO

Redding

Sacramento

Napa

Oakland
San Francisco

Stockton

Merced

Fresno

San Luis Obispo

Bakersfield

Los Angeles

San Bernardino

San Diego

El Centro

40°N
35°N
125°W
120°W

Legend:

Almond		Cotton	
Apple		Grape	
Apricot		Olive	
Asparagus		Orange	
Avocado		Peach	
Bean		Pear	
Broccoli		Plum	
Cantaloupe		Sugar beet	

→ Migrant labor route

— County boundary

0   50   100 mi.
0   50   100 km
Lambert Conformal Conic Projection

Farmers use machines to process tomatoes at this tomato cannery in Sacramento. California leads the nation in tomato processing. It also leads the nation in the production and sale of almonds, pictured below.

Growers always worried about having enough pickers when crops were ripe. The farmers' worries led to two big changes on the farms. One was the start of the bracero (*bruh SAIR oh*) program. Under this program, Mexico agreed to provide California growers with workers. These workers were called braceros, which means "laborers" in Spanish. In return, growers promised to feed, house, and pay the workers.

The science and technology developed at California universities helped to improve agriculture in many ways during this time. In the 1940s, for example, a plant disease nearly wiped out California's orange crop. After two years of study, scientists at the University of California's Citrus Experiment Station at Riverside found a cure that saved the orange industry.

The research in the universities also helped to develop faster, better farm machines. One new tomato picker was so gentle it could pick up an egg and place it uncracked in a box. Another could shake ripe fruits and nuts from trees. Together, machines and people helped make California's agriculture industry the largest and richest in the nation. ■

■ *How did California farming change after World War II?*

R E V I E W

1. **FOCUS** How did new technology benefit California from 1945 to 1965?
2. **CONNECT** Why do you think aviation grew in California after World War II, while shipbuilding did not?
3. **ECONOMICS** Explain how the bracero program helped California agriculture grow.
4. **CRITICAL THINKING** What did Francis Shepard find when he explored the ocean bottom?
5. **ACTIVITY** Draw a picture of divers exploring the ocean floor.

L E S S O N   3

New Ways of Living

How was life in the suburbs different from life in the cities after World War II?

Key Terms

- suburb
- barrio

➤ *In the 1950s, people saw plastic as a material that would last forever. The bubble-shaped House of the Future was built almost entirely of plastic. Even the furniture in the house was made of plastic.*

"Someday, push buttons will replace the telephone dial." The wonderful new push-button phone was one of the modern features proudly displayed in the Walt Disney theme park's House of the Future in 1957. Of course, no one would give the phone a second look today. But to people of the 1950s it brought gasps of delight. The home boasted all kinds of new inventions that few people had ever seen before. There was a garbage disposal and a microwave oven. Most of the house was made of plastic. This new building material looked clean and modern. Visitors were amazed.

You're not amazed? Then consider these other items. The dishwasher used sound waves to shake food off the dishes. A panel in each room controlled the air temperature and added the scent of pine, flowers, or sea breezes. The oven disappeared into the wall at the touch of a button. More than 30 years after these items were designed, they are still new ideas.

Walt Disney loved new ideas. When he built his theme park in 1955, he wanted to create a place of fantasy and fun. But in features like the House of the Future, Disney also celebrated human progress.

Growth of the Suburbs

Walt Disney wasn't the only one to be fascinated by the new technology of his time. Many of the things we never give a thought to today, like freezers and freeways, were exciting to people of the 1950s. A time of progress came after years of depression and war. Now people were eager to have a comfortable life. They wanted good jobs and modern homes.

California had all the ingredients for this good life. The state had room to grow. It had beauty and warmth. And it had jobs. Industries like aerospace offered high-paying jobs to college graduates. These job opportunities drew about 1,500 people a day to come to California in the years after the war. To find out how quickly California's population grew, see the Minipedia, page 311.

The new Californians began building thousands of new homes. Before this time, houses were usually built one at a time. But now people needed lots of new homes at once. So builders planned communities with hundreds of homes. Matching houses stood side by side on small pieces of land.

Many of these new housing areas grew up just outside major cities. These communities near the cities were called **suburbs**. As suburbs got larger, many became separate towns. They had shopping centers, modern schools, and movie theaters. Often, suburbs spread across land where farms had once been. Rows of houses replaced rows of orange trees in areas like Orange County.

Row after row of houses spread across suburbs like the Los Angeles suburb pictured here.

How Do We Know?

HISTORY *Television programs of the 1950s tell a lot about how people thought of California. In the Hollywood TV shows, Mom, Dad, the kids, and the dog lived a happy life in a comfortable house in a nice town. Television brought the California dream to people around the country.*

◄ *Cruising in the California sun in a shiny new car was part of the good life people wanted.*

▼ *Californians have long been in love with their cars. Use the chart below to find out how many more cars there were in 1960 than in 1930.*

Automobiles in California

= 1 Million

Year

1930

1940

1950

1960

| 0 | 1 | 2 | 3 | 4 | 5 | 6 | 7 |

Number of Cars (in millions)

◼ *What were the reasons for the growth of the suburbs?*

➤ *Hispanic children in a city neighborhood play at breaking a piñata. The colorful piñata is filled with candies, fruits, and toys.*

Building New Roads

Suburbs and freeways grew up together. The Pasadena freeway near Los Angeles was built in 1940. The nine-mile road was the state's first freeway. By the end of the 1950s, California was spending over a million dollars a day on the construction of new freeways. Californians could have chosen to link the trolleys and railroads in the big cities with the new suburbs. But Californians enjoyed the freedom of driving their own cars. So they built freeways. As the chart on the left shows, the number of cars in California grew quickly from 1930 to 1960. The choice between trolleys and cars is explained in Making Decisions, pages 264–265.

People took the fast freeways from their homes in the suburbs to jobs in the cities. The freeways cut through city neighborhoods that most suburban people knew little about. In these city communities, life was very different from life in the suburbs. ◼

Growth of the Cities

It is almost evening in the city. Dark-haired, giggling children play tag in the streets. The houses on this hillside are painted in the colors of a piñata—bright yellow, pink, and white. Old cars rumble past small shops whose signs are written in Spanish.

This is East Los Angeles, and the community is called a **barrio** (*BAH ree oh*). This means neighborhood in Spanish. After World War II the East Los Angeles barrio grew into the third largest Mexican community in the world. New people arrived all the time. Many spoke no English. The barrio gave them a feeling of comfort and protection.

People from many different cultures and ethnic groups gather in Los Angeles's festive Chinatown.

Ethnic Neighborhoods

The people who came to California after the war caused cities to grow quickly. Often cities were made up of many ethnic neighborhoods—black, Armenian, Chinese, Jewish, Italian, and Mexican. Large neighborhoods became cities within cities. Some neighborhoods were poorer than others.

Black Americans often lived in the worst areas. Discrimination against blacks was strong in California during this time. Blacks got little money or help for improving their neighborhoods. Because of discrimination, they couldn't move into better areas like the suburbs. In the black communities, a quiet anger began to grow.

As California moved into the 1960s, people became more concerned about the difference between life in the suburbs and life in the cities. Black Americans and other ethnic groups wanted to find a way to save the culture of their communities. And they wanted to make their neighborhoods better places to live. ■

■ *What caused the barrios and other city neighborhoods to grow?*

R E V I E W

1. **FOCUS** How was life in the suburbs different from life in the cities after World War II?

2. **CONNECT** Compare San Francisco's Chinese neighborhood in the late 1800s to the Los Angeles barrio after World War II. Why were people attracted to these communities?

3. **ECONOMICS** What effects did the car have on life in California?

4. **CRITICAL THINKING** In the 1950s, there was a big increase in tourism in California. In what ways do you think new technology helped people to tour more of the state?

5. **ACTIVITY** Draw a picture of three things that were a part of life in California suburbs.

263

World War II and Beyond

Trolleys or Cars?

A*merica lives on wheels, and we have to provide the highways to keep . . . the kind and form of life we want.*

George M. Humphrey, former U.S. Treasury Secretary

N*early everyone was sure highways were the only answer to transportation problems. . . . But we were wrong.*

Francis Sargent, former Massachusetts Governor

Background

Los Angeles without cars is as hard to imagine as southern California without sunshine. It wasn't always that way, though. From 1880 to 1920, when the city was smaller, most people rode trolleys, like the one below. Most people in Los Angeles lived within four blocks of a trolley line.

Automobiles arrived in about 1900. At the same time, Los Angeles began to spread out. The trolleys couldn't serve everyone, and many people started buying cars. Trolley companies began losing money. One by one they shut down.

Cars brought problems to Los Angeles. Huge traffic jams became a part of daily life. The sky was dirty with car fumes. The city tried to fix traffic problems by building freeways. But that just made it easier for people to live in suburbs far from the city and to drive their cars even more.

▲ *At first the people of Los Angeles traveled on horse-drawn railways. Later they used trolley cars like the one here. These trolleys were much like the cable cars still used in San Francisco today.*

Conflict Over How to Spend Money

Something had to be done. In the 1960s, some city officials suggested forcing people to drive their cars less and use other ways to travel. Officials wanted to spend less government money on building freeways and more on mass transit. Buses, railroads, and subways are types of mass transit because they carry masses, or large groups of people. It costs about $100 million to build just one mile of a mass transit line. Since some Los Angeles suburbs are up to 25 miles away from the center of the city, the cost would be high.

Many car owners didn't want to pay higher taxes to build a transportation system that they wouldn't use. They complained that transit lines wouldn't reach enough places, and they would have to wait too long to catch the bus or train. Spend our tax dollars on new and better freeways instead, the car owners urged.

The city is still trying to find an answer to its transportation problems. Meanwhile, the freeways grow more crowded, and the skies grow grayer and dirtier.

Decision Point

1. What are the good and bad effects of using mass transit?
2. What are the good and bad effects of using cars?
3. What do people who want mass transit value most?
4. What do people who prefer car travel value most?
5. What are some creative solutions to the car problem in Los Angeles? Draw a picture of your favorite one.

What form of transportation should Los Angeles depend on in the future?

Mass transit:
- causes less smog
- reduces traffic jams
- uses less fuel

Car travel:
- go when you want
- go where you want
- more comfortable

Build new mass-transit systems.

Build more freeways.

Chapter Review

Reviewing Key Terms

aerospace (p.256)   manufacturing (p.251)
aviation (p.256)   shipyard (p.252)
barrio (p.263)   suburb (p.261)

A. Choose the key term that best completes each sentence.

1. During World War II, California's ____ industries included shipbuilding and aircraft construction.
2. Charles Lindbergh's flight across the Atlantic Ocean was an important event in the history of _____.
3. Kaiser's new system helped each _____

in Richmond to manufacture one new Liberty Ship every 10 days.

4. _____ is the Spanish word that means neighborhood.

B. Write a sentence for each pair of words below. Then write a sentence telling how the words in each pair are related.

1. barrio, neighborhood
2. manufacturing, ships
3. rockets, aerospace
4. city, suburb

Exploring Concepts

A. Copy the timeline below on a separate piece of paper. Extend it to 1965. Then add the following events to your timeline:

1. 1947—Chuck Yeager travels faster than the speed of sound.
2. 1955—Walt Disney builds a theme park in Anaheim.

3. 1964—Francis P. Shepard explores the ocean in a diving saucer.

B. Write one or two sentences to answer each question below. Use details from this chapter to support your answers.

1. Why is December 7, 1941 an important date in United States history?
2. Why were Japanese families taken from their homes and sent to internment camps?
3. What new jobs were created because of World War II?
4. What changes in the agriculture industry have been brought by harvesting machines?
5. How did California's freeways change life in the cities and suburbs?

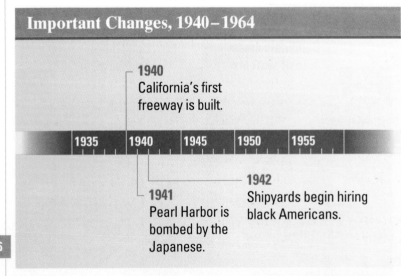

Important Changes, 1940–1964

1940 California's first freeway is built.

1935   1940   1945   1950   1955

1941 Pearl Harbor is bombed by the Japanese.

1942 Shipyards begin hiring black Americans.

Reviewing Skills

1. Pretend you are going to interview someone who writes a television show. What do you want to know about how a television show is made? Write a list of questions you will ask. Be sure to include questions that ask *who*, *what*, *when*, *where*, *why*, and *how*.
2. Look at the line graph at the right. In 1945, about how many miles of freeway were there in California? How many miles were there in 1965?
3. The American photographer, Dorothea Lange, took many pictures of people involved in World War II. Where would you look for information about this important artist?

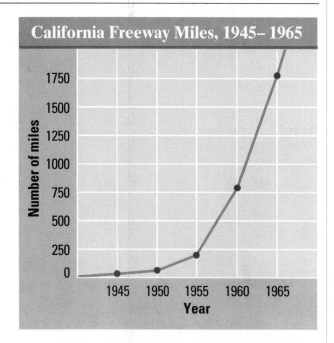

California Freeway Miles, 1945–1965

Using Critical Thinking

1. As California's cities grew, separate neighborhoods of black Americans, Mexican Americans, Japanese Americans, and other ethnic groups developed. Each ethnic group tried to continue its own cultural traditions. How do today's neighborhoods show the cultures of the people who live there now or who lived there in the past? If possible, base your answer on details about your own neighborhood.
2. "Laborers will go where they can get good jobs." Based on what you learned in this chapter, do you agree with this statement? What special jobs do people do in the area where you live?

Preparing for Citizenship

1. **COLLECTING INFORMATION** Californians use many other kinds of transportation besides cars. Collect pictures from magazines and newspapers showing how people in California travel from one place to another. Paste the pictures you find onto a large piece of paper, and label the pictures. Include a picture that shows the way you travel between home and school.
2. **COLLABORATIVE LEARNING** As a class project, make a mural that shows your class's idea of "California in the Future." Before you begin, discuss how the mural will look. All members of the class should tell what they might like to see in the future. Ideas should cover the following topics: transportation, cities, parks, houses, recreation, jobs, and schools. Work in small groups to plan different parts of the mural by drawing sketches in pencil. Then all students should color in the drawings. Share your class's finished mural with the rest of the school.

Chapter 12
New Steps Forward

Progress doesn't always mean building houses or roads. Sometimes it means making life better for people. In the 1960s and 1970s, Californians worked hard to stop the discrimination that had long been a part of the state's history. Sometimes the battles were difficult. But they made California a better place for everyone.

California has led the way in education. The state opened up its college and university system to all students who make good grades.

The United States government changed its laws to allow more Asians and other immigrants into the country.

1965	1970	1975	1980

1965

1980 Personal computers begin to sell in great numbers, causing a boom in California's Silicon Valley.

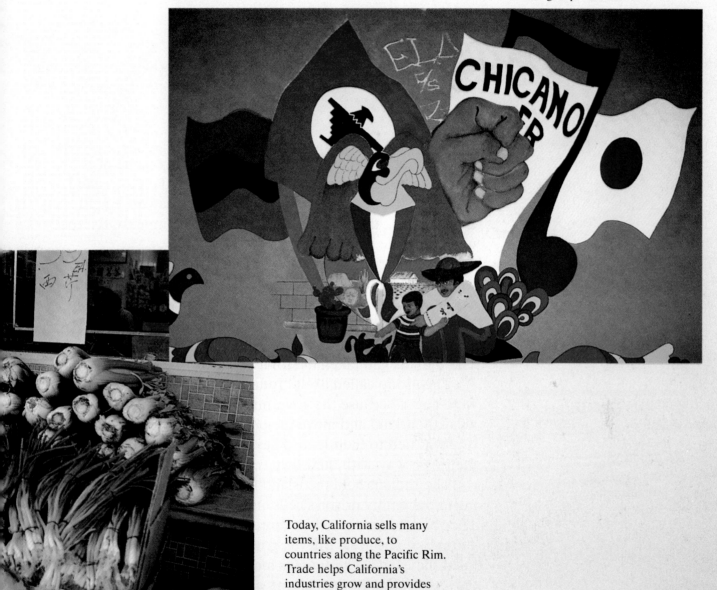

The many murals, or wall paintings, found throughout Los Angeles, show the pride of the city's different ethnic groups and cultures.

Today, California sells many items, like produce, to countries along the Pacific Rim. Trade helps California's industries grow and provides many jobs.

1985   1990   1995   2000

1986 California admits 21,984 immigrants from southeastern Asia. Immigrants from this region pour into the state throughout the 1980s, making Southeast Asians California's fastest-growing immigrant population.

2000

LESSON 1

A Struggle for Rights

THINKING
FOCUS

What civil rights did minorities fight for during the 1960s and 1970s?

Key Terms

- civil rights
- minority
- protest
- labor union
- strike
- boycott

➤ *Many people from San Francisco helped the Indians to stay on the island. They sent food, water, and clothing.*

Most people knew the frightening name of Alcatraz. The prison that stood on the island of Alcatraz in San Francisco Bay once held the nation's most dangerous criminals. Escape was said to be impossible.

But the prison had closed in 1963. And the 80 Indians who rowed a boat to Alcatraz in November 1969 wanted to get on the island, not to escape from it. In the dark of night they pulled their boat ashore and climbed the island's rocky walls. Then they set up camp around the deserted prison. The Indians had taken over Alcatraz.

The group called itself "Indians of All Tribes." They were angry because the government was trying to take away their land and move them into cities. The Indians' culture was tied to their land. They wanted the right to live in their own way, with their own traditions.

The Indians held the island for nearly two years, sleeping in the empty prison's cells and cooking over open fires. They had hoped to build a center for the study of Indian culture on Alcatraz. But the government would not sell them the island. The Indians may have lost Alcatraz, but they had captured the nation's attention. Now people everywhere knew about the troubles of the Indians.

Blacks Seek Equal Rights

The Indians were not the only people who were tired of being treated unfairly. People like Odis Jackson were tired of it too. In 1963, Jackson, a 30-year-old lawyer, tried to buy a house in a Los Angeles suburb. But because Jackson was black, the owner refused to sell him the house. Such dis-

crimination was not unusual. Many whites did not want black Americans in their new suburbs. They refused to sell or rent houses to blacks. Blacks were also kept out of the higher-paying jobs and the better schools.

In the 1940s and 1950s, blacks tried to stop discrimination by getting the government to pass new laws. But these laws were often ignored. It seemed as if all their work had been for nothing. So, in the 1960s, blacks began to fight even harder for their **civil rights**—their freedoms as citizens.

◄ *A black woman holds a sign calling for integration. Blacks were fighting for their right to live in white neighborhoods and attend white schools.*

UNDERSTANDING CIVIL RIGHTS

Odis Jackson wanted the freedom to live where he chose. All Rosa Parks wanted was to rest her tired feet. Both became fighters for their civil rights.

In 1955, Parks, a black woman from Montgomery, Alabama, sank into a seat at the front of the city bus. But the front seats were for white people only. "Back of the bus," the driver ordered her. Parks was weary, and she didn't want to move. So she was arrested and put in jail. Her protest started a nationwide battle. After many bitter struggles, blacks won new laws that ended the "whites only" sections in buses, restaurants, and movie theaters.

The right of blacks to be treated the same as whites is a civil right. Civil rights are the freedoms that the laws of the United States give to each citizen. For example, people have the right to say what they think, to choose their religion, and to own land. And all citizens must be treated equally and fairly. That includes blacks and whites, rich people and poor, men and women.

In the 1960s and 1970s, people began to speak up for their civil rights. Women fought for their right to work in jobs such as judges, TV reporters, and doctors. These jobs were usually given to men, until women stood up for their civil rights.

▲ Blacks, whites, and other groups joined in this civil rights protest.

▲ In 1972, Yvonne Braithwaite Burke became the first black woman ever elected to the United States Congress from California. Before this, she served on the committee that looked into the Watts riots.

■ How did protests help blacks win their civil rights?

Civil rights include such freedoms as voting, saying what you believe, and living where you want. Across the country, blacks and nonblacks joined in the struggle for civil rights.

The Civil Rights Struggle in California

California played a big part in winning new freedoms for minorities. A **minority** is a group of people, like an ethnic group, that is a smaller part of the whole population. In Los Angeles, people decided to **protest** when Odis Jackson could not buy his house. This means they wanted to show the owner and the public that they objected to the way Jackson had been treated. They protested by carrying signs and marching down the streets of the neighborhood. Finally, the owner gave in and agreed to sell Jackson a house.

Groups protested against discrimination all over the state. In San Francisco, people protested against a supermarket chain that wouldn't hire blacks. They filled shopping carts with cold and frozen food and left them at checkout lines.

But not everyone protested in peaceful ways. In 1965, a violent riot broke out in the Los Angeles neighborhood of Watts. Angry blacks wrecked stores and set fire to many houses. The riot, which left 34 people dead, shocked the nation. People began to see that it was time for change.

The work of groups and individuals in California brought about progress for minorities. But the fight is not over. As Congresswoman Yvonne Braithwaite Burke put it, "Our job is before us in making opportunities and a pleasant place for children to live." ■

272

Farm Workers Organize

Outside the cities, in the open fields of California's farms, another group fought for its civil rights. Migrant farm workers led by Cesar Chávez worked together for fair wages and better working conditions.

Chávez knew well the hard life of California's migrant laborers. When Chávez was 10 years old, his family had to give up its farm and become migrant workers. They worked long hours in the fields picking box after box of fruits and vegetables. This was during the Great Depression. Sometimes Chávez's parents did not make enough money in a day to pay the 70-cent bus fare to and from the fields. Chávez remembers walking along the highway with his brother, looking for the tinfoil from cigarette packs. They gathered the foil in a ball and sold it to junk dealers.

Being poor was not the only hardship migrant laborers faced. Families moved often in their search for work. Because of this, their children did not receive a good education. Chávez himself attended over 35 schools and only got through the eighth grade. Migrant laborers also made low wages. Many growers charged workers high rents to live in rundown shacks, and high prices for the food they ate. On one farm, the field boss made workers pay 25 cents for a glass of water.

Standing beside a grape field, Chávez protests with migrant laborers. The protest sign and the union flag pictured below say "Huelga." That means strike in Spanish.

Organizing the People

Chávez wanted to improve the lives and working conditions of the migrant laborers. But he knew he could not do it alone. So he drove from town to town and talked to all the people that would listen. Chávez wanted to organize migrant laborers into a group to work toward a shared goal. He felt that if he organized, or gathered, enough people together, they would grow powerful enough to win their rights. The idea, Chávez explained, was like picking grapes:

273

The chart below shows that Hispanic people are California's largest minority group. Hispanics are people whose families are originally from Spanish-speaking countries.

*I*f you talk to people, you're going to organize them. But people aren't going to come to you. You have to go to them. It takes a lot of work. When you pick grapes, you pick a bunch at a time. Eventually you pick the whole vineyard. Organizing is no different.

Cesar Chávez: *Autobiography of La Causa*, 1975

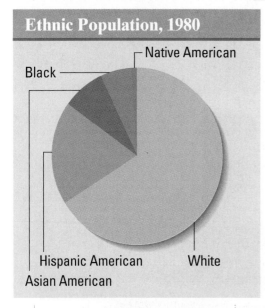

Ethnic Population, 1980

- Native American
- Black
- Hispanic American
- Asian American
- White

Chávez did convince enough workers to join with him. Together they formed a labor union. A **labor union** is a group of workers joined together to protect their own rights. Workers who don't belong to a union can lose their jobs if they complain when they have been treated unfairly. But union members know they can complain because their union will stand behind them.

The Grape Boycott

In 1965, Chávez and the union asked grape pickers to **strike.** This meant that they would refuse to do any more work until the growers had agreed to what the union wanted. The workers asked for better pay and better working conditions. They also wanted growers to agree to deal with the union. The growers refused.

Chávez also asked the public to join in a grape **boycott.** This meant that people could support the union strike by refusing to buy or eat grapes. People across the country joined the boycott. Dockworkers refused to load grapes onto ships. Children also helped by not eating grapes.

In 1976, grape growers finally gave in to the union. They promised to give workers better pay, free housing, and safer working conditions. Chávez's hard work had paid off. The union had fought the growers and won workers' rights. ■

➤ *People joined the boycott and wore buttons like the one pictured at the right.*

■ *How did migrant laborers force owners to improve the conditions for laborers on California's farms?*

R E V I E W

1. **FOCUS** What civil rights did minorities fight for during the 1960s and 1970s?
2. **CONNECT** Compare the life of Cesar Chávez's family to the life of the Dust Bowl farmers who came to California during the Great Depression. How were they alike?
3. **CITIZENSHIP** Why did blacks feel that they had

to protest in order to win their civil rights?
4. **CRITICAL THINKING** What kinds of opportunities do you think minorities have today that they didn't have in the 1960s?
5. **WRITING ACTIVITY** Write a news story covering one event from the lesson. Read your article in a broadcast to the class.

Comparing Parts of a Whole

Here's Why

When you read a circle graph that gives information about California agriculture, you can learn a lot in just one glance. A circle graph shows how a whole thing is divided into parts. It also shows how the parts compare in size.

Here's How

A circle graph is sometimes called a "pie chart," because it looks like a pie that has been cut into pieces. The parts

Workers in Agriculure

Farm owners — Farm managers

Farm laborers

of the graph are usually different sizes. Look at the graph above. The whole that this graph shows is the number of workers in California agriculture in 1975. Its three parts are farm owners, farm managers, and farm laborers. Which part is the largest? The parts that show the numbers of owners and managers are both small. The part that shows the number of laborers is much larger than both of the other parts put together. The graph shows that in 1975 California had

many more farm laborers than farm owners and managers.

Try It

Look at the circle graph below. It shows the amounts of table grapes that were grown in seven areas of California in 1988. Which area grew the most grapes in that year? Which grew the least? How do the sizes of the other parts of the graph compare?

Apply It

Look in encyclopedias for circle graphs showing information about a state, a country, or a topic such as agriculture. What whole does the graph show? What are its parts? How do the parts compare in size?

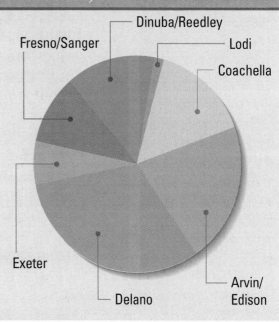

California Table Grape Production, 1988

Fresno/Sanger — Dinuba/Reedley — Lodi — Coachella — Exeter — Delano — Arvin/Edison

LESSON 2

A New Wave of Immigrants

THINKING FOCUS

Why was the new wave of immigrants good for the newcomers and for California?

Key Terms

- refugee
- custom

► *The Hmong people wove beautiful storycloths that told the tales of their culture through pictures.*

When the villagers first arrived, the roar and glitter of California frightened them. They had never seen so many cars, bright lights, and tall buildings. The Hmong (*mahng*) people had come from a place where there were no cars or freeways. In their mountain villages, the Hmong didn't own land. They just lived wherever they wanted to. They grew all their own food and cooked it over open fires.

The Hmong had left their country, Laos (*LAH ohs*), to escape violence and destruction. War had torn apart the region, and many people lost their homes. Families scattered and fled the country.

Many Hmong decided to live in California's Central Valley. Large farms stretched for miles in this flat valley. It looked very different from the mountain villages the Hmong had left behind. They had no money to buy land to farm, so they had to learn English and find other jobs.

The changes they went through were hard, but the Hmong faced their new lives in California eagerly. Some churches, universities, and citizens helped them find jobs and homes. Today the children of the Hmong villagers call California their home.

The Nation Welcomes New Immigrants

In 1965, the United States government passed a law that sent a message to people in many parts of the world. That message was "Welcome." The new law made it possible for many more immigrants from China, Japan, and Mexico to come to the United States. The law also welcomed new groups from countries along the Pacific Rim, shown in the map below.

One of the largest groups of new immigrants came from countries in a region known as Southeast Asia. In the 1960s and 1970s, the United States was involved in a war in Vietnam, a small country in Southeast Asia. The destruction caused by this war spread to other countries in the region, such as Cambodia, Thailand, and Laos. The people in Southeast Asia suffered great hardships during this time.

The Refugees of the War

The war created hundreds of thousands of refugees. A **refugee** is a person who flees his or her homeland to find safety or freedom. People often become refugees to escape the violence of war or to get away from unfair treatment by their governments.

The Hmong people were refugees. Many Hmong and other Southeast Asian refugees fled their region by boat. They were called boat people. Their long journeys to find

▼ *Boat people faced many dangers. Pirates often robbed them, and many boats were lost at sea.*

▼ *Many immigrants to California come from countries along the Pacific Ocean. The area is known as the Pacific Rim.*

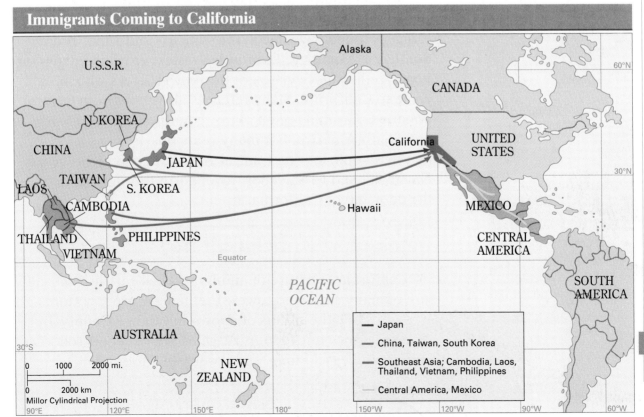

Immigrants Coming to California

Alaska
U.S.S.R.
CANADA
60°N
N. KOREA
California
UNITED STATES
CHINA
JAPAN
30°N
TAIWAN
S. KOREA
LAOS
CAMBODIA
Hawaii
MEXICO
THAILAND
PHILIPPINES
CENTRAL AMERICA
VIETNAM
Equator
SOUTH AMERICA
PACIFIC OCEAN
30°S
AUSTRALIA
NEW ZEALAND

— Japan
— China, Taiwan, South Korea
— Southeast Asia; Cambodia, Laos, Thailand, Vietnam, Philippines
— Central America, Mexico

0   1000   2000 mi.
0   2000 km
Millor Cylindrical Projection
90°E   120°E   150°E   180°   150°W   120°W   90°W   60°W

Many Asian immigrants have found work in California's computer industry. These people are working in a chip manufacturing company in Sunnyvale. Below, a family of Cambodian immigrants reads together.

welcoming countries were very dangerous. In the 1980 book *Wrapped in the Windshawl,* one Vietnamese refugee remembered his journey out of Vietnam on a boat:

> The boat was 36 feet long and 6 feet wide, and there were 174 people on board. When I got on I had to sit with my knees drawn up so there would be room for others. . . . We sailed at night. . . carrying hardly any food or water because we wanted to make as much room as possible. We even threw some of the food overboard to make room. In two days we were drinking the water used to cool the boat's engine.

After months and often years of hardship, many refugees found welcome in the state of California. Today Southeast Asians are California's fastest growing immigrant population. But they are not the only refugees who have come to California. Many refugees also come from Central America. This is a region of tiny countries between North and South America. For many years this area has been torn by war. People leaving Central American countries such as Nicaragua and El Salvador travel north through Mexico to the doorstep of California. ■

■ *Why did new immigrants pour into California after 1965?*

Immigrants Enrich Culture

California's mixture of immigrants has enriched the culture of many cities and towns. Vietnamese grocery stores and shops line the streets of a town in Orange County. In Artesia, a town outside Los Angeles, shopkeepers sell Indian candies, clothing, and jewelry in a four-block

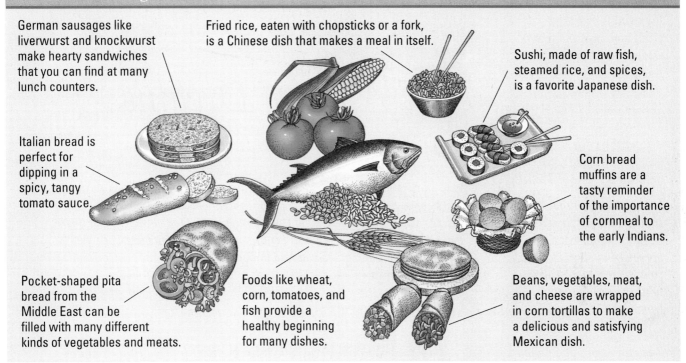

German sausages like liverwurst and knockwurst make hearty sandwiches that you can find at many lunch counters.

Fried rice, eaten with chopsticks or a fork, is a Chinese dish that makes a meal in itself.

Sushi, made of raw fish, steamed rice, and spices, is a favorite Japanese dish.

Italian bread is perfect for dipping in a spicy, tangy tomato sauce.

Corn bread muffins are a tasty reminder of the importance of cornmeal to the early Indians.

Pocket-shaped pita bread from the Middle East can be filled with many different kinds of vegetables and meats.

Foods like wheat, corn, tomatoes, and fish provide a healthy beginning for many dishes.

Beans, vegetables, meat, and cheese are wrapped in corn tortillas to make a delicious and satisfying Mexican dish.

neighborhood. And in Gardena, a city south of Los Angeles, a large Japanese community runs its own cable television station.

The customs that immigrants bring have also enriched California's culture. A **custom** is a habit, tradition, or way of life that belongs to the people of one country or culture. For instance, it is a Japanese custom to bow when greeting someone. People from around the world bring their customs to California. Their art, music, games, and dances add interest and beauty to California's culture.

You can see signs of immigrant culture everywhere in California. For example, the immigrant foods shown above have changed the way many Californians eat. Have you ever had a tortilla, a bagel, or an egg roll? Then you've had a taste of immigrant culture. ■

■ *What kinds of customs do immigrants bring to California?*

R E V I E W

1. **FOCUS** Why was the new wave of immigrants good for the newcomers and for California?
2. **CONNECT** How was the immigration wave from 1965 to 1980 different from the one between 1849 and 1910?
3. **GEOGRAPHY** Why do you think so many refugees along the Pacific Rim went to California, instead of to some other place?
4. **CRITICAL THINKING** Why might immigrants keep some of the customs of their old countries rather than those of the United States?
5. **WRITING ACTIVITY** List things about your neighborhood that have been affected by immigrants.

279

New Steps Forward

A Jar of Dreams

Yoshiko Uchida

Young Rinko and her family live in America now. When Aunt Waka comes to visit from Japan and brings a gift of a kimono, Rinko has mixed feelings about her Japanese family and her life in the United States. Her thoughts and actions tell of the difficulties many immigrants feel when they move to a new country. As you read this story, try to imagine how it would feel to be in Rinko's place.

Like Rinko and her family, many of the immigrants discussed in this chapter have borrowed customs from their new country while keeping others from their homelands.

rice paper thin paper made from an Asian tree

brocade a heavy cloth with a rich design

peonies large flowers

promise is a promise, so on Sunday after dinner, I got out the kimono Aunt Waka had brought me. It was in my bureau drawer still folded nice and flat inside its soft rice paper wrapping.

One good thing about kimonos is that they don't wrinkle if you fold them properly on the seams. Also almost anybody can wear the same size because there are no buttons or snaps. If you're short, you just pull up more to make a tuck and tie it in place with a silk cord. I thought that was pretty clever when Aunt Waka pointed it out to me.

She had to help me get dressed in the kimono because I certainly couldn't do it by myself. She made sure I overlapped the left side over the right (boys do the opposite), and she wound the wide brocade obi around and around my middle and tied an enormous knot in back.

I felt as if I was bound up in a silk cocoon and could hardly bend down to put the white tabi socks on my feet. It was hard to walk, too, with the thongs of the zori —the sandals—digging in between my toes, and I discovered why Aunt Waka took those small steps when she walked. You have to, with the long narrow kimono coming down to your ankles.

"There, you look beautiful," Aunt Waka said, when she'd finished. "Go look at yourself in the mirror."

I padded over in small steps to the bureau and looked at myself. I held out my arms to look at the white peonies blooming on the long blue silky sleeves. I turned around and twisted my head to look at the knot of the obi in back. I knew then exactly how Aunt Waka felt when we made her get into her western clothes.

"That's not me," I said.

Aunt Waka smiled. "I know how you feel, but it's you all right."

Then she hurried me out to the parlor to show Mama and Papa how I looked.

Mama's eyes really lit up when she saw me. "Why, Rinko, you look so pretty." And then she said, "Stand up straight now." But she didn't say it the way she usually does in order to improve my posture. She said it as though she wanted me to feel proud of myself.

I guess Papa was about as pleased as Mama. He stood back and studied me as though he was taking a picture of me.

"I suppose you wouldn't consider going to the hospital to show Uncle Kanda how you look, would you? That would really cheer him up, you know."

"Never in a million years," I said.

So Papa told Joji to get the box camera he got for Christmas and take my picture for Uncle Kanda. Aunt Waka got her camera too. We all trooped outside, and I stood beside the peach tree squinting at the sun.

"Stop squinting, Rinky Dink," Joji said.

"Don't you call me that, Joji Tsujimura," I said. I raised my arm to give him a whack and that's when he took my picture.

"Smile," Aunt Waka said, focusing her camera.

I blinked, and that's when she squeezed the shutter.

Mama wanted a picture with all of us in it, so I went over to get Mrs. Sugar. She looked exactly the way I thought she would when she saw me wearing a kimono. Her mouth made a big O, but no sound came out.

Then she said, "Why, it's my sweet little Japanese Rinko," and she gave me a hug. But it was hard to hug her back being wrapped up like a package in all that stiff brocade.

Mrs. Sugar lined us up in front of Papa's garage and made sure she got his big sign in the picture too.

"There," she said when she'd taken three pictures. "This will be a fine commemoration of your aunt's visit."

She sounded just like the people at church. They are always taking pictures to commemorate Easter or Memorial

shutter part of a camera that opens the lens to expose the film

281

circulation the movement of blood through the body

mothballs small balls stored with clothes to keep away moths

Day or somebody's baptism or even somebody's funeral.

I could hardly wait to get out of the kimono when we were finished with all the picture-taking. Aunt Waka untied and unwound everything, and I shook my bones loose to get my circulation going again.

"Boy, am I glad to get out of that thing," I said.

Then I remembered the kimono was a present from Aunt Waka, and I tried to think of something nicer to say.

"I'll have Mama put it in her trunk and cover it with mothballs," I said.

I guess that wasn't exactly what Aunt Waka wanted to hear either. I thought she probably would've liked me to say I'd get it out and wear it once in a while.

But she didn't say that. She just smiled and said, "Ah, Rinko, you certainly are a child of America." Then she turned serious and said, "But don't ever forget, a part of you will always be Japanese too, even if you never wear a kimono again."

"I know," I said. "It's the part that makes me feel different and not as good as the others."

It was the strangest thing. Suddenly, it was as if I'd opened a faucet in my head and everything inside came pouring out. I told Aunt Waka all about how I felt at school—how the boys called me names and the girls made me feel left out. And I told her a terrible secret I'd kept to myself and never told anybody, ever.

Once when there was going to be a PTA meeting at school and we had notes to bring home, I tore up my note and never gave it to Mama. I did it because I didn't want Mama to go. I didn't want her bowing to all my teachers and talking to them in the funny English she sometimes uses. I didn't want Mama to be ignored by everybody and left sitting in a corner. I guess maybe I was a little bit ashamed of Mama. But mostly I was ashamed of myself.

"I hate always being different and left out," I told Aunt Waka.

Aunt Waka was folding my kimono and obi on top of my bed, smoothing them out carefully so there would be no wrinkles. She wrapped them up again in the soft rice paper and tied them up just the way they were when she'd brought them. Then she put them aside and sat down on my bed.

"I think I understand how you feel, Rinko," she said in a soft whispery voice. "When I was young and couldn't run or play with my friends, they used to tease me and call me a cripple. They often made me cry."

I thought of the old photograph of Aunt Waka standing with the crutch. "But you were smiling anyway," I said, as if she'd know what I was remembering.

"Just because you're different from other people doesn't mean you're not as good or that you have to dislike yourself," she said.

She looked straight into my eyes, as if she could see all the things that were muddling around inside my brain.

"Rinko, don't ever be ashamed of who you are," she said. "Just be the best person you can. Believe in your own worth. And someday I know you'll be able to feel proud of yourself, even the part of you that's different...the part that's Japanese.

I was still in my slip sitting next to Aunt Waka and wriggling my toes as I listened to her. And then it happened, like a light bulb had been switched on in my head. At that very minute I finally knew what made Aunt Waka seem so special. She was exactly the kind of person she was telling me to be. She believed in herself and she liked herself. But mostly, I guess she was proud of who she was.

cripple a person who is partly disabled or lame

wriggling turning and twisting

Further Reading

Dragonwings. Laurence Yep. This is the story of Moon Shadow, a Chinese immigrant boy who helps his father test their homemade airplane.

Sunday for Sona. Gladys Yessayan Cretan. Sona's work on a sailboat brings her into conflict with her strict Armenian grandmother.

Soy Chicano: I Am a Mexican-American. Bob Fitch and Lynne Fitch. This book tells about Guadalupe Maria Saludo and the Mexican-American farm laborers of California.

Journey Home. Yoshiko Uchida. Yuki and her family return to California after World War II.

L E S S O N   3

A Growing California

THINKING FOCUS

In what ways have technology, trade, and education helped California to grow in the last 25 years?

Key Terms

- export
- import

➤ *The tiny ant holds the even tinier silicon computer chip in its mouth.*

284

The first computers were monsters. They were as big as your classroom, they were slow, and they were expensive. But in 1959, something barely the size of an oatmeal flake changed all that.

It was the silicon chip, and it was born in California. The chip is so tiny that the ant in the picture below is actually holding one in its mouth. The chip is the brain of a computer and has millions of pieces of information stored in its memory. It tells the computer how to solve very difficult problems in a flash. The tiny chip may contain the instructions for playing a computer game, for figuring out math problems, or for building a skyscraper.

The small personal computer changed the world, but it especially changed California. The birthplace of many of the new computers was an area south of San Francisco called Santa Clara Valley. Fruit trees once spread across the valley, and people called it the "Valley of Heavenly Delights." But in the 1970s and 1980s, computer companies replaced mile after mile of plum, apricot, and cherry orchards. Now people call the area "Silicon Valley" because of the chip that made the valley famous.

Technology and the Trade Boom

Computers brought a boom to California industry, just as gold, oil, and aerospace had in the past. People all over the world use computers and computer technology made in Silicon Valley. A Moment in Time on the next page shows how a scientist uses computer technology. The computer boom brought new growth and many jobs to the state.

California teenagers were part of this boom. In the late 1960s, some smart and curious kids began to tinker with computers in their garages and basements. They took computers apart, studied them, and found better ways to build and work with them. Their discoveries helped to make California's computer industry one of the biggest in the world.

Computer technology has helped another big California industry, movie-making. Once again, it was bright young people who made progress possible. They were interested in using computers to create "special effects." These are the tricks that make laser beams, spaceships, and creatures from other planets, like E.T., look like real life. Young moviemakers have dared to try new ideas. Their courage has led to an exciting new period in film making.

Exports and Imports

Computers and Hollywood films are among California's leading **exports**. These are the products that California sells to other countries. Just as the Indians of the past traded food and goods with neighboring tribes, modern countries trade their products with one another.

Across Time & Space

During World War II many of Japan's factories were ruined. But with help from the United States, Japan made a comeback. Now, products from Japan, like cameras, televisions, and cars, are known for their high quality.

▼ *Action! The clap of a slate means the cameras are rolling and the scene can begin.*

HOLLYWOOD

PRODUCTION _____

DIRECTOR _____

CAMERA _____

DATE | SCENE | TAKE

Deep-Sea Cameraman

5:07 A.M., April 7, 1989
Four miles offshore in
Monterey Bay

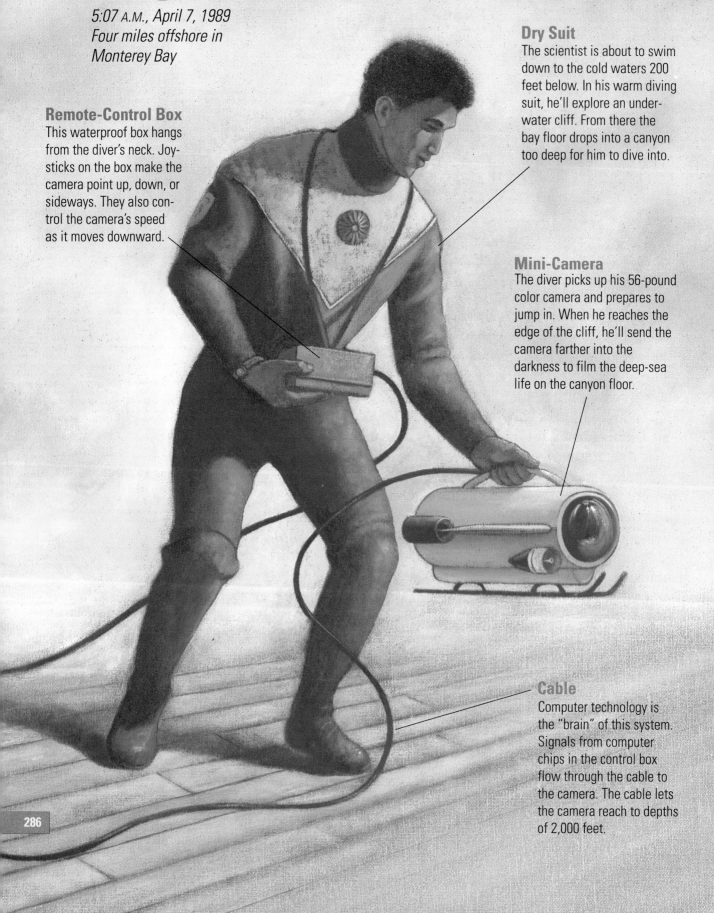

Dry Suit
The scientist is about to swim down to the cold waters 200 feet below. In his warm diving suit, he'll explore an underwater cliff. From there the bay floor drops into a canyon too deep for him to dive into.

Remote-Control Box
This waterproof box hangs from the diver's neck. Joysticks on the box make the camera point up, down, or sideways. They also control the camera's speed as it moves downward.

Mini-Camera
The diver picks up his 56-pound color camera and prepares to jump in. When he reaches the edge of the cliff, he'll send the camera farther into the darkness to film the deep-sea life on the canyon floor.

Cable
Computer technology is the "brain" of this system. Signals from computer chips in the control box flow through the cable to the camera. The cable lets the camera reach to depths of 2,000 feet.

Other California exports include oil, blue jeans, agricultural products, and airplanes.

But California cannot make every product that the people of the state need. So California buys **imports** from other countries. These products come from countries along the Pacific Rim. Many of the cars, cameras, and silk fabrics that Americans buy are imports from countries such as Japan, Korea, and Taiwan. ■

■ *Why are the computer and film industries important to California?*

Education Provides Opportunities

Talented young people have been a big part of the growth and success of California's computer and film industries. California leaders have long known the importance of providing the state's young people with a good education. This is why California created the largest system of higher education in the country. This system is made up of twenty universities.

◄ *This T-shirt is from the University of California at Berkeley. The school, which opened in 1868, is one of California's first universities.*

State leaders have also realized that it is important for everyone to have the chance to go to college. New immigrants, minorities, and children from families with little money may not be able to afford the costs of college. In 1960, state lawmakers passed a new law to help these students. The law said that all high school graduates with good grades can go on to college, whether or not they have the money to pay for it.

California's system of higher education is good for the state and the people, as well as for the rest of the country and the world. Education is a very important part of California's growth, progress, and success. ■

■ *Why did California change its university system in 1960?*

R E V I E W

1. **FOCUS** In what ways have technology, trade, and education helped California to grow in the last 25 years?

2. **CONNECT** What other industries besides computers have brought a boom to California?

3. **ECONOMICS** Why did the tiny computer chip have such a big effect on California?

4. **CRITICAL THINKING** How do you think California's universities benefit minorities, new immigrants, and export trade?

5. **ACTIVITY** How many imports can you find in your home and classroom? Make a list of them. Hint: Start by checking the labels on your clothing and shoes.

Chapter Review

Reviewing Key Terms

boycott (p.274)
civil rights (p.271)
customs (p.279)
export (p.285)
import (p.285)

labor union (p.274)
minority (p.272)
protest (p.272)
refugee (p.277)
strike (p.274)

A. Write the key term for each definition below:

1. a group of workers who join together to protect their rights
2. a small part of the rest of the population
3. a product bought from another country
4. a refusal to buy or eat a product
5. a product sold to other countries
6. habits, practices, or ways of life

B. Choose the key term that best completes each sentence.

1. Cesar Chávez led the grape pickers to _____ until the growers agreed to change working conditions.
2. People in San Francisco _____ed against a supermarket chain because it wouldn't hire blacks.
3. Minorities in the United States have often had to fight for their _____.
4. The Hmong people were _____s who fled their country because of war.
5. People supported Cesar Chávez's labor union by joining in a grape _____.
6. The art, music, and _____ that immigrants bring enrich California's culture.

Exploring Concepts

Group	Cause	Effect
Indians		They took over Alcatraz.
Migrant laborers	Working conditions were poor.	
Blacks		
Asian immigrants		
People who worked with computers	Computer chip was created.	

A. Complete the chart at the left on a separate paper by adding causes and effects. Each cause should be something that happened to the people in each group. Each effect should be something that happened as a result.

B. Write one or two sentences to answer each question below. Use details from this chapter to support your answers.

1. Why did migrant laborers join Cesar Chávez's union?
2. Why do refugees from Southeast Asia and Central America come to live in California?
3. How did the computer chip change the Santa Clara Valley?
4. How does California help its youth?

Reviewing Skills

1. Look at the circle graph at the right. Write the answers to these questions: What is the whole that is divided into parts? How many parts are shown? What does the graph tell you about California as a state that produces movies? What state made the second-largest number of movies in 1988? How many states are included in the part called "Other?"

2. Read the sentences below. On a separate piece of paper, tell which sentences state facts and which sentences state opinions. Write a sentence to explain each answer you give.

   a. Alcatraz is an island located in San Francisco Bay.
   b. You can buy clothes from India in a town near Los Angeles.
   c. Grapes are the most delicious fruit grown in California.

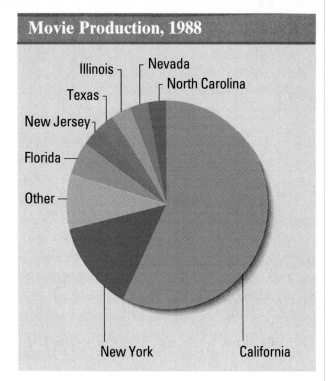

Movie Production, 1988

Illinois — Nevada
Texas — North Carolina
New Jersey —
Florida —
Other —
New York
California

   d. I agree that the mountains in California are prettier than the desert.

Using Critical Thinking

1. There is often more than one way to solve a problem. What were some of the problems in the lives of migrant laborers? What ways did Cesar Chávez think of to solve these problems?

2. In the United States, one civil right is the right to say what you think. How have people used this right to change how they are treated? How is that civil right important to you?

Preparing for Citizenship

1. **INTERVIEWING** Consider this question: What does being a citizen of the United States mean to you? Interview several people to learn their answers to this question. Take notes during the interviews. Write a summary of each person's answer.

2. **COLLABORATIVE LEARNING** As a class, form a welcoming committee to welcome new students to your school. Think especially about students who are immigrants or who have recently arrived in California. Discuss what items you could give these students to help them learn about the school. You might include a school map, the names of students who speak their language, and a "Welcome!" sign autographed by each member of the class. Work in small groups to make the materials you have discussed.

Chapter 13

Decisions for the Future

People like to dream about the future. Their dreams don't always come true, of course. But throughout history, the dreams, visions, and hopes of Californians have helped bring about progress. Decisions we make today will shape the California of tomorrow.

Artist David Em used a computer to make this picture. New computer technology like this can now help people plan for the future.

1900	1930	1960

└ **1941** Los Angeles begins taking water from Mono Lake, causing damage to the lake's environment.

1900

Windmills use the wind to make electricity, instead of burning fuels that make the air dirty. In windfarms near places like Livermore and Palm Springs, fields of windmills give the state part of its electricity and help make California skies cleaner.

How will this California classroom be different in the future?

1990	2020	2050

1990 With the help of the state government, Los Angeles gets ready to put into action the toughest anti-smog plan in the country.

2050

L E S S O N   1

The Past Shapes the Future

Key Terms

* environment
* conservation

▼ *When you step out of the time machine in the year 2050, the first thing you might do is look at your watch to check the day and the time.*

11:33AM
10.16.2050

You have been a traveler in time, visiting some of the most important events in California's history. You were there when the Miwok ground acorns into meal. You saw Father Junípero Serra raise a large cross above the ground to claim California for Christianity and for Spain. You watched a forty-niner strike it rich.

Your journey has taken you through some very sad times. You felt the sorrow of the Californios as they lost their ranchos, and the hunger of Dust Bowl families on the road to California. But there were also many exciting times. When Gusher Charlie danced in the raining oil, you danced with him. And you flew with Chuck Yeager at speeds faster than sound.

These are your memories of times past. But what about times to come? Using your imagination, you can travel into the future. Imagine taking a ride in a time machine. You speed through thousands of days and nights to the year 2050. When the time machine stops, you find yourself in a place you hardly recognize. You have landed in the California of the future.

This is your old neighborhood, all right, but it looks very different. There's a new school where your old one used to be. People pass by you in strange clothing, and the cars look like something out of a science fiction movie. There are no newspapers. Instead, a place called "The Information Center" has rows of computers that show news from all over the state and the world.

What do the newspaper headlines tell you about this future California? Is it a better place to live? Who are the heroes of this time?

The Past Affects the Present

Sometimes events in history seem like a row of dominoes. If you tap the first one, it knocks over the next and the next, until the last one falls. Like the falling dominoes, events in history can be connected. A decision made in the past can set off a chain of events that ripples through the years. California's water wars are an example of this chain of events.

In 1906, when the Los Angeles Aqueduct was being built, people thought their water troubles were over. The *Los Angeles Times* proudly said, "The Victory for Los Angeles Is Complete." But, the decision to build the aqueduct was like that first falling domino. It started a chain of events that continues today.

Aqueduct Brought Harm and Help

Look at the effect the aqueduct decision has had on present-day life in California. Dust storms now swirl over the Owens Valley, where cattle used to graze and crops grew plentifully. But the decision also made tremendous growth possible in Los Angeles. The water supply helped it become a large and important city.

Imagine what might have happened if Los Angeles had decided not to build the aqueduct. The city might have run out of water and become a ghost town. In its place, the Owens Valley, with rich soil and plenty of water, might have become the state's farming center. Quiet valley towns like Bishop or Independence might have become California's biggest cities.

▼ *The larger picture shows part of the aqueduct that brings water to Los Angeles. The dust storms in the small picture are now common in the Owens Valley.*

The Water Search Continues

The next domino in this chain fell in 1941. Los Angeles again needed more water, so the city extended its aqueduct farther north to Mono Lake. Five freshwater streams filled the lake. But the lake itself was very salty. Few people used it. When writer Mark Twain visited the lake in the 1860s, he had nothing nice to say about it. He described the lake in his book *Roughing It:*

> There are no fish in Mono Lake—no frogs, no snakes, no polliwogs—nothing, in fact, that goes to make life desirable. Millions of wild ducks and sea gulls swim about the surface, but no living thing exists *under* the surface, except a white feathery sort of worm.

Actually, it wasn't a worm, but a kind of shrimp. The shrimp provided food for the birds that nested on Negit Island in the middle of Mono Lake. In 1941, people were not worried about what the aqueduct might do to the wildlife of the lake. So the fresh water from four of the lake's five streams was directed into the aqueduct. Now, you can see the effects of this decision. The water level at Mono Lake has dropped more than 40 feet since 1941, making the water even saltier. This threatens to kill the shrimp, which the birds need for food.

Sometimes meeting the needs of people can cause damage to the soil, water, animals, plants, and other parts of nature that make up the **environment**. But in 1941, few people thought about what the aqueduct would do to the environment of Mono Lake. That question was left for the people of today. ■

▼ *This chart shows how much people depend on water. The foods people eat need lots of water to live and grow.*

Water Needed to Grow Crops

Gallons of Water

140	
120	
100	
80	
60	
40	
20	
0	

1 pound of potatoes   1 pound of tomatoes   1 loaf of bread

■ *How did the loss of water change the environment of the Owens Valley and Mono Lake?*

The Present Affects the Future

The chain of dominoes continues as Californians make new decisions that will ripple through the future. In recent years, the people of California have begun to think more

about conservation when they make their decisions. **Conservation** is the protection of natural resources, like water and forests. People now realize that conservation is important for the present and for the future. In 1989, the city of Los Angeles agreed to take less water from Mono Lake to help protect, or conserve, it. In another important decision, the city promised to share some of the Owens River water with the people of the Owens Valley.

Then where will the city find more water? Will new water sources bring more damage to the environment? This question will continue far into the future.

In addition to environmental issues, your generation will decide many other questions that will affect the people of the future. Californians have a lot of power to solve problems. The rest of this chapter will look at how people can make California better. One way is through state government, which is explored in Lesson 2. Another way is to get lots of people involved in an issue. Lesson 3 looks at the power of people working together. It also shows how much just one person can do to change the world.

The work is not easy, but it can be very exciting. And the people of the future—the people you visited in your time machine—may thank you for it. ■

■ *How will today's decisions on water conservation affect the future?*

R E V I E W

1. **FOCUS** How has bringing water to Los Angeles affected the city's growth as well as California's environment?

2. **CONNECT** How have Californians' feelings about the environment changed from 1906 to today?

3. **ECONOMICS** Name three kinds of natural resources that California needs to conserve.

4. **CRITICAL THINKING** Do you think Mono Lake was valuable, even though people didn't use it very much? Explain your answer.

5. **WRITING ACTIVITY** Pretend you've traveled in a time machine to the year 2050. Write a story about what you saw on your journey.

Decisions for the Future

L E S S O N   2

California Fights Smog

THINKING FOCUS

How does state government help solve problems?

Key Terms

- legislative branch
- governor
- executive branch
- judicial branch
- pollution

➤ *The mountains around Los Angeles keep much of the smog trapped over the city.*

When the Spanish explorer Cabrillo entered San Pedro Bay in 1542, he came upon a strange sight. The land ahead was covered with a blanket of smoke so thick that he could barely see the mountains in the distance. Cabrillo named these waters *La Bahia de Los Fumos,* which is Spanish for "The Bay of Smokes." The smoke that the Spanish explorer saw was from Indian fires.

Those fires died out long ago. But today the modern city of Los Angeles is still wrapped in a heavy haze that hides the San Bernardino Mountains. The haze looks like a mixture of smoke and fog. People have named it smog.

Smog comes mainly from the burning of fuel, like the gasoline burned in car engines. As Los Angeles grew and spread out, people needed their cars more than ever. Now the city has the country's worst smog problem.

People have come up with some wild ideas for getting rid of the city's smog. One plan was to dig tunnels through the mountains, and then put giant fans in the tunnels. The fans would pull the smog through the tunnels and blow it over to the other side of the mountains. Couldn't anyone come up with a better way?

How State Government Works

Smog doesn't just stay in one place. The winds can spread it for miles. So the smog caused by cars, factories— even backyard barbecues—affects most of California. When a problem affects the whole state, the people of the state have to work together to find a solution.

That's why California has a state government. The people who run the state, or govern it, make up its government. That includes everybody from the top leaders you see in the news to the state police officers on the roads. Many schools, hospitals, and prisons are run by the state government. The state builds freeways, helps needy people, and handles big problems like smog.

Hundreds of thousands of people work in the state government. But most of the state's highest officials work in Sacramento. This northern city is the capital, or government center, of California.

California's state government is divided into three parts called branches. The **legislative branch** is made up of lawmakers chosen by the citizens of California. Members of

▲ *The legislative branch meets to decide on state laws. They do their work in the state capitol in Sacramento.*

How Do We Know?

HISTORY *The state government produces mountains of paperwork. One law alone can be as thick as this book. All of California's official documents are kept in a place called the state archives (AR kyvz).*

Three Branches of State Government

Legislative Branch
Citizens elect the members of the legislative branch. Legislators help to make new laws. Legislators speak and act for the people who elect them. They also help to decide how the state will spend its money.

Executive Branch
The governor heads the executive branch. He or she is the highest official in state government, and is in charge of seeing that laws are carried out. State agencies are part of the executive branch.

Judical Branch
State courts and judges decide if the law has been broken, and they punish lawbreakers. They also decide if a law agrees with the state's constitution. The supreme court heads the judicial branch. It is the state's highest court.

the legislative branch, legislators, write bills. Bills are ideas for a new law that will help the citizens of the state. Some legislators will be for a new law and some will be against it. So they debate, or argue, the bill's good and bad points. Then they vote on whether or not to make the bill a law.

If most of the legislators vote in favor of a suggested law, the legislative branch passes it to the governor for approval. A law becomes official when the governor signs it. The **governor** is the highest official in state government. He or she is head of the **executive branch.** This branch is made up of departments that make sure the state laws are being carried out. For instance, there are departments in charge of working to solve the state's smog problem.

Sometimes people think that a new law is not needed or is not fair. They have the right to challenge the law in court. This involves the **judicial branch** of the state government, which is made up of courts and judges. California courts decide on questions like whether a law is fair. If a law is unfair, the courts can throw out the law. State courts also punish people who break the laws. To learn more about state government, see the Minipedia, page 315. ■

■ Name the three branches of state government and explain what each branch does.

UNDERSTANDING REPRESENTATION

Once upon a time, California had a king. He ruled the Kingdom of California and all the people in it. If he was in a good mood, he made good laws. But when he was in a bad mood, he made terrible laws!

This is a fairy tale, of course. The state of California never had a king. Giving all the power to one person would not be wise. California has a better system of government. It's called representation.

The citizens of California choose people to represent them—that is, to take action and make decisions for them. They choose their representatives by voting for them in an election. California citizens elect the members of the state Legislature. They also elect the governor and many judges.

Representation works well when people elect honest men and women who will make good decisions. Voters need to know what's going on around the state. Then they'll know if their representatives are making good decisions on the issues. If you have strong views on an issue, you should let your representatives know how you feel. That way you'll have a voice in how your government is run.

State Government Gets Tough on Smog

One of the most important and difficult problems that California's state government must solve is smog. It is a serious problem in many parts of California. Smog is harmful to people and plants. Scientists say that smog damage to crops costs the state almost one billion dollars each year. The picture on this page shows how smog can harm plants.

The geography of Los Angeles is a big part of the smog problem. The city lies in a bowl-shaped piece of land called a basin. The tall mountains surrounding Los Angeles form the sides of the bowl. They trap the smog produced by the cars, factories, people, and businesses in the city.

Many people who live in Los Angeles are used to seeing smog covering their city. But visitors and newcomers are surprised when they see the thick blanket of smog overhead. In 1979, one visiting reporter wrote a description of the yellowish haze that covers Los Angeles.

From the time it came up that day, the sun was … a reddish smear in the smog. By midmorning the air was like mustard gas. Nothing stirred up there. Around five o'clock, Los Angeles lay… under a layer of smog so thick and noxious [poisonous] that even those with healthy hearts and lungs were cautioned to stay indoors.

▼ In 1982, scientists did an experiment to see how plants grew in clean air and how they grew in smoggy air. The Timothy plant, shown below, grew to several inches below its normal height in smoggy air.

Smog-Control Laws

The smog in Los Angeles and other California cities caused the state government to take action. In 1960, California legislators passed the nation's first smog-control act. The law said that all new cars and trucks must be made with a device that trapped the pollution from engine exhaust. **Pollution** is the smoke, dirt, and gases that make the air unclean and smoggy. More recent laws have made car exhaust become even cleaner.

California's smog-control laws have been very successful. Today there are eight million cars in Los Angeles. They add about as much smog to the air as the two-and-a-half million cars did in the 1950s. This is because cars then had no pollution-control devices in their engines. Also, today's cars are built to burn less gas than the bigger cars of the 1950s.

299

➤ *This solar-powered car runs on energy from the sun. With the help of state government, many Californians may one day be driving nonpolluting cars.*

The "L.A. Plan"

Each year a half million people move to California. Most of these people drive cars. State lawmakers must continue to look at new ways to solve the smog problem. In the late 1980s, legislators made a new plan to cut down on smog in the Los Angeles region even more by 2007.

The "L.A. plan," as it is called, is 5,500 pages long and stands three feet high. It puts controls on almost every cause of smog. Among other things, the plan will require that car engines send out even fewer poisonous fumes. Many drivers will be forced to use cleaner forms of fuel by 1998. Also, when people must drive long distances to work, the plan will require three or four people from the same office to share one car for the ride to and from work.

This plan will affect every citizen and every company in the Los Angeles area. Each branch of government will take part in making sure that the rules of the plan are followed and that the changes are fair. With this tough new plan, the state continues to serve as an example for the rest of the country in its fight against smog. ■

■ *How is state government fighting the smog problem in California?*

R E V I E W

1. **FOCUS** How does state government help solve problems?
2. **CONNECT** How might the state government help solve California's water problems?
3. **SOCIAL SYSTEMS** In what ways might the "L.A. plan" change the lives of people living in the Los Angeles area?
4. **CRITICAL THINKING** What would it be like if there were only one branch of state government and the members of that branch were not elected by the citizens of California?
5. **WRITING ACTIVITY** Write a letter to the governor of California, stating your view on an issue you think is important.

Chapter 13

Looking for Information

Here's Why

Knowing how to find the right information will help you to write good reports. Suppose you want to write a research report on smog. You can look for information in the library. Then you must decide if this information fits your topic and if it is correct.

Here's How

You can learn about smog by reading nonfiction books. For specific facts about smog, you can also look in different types of reference books.

An almanac gives up-to-date facts. It is published every year.

An atlas contains many different kinds of maps.

Encyclopedias have information on people, places, things, and events. The topics are arranged alphabetically.

A biographical dictionary gives facts about famous people.

A geographical dictionary has facts about places throughout the world.

When researching information about your topic, ask these questions:

1. Does this information tell me something important or interesting about my topic?
2. What other references can I use?
3. Are these the most up-to-date facts?
4. What information do other books give about the same topic?

Try It

Carbon monoxide, which is a poisonous gas, adds to the problem of smog. The circle graph to the right tells where carbon monoxide in the air comes from.

The graph shows five sources. Which source is the largest? Which source is the second largest?

This graph is from a 1983 encyclopedia. What other books could you look in to find out about smog? Where could you find information that is more up to date? Which type of reference book in the list at the left would not be at all useful for a report on smog?

Apply It

Read "State Government Gets Tough on Smog" on page 299. Then find three books in the library with information about smog. Look for one nonfiction book and two reference books. Ask yourself the questions about looking for information. Write your answers. Share your facts about smog with the class.

Sources of Carbon Monoxide

Other fires and chemical sprays
Industry
Trash and leaf fires
Fuel burning in homes, offices, and power plants
Motor vehicles

LESSON 3

People Take Action

THINKING
FOCUS

In what ways can individuals and groups work to improve California's future?

Key Terms

- endangered species

On a chalkboard, draw a line nine feet long. Now imagine a bird with wings that stretch nine feet as it soars over mountaintops. Long ago, Indians worshiped this bird. They believed its flapping wings created thunder and that lightning flashed in its eyes. This animal is the largest flying bird in North America—the California condor.

California condors almost disappeared from the earth. Over the years many were killed by hunters. Others died as growing cities destroyed their natural environment. So in 1987, scientists trapped a few of the remaining birds so they could be raised in protected areas. Two years later, four new condor chicks were hatched at the San Diego Zoo. The birds are being cared for, so that one day they may be returned to the wild.

This work is expensive. Some money comes from the government, but that's not enough. In a San Diego program called "Cans for Critters," kids collect used cans and donate the deposit money to protect animals.

Who would think that picking up a soda can could make such a difference? Cans for Critters shows how much power people have when they work together.

➤ *San Diego Zoo keeper Don Sterner feeds baby condors using a puppet that looks like a mother condor.*

The Power of Many People

In Lesson 2 you saw how people in state government work to solve problems. But you don't have to be in government to get things done. Many groups of people, like the children in San Diego, are trying to make California better.

Groups worked together in California's Coachella Valley, home to an odd little animal called the fringe-toed lizard. The lizard runs across the desert sand on feet that act like snowshoes. It can also dive into the sand and swim like a fish in water.

In the 1920s, golf courses, homes, and hotels began to spread across the Coachella Valley. By 1980, the fringe-toed lizard had become an **endangered species**. That meant it was in danger of disappearing forever, like the condor. Some people wanted all new construction to stop. Builders wanted to keep building because many people wanted to move to the valley.

Finally, everyone decided to work together. Scientists, government officials, builders, environmental groups, and the people who lived in the valley came up with a plan. In 1986, they divided up the Coachella Valley. Part of the land was kept for the builders, and part was set aside for the lizard. The agreement was so good that it set an example for groups across the country. ■

Across Time & Space

In Tennessee, concern about a tiny fish called the snail darter delayed the building of Tellico Dam in the 1970s. The issue showed the need to protect even the smallest creatures to keep nature's balance.

▼ *The Coachella Valley Preserve was set aside as a permanent home for the fringe-toed lizard, shown at left.*

Coachella Valley Preserve

0 — 50 mi.
0 — 50 km
Lambert Conformal Conic Projection

Oregon | Idaho
Nevada
California
Los Angeles
San Diego
PACIFIC OCEAN

MOJAVE DESERT

COAST RANGES

San Bernardino
Los Angeles
COACHELLA VALLEY
Palm Springs
Coachella Valley Preserve
Indio
Route 10
Colorado River Aqueduct
Colorado River
San Diego Aqueduct
Salton Sea
IMPERIAL VALLEY

PACIFIC OCEAN

San Diego

MEXICO

34°N
33°N
119°W
118°W

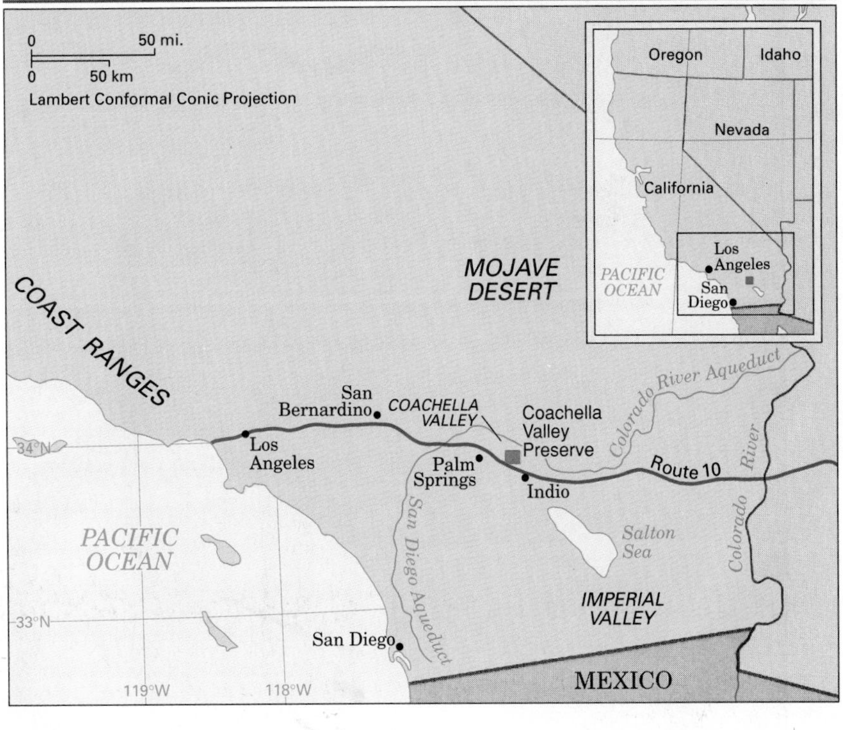

The Power of One Person

But you're just one California fourth-grader. How can you have an effect on anything? Believe it or not, you're already making decisions that affect California. A Closer Look at a You and the Environment, on the next page, explains what happens when you use or buy different items.

■ *How did different groups benefit from the Coachella Valley solution?*

303

You and the Environment

What you do every day changes the world you live in. Let's peek inside a student's backpack to see how the choices you make affect the land, water, and air of your environment.

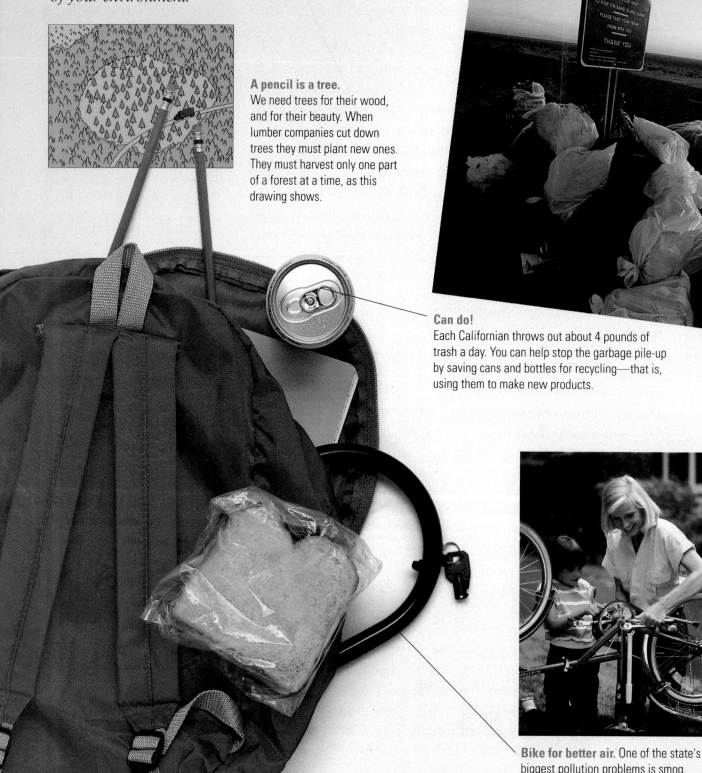

A pencil is a tree. We need trees for their wood, and for their beauty. When lumber companies cut down trees they must plant new ones. They must harvest only one part of a forest at a time, as this drawing shows.

Can do! Each Californian throws out about 4 pounds of trash a day. You can help stop the garbage pile-up by saving cans and bottles for recycling—that is, using them to make new products.

Bike for better air. One of the state's biggest pollution problems is smog. When you bike or walk instead of ride in a car, you're battling smog.

At the Mt. Palomar observatory in the mountains north of San Diego, California scientists photograph the world and the universe around us.

The Earth from space. Will it be a better place in the future?

Sometimes your choices help put people to work in industry. But some items that you buy also create pollution. You can make choices that help to stop pollution. This means that you have the power to bring about change.

In San Diego, children's love of animals moved them to help. What kinds of issues do you care about? Perhaps you love the water. Then you can help make California's water plentiful and clean. Start with individual action. Decide to take shorter showers and to turn off faucets, so less clean water will be wasted. Do not throw trash into rivers and lakes. Next, take group action. Start a project in your school to save water.

Continue by finding out what state government is doing to stop water pollution. Then you can write to your representative to show your support for clean water. You'll find that you can make decisions that affect your home, your school, your neighborhood, your state, and your world.

When you first opened this book many months ago, you saw a big blue ball. That was the earth. When you care for California, you are helping to care for the earth. In 2050, when the space shuttles of the future circle high above the earth, the astronauts may look down on a world that is a little cleaner, a little healthier, and a little nicer because you helped make it that way. ■

■ How can people's decisions affect the future of California?

R E V I E W

1. **FOCUS** In what ways can individuals and groups work to improve California's future?

2. **CONNECT** How does Lesson 1 show Californians learning to work together on a problem?

3. **CITIZENSHIP** How can you have an effect on water pollution?

4. **CRITICAL THINKING** What kind of job would you like to have when you grow up, and how do you think that job will affect the future?

5. **WRITING ACTIVITY** Pretend you are a character in this book. Write an autobiography that tells how you changed California's future.

305

Decisions for the Future

Planning a Project

Here's Why

By having a discussion, a group of people can decide on a project to do together. When people work as a group, they can do jobs that one person alone could not do. Working together, people can help to protect the environment.

Here's How

To have a discussion in a group, follow these guidelines.

1. Keep the discussion topic in mind, and stick to it.
2. Join in the discussion. Give your ideas, and ask questions about points that are not clear to you.
3. Listen politely to the ideas of others. Wait your turn quietly. Do not interrupt when someone else is speaking.
4. Think before you speak. Speak so that everyone can understand you.

Mr. Nakamura's fourth-grade class wanted to help protect the environment. They had a discussion to decide on a project. As you read their comments, keep the discussion guidelines in mind.

Jill: Let's tell people to recycle paper.
Lee: That's a silly idea!
Jo: I think —
Sam: Did you read the comics today?
Jill: What did you want to say, Jo?
Carlo: Jill's idea about recycling paper is good. How could we tell people, Jill?

Some students are following the guidelines. Who is not? Explain.

Try It

Have a discussion with four or five students in a group. Discuss ways to inform your neighbors and friends why it is important to recycle paper. Include an explanation of what happens when paper is recycled. Make sure that everyone follows the guidelines for discussion.

Apply It

Meet with five classmates to discuss a project you can do to improve the environment in your community. Follow the discussion guidelines. When you have decided on a project, plan how to do it. Share your plan with the class, and put your plan into action.

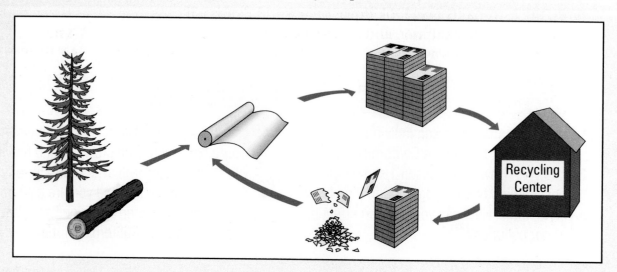

Chapter Review

Reviewing Key Terms

conservation (p.295)
endangered species
  (p. 303)
environment (p. 294)
executive branch
  (p.298)

governor (p. 298)
judicial branch (p. 298)
legislative branch (p. 297)
pollution (p. 299)

will disappear from the earth.

4. People in the ___ of state government vote on new laws for the state.
5. The ___ of the state is the highest official in state government.
6. Courts and judges are in the ___ of state government.

A. Choose the key term that best completes each sentence.

1. Taking care of the ___ is as important as taking care of the needs of people.
2. The ___ of California's state government is in charge of seeing that laws are carried out.
3. Unless we work to protect it, an ___

B. Write the definition of each key term below. Then write one or two sentences telling how the four terms are related.

1. conservation
2. endangered species
3. environment
4. pollution

Exploring Concepts

A. Complete the chart below on a separate piece of paper. Use details from the chapter to answer the questions.

B. For each event below, write a list of good effects and a list of bad effects.
  1. In 1941, the city of Los Angeles began

to use water from Mono Lake.
2. Many people in California prefer to travel by car.
3. Homes, hotels, and golf courses have been built in the Coachella Valley.
4. Endangered species used to living in the wild are being cared for in a zoo.

Problem	What caused the problem?	How is it being solved?	Who took action?	What has been the result?
Smog				
Animal species in danger of dying out				

Reviewing Skills

1. Read the five questions below. Then decide what kind of book you would use to answer each question. On a separate sheet of paper, write whether the book would be an almanac, an atlas, an encyclopedia, a biographical dictionary, or a geographical dictionary.
   a. When and where was the Spanish explorer Cabrillo born?
   b. How does an aqueduct work?
   c. What roads lead to Mono Lake?
   d. How high are the San Bernardino Mountains?
   e. How many people lived in San Diego in 1982?

2. Suppose you are having a group discussion about state government. You hear the term *legislator* used, and you do not understand what the word means. What should you do?

3. Pretend that you are going to interview a person who cares for the California condors in the San Diego Zoo. Think about what you would like to know about the job and about the birds. Then prepare a list of questions you would ask.

4. What type of books could you use to find out more information about the California condor?

Using Critical Thinking

1. Like the government of the United States, the government of California has three branches. Why is having three branches of government better than having only one?

2. The first Californians were Indians who lived closely with the land. If these early people could see California today, what might they think of how the land has been treated?

3. Because Los Angeles is built on a desert, the city has always had trouble finding enough water to meet the needs of its people. What solutions to this problem can you think of for the future?

Preparing for Citizenship

1. ART ACTIVITY Find out about a California animal that is an endangered species. Make a poster that shows information about the animal. Draw a picture of what the animal looks like, or find a picture in a magazine to glue on your poster. Also show where the animal lives, what it eats, and why it is special. Include a picture of what has caused the species to become endangered.

2. COLLABORATIVE LEARNING As a class, make an album of pictures that show some of the history of California. Using the chapters of this book as a guide, discuss what important events you will include. Then work in small groups to illustrate the events. Some students in each group can draw a picture for each event. Others can write two or three sentences to explain each picture.

   When all the groups are finished, put the pictures and explanations together in an album called *The History of California*. Choose one person to make a cover for the book. You can share your class's album with other students by putting it in the school library.

Decisions for the Future

Time/Space Databank

California in brief

Symbols of California

The state flag, adopted in 1911, shows a grizzly bear and a single red star. On the state seal, adopted in 1849, a grizzly bear representing California stands next to Minerva, the Roman goddess of wisdom. A sheaf of wheat and clusters of grapes symbolize agriculture, and a miner laboring with a pick stands for mining. Ships represent commerce. The peaks in the background symbolize the Sierra Nevada.

State flag

State seal

California (brown) ranks third in size among all the states and is the largest of the Pacific Coast States (yellow).

General information

Statehood: Sept. 9, 1850, the 31st state.
State abbreviations: Calif. (traditional); CA (postal).
State motto: *Eureka* (I Have Found It).
State song: "I Love You, California." Words by F. B. Silverwood; music by A. F. Frankenstein.

The State Capitol is in Sacramento, California's capital since 1854. Monterey, San Jose, Vallejo, Benicia, and San Francisco were temporary capitals between 1850 and 1854.

Land and climate

Area: 158,706 sq. mi. (411,049 km²), including 2,407 sq. mi. (6,234 km²) of inland water but excluding 69 sq. mi. (179 km²) of Pacific coastal water.
Elevation: *Highest*—Mount Whitney, 14,495 ft. (4,418 m) above sea level. *Lowest*—282 ft. (86 m) below sea level in Death Valley.
Coastline: 840 mi. (1,352 km).
Record high temperature: 134° F. (57° C) at Greenland Ranch in Death Valley on July 10, 1913.
Record low temperature: −45° F. (−43° C) at Boca, near Truckee, on Jan. 20, 1937.
Average July temperature: 75° F. (24° C).
Average January temperature: 44° F. (7° C).
Average yearly precipitation: 22 in. (56 cm).

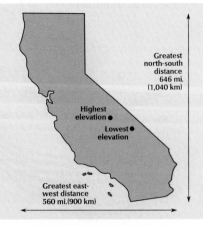

Greatest north-south distance 646 mi. (1,040 km)

Highest elevation ●

Lowest ● elevation

Greatest east-west distance 560 mi. (900 km)

Important dates

Junípero Serra established the first Franciscan mission in California near present-day San Diego.

James W. Marshall discovered gold at Sutter's Mill.

| 1542 | 1769 | 1846 | 1848 |

Juan Rodríguez Cabrillo, a Portuguese sailor employed by Spain, explored San Diego Bay.

United States forces conquered California during the Mexican War.

State bird
California valley quail

State flower
Golden poppy

State tree
California
redwood

People

Population: 23,667,826 (1980 census)
Rank among the states: 1st
Density: 149 persons per sq. mi. (58 per km²), U.S. average 67 per sq. mi. (26 per km²)
Distribution: 91 per cent urban, 9 per cent rural
Largest cities in California

Los Angeles	2,968,579
San Diego	875,538
San Francisco	678,974
San Jose	629,531
Long Beach	361,355
Oakland	339,337

Source: U.S. Bureau of the Census.

Population trend

*All figures are census figures except 1985, which is an estimate.

Millions

Year	Population*
1985	26,365,000
1980	23,667,826
1970	19,971,069
1960	15,717,204
1950	10,586,223
1940	6,907,387
1930	5,677,251
1920	3,426,861
1910	2,377,549
1900	1,485,053
1890	1,213,398
1880	864,694
1870	560,247
1860	379,994
1850	92,597

Source: U.S. Bureau of the Census.

Economy

Chief products

Agriculture: milk, beef cattle, greenhouse and nursery products, cotton, grapes, hay, tomatoes.
Manufacturing: electrical equipment, transportation equipment, food products, machinery.
Mining: petroleum, natural gas.

Gross state product

Value of goods and services produced in 1986, $533,816,000,000. *Services* include community, business, and personal services; finance; government; trade; and transportation, communication, and utilities. *Industry* includes construction, manufacturing, and mining. *Agriculture* includes agriculture, fishing, and forestry.

Source: U.S. Bureau of Economic Analysis.

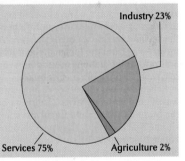

Industry 23%

Services 75%

Agriculture 2%

Government

State government

Governor: 4-year term
State senators: 40; 4-year terms
Members of the Assembly: 80; 2-year terms
Counties: 58

Federal government

United States senators: 2
United States representatives: 45
Electoral votes: 47

Sources of information

Tourism: California Office of Tourism, P.O. Box 9278, Van Nuys, CA 91409
Economy: Department of Finance, 1025 P Street, Sacramento, CA 95814
Government: Secretary of the Senate, Room 3044, State Capitol, Sacramento, CA 95814
History: Secretary of the Senate, Room 3044, State Capitol, Sacramento, CA 95814

International expositions at San Diego and San Francisco marked the opening of the Panama Canal.

California became the state with the largest population.

1850	1915	1960	1963

California became the 31st state on September 9.

The state legislature provided funds to bring water from the northern mountains to coastal cities and southern California.

Earthquake

Earthquake is a sudden shaking or shock in the earth. There may be as many as a million earthquakes in a single year. Most of them take place beneath the surface of the sea. Few of these cause any damage. But those that occur near large cities cause much damage and loss of life, especially if the cities rest on soft ground. The energy released by a large earthquake may equal that of about 200 million short tons (180 million metric tons) of TNT. Its energy may be 10,000 times as great as that of the first atomic bomb. The strength of an earthquake is often measured on a scale of numbers called the *Richter scale.* The largest earthquakes are commonly measured using figures called *strain-energy magnitudes.*

Large earthquakes cause violent motions of the earth's surface. Coastal earthquakes may cause huge sea waves that sweep up on land and add to the general destruction. Such waves often occur in the Pacific Ocean, where coastal earthquakes are most common. Geologists use a Japanese word, *tsunami,* for these destructive waves.

Why earthquakes occur. According to the *plate tectonics* theory, the earth's surface consists of seven large rigid plates and about as many smaller ones that are in slow, continuous motion. This motion squeezes and stretches rocks at the plates' edges. If the force becomes too great, the rocks *rupture* (break) and shift, causing an earthquake. Most of these ruptures, or *faults,* lie beneath the surface. But some, such as the San Andreas Fault in California, are visible.

Much of the energy released in an earthquake travels away from the fault in waves called *seismic waves.* Near the *focus* (place where the rupture begins), vibrations of the seismic waves can be destructive. As the waves travel away from the focus, their vibrations weaken. Seismographic stations around the world record seismic waves from a great earthquake.

Seismic waves consist of compressional waves, shear waves, and surface waves. *Compressional waves* are really sound waves, and travel at a speed of 5 miles (8 kilometers) a second. They pass through the earth in about 20 minutes. The rocks vibrate in the direction traveled by the wave from inside the earth. This causes the

Causes and effects of earthquakes

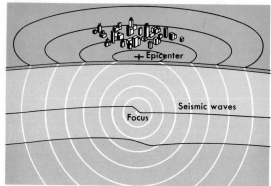

WORLD BOOK diagram by Mas Nakagawa

An earthquake occurs when forces inside the earth cause a sudden rock movement. The site of the movement is the quake's *focus.* Seismic waves created by the quake are strongest at the *epicenter,* the point on the surface above the focus.

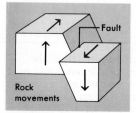 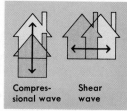

WORLD BOOK diagrams

An earthquake focus is centered in rocks that have broken and slid past one another. Geologists call such places *faults.*

Seismic waves include *compressional waves,* which shake buildings vertically, and *shear waves,* which move them horizontally.

rocks to change volume. *Shear waves* travel about half as fast as compressional waves. The rocks vibrate at right angles to the direction traveled by the wave from inside the earth. This causes the rocks to change shape.

Strongest earthquakes since 1900

Year	Location	Magnitude*	Year	Location	Magnitude*
1905	Northern India	8.0	1958	Southeastern Alaska	8.1
	Western Mongolia	8.4		Kuril Islands	8.4
1906	San Francisco	8.1	1960	Southern Chile	9.7
1920	Gansu, China	8.4	1963	Kuril Islands	8.3
1923	Kamchatka, Soviet Union	8.5	1964	Southern Alaska	9.2
1933	Pacific Ocean floor, near Japan	8.3	1965	Aleutian Islands	8.5
1934	Nepal	8.3	1966	Western Peru	8.0
1938	Banda Sea floor, near Indonesia	8.6	1968	Pacific Ocean floor, near Japan	8.1
1939	Eastern Turkey	8.0	1969	Kuril Islands	8.0
1944	Southern Honshu, Japan	8.0	1970	Western Peru	7.9
1946	Aleutian Islands	8.3	1972	Southeastern Alaska	7.9
	Pacific Ocean floor, near Japan	8.0	1976	Mindanao, Philippines	7.9
1949	Queen Charlotte Islands, British Columbia	8.2	1977	Lesser Sunda Islands, Indonesia	8.8
1950	Assam, India	8.8	1983	New Ireland, Papua New Guinea	7.9
1952	Pacific Ocean floor, Japan	8.7	1985	Mexico City	8.1
	Kamchatka, Soviet Union	8.9	1986	Aleutian Islands	8.3
1957	Aleutian Islands	9.1		Kermadec Islands, South Pacific	8.4
	Southwestern Mongolia	8.1	1989	Pacific Ocean floor, near New Zealand	8.5

*Magnitudes given are strain-energy magnitudes, which measure strong earthquakes more accurately than Richter magnitudes.
Sources: G. Purcaru and H. Berckhemer in *Tectonophysics* 49 (1978), © Elsevier Scientific Publishing Company, Amsterdam; U.S. National Geophysical Data Center.

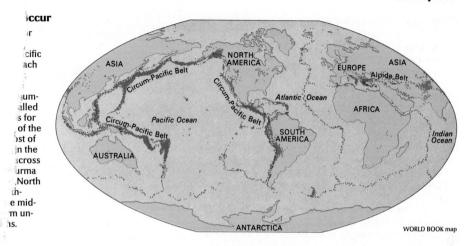

WORLD BOOK map

...ccur

...r

...cific
...ach

...jum-
...alled
...s for
...of the
...st of
...n the
...cross
...urma
...North
...th-
...e mid-
...m un-
...hs.

...el slightly slower than shear waves. ...to the earth's surface in much the same way that ocean waves are limited to the surface of the sea. By measuring the speed of seismic waves, scientists can obtain some idea of the kinds of rocks that are found below the surface of the earth.

Location of earthquakes. Seismologists use the time intervals between different seismic waves to compute the distance of the focus from a seismographic station (see **Seismograph**). To locate the focus more precisely, they draw circles on a map to show the distance of the earthquake from several stations. The earthquake is located where the circles intersect. The focus of most earthquakes occurs less than 25 miles (40 kilometers) beneath the surface of the earth. Some may occur at depths as great as 400 miles (640 kilometers).

Most earthquakes occur along the boundaries where plates separate, collide, or slide past each other. These places are the earth's most geologically active regions. Volcanoes, new mountain ranges, and deep ocean trenches—in addition to earthquakes—occur along the edges of the plates. In contrast, the flat parts of the continents and sea floor are stable regions that have few quakes. Most earthquakes take place within two belts. The *circum-Pacific* belt lies along plate boundaries around the Pacific Ocean. The *Alpide* belt follows plate boundaries across southern Europe and Asia.

Prediction of earthquakes is not yet possible, but scientists are optimistic that they will find a method. Scientists know the regions where earthquakes are likely to occur. They may use the history of previous earthquakes to estimate how often a certain region may expect earthquakes. For example, California may expect a catastrophic earthquake once every 50 to 100 years. In such regions, engineers have developed buildings to withstand the severest earthquakes.

Seismologists are closely monitoring selected areas where large earthquakes are expected. They hope to record small earthquakes or distortions in the ground which might signal that a large earthquake is about to occur. However, progress toward successful earthquake prediction is slow.

Damage by earthquakes. Most earthquakes pass unnoticed. Light earthquakes may be mistaken for the rumbling of a truck. But large, destructive earthquakes do occur from time to time. Most of the destruction takes place shortly after the first tremor is felt.

Most deaths and damage from an earthquake result from the collapse of buildings or other structures. The earthquake may loosen the bricks in a chimney or cause a wall or roof to cave in. Falling material may kill or injure someone or damage other property. Earthquakes may also topple bridges, break water pipes, cut electric lines, and rupture gas mains. Fire is one of the greatest dangers in an earthquake.

San Andreas Fault, *SAN an DRAY uhs,* is a long fracture in the earth's crust marked by a zone of disrupted land in California. The fault extends more than 750 miles (1,210 kilometers) from off the coast of northwestern California to the southeastern part of the state near the Mexican border.

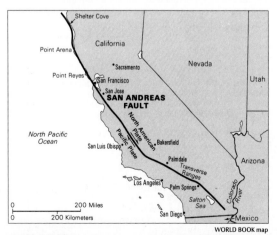

WORLD BOOK map

The San Andreas Fault is a fracture in the earth's crust that extends through much of California. Sudden crustal movements along the fault have resulted in severe earthquakes.

Panama Canal

Panama Canal is a waterway that cuts across the Isthmus of Panama and links the Atlantic Ocean and the Pacific Ocean. It ranks as one of the greatest engineering achievements in the world. Upon its completion in 1914, the canal shortened a ship's voyage between New York City and San Francisco to less than 5,200 miles (8,370 kilometers). Previously, ships making this trip had to travel around South America—a distance of more than 13,000 miles (20,900 kilometers).

The United States built the Panama Canal at a cost of about $380 million. Thousands of laborers worked on it for about 10 years, using steam shovels and dredges to cut through jungles, hills, and swamps. They had to conquer such tropical diseases as malaria and yellow fever.

The Panama Canal extends 50.72 miles (81.63 kilometers) from Limón Bay on the Atlantic Ocean to the Bay of Panama on the Pacific Ocean. A ship traveling through the canal from the Atlantic to the Pacific sails from northwest to southeast. The ship actually leaves the canal 27 miles (43 kilometers) east of where it entered.

The canal has three sets of waterfilled chambers called *locks,* which raise and lower ships from one level to another. The locks were built in pairs to allow ships to pass through in both directions at the same time. Each lock has a usable length of 1,000 feet (300 meters), a width of 110 feet (34 meters), and a depth of about 70 feet (21 meters). The dimensions of the locks limit the size of ships that can use the canal. For example, commercial supertankers and the supercarriers of the U.S. Navy cannot pass through it.

A 1903 treaty between the United States and Panama gave the United States the right to build and operate the waterway. The United States also received the right to govern an area of land called the Panama Canal Zone on both sides of the canal. For many years, Panama tried to gain control of the canal and the zone. In 1977, Panama and the United States signed a new treaty. As a result of this treaty, Panama received territorial jurisdiction over the zone in 1979. The United States kept administrative control of some military installations and areas necessary to operate and defend the canal. The treaty also provided for Panama to take control of the operations of the canal and its associated military installations on Dec. 31, 1999. A second treaty gave the United States the right to defend the neutrality of the canal.

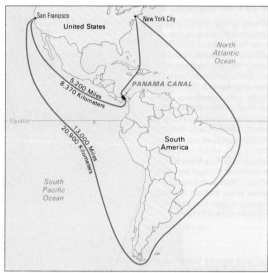

WORLD BOOK map

The Panama Canal shortens sea voyages between the Atlantic and Pacific oceans. A ship sailing between New York City and San Francisco saves about 7,800 miles (12,600 kilometers) by using the canal rather than traveling around South America.

Importance of the canal

The Panama Canal is a vital commercial and military waterway. About 12,000 oceangoing vessels travel through it yearly—an average of about 33 per day. The ships carry about 168 million short tons (152 million metric tons) of cargo annually.

About 70 per cent of the ships that sail through the canal are traveling to or from U.S. ports. Other frequent users of the canal include Canada and Japan.

The United States maintains several military bases to defend the canal. The U.S. Southern Command, which directs all U.S. military units in the Caribbean area, has its headquarters near the canal. Huge quantities of war materials and thousands of troops passed through the canal during World War II, the Korean War, and the Vietnam War.

A profile of the Panama Canal shows a ship's course through the waterway. A ship from the Atlantic Ocean is lifted by the Gatun Locks to the level of Gatun Lake. The ship crosses the lake and passes through the Gaillard Cut channel. The Pedro Miguel and Miraflores locks lower it to the level of the Pacific. The raising and lowering process is reversed for a ship from the Pacific.

WORLD BOOK diagram

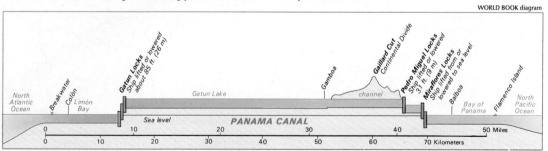

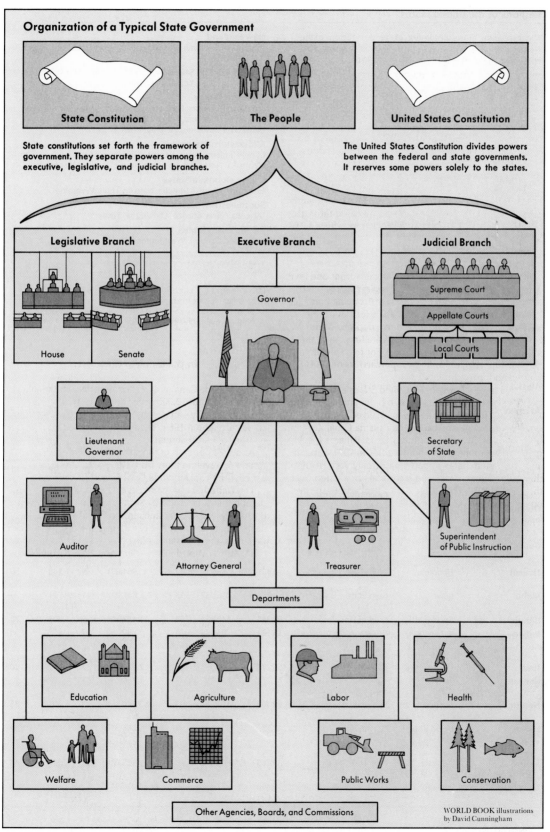

Organization of a Typical State Government

State Constitution

The People

United States Constitution

State constitutions set forth the framework of government. They separate powers among the executive, legislative, and judicial branches.

The United States Constitution divides powers between the federal and state governments. It reserves some powers solely to the states.

Legislative Branch

House

Senate

Executive Branch

Governor

Judicial Branch

Supreme Court

Appellate Courts

Local Courts

Lieutenant Governor

Secretary of State

Auditor

Attorney General

Treasurer

Superintendent of Public Instruction

Departments

Education

Agriculture

Labor

Health

Welfare

Commerce

Public Works

Conservation

Other Agencies, Boards, and Commissions

WORLD BOOK illustrations by David Cunningham

United States

Regions of the United States

The map below shows the location of the seven regions of the continental United States that are discussed in this section. The table at the right lists the states within each region.

WORLD BOOK map

New England
Connecticut, Maine, Massachusetts, New Hampshire, Rhode Island, Vermont

Middle Atlantic States
New Jersey, New York, Pennsylvania

Southern States
Alabama, Arkansas, Delaware, Florida, Georgia, Kentucky, Louisiana, Maryland, Mississippi, North Carolina, South Carolina, Tennessee, Virginia, West Virginia

Midwestern States
Illinois, Indiana, Iowa, Kansas, Michigan, Minnesota, Missouri, Nebraska, North Dakota, Ohio, South Dakota, Wisconsin

Rocky Mountain States
Colorado, Idaho, Montana, Nevada, Utah, Wyoming

Southwestern States
*Arizona, *New Mexico, Oklahoma, Texas

Pacific Coast States
California, Oregon, Washington

*Arizona and New Mexico are often grouped with the Rocky Mountain States.

Facts in brief about the states

State	Capital	Popular name	Area (sq. mi.)	Area (km²)	Rank in area	Population*	Rank in pop.*	Population density* (sq. mi.)	Population density* (km²)
Alabama	Montgomery	Yellowhammer State	51,705	133,915	29	3,893,978	22	75	29
Alaska	Juneau	Last Frontier	591,004	1,530,700	1	401,851	50	0.7	0.3
Arizona	Phoenix	Grand Canyon State	114,000	295,260	6	2,718,425	29	24	9
Arkansas	Little Rock	Land of Opportunity	53,187	137,754	27	2,286,419	33	43	17
California	Sacramento	Golden State	158,706	411,049	3	23,668,562	1	149	58
Colorado	Denver	Centennial State	104,091	269,595	8	2,889,964	28	28	11
Connecticut	Hartford	Constitution State	5,018	12,977	48	3,107,576	25	619	239
Delaware	Dover	First State	2,044	5,295	49	594,338	47	291	112
Florida	Tallahassee	Sunshine State	58,664	151,939	22	9,746,421	7	166	64
Georgia	Atlanta	Empire State of the South	58,910	152,576	21	5,463,087	13	93	36
Hawaii	Honolulu	Aloha State	6,471	16,759	47	964,691	39	149	58
Idaho	Boise	Gem State	83,564	216,432	13	944,038	41	11	4
Illinois	Springfield	Land of Lincoln	56,345	145,934	24	11,427,414	5	203	78
Indiana	Indianapolis	Hoosier State	36,185	93,720	38	5,490,260	12	152	59
Iowa	Des Moines	Hawkeye State	56,275	145,753	25	2,913,808	27	52	20
Kansas	Topeka	Sunflower State	82,277	213,098	14	2,364,236	32	29	11
Kentucky	Frankfort	Bluegrass State	40,409	104,660	37	3,660,257	23	91	35
Louisiana	Baton Rouge	Pelican State	47,752	123,677	31	4,206,098	19	88	34
Maine	Augusta	Pine Tree State	33,265	86,156	39	1,125,030	38	34	13
Maryland	Annapolis	Old Line State	10,460	27,092	42	4,216,941	18	403	156

*1980 census

The *Pacific Coast States Region,* which borders the Pacific Ocean, is known for its dense forests, rugged mountains, and dramatic ocean shore. The scenic beauty and relatively mild climate encourage an outdoor life style enjoyed by both residents and tourists.

Fertile valleys in the Pacific Coast States Region produce a large part of the nation's fruits, nuts, vegetables, and wine grapes. The region also has abundant timber, minerals, and fish. Much manufacturing takes place in its large cities, which include—in order of size—Los Angeles, San Diego, San Francisco, San Jose, and Seattle.

The discovery of gold and the opening of the Oregon Territory in the mid-1800's brought a stream of settlers to the Pacific Coast. New residents have continued to pour in ever since. Today, the population includes people of European ancestry, and black and Mexican-American minority groups. The region also has more people of Asian ancestry than any other part of the United States, and a large number of American Indians.

Main outlying areas of the United States

Name	Acquired	Status
American Samoa	*	Unorganized unincorporated territory
Baker Island and Jarvis Island	1856	Unincorporated territory
Guam	1898	Organized unincorporated territory
Howland Island	1856	Unincorporated possession
Johnston Island and Sand Island	1858	Unincorporated territory
Kingman Reef	1922	Unincorporated territory
Midway Island	1867	Unincorporated territory
Northern Mariana Islands	1947	Commonwealth
Palmyra Island	1898	Unincorporated possession
Puerto Rico	1898	Commonwealth
Trust Territory of the Pacific Islands	1947	UN trust territory (U.S. administration)
Virgin Islands of the United States	1917	Organized unincorporated territory
Wake Island	1898	Unincorporated possession

*Acquired in stages between 1900 and 1925.

State abbreviation	State bird	State flower	State tree	State song	Admitted to the Union	Order of admission	Members of Congress Senate	House
Ala.	Yellow-hammer	Camellia	Southern pine (Longleaf pine)	"Alabama"	1819	22	2	7
†	Willow ptarmigan	Forget-me-not	Sitka spruce	"Alaska's Flag"	1959	49	2	1
Ariz.	Cactus wren	Saguaro (Giant cactus)	Paloverde	"Arizona"; "I Love You Arizona"	1912	48	2	5
Ark.	Mockingbird	Apple blossom	Pine	"Arkansas"	1836	25	2	4
Calif.	California valley quail	Golden poppy	California redwood	"I Love You, California"	1850	31	2	45
Colo.	Lark bunting	Rocky Mountain columbine	Blue spruce	"Where the Columbines Grow"	1876	38	2	6
Conn.	Robin	Mountain laurel	White oak	"Yankee Doodle"	1788	5	2	6
Del.	Blue hen chicken	Peach blossom	American holly	"Our Delaware"	1787	1	2	1
Fla.	Mockingbird	Orange blossom	Cabbage (Sabal) palm	"Old Folks at Home" ("Swanee River")	1845	27	2	19
Ga.	Brown thrasher	Cherokee rose	Live oak	"Georgia on My Mind"	1788	4	2	10
†	Nene (Hawaiian goose)	Hibiscus	Kukui	"Hawaii Ponoi" (Hawaii's Own)	1959	50	2	2
Ida.	Mountain bluebird	Syringa (Mock orange)	Western white pine	"Here We Have Idaho"	1890	43	2	2
Ill.	Cardinal	Native violet	White oak	"Illinois"	1818	21	2	22
Ind.	Cardinal	Peony	Tulip tree, or yellow poplar	"On the Banks of the Wabash, Far Away"	1816	19	2	10
Ia.	Eastern goldfinch	Wild rose	Oak	"The Song of Iowa"	1846	29	2	6
Kans. or Kan.	Western meadowlark	Sunflower	Cottonwood	"Home on the Range"	1861	34	2	5
Ky. or Ken.	Kentucky cardinal	Goldenrod	Kentucky coffeetree	"My Old Kentucky Home"	1792	15	2	7
La.	Brown pelican	Magnolia	Bald cypress	"Give Me Louisiana"; "You Are My Sunshine"	1812	18	2	8
Me.	Chickadee	White pine cone and tassel	White pine	"State of Maine Song"	1820	23	2	2
Md.	Baltimore oriole	Black-eyed Susan	White oak (Wye oak)	"Maryland, My Maryland"	1788	7	2	8

†The state has no traditional abbreviation.

United States

State	Capital	Popular name	Area (sq. mi.)	Area (km²)	Rank in area	Population*	Rank in pop.*	Population density* (sq. mi.)	Population density* (km²)
Massachusetts	Boston	Bay State	8,284	21,456	45	5,737,081	11	693	268
Michigan	Lansing	Wolverine State	58,527	151,586	23	9,262,070	8	158	61
Minnesota	St. Paul	Gopher State	84,402	218,601	12	4,075,970	21	48	19
Mississippi	Jackson	Magnolia State	47,689	123,515	32	2,520,631	31	53	20
Missouri	Jefferson City	Show Me State	69,697	180,516	19	4,916,759	15	71	27
Montana	Helena	Treasure State	147,046	380,848	4	786,690	44	5	2
Nebraska	Lincoln	Cornhusker State	77,355	200,350	15	1,569,825	35	20	8
Nevada	Carson City	Silver State	110,561	286,532	7	799,184	43	7	3
New Hampshire	Concord	Granite State	9,297	24,032	44	920,610	42	99	38
New Jersey	Trenton	Garden State	7,787	20,169	46	7,365,011	9	946	365
New Mexico	Santa Fe	Land of Enchantment	121,593	314,925	5	1,303,445	37	11	4
New York	Albany	Empire State	49,108	127,189	30	17,558,072	2	358	138
North Carolina	Raleigh	Tar Heel State	52,669	136,413	28	5,881,813	10	112	43
North Dakota	Bismarck	Flickertail State	70,702	183,119	17	652,717	46	9	3
Ohio	Columbus	Buckeye State	41,330	107,044	35	10,797,624	6	261	101
Oklahoma	Oklahoma City	Sooner State	69,956	181,186	18	3,025,495	26	43	17
Oregon	Salem	Beaver State	97,073	251,419	10	2,633,149	30	27	10
Pennsylvania	Harrisburg	Keystone State	45,308	117,348	33	11,864,751	4	262	101
Rhode Island	Providence	Ocean State	1,212	3,140	50	947,154	40	781	302
South Carolina	Columbia	Palmetto State	31,113	80,582	40	3,122,814	24	100	39
South Dakota	Pierre	Sunshine State	77,116	199,730	16	690,768	45	9	3
Tennessee	Nashville	Volunteer State	42,114	109,152	34	4,591,120	17	109	42
Texas	Austin	Lone Star State	266,807	691,030	2	14,227,574	3	53	20
Utah	Salt Lake City	Beehive State	84,899	219,889	11	1,461,037	36	17	7
Vermont	Montpelier	Green Mountain State	9,614	24,900	43	511,456	48	53	20
Virginia	Richmond	Old Dominion	40,767	105,586	36	5,346,797	14	131	51
Washington	Olympia	Evergreen State	68,139	176,479	20	4,132,204	20	61	24
West Virginia	Charleston	Mountain State	24,231	62,759	41	1,950,258	34	80	31
Wisconsin	Madison	Badger State	56,153	145,436	26	4,705,642	16	84	32
Wyoming	Cheyenne	Equality State	97,809	253,326	9	469,557	49	5	2

*1980 census

State abbreviation†	State bird	State flower	State tree	State song	Admitted to the Union	Order of ad-mission	Members of Congress Senate	House
Mass.	Chickadee	Mayflower	American elm	"All Hail to Massa-chusetts"	1788	6	2	11
Mich.	Robin	Apple blossom	White pine	"Michigan, My Michigan"**	1837	26	2	18
Minn.	Common loon	Pink and white lady's-slipper	Norway, or red, pine	"Hail! Minnesota"	1858	32	2	8
Miss.	Mockingbird	Magnolia	Magnolia	"Go Mis- sis- sip- pi"	1817	20	2	5
Mo.	Bluebird	Hawthorn	Flowering dogwood	"Missouri Waltz"	1821	24	2	9
Mont.	Western meadowlark	Bitterroot	Ponderosa pine	"Montana"	1889	41	2	2
Nebr. or Neb.	Western meadowlark	Goldenrod	Cottonwood	"Beautiful Nebraska"	1867	37	2	3
Nev.	Mountain bluebird**	Sagebrush**	Single-leaf piñon	"Home Means Nevada"	1864	36	2	2
N.H.	Purple finch	Purple lilac	White birch	"Old New Hamp-shire"	1788	9	2	2
N.J.	Eastern goldfinch	Purple violet	Red oak	None	1787	3	2	14
N. Mex. or N.M.	Roadrunner	Yucca flower	Piñon, or nut pine	"O, Fair New Mexico"	1912	47	2	3
N.Y.	Bluebird	Rose	Sugar maple	"I Love New York"	1788	11	2	34
N.C.	Cardinal	Flowering dogwood	Pine	"The Old North State"	1789	12	2	11
N. Dak. or N.D.	Western meadowlark	Wild prairie rose	American elm	"North Dakota Hymn"	1889	39	2	1
O.	Cardinal	Scarlet carnation	Buckeye	"Beautiful Ohio"	1803	17	2	21
Okla.	Scissor-tailed flycatcher	Mistletoe	Redbud	"Oklahoma!"	1907	46	2	6
Ore. or Oreg.	Western meadowlark	Oregon grape	Douglas fir	"Oregon, My Oregon"	1859	33	2	5
Pa. or Penn.	Ruffed grouse	Mountain laurel	Hemlock	None	1787	2	2	23
R.I.	Rhode Island Red	Violet	Red maple	"Rhode Island"	1790	13	2	2
S.C.	Carolina wren	Carolina jessamine	Palmetto	"Carolina"	1788	8	2	6
S. Dak. or S.D.	Ring-necked pheasant	American pasqueflower	Black Hills spruce	"Hail, South Dakota"	1889	40	2	1
Tenn.	Mockingbird	Iris	Tulip poplar	"My Homeland, Ten-nessee"; "My Ten-nessee"; "Rocky Top"; "The Tennessee Waltz"; "When It's Iris Time in Tennessee"	1796	16	2	9
Tex.	Mockingbird	Bluebonnet	Pecan	"Texas, Our Texas"	1845	28	2	27
Ut.	Sea Gull	Sego lily	Blue spruce	"Utah, We Love Thee"	1896	45	2	3
Vt.	Hermit thrush	Red clover	Sugar maple	"Hail, Vermont!"	1791	14	2	1
Va.	Cardinal	Dogwood	Dogwood	"Carry Me Back to Old Virginia"	1788	10	2	10
Wash.	Willow goldfinch	Coast rhodo-dendron	Western hemlock	"Washington, My Home"	1889	42	2	8
W. Va.	Cardinal	Rhododendron	Sugar maple	"The West Virginia Hills"; "This is My West Virginia"; "West Virginia, My Home Sweet Home"	1863	35	2	4
Wis.	Robin	Wood violet	Sugar maple	"On, Wisconsin!"	1848	30	2	9
Wyo.	Meadowlark	Indian paintbrush	Cottonwood	"Wyoming"	1890	44	2	1

WORLD: *Political*

ABBREVIATIONS

CEN. AFR. REP.
    Central African Republic
DEN. Denmark
FR. France
GR. Greece
IT. Italy
N. North, Northern
NETH. Netherlands
P.D.R. YEMEN
    People's Democratic
    Republic of Yemen
PORT. Portugal
S. South
SP. Spain
TERR. Territory
U.A.E. United Arab
    Emirates
U.K. United Kingdom
U.S. United States
W. Western

— National boundary

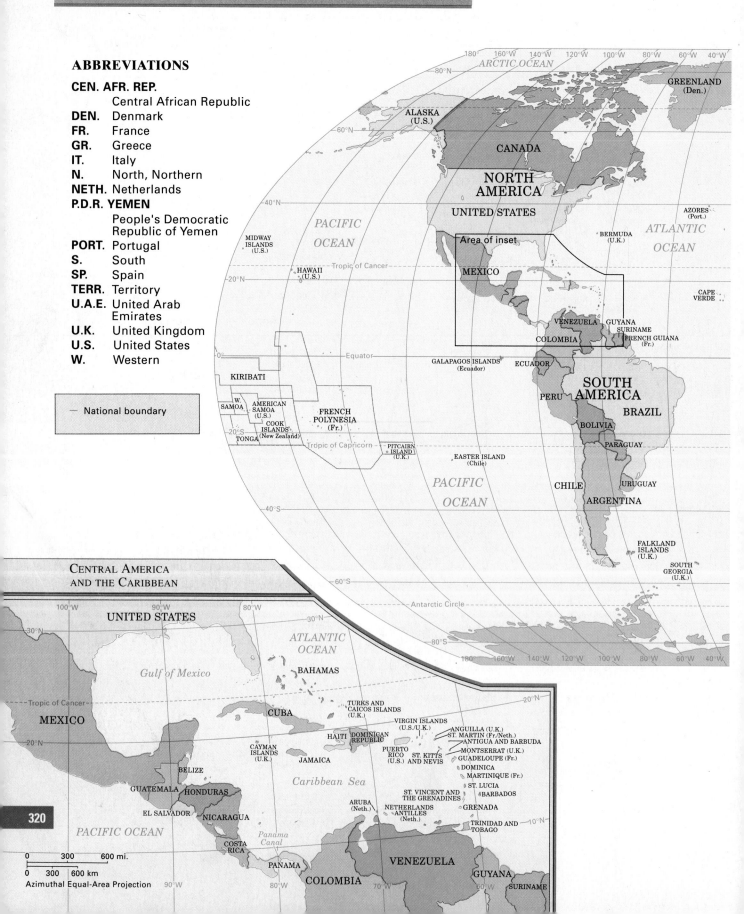

CENTRAL AMERICA
AND THE CARIBBEAN

0   300   600 mi.
0   300   600 km
Azimuthal Equal-Area Projection

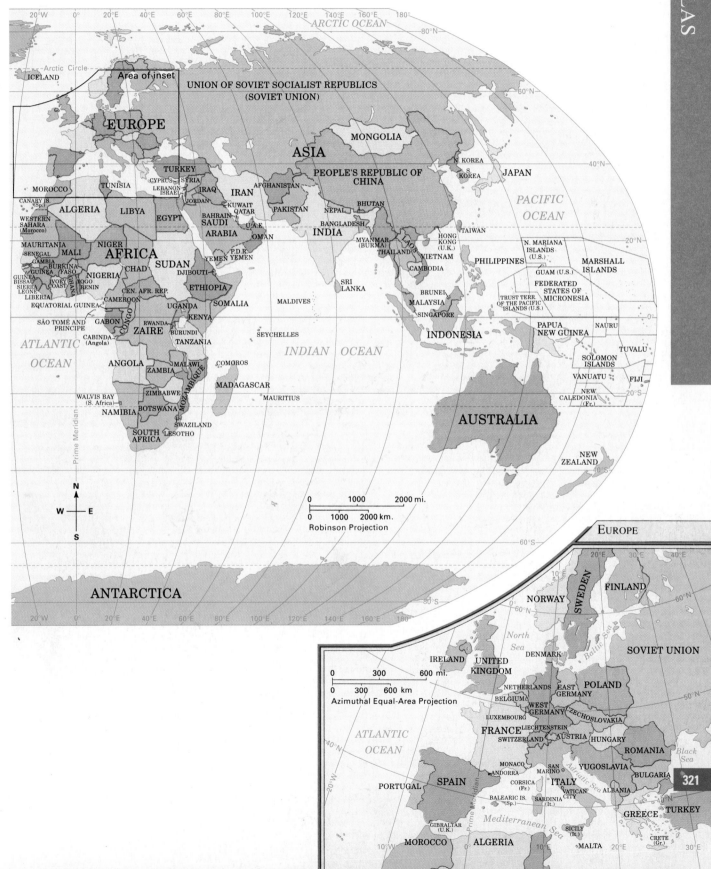

20°W 0° 20°E 40°E 60°E 80°E 100°E 120°E 140°E 160°E 180°

ARCTIC OCEAN

80°N

Arctic Circle

ICELAND

Area of inset

UNION OF SOVIET SOCIALIST REPUBLICS
(SOVIET UNION)

60°N

EUROPE

MONGOLIA

ASIA

N. KOREA
S. KOREA

JAPAN

40°N

TURKEY

PEOPLE'S REPUBLIC OF
CHINA

CYPRUS SYRIA
LEBANON
ISRAEL

MOROCCO TUNISIA

IRAQ IRAN AFGHANISTAN

JORDAN

PACIFIC
OCEAN

CANARY IS.
(Sp.)

ALGERIA LIBYA EGYPT

KUWAIT
QATAR

BHUTAN

TAIWAN

20°N

WESTERN
SAHARA
(Morocco)

SAUDI
ARABIA

BAHRAIN
U.A.E

PAKISTAN NEPAL

BANGLADESH

HONG
KONG
(U.K.)

N. MARIANA
ISLANDS
(U.S.)

OMAN

INDIA

MYANMAR
(BURMA)

MARSHALL
ISLANDS

MAURITANIA NIGER

P.D.R.
YEMEN YEMEN

MALI AFRICA

LAOS

GUAM (U.S.)

SENEGAL

THAILAND

VIETNAM

GAMBIA

CHAD SUDAN

CAMBODIA

PHILIPPINES

FEDERATED
STATES OF
MICRONESIA

0°

GUINEA
BISSAU

BURKINA
FASO

GUINEA

NIGERIA

DJIBOUTI

SIERRA
LEONE

IVORY
COAST

TOGO
BENIN

CEN. AFR. REP.

ETHIOPIA

SRI
LANKA

BRUNEI

LIBERIA

GHANA

MALDIVES

TRUST TERR.
OF THE PACIFIC
ISLANDS (U.S.)

EQUATORIAL GUINEA

CAMEROON

UGANDA

MALAYSIA

SÃO TOMÉ AND
PRINCIPE

GABON

KENYA

SINGAPORE

NAURU

CONGO

ZAIRE

RWANDA
BURUNDI

SEYCHELLES

INDONESIA

PAPUA
NEW GUINEA

CABINDA
(Angola)

TANZANIA

INDIAN OCEAN

ATLANTIC

OCEAN

ANGOLA

ZAMBIA

MALAWI

COMOROS

SOLOMON
ISLANDS

TUVALU

WALVIS BAY
(S. Africa)

ZIMBABWE

MOZAMBIQUE

MADAGASCAR

MAURITIUS

VANUATU

FIJI

20°S

NAMIBIA BOTSWANA

SWAZILAND

NEW
CALEDONIA
(Fr.)

SOUTH
AFRICA

LESOTHO

AUSTRALIA

Prime Meridian

N
W   E
S

0   1000   2000 mi.

0   1000   2000 km.

Robinson Projection

NEW
ZEALAND

40°S

60°S

ANTARCTICA

80°S

20°W 0° 20°E 40°E 60°E 80°E 100°E 120°E 140°E 160°E 180°

EUROPE

20°E 30°E 40°E

10°E

SWEDEN FINLAND

0° NORWAY

60°N

North
Sea

DENMARK

Baltic Sea

SOVIET UNION

IRELAND UNITED
KINGDOM

NETHERLANDS EAST
GERMANY

POLAND

50°N

0   300   600 mi.

0   300   600 km.

Azimuthal Equal-Area Projection

BELGIUM

LUXEMBOURG

WEST
GERMANY

CZECHOSLOVAKIA

FRANCE LIECHTENSTEIN

SWITZERLAND AUSTRIA HUNGARY

ROMANIA

ATLANTIC

OCEAN

40°N

MONACO

ANDORRA

SAN
MARINO

YUGOSLAVIA

Black
Sea

BULGARIA

321

PORTUGAL SPAIN

CORSICA
(Fr.)

ITALY

VATICAN
CITY

ALBANIA

Adriatic Sea

BALEARIC IS.
(Sp.)

SARDINIA
(It.)

GREECE TURKEY

GIBRALTAR
(U.K.)

Prime Meridian

SICILY
(It.)

CRETE
(Gr.)

MOROCCO ALGERIA

MALTA

Mediterranean Sea

10°W 0° 10°E 20°E 30°E

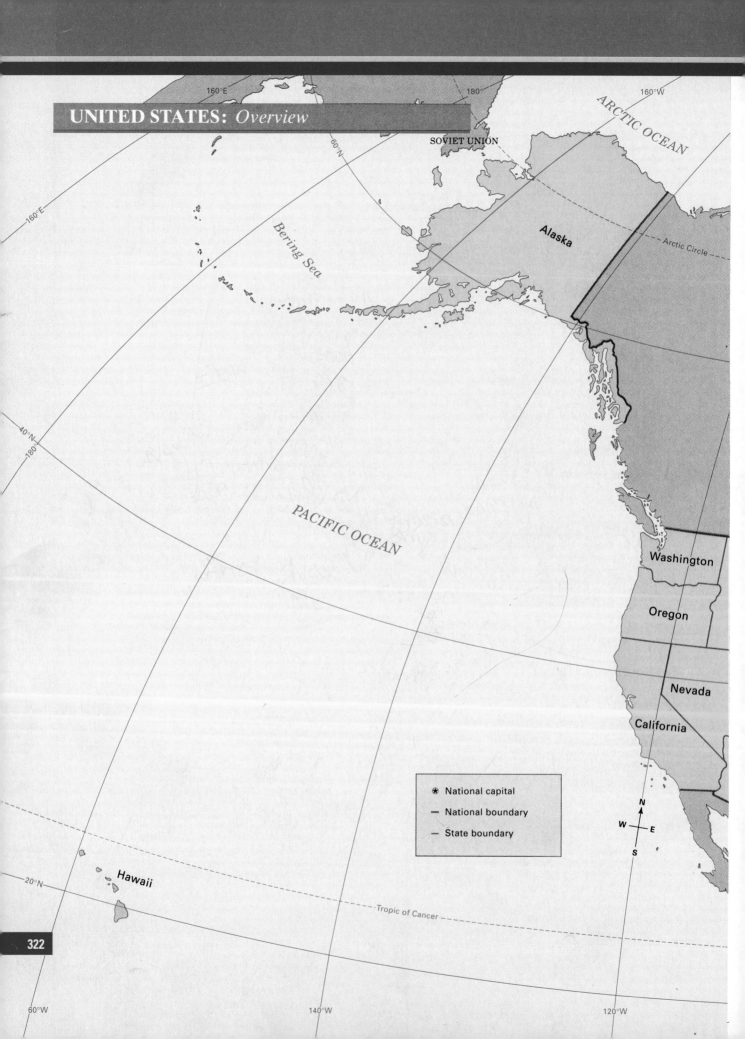

160°E

180°

160°W

ARCTIC OCEAN

SOVIET UNION

60°N

Alaska

Arctic Circle

Bering Sea

160°E

40°N

180

PACIFIC OCEAN

Washington

Oregon

Nevada

California

⊛ National capital

— National boundary

— State boundary

N

W   E

S

20°N

Hawaii

Tropic of Cancer

60°W

140°W

120°W

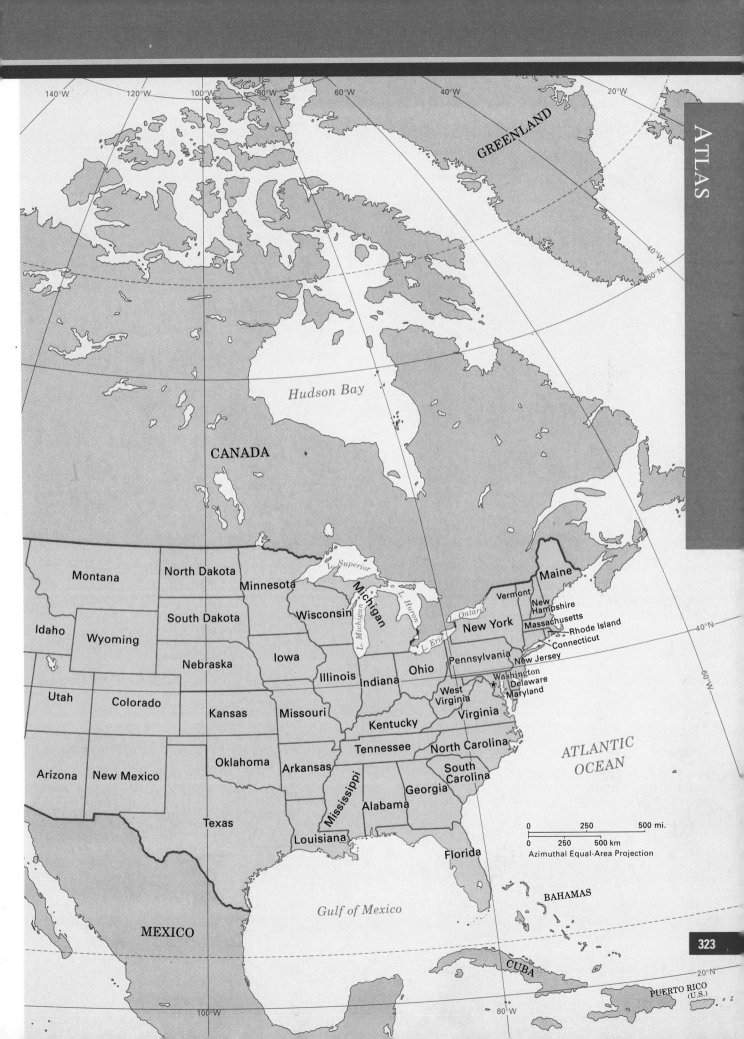

GREENLAND

Hudson Bay

CANADA

L. Superior

North Dakota

Montana

Minnesota

Michigan

L. Huron

Maine

Vermont

New Hampshire

Idaho

Wyoming

South Dakota

Wisconsin

L. Michigan

L. Ontario

New York

Massachusetts

Rhode Island

Connecticut

Nebraska

Iowa

L. Erie

Pennsylvania

New Jersey

Utah

Colorado

Illinois

Indiana

Ohio

West Virginia

Washington

Delaware

Maryland

Kansas

Missouri

Virginia

Kentucky

Arizona

New Mexico

Oklahoma

Arkansas

Tennessee

North Carolina

ATLANTIC OCEAN

South Carolina

Mississippi

Alabama

Georgia

Texas

Louisiana

Florida

0	250	500 mi.
0	250	500 km

Azimuthal Equal-Area Projection

BAHAMAS

MEXICO

Gulf of Mexico

CUBA

PUERTO RICO (U.S.)

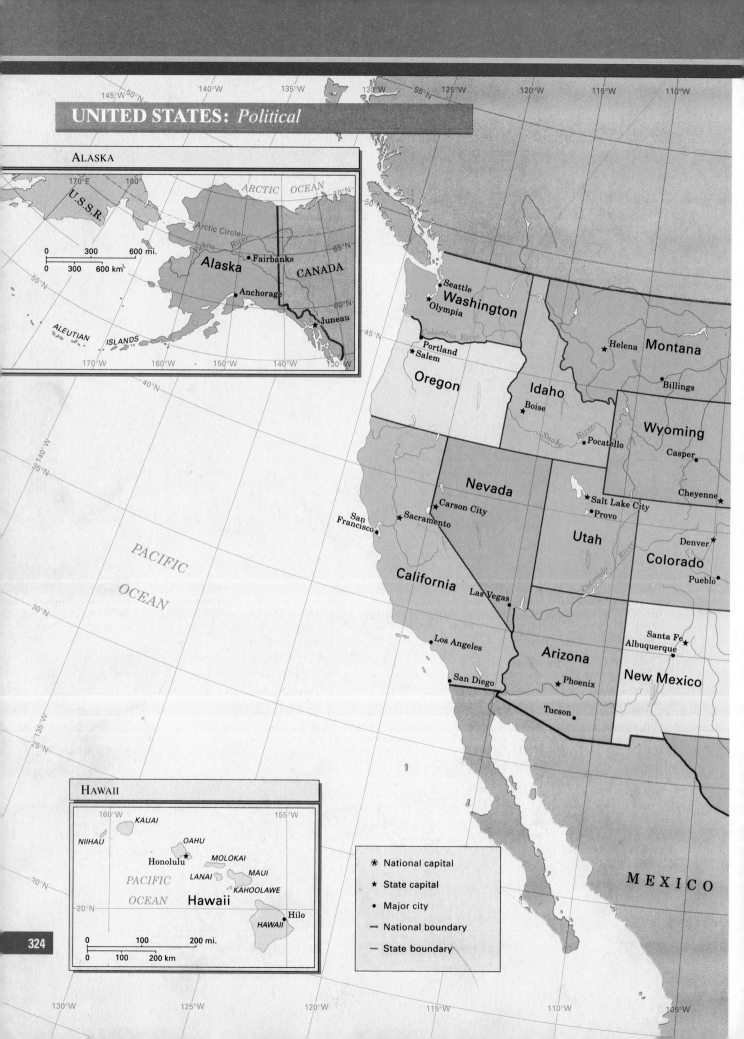

UNITED STATES: *Political*

ALASKA

170°E 180° 170°N
ARCTIC OCEAN
U.S.S.R.
Arctic Circle
Yukon River
Fairbanks
Alaska
CANADA
65°N
Anchorage
60°N
Juneau
ALEUTIAN ISLANDS
55°N
170°W 160°W 150°W 140°W 130°W

0 300 600 mi.
0 300 600 km

PACIFIC OCEAN

Seattle
Washington
Olympia
Columbia River
Portland
Salem
Oregon

Helena
Montana
Billings

Idaho
Boise
Snake River
Pocatello

Wyoming
Casper

Nevada
Carson City

Salt Lake City
Provo
Utah
Colorado River

Cheyenne

Denver
Colorado
Pueblo

San Francisco
Sacramento

California
Las Vegas

Los Angeles

San Diego

Arizona
Phoenix
Tucson

Santa Fe
Albuquerque
New Mexico

MEXICO

HAWAII

160°W 155°W
KAUAI
NIIHAU
OAHU
Honolulu
MOLOKAI
LANAI
PACIFIC
OCEAN
MAUI
KAHOOLAWE
Hawaii
HAWAII
Hilo

0 100 200 mi.
0 100 200 km

✪	National capital
★	State capital
•	Major city
—	National boundary
—	State boundary

324

CANADA

North Dakota
Bismarck ★
Fargo •

Minnesota
Minneapolis • ★ St. Paul

South Dakota
Pierre ★
Sioux Falls •

Lake Superior

Michigan

Lake Huron

Wisconsin
Milwaukee •
Madison ★

Lansing ★

Maine
Augusta ★

Vermont
Burlington •
Montpelier ★
New Hampshire
Concord ★
Portland •

Nebraska
Lincoln ★
Omaha •

Sioux City •

Iowa
Des Moines ★

Chicago •

Detroit •

Lake Erie

New York
Albany ★

Massachusetts
Hartford ★
New Haven •
Boston ★
Providence ★
Rhode Island
Connecticut

Lake Ontario

Lake Michigan

Missouri River
Platte River

Illinois
Springfield ★

Indiana
Indianapolis ★

Ohio
Columbus ★
Cleveland •

Pennsylvania
Harrisburg ★
Pittsburgh •

New York •
New Jersey
Trenton ★
Philadelphia •
Wilmington •
Dover ★
Delaware
Baltimore •
Washington •
Annapolis ★
Maryland

Kansas
Topeka ★
Wichita •

Kansas City •

St. Louis •

Louisville •

Frankfort ★

West Virginia
Charleston ★

Virginia
Richmond ★
Norfolk •

Arkansas River

Jefferson City ★

Missouri

Evansville •

Kentucky

Nashville •

Raleigh ★

North Carolina
Charlotte •

Oklahoma
Oklahoma City ★
Tulsa •
Fort Smith •
Little Rock ★

Arkansas

Tennessee
Memphis •

Mississippi River

South Carolina
Columbia ★
Charleston •

Red River

Greenville •

Birmingham •

Atlanta ★

Georgia
Savannah •

Texas
Dallas •
Austin ★
Houston •

Louisiana
Baton Rouge ★
New Orleans •

Jackson ★

Mississippi

Alabama
Montgomery ★

Tallahassee ★

ATLANTIC OCEAN

Florida
Tampa •
Miami •

BAHAMAS

Rio Grande

Gulf of Mexico

N
W — E
S

CUBA

0   200   400 mi.
0   200   400 km
Albers Equal-Area Projection

105°W 100°W 95°W 90°W 85°W 80°W 75°W 70°W 65°W 60°W
55°N 50°N 45° 40°N 35°N 30°N 25°N 20°N
70°W 75°W

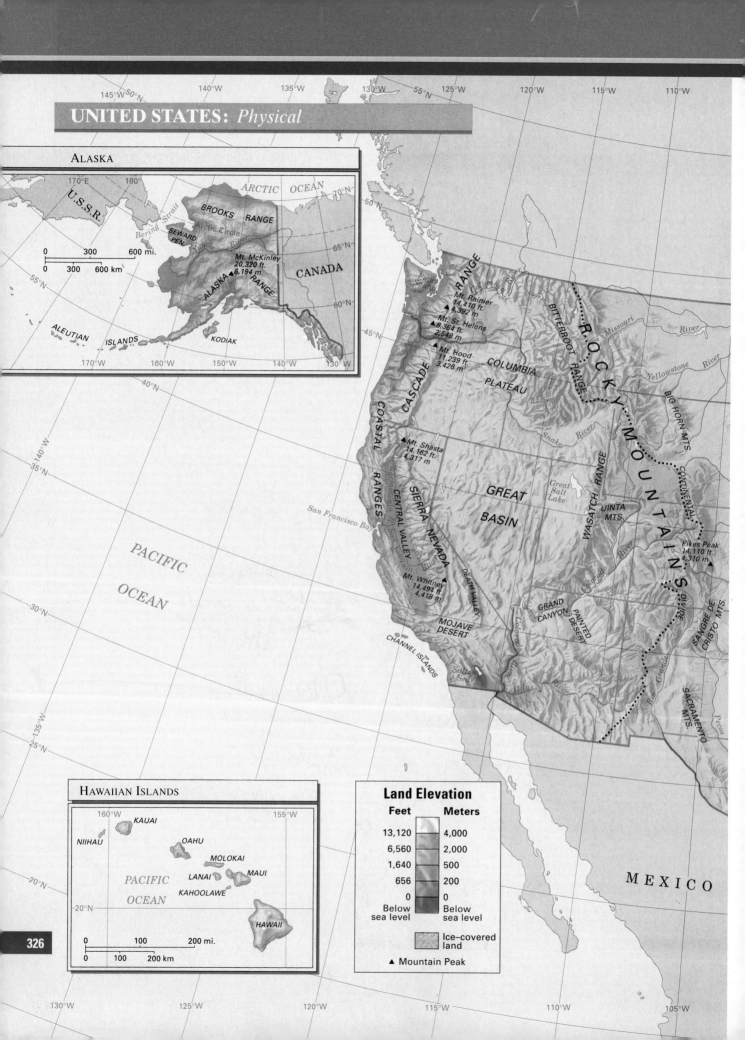

ALASKA

ARCTIC OCEAN

U.S.S.R.

BROOKS RANGE

Bering Strait

Arctic Circle

SEWARD PEN.

CANADA

Mt. McKinley
20,320 ft.
6,194 m

ALASKA RANGE

ALEUTIAN ISLANDS

KODIAK

0   300   600 mi.
0   300   600 km

Mt. Rainier
14,410 ft.
4,392 m

Mt. St. Helens
8,364 ft.
2,549 m

Mt. Hood
11,239 ft.
3,426 m

CASCADE RANGE

COLUMBIA PLATEAU

BITTERROOT RANGE

ROCKY MOUNTAINS

Missouri River

Yellowstone River

BIG HORN MTS.

CONTINENTAL

COASTAL RANGES

Mt. Shasta
14,162 ft.
4,317 m

Snake River

GREAT BASIN

Great Salt Lake

WASATCH RANGE

UINTA MTS.

SIERRA NEVADA

CENTRAL VALLEY

San Francisco Bay

Mt. Whitney
14,494 ft.
4,418 m

DEATH VALLEY

Pikes Peak
14,110 ft.
4,310 m

DIVIDE

SANGRE DE CRISTO MTS.

Colorado River

GRAND CANYON

PAINTED DESERT

CHANNEL ISLANDS

MOJAVE DESERT

Salton Sea

Gila River

Rio Grande

Pecos River

SACRAMENTO MTS.

PACIFIC OCEAN

MEXICO

HAWAIIAN ISLANDS

KAUAI

NIIHAU

OAHU

MOLOKAI

LANAI

MAUI

KAHOOLAWE

PACIFIC OCEAN

HAWAII

0   100   200 mi.
0   100   200 km

Land Elevation

Feet	Meters
13,120	4,000
6,560	2,000
1,640	500
656	200
0	0
Below sea level	Below sea level

Ice-covered land

▲ Mountain Peak

105°W 100°W 95°W 90°W 85°W 80°W 75°W 70°W 55°N 65°W 60°W

CANADA

GREAT PLAINS

MESABI RANGE

Lake of the Woods

Lake Superior

Red River

Lake Michigan

Lake Huron

Lake Ontario

Lake Erie

ADIRONDACK MTS.

CATSKILL MTS.

WHITE MTS.

Mt. Washington 6,288 ft. 1,917 m

St. Lawrence River

NANTUCKET

MARTHA'S VINEYARD

LONG ISLAND

BLACK HILLS

BADLANDS

SAND HILLS

Missouri River

Mississippi River

Des Moines River

Platte River

CENTRAL PLAINS

ALLEGHENY PLATEAU

APPALACHIAN MOUNTAINS

Susquehanna River

Hudson River

Delaware Bay

Chesapeake Bay

Arkansas River

OZARK PLATEAU

Wabash River

Ohio River

CUMBERLAND PLATEAU

BLUE RIDGE MTS.

Mt. Mitchell 6,684 ft. 2,037 m

FALL LINE

ATLANTIC COASTAL PLAIN

ATLANTIC OCEAN

70°W

LLANO ESTACADO

OUACHITA MOUNTAINS

Red River

Arkansas River

Tennessee River

Tombigbee River

Savannah R.

Chattahoochee River

EDWARDS PLATEAU

Brazos River

Colorado River

Sabine River

Red River

Altamaha R.

Alabama River

Pearl River

GULF COASTAL PLAIN

Mobile Bay

Pensacola Bay

Rio Grande

Galveston Bay

Gulf of Mexico

N W E S

Tampa Bay

Lake Okeechobee

EVERGLADES

BAHAMAS

FLORIDA KEYS

CUBA

50°N 45°N 40°N 35°N 30°N 25°N 20°N

0 200 400 mi.
0 200 400 km
Albers Equal-Area Projection

327

100°W 95°W 90°W 85°W 80°W 75°W

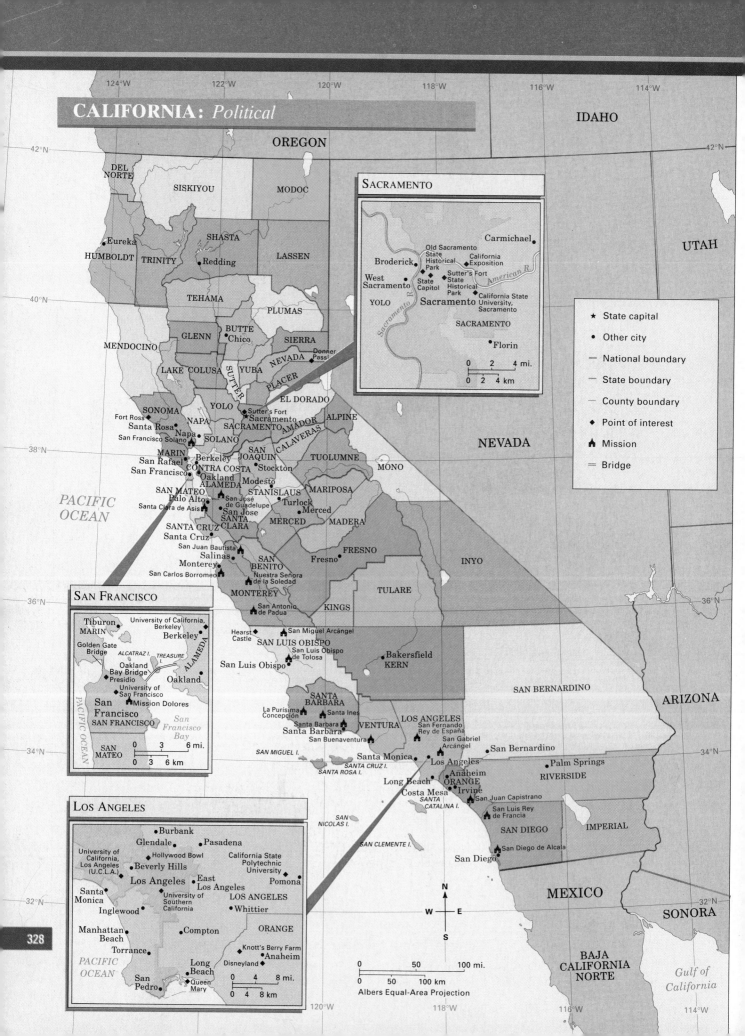

CALIFORNIA: *Political*

OREGON
IDAHO

DEL NORTE
SISKIYOU
MODOC

UTAH

Eureka
HUMBOLDT TRINITY SHASTA
Redding
LASSEN

TEHAMA

PLUMAS

MENDOCINO GLENN BUTTE
Chico
SIERRA
Donner Pass
LAKE COLUSA YUBA NEVADA
SUTTER
PLACER

YOLO
EL DORADO
Sutter's Fort
SONOMA NAPA ★Sacramento AMADOR ALPINE
Fort Ross SACRAMENTO
Santa Rosa Napa SOLANO CALAVERAS
San Francisco Solano MARIN SAN JOAQUIN TUOLUMNE
Berkeley
San Rafael CONTRA COSTA Stockton
San Francisco Oakland MONO
ALAMEDA Modesto
SAN MATEO STANISLAUS MARIPOSA
Palo Alto San José de Guadalupe Turlock
Santa Clara de Asis SANTA CLARA Merced MADERA
San Jose MERCED
SANTA CRUZ
Santa Cruz
San Juan Bautista FRESNO
Salinas SAN BENITO Fresno FRESNO
Monterey INYO
San Carlos Borromeo Nuestra Señora de la Soledad
MONTEREY TULARE
San Antonio de Padua KINGS

PACIFIC OCEAN

SACRAMENTO

Carmichael
Old Sacramento State Historical Park
Broderick California Exposition
West Sacramento Sutter's Fort
State Capitol State Historical Park
YOLO California State University, Sacramento
Sacramento
SACRAMENTO
American R.
Sacramento R.

Florin

| 0 | 2 | 4 mi. |
| 0 | 2 | 4 km |

NEVADA

Legend
★ State capital
● Other city
— National boundary
— State boundary
— County boundary
◆ Point of interest
⌂ Mission
= Bridge

SAN FRANCISCO

Tiburon University of California, Berkeley
MARIN Berkeley
Golden Gate Bridge ALCATRAZ I. TREASURE I.
Oakland Bay Bridge ALAMEDA
Presidio Oakland
University of San Francisco
San Francisco Mission Dolores
SAN FRANCISCO San Francisco Bay
SAN MATEO
PACIFIC OCEAN

| 0 | 3 | 6 mi. |
| 0 | 3 | 6 km |

Hearst Castle San Miguel Arcángel
SAN LUIS OBISPO
San Luis Obispo de Tolosa
San Luis Obispo Bakersfield
KERN

SANTA BARBARA
La Purisima Concepción Santa Ines
Santa Barbara VENTURA
Santa Barbara
San Buenaventura

SAN MIGUEL I.
SANTA CRUZ I.
SANTA ROSA I.

LOS ANGELES
San Fernando Rey de España
San Gabriel Arcángel
Santa Monica Los Angeles San Bernardino
SAN BERNARDINO

Palm Springs
Anaheim RIVERSIDE
Long Beach ORANGE
Costa Mesa Irvine
SANTA CATALINA I. San Juan Capistrano
San Luis Rey de Francia
IMPERIAL
SAN DIEGO
San Diego de Alcala
San Diego

ARIZONA

SAN NICOLAS I.
SAN CLEMENTE I.

MEXICO
SONORA

LOS ANGELES

Burbank
Glendale Pasadena
University of California, Los Angeles (U.C.L.A.) Hollywood Bowl
Beverly Hills California State Polytechnic University
Los Angeles East Los Angeles Pomona
Santa Monica University of Southern California LOS ANGELES
Inglewood Whittier
Manhattan Beach Compton ORANGE
Torrance Knott's Berry Farm
Long Beach Anaheim
Disneyland
San Pedro Queen Mary
PACIFIC OCEAN

| 0 | 4 | 8 mi. |
| 0 | 4 | 8 km |

N
W E
S

| 0 | 50 | 100 mi. |
| 0 | 50 | 100 km |
Albers Equal-Area Projection

BAJA CALIFORNIA NORTE
Gulf of California

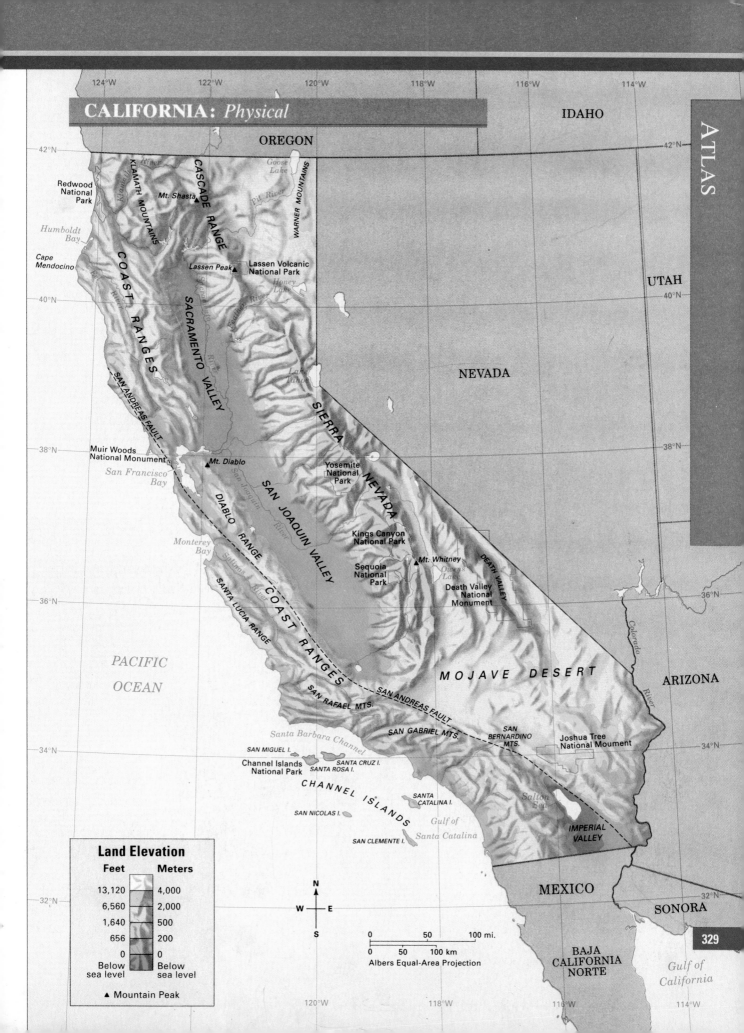

CALIFORNIA: *Physical*

IDAHO

OREGON

Redwood
National
Park

*Humboldt
Bay*

Cape
Mendocino

KLAMATH MOUNTAINS

Klamath River

Mt. Shasta ▲

CASCADE RANGE

*Goose
Lake*

Pit River

WARNER MOUNTAINS

Lassen Peak ▲

Lassen Volcanic
National Park

*Honey
Lake*

SACRAMENTO VALLEY

Feather River

COAST RANGES

Eel River

SAN ANDREAS FAULT

UTAH

NEVADA

*Lake
Tahoe*

SIERRA NEVADA

Muir Woods
National Monument

*San Francisco
Bay*

Mt. Diablo ▲

San Joaquin River

SAN JOAQUIN VALLEY

DIABLO RANGE

Yosemite
National
Park

*Monterey
Bay*

Salinas River

SANTA LUCIA RANGE

COAST RANGES

Kings Canyon
National Park

Sequoia
National
Park

Mt. Whitney ▲

*Owens
Lake*

DEATH VALLEY

Death Valley
National
Monument

PACIFIC
OCEAN

SAN RAFAEL MTS.

SAN ANDREAS FAULT

MOJAVE DESERT

Colorado River

ARIZONA

SAN GABRIEL MTS.

SAN
BERNARDINO
MTS.

Joshua Tree
National Monument

Santa Barbara Channel

SAN MIGUEL I.

Channel Islands
National Park

SANTA ROSA I.

SANTA CRUZ I.

*Salton
Sea*

IMPERIAL
VALLEY

CHANNEL ISLANDS

SANTA
CATALINA I.

SAN NICOLAS I.

*Gulf of
Santa Catalina*

SAN CLEMENTE I.

MEXICO

SONORA

BAJA
CALIFORNIA
NORTE

*Gulf of
California*

Land Elevation

Feet		Meters
13,120		4,000
6,560		2,000
1,640		500
656		200
0		0
Below sea level		Below sea level

▲ Mountain Peak

N
W E
S

| 0 | 50 | 100 mi. |
| 0 | 50 | 100 km |

Albers Equal-Area Projection

329

UNITED STATES: *Climate*

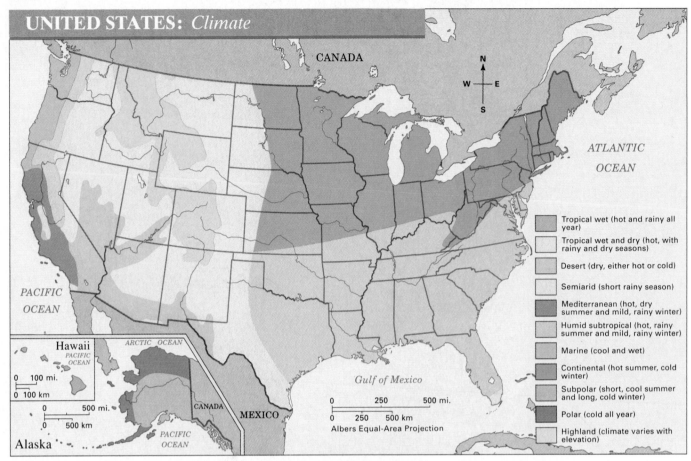

CANADA

N
W   E
S

ATLANTIC OCEAN

PACIFIC OCEAN

Gulf of Mexico

Hawaii
PACIFIC OCEAN
0   100 mi.
0   100 km

ARCTIC OCEAN

0   500 mi.
0   500 km

CANADA

MEXICO

PACIFIC OCEAN

Alaska

0   250   500 mi.
0   250   500 km
Albers Equal-Area Projection

Tropical wet (hot and rainy all year)

Tropical wet and dry (hot, with rainy and dry seasons)

Desert (dry, either hot or cold)

Semiarid (short rainy season)

Mediterranean (hot, dry summer and mild, rainy winter)

Humid subtropical (hot, rainy summer and mild, rainy winter)

Marine (cool and wet)

Continental (hot summer, cold winter)

Subpolar (short, cool summer and long, cold winter)

Polar (cold all year)

Highland (climate varies with elevation)

UNITED STATES: *Vegetation*

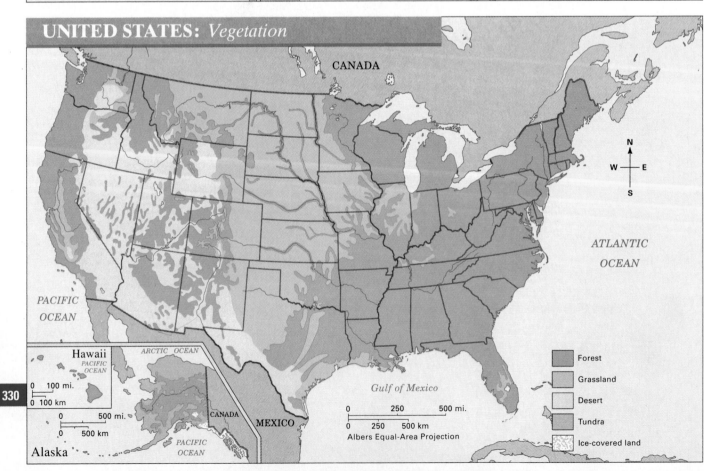

CANADA

N
W   E
S

ATLANTIC OCEAN

PACIFIC OCEAN

Gulf of Mexico

Hawaii
PACIFIC OCEAN
0   100 mi.
0   100 km

ARCTIC OCEAN

0   500 mi.
0   500 km

CANADA

MEXICO

PACIFIC OCEAN

Alaska

0   250   500 mi.
0   250   500 km
Albers Equal-Area Projection

Forest

Grassland

Desert

Tundra

Ice-covered land

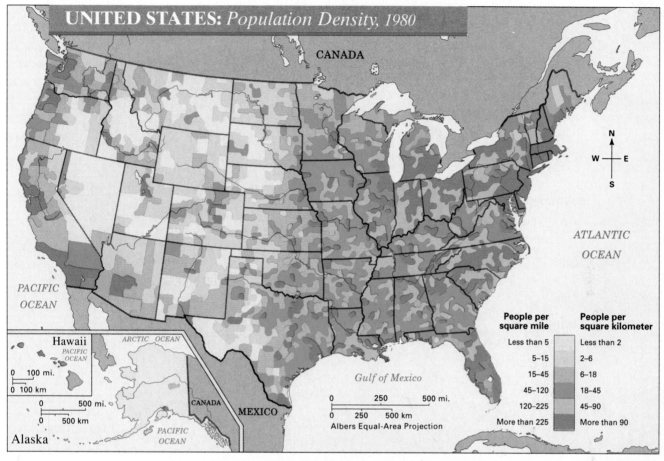

UNITED STATES: *Population Density, 1980*

CANADA

CONTEXTLESS MAP LABELS:

PACIFIC
OCEAN

ATLANTIC
OCEAN

Hawaii
ARCTIC OCEAN
PACIFIC
OCEAN

0 100 mi.
0 100 km

0   500 mi.
0   500 km

CANADA

Alaska

PACIFIC
OCEAN

MEXICO

Gulf of Mexico

0   250   500 mi.
0   250   500 km
Albers Equal-Area Projection

People per square mile	**People per square kilometer**
Less than 5	Less than 2
5–15	2–6
15–45	6–18
45–120	18–45
120–225	45–90
More than 225	More than 90

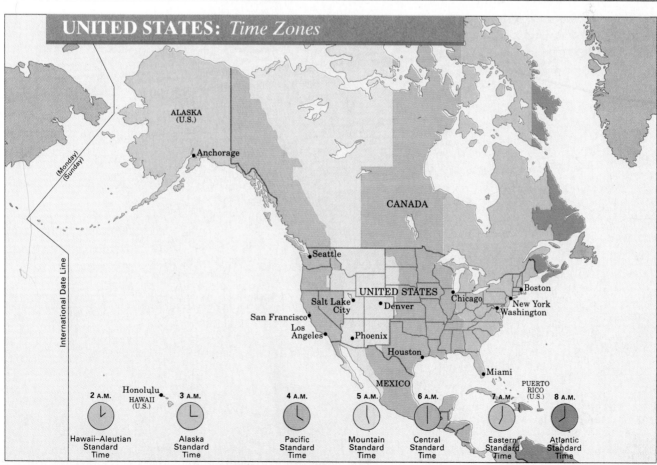

UNITED STATES: *Time Zones*

ALASKA
(U.S.)
• Anchorage

(Monday)
(Sunday)

CANADA

International Date Line

• Seattle

UNITED STATES

Salt Lake
City •   • Denver   Chicago •   • Boston
San Francisco •   • New York
Los   • Washington
Angeles •   • Phoenix

• Houston

MEXICO   • Miami

PUERTO
RICO
(U.S.)

2 A.M.   Honolulu •   **3** A.M.   **4** A.M.   **5** A.M.   **6** A.M.   **7** A.M.   **8** A.M.
                   HAWAII
                   (U.S.)

Hawaii–Aleutian   Alaska   Pacific   Mountain   Central   Eastern   Atlantic
Standard   Standard   Standard   Standard   Standard   Standard   Standard
Time   Time   Time   Time   Time   Time   Time

GLOSSARY OF GEOGRAPHIC TERMS

glacier
a large ice mass that moves slowly down a mountain or over land

mountain
a steeply raised mass of land, much higher than the surrounding country

ocean or **sea**
a salty body of water covering a large area of the earth

mountain range
a row of mountains

tree line
on a mountain, the area above which no trees grow

mountain pass
a gap between mountains

valley
low land between hills or mountains

basin
a bowl-shaped area of land surrounded by higher land

mesa
a wide, flat-topped mountain with steep sides, found mostly in dry areas

hill
a raised mass of land, smaller than a mountain

prairie
a large, level area of grassland without trees

desert
a dry area where few plants grow

cliff
the steep, almost vertical, edge of a hill, mountain, or plain

plain
a broad, flat area of land

volcano
an opening in the earth, often raised, through which lava and gasses from the earth's interior escape

sea level
the level of the surface of the ocean

strait
a narrow channel of water connecting two large bodies of water

harbor
a sheltered body of water where ships can safely dock

coast
the land next to an ocean

bay
part of a lake or ocean extending into the land

peninsula
land mostly surrounded by water but connected to the mainland

island
a body of land completely surrounded by water

isthmus
a narrow strip of land connecting two large bodies of land

river
a large stream that runs into a lake, ocean, or another river

lake
a body of water completely surrounded by land

333

This Gazetteer will help you locate many of the places discussed in this book. Latitude and longitude given for large areas of land and water refer to the centermost point of the area; latitude and longitude of rivers refer to the river mouth. The page number tells you where to find each place on a map.

PLACE	LAT.	LONG.	PAGE
A			
Alabama (state)	32°N	87°W	**323**
Alaska (state)	64°N	150°W	**322**
Alta California (original Spanish name for present-day California)	38°N	121°W	**68**
American River (in California)	38°N	120°W	**136**
Arizona (state)	34°N	113°W	**323**
Arkansas (state)	34°N	93°W	**323**
B			
Baja California (peninsula in western Mexico)	29°N	116°W	**68**
Bering Strait (waterway linking Pacific Ocean and Arctic Ocean)	64°N	169°W	**33**
Brazil (country in South America)	95°N	53°W	**320**
C			
California (state)	38°N	121°W	**7**
Cambodia, (country in Southeast Asia)	13°N	105°E	**321**
Canada (country in North America)	50°N	100°W	**325**
Cape Horn (southern tip of South America)	56°S	67°W	**59**
Caribbean Sea (body of water east of Central America)	14°N	75°W	**320**
Cascade Mountains (range in northern California)	42°N	122°W	**8**
Central America (southern region of North America)	10°N	87°W	**320**
Central Valley (river valley in central California)	38°N	122°W	**13**
China (country in Asia)	36°S	93°E	**321**
Coachella Valley (area in southern California)	33°N	115°W	**303**
Coast Ranges (mountains along California's western coast)	41°N	123°W	**329**
Colorado (state)	39°N	106°W	**322**
Colorado Desert (dry area in southeastern California)	36°N	109°W	**19**
Colorado River (in southwestern U.S.)	32°N	115°W	**326**

PLACE	LAT.	LONG.	PAGE
Connecticut (state)	41°N	73°W	**323**
Cuba (island country in Caribbean Sea)	22°S	79°W	**320**
D			
Death Valley (desert area in California; lowest point in U.S.)	36°N	117°W	**329**
Delaware (state)	38°N	75°W	**323**
E			
El Camino Real (old road on which missions were located)			**74**
F			
Florida (state)	28°N	82°W	**323**
Fresno (city in central California)	36°N	119°W	**207**
G			
Georgia (state)	32°N	83°W	**323**
Golden Gate Strait (waterway linking San Francisco Bay to Pacific Ocean)	37°N	122°W	**230**
Great Lakes (freshwater lakes bordering U.S. and Canada)			**327**
Great Plains (grassland region in central U.S.)	45°N	104°W	**326**
Great Salt Lake (saltwater lake in northern Utah)	41°N	112°W	**326**
Gulf of Mexico (part of Atlantic Ocean, east of Mexico, south of U.S.)	25°N	93°W	**327**
H			
Hawaii (state)	20°N	157°W	**324**
Hispaniola (island in West Indies)	19°N	72°W	**59**
Hudson Bay (body of water in north central Canada)	52°N	102°W	**323**
Hudson River (in eastern New York)	41°N	73°W	**327**

PLACE	LAT.	LONG.	PAGE
I			
Idaho (state)	44°N	115°W	**323**
Illinois (state)	40°N	90°W	**323**
Imperial Valley (farm area in southern California)	33°N	115°W	**8**
Indiana (state)	39°N	86°W	**323**
Iowa (state)	42°N	94°W	**323**
Ireland (country in western Europe)	53°N	8°W	**321**
Isthmus of Panama (land in Central America connecting North and South America)	9°N	81°W	**320**
Italy (country in southern Europe)	43°N	11°E	**321**
J			
Jamaica (island in West Indies)	17°N	70°W	**320**
Japan (island country in East Asia)	17°N	78°E	**321**
K			
Kansas (state)	38°N	99°W	**323**
Kentucky (state)	37°N	87°W	**323**
Kern River (in California)	35°N	118°W	**329**
Klamath River (in northern California)	41°N	124°W	**329**
Korea (country in East Asia)	38°N	128°E	**321**
L			
Lake Tahoe (freshwater lake bordering California and Nevada)	39°N	120°W	**8**
Laos (country in Southeast Asia)	20°N	102°E	**321**
Los Angeles (city in southern California)	34°N	118°W	**230**
Louisiana (state)	30°N	92°W	**323**
M			
Maine (state)	45°N	69°W	**323**
Marin County (section of nothern California)	38°N	122°W	**329**
Maryland (state)	39°N	76°W	**323**
Massachusetts (state)	42°N	72°W	**323**

PLACE	LAT.	LONG.	PAGE
Mexican Cession (land ceded by Mexico to U.S.)			**119**
Mexico (country in North America)	23°N	104°W	**320**
Michigan (state)	45°N	87°W	**323**
Minnesota (state)	46°N	90°W	**323**
Mississippi (state)	32°N	89°W	**323**
Mississippi River (in central U.S.)	31°N	91°W	**327**
Missouri River (in central and western U.S.)	40°N	96°W	**327**
Mojave Desert (dry region in southern California)	35°N	117°W	**329**
Mono Lake (saltwater lake in eastern California)	38°N	119°W	**8**
Montana (state)	47°N	111°W	**323**
Monterey (coastal city in California)	36°N	121°W	**207**
Mount Lassen (volcanic peak in northern California)	40°N	121°W	**329**
Mount McKinley (mountain in central Alaska, highest point in U.S. and North America)	63°N	151°W	**326**
Mount Shasta (peak in northern California)	41°N	122°W	**329**
Mount Whitney (mountain in eastern California)	36°N	118°W	**329**
N			
Nebraska (state)	41°N	101°W	**323**
Nevada (state)	39°N	117°W	**323**
New Hampshire (state)	43°N	71°W	**323**
New Jersey (state)	40°N	74°W	**323**
New Mexico (state)	34°N	107°W	**323**
New Spain (original name for lands ruled by Spain from Mexico City)			**59**
New York (state)	42°N	78°W	**323**
North Carolina (state)	35°N	81°W	**323**
North Dakota (state)	47°N	101°W	**323**
O			
Oakland (city in California)	37°N	122°W	**328**
Ohio (state)	40°N	83°W	**323**
Oklahoma (state)	36°N	98°W	**323**
Orange County (section of southern California)	33°N	117°W	**328**
Oregon (state)	43°N	121°W	**323**

PLACE	LAT.	LONG.	PAGE
Owens River Valley (water source for Los Angeles)	37°N	118°W	**229**

P

PLACE	LAT.	LONG.	PAGE
Panama Canal (waterway linking Atlantic and Pacific Oceans)	9°N	81°W	**314**
Pasadena (city in California)	34°N	118°W	**328**
Pennsylvania (state)	41°N	78°W	**323**
Philippines (Pacific island country in Southeast Asia)	14°N	125°E	**277**
Portugal (country in southern Europe)	38°N	8°W	**321**

R

PLACE	LAT.	LONG.	PAGE
Rhode Island (state)	41°N	323°W	**323**
Rio Grande (river border between U.S. and Mexico)	29°N	100°W	**326**
Rocky Mountains (mountain range in western U.S.)	50°N	114°W	**326**

S

PLACE	LAT.	LONG.	PAGE
Sacramento (city in northern California; state capital)	38°N	121°W	**324**
Sacramento River (in northern California)	38°N	122°W	**40**
Salton Sea (man-made lake in southern California)	33°N	115°W	**329**
San Andreas Fault (a long break in the earth's crust running through California)	37°N	122°W	**329**
San Bernadino Mountains (range in southern California)	32°N	117°W	**329**
San Diego (coastal city in southern California)	32°N	117°W	**74**
San Francisco (coastal city in central California)	37°N	122°W	**230**
San Joaquin (river in central California)	38°N	122°W	**136**
San Luis Obispo (mission city on California coast)	35°N	120°W	**74**
San Pedro (harbor of Los Angeles)	33°N	118°W	**230**
Santa Barbara (coastal city in California)	34°N	119°W	**328**
Santa Clara (mission city in California)	37°N	121°W	**74**

Sequoia National Forest (national park in California) 36°N 118°W **329**

PLACE	LAT.	LONG.	PAGE
Sierra Nevada (range in eastern California)	39°N	120°W	**326**
Sonora (state in Mexico)	29°N	111°W	**328**
South Carolina (state)	34°N	81°W	**323**
South Dakota (state)	44°N	101°W	**323**
Soviet Union (country in Europe and Asia)	60°N	64°E	**321**
Spain (country in southern Europe)	40°N	3°W	**321**
Strait of Magellan (waterway in South America)	53°N	70°W	**59**

T

PLACE	LAT.	LONG.	PAGE
Tennessee (state)	35°N	88°W	**323**
Texas (state)	31°N	101°W	**323**
Thailand (country in Southeast Asia)	17°N	100°E	**321**

U

PLACE	LAT.	LONG.	PAGE
United Kingdom (countries of British Isles, except Ireland)	56°N	0°W	**321**
United States (country in central North America)	38°N	110°W	**324**
Utah (state)	99°N	112°W	**323**

V

PLACE	LAT.	LONG.	PAGE
Vermont (state)	43°N	72°W	**323**
Vietnam (country in Southeast Asia)	18°N	107°E	**277**
Virginia (state)	37°N	80°W	**323**

W/Y

PLACE	LAT.	LONG.	PAGE
Washington (state)	47°N	121°W	**323**
Washington, D.C. (city on Potomac River; Capital of United States)	38°N	77°W	**7**
West Indies (islands in Caribbean Sea)	20°N	78°W	**6**
West Virginia (state)	39°N	80°W	**322**
Wisconsin (state)	44°N	91°W	**323**
Wyoming (state)	42°N	108°W	**322**
Yosemite Valley (valley in the Sierra Nevada)	38°N	119°W	**329**

Pronunciation Key

This chart presents the system of phonetic respellings used to indicate pronunciation in the Biographical Dictionary and in the chapters of this book.

Spellings	Symbol	Spellings	Symbol	Spellings	Symbol
pat	a	kick, cat, pique	k	thin, this	th
pay	ay	lid, needle	l	cut	uh
care	air	mum	m	urge, term, firm, word, heard	ur
father	ah	no, sudden	n		
bib	b	thing	ng	valve	v
church	ch	pot, horrid	ah	with	w
deed, milled	d	toe	oh	yes	y
pet	eh	caught, paw, for	aw	zebra, xylem	z
bee	ee	noise	oy	vision, pleasure, garage	zh
life, phase, rough	f	took	u		
gag	g	boot	oo	about, item, edible, gallop, circus	uh
hat	h	out	ow		
which	hw	pop	p	butter	ur
pit	ih	roar	r		
pie, by	ih	sauce	s	Capital letters indicate stressed syllables.	
pier	ihr	ship, dish	sh		
judge	j	tight, stopped	t		

A

Anza, Juan Bautista *(bah TEE stuh)* **de** 1735–1788(?), Spanish soldier; led a party of 240 settlers to start a mission in San Francisco (p. 68).

B

Burbank, Luther 1849–1926, agricultural scientist; developed many new breeds of fruits, vegetables, and flowers (p. 186).

Burke, Yvonne Braithwaite b. 1932, congresswoman; was the first black woman elected to Congress from California and first black woman to act as Los Angeles County Supervisor (p. 272).

Burton, Maria Amparo Ruiz de d. 1894, author; wrote about the lives and hardships of the Californios (p. 215).

Butterfield, John 1801–1869, businessman; owned cross-country stagecoach line (p. 166).

C

Cabrillo *(cah BREE yoh),* **Juan Rodríguez** d. 1543, Spanish explorer; first European to explore California (p. 60).

Casey, James d. 1856, San Francisco politician; shot newspaper reporter James King (p. 147).

Chaffey, George 1848–1932, engineer; built irrigation system in the Colorado Desert (p. 196).

Chávez, Cesar b. 1927, migrant laborer and union organizer; founded the United Farm Workers of America (p. 273).

Colton, Walter 1797–1857, alcalde of Monterey; founded *The Californian,* the region's first newspaper (p. 134).

Columbus, Christopher 1451–1506, Italian explorer; discovered North America (p. 59).

Cortés *(kor TEHZ),* **Hernando** 1485–1547, Spanish conquistador; conquered the Aztecs and claimed Mexico for Spain (p. 58).

Crippen, Robert b. 1937, astronaut; rode on the first flight of space shuttle *Columbia* (p. 8).

Crocker, Charles 1822–1888, one of the Central Pacific Railroad's leaders; supervised the laying of tracks for the railroad (p. 171).

D

Dana, Richard Henry 1815–1882, author; wrote *Two Years Before the Mast* (p. 86).

Disney, Walt 1901–1966, creator of cartoon characters and films; formed film studio; developed several theme parks; founded California Institute of the Arts (p. 260).

Dominguez, Manuel 1803–1882, delegate at California's constitutional convention. (p. 143).

Drake, Sir Francis 1540(?)–1596, English explorer; claimed land in northern California for England *(p. 62).*

E

Elizabeth I 1533–1603, Queen of England,1558-1603; raised England to a world power (p. 62).

F

Fages *(FAH hays)*, **Pedro** 1730–1794, governor of Alta California, 1770–1791; led many expeditions to Alta California (p. 66).

Fillmore, Millard 1800–1874, 13th President of the United States, 1850–1853; held office when California became a state (p. 144).

Frémont, John C. 1813–1890, a leader of the Bear Flag Revolt; later became California's first U.S. senator (p. 117).

Frémont, Jessie Benton 1824–1902, writer; helped husband John Frémont write accounts of his Western explorations (p. 106).

G

Galvez *(gahl VEHZ)*, **José de** 1729–1787, governor of New Spain, 1765–1771; developed a chain of missions in Alta California (p. 66).

Ghirardelli *(gihr uhr DEH lee)*, **Domingo** 1817–1894, confectioner; founded Ghirardelli Chocolate Company in San Francisco (p. 214).

Gilman, Charlotte Perkins 1860–1935, author; wrote many books and articles about women's issues (p. 235).

Guerra, Pablo de la 1819–1874, delegate to California's constitutional convention; later became state senator (p. 143).

H

Hearst, William Randolph 1863–1951, publisher and politician; owned newspapers, radio stations, and movie companies (p. 233).

Hopkins, Mark 1813–1878, one of the Central Pacific Railroad's leaders; was treasurer for the railroad (p. 171).

Huntington, Collis P. 1821–1900, a leader of the Central Pacific Railroad; managed the railroad's business dealings (p. 171).

I

Ishi 1860(?)–1916, Yahi Indian; last survivor of the Yahi tribe (p. 210).

J

Johnson, Hiram 1866–1945, governor of California, 1911–1917; fought the Southern Pacific Railroad's power (p. 234).

Judah, Anna 1828–1895, strong supporter of husband Theodore Judah's plans for a transcontinental railroad (p. 168).

Judah, Theodore 1826–1863, engineer; planned route for the first transcontinental railroad; founded the Central Pacific Railroad Company (p. 168).

K

Kaiser, Henry 1882–1967, manufacturer; built ships for World War II at his shipyards around San Francisco Bay (p. 252).

Kearny, Stephen W. 1794–1848, general in the U.S. Army; commanded the Army of the West in the Mexican War (p. 118).

King, James 1822–1856, newspaper owner; wrote about San Francisco's crime problems; murdered by James Casey (p. 147).

King, Jr., Rev. Dr. Martin Luther 1929–1968, minister and civil rights leader; spoke for and promoted the cause of civil rights (p. 271).

L

Lange, Dorothea 1895–1965, photographer; known for her pictures of workers and farmers during the Great Depression (p. 244).

Lincoln, Abraham 1809–1865, 16th U.S. President, 1861–1865; held office during the Civil War (p. 164).

Love, Harry S. 1809(?)–1868, captain of the California Rangers; hunted the legendary bandit Joaquin Murieta (p. 146).

M

Marshall, James W. 1810–1885, settler; discovered the first gold found in California (p. 121).

Mason, Biddy 1815(?)–1891, California citizen born into slavery; known for her work supporting the black community (p. 145).

Muir, John 1838–1914, naturalist; studied and wrote about Yosemite, the Sierra Nevada, and other wilderness areas; worked to save forest lands; founded the Sierra Club (p. 16).

Mulholland, William 1835–1935, head of the Los Angeles water department; engineered the Los Angeles aqueduct project (p. 228).

Murieta, Joaquin d. 1853(?), the name given to a legendary bandit who was blamed for many robberies and murders in California (p. 146).

N

Ng Poon Chew *(nn poon CHEE oo)* 1866–1931, newspaper publisher; published and edited *Chung Sai Yat Po,* the first Chinese-American newspaper (p. 217).

Norris, Frank 1870–1902, author; wrote *The Octopus,* a story of the railroad's great power in California (p. 184).

P

Parks, Rosa b. 1913, civil rights activist; protested against a law that required blacks to sit at the backs of buses (p. 271)

Polk, James K. 1795–1849, 11th President of the United States, 1845–1849; held office during the Mexican War, and saw California annexed to the Union (p. 122).

Portolá *(pohr toh LAH),* **Gaspar de** 1723–1784, governor of New Spain; is said to have discovered San Francisco Bay (p. 66).

R

Ride, Sally b. 1951, astronaut; was the first American woman to travel in space (p. 4).

Riley, Gen. Bennett 1787–1853, military governor of California; organized California's constitutional convention *(p. 137)*

Rivera, Fernando 1711–1782, captain; led first overland party to Alta California (p. 66).

Roosevelt, Franklin Delano 1882–1945, 32nd President of the United States, 1933–1945; held office during the Great Depression and World War II (p. 245).

Royce, Sarah 1819–1891, author; wrote about her overland journey to California (p. 145).

S

Schmitz, Eugene 1864–1928, mayor of San Francisco, 1902–1907; was accused of taking bribes and forced out of office (p. 233).

Semple, Robert 1806–1854, a leader of the Bear Flag Revolt and president of California's constitutional convention (p. 141).

Serra, Junípero *(hoo NEE peh roh)* 1713–1784, Spanish priest and missionary; founded first mission in Alta California (p. 66).

Shepard, Francis P. 1897–1985, oceanographer; was the first American to explore the ocean floor in a deep-sea submarine (p. 257).

Smith, Jedediah 1799–1831, fur trapper and pioneer; led the first party of pioneers across the Sierra Nevada (p. 108).

Stanford, Leland 1824–1893, president of the Central Pacific Railroad Company; founded Stanford University (p. 171).

Stearns, Abel 1789–1871, trader and pioneer; helped Californios increase their trade (p. 110).

Strong, Harriet Russell 1844–1929, rancher and feminist; supported women's rights and water supply reform (p. 196).

Sutter, John 1803–1880, pioneer; started a settlement and trading post near Sacramento; gold was discovered at his mill (p. 110).

T

Todd, William 1818–1880(?), a leader of the Bear Flag Revolt; designed and painted the Bear Flag, whose symbols were used in California's present flag (p. 117)

Toypurina 1761–1799, Gabrielino Indian; she led Indians from six rancherias in a revolt against San Gabriel Mission (p. 79).

Twain, Mark 1835–1910, author; (real name: Samuel L. Clemens); wrote about life in California during the 1860s (p. 294).

V

Vallejo *(vah YEH hoh),* **Gen. Mariano** 1808–1890, military leader; served as a delegate to California's constitutional convention (p. 116).

W

Walker, James 1818–1889, artist; painted scenes of Californio life (p. 93).

Y

Yeager, Chuck b. 1923, World War II fighter pilot and test pilot; first person to fly an airplane faster than the speed of sound (p. 255).

GLOSSARY

A

aerospace (âr´ō-spās´) the technology used to design, construct, and fly aircraft and space-craft (p. 256).

agriculture (ăg´rĭ-kŭl´chər) the science and business of growing crops and raising livestock (p. 76).

aqueduct (ăk´wĭ-dŭkt´) a large pipe that brings great amounts of water to a dry region (p. 228).

archaeologist (är´kē-ŏl´ə-jĭst) a scientist who studies ancient cultures by examining their old tools, pottery, and buildings (p. 34).

aviation (ā´vē-ā´shən) the production and flying of aircraft (p. 256).

B

barrio (bä´rē-ō´) a Spanish-speaking community in a city, such as the community in East Los Angeles (p. 263).

barter (bär´tər) to trade one good or service for another without using money (p. 88).

boom (bo͞om) a sudden period of rapid growth or activity (p. 193).

border (bôr´dər) the manmade or naturally occurring line that separates two areas (p. 6).

boycott (boi´kŏt´) to refuse to buy or use a good or service as an act of protest (p. 274).

bribe (brīb) money or valuable objects offered to persuade someone to act dishonestly (p. 233).

C

canal (kə-năl´) a waterway built to join one body of water to another, so ships can pass through (p. 230).

ceremony (sĕr´ə-mō´nē) a formal event that celebrates a special occasion (p. 45).

civil rights (sĭv´əl rīts) the fair and equal treatment promised by law to citizens of a democratic nation (p. 271).

claim (klām) the small piece of land on which a miner digs for gold (p. 125).

climate (klī´mĭt) the type of weather that occurs in an area (p. 14).

colony (kŏl´ə-nē) an area of land that is ruled by or belongs to another country (p. 59).

commission (kə-mĭsh´ən) a group that is chosen to make an important decision or do a certain job (p. 157).

communication (kə-myo͞o´nĭ-kā´shən) the movement or exchange of news, messages, and information (p.165).

community (kə-myo͞o´nĭ-tē) a group of people who live together in one area and share the same government (p. 39).

competition (kŏm´pĭ-tĭsh´ən) when two or more companies work against each other in order to win the most customers (p. 193).

conservation (kŏn´sûr-vā´shən) the careful use and protection of the environment and natural resources (p. 295).

constitution (kŏn´stĭ-tōō´shən) an important agreement that states the basic laws and rules by which a government will run a country or state (p. 143).

construction (kən-strŭk´shən) the business or act of building a structure (p. 173).

continent (kŏn´tə-nənt) one of the seven large land masses of the earth; they are Africa, Antarctica, Asia, Australia, Europe, North America, and South America (p. 5).

convention (kən-vĕn´shən) a meeting where delegates or other representatives discuss important issues and make decisions (p. 137).

culture (kŭl´chər) the beliefs and way of life of a group of people (p. 76).

custom (kŭs´təm) a habit, practice, or tradition of the people from one country or culture (p. 279).

D

delegate (dĕl´ĭ-gāt´) a person who is chosen to speak and act for the citizens on important matters (p. 137).

discrimination (dĭ-skrĭm´ə-nā´shən) the unfair treatment of certain people for reasons such as their religion, skin color, physical disabilities, or country of origin (p. 210).

Dust Bowl (dŭst bōl) a region in the middle United States that suffered from extreme wind storms and drought in the 1930s (p. 243).

E

endangered species (ĕn-dān´jərd spē´shēz) a type of animal or plant that is in danger of disappearing forever from the earth (p. 303).

engineering (ĕn´jə-nîr´ĭng) the use of science and mathematics in the planning and building of structures (p. 175).

environment (ĕn-vī´rən-mənt) natural surroundings, including the soil, plants, animals, water, and air (p. 294).

ethnic group (ĕth´nĭk grōōp) a group of people who share a common culture, religion, race or nationality (p. 215).

executive branch (ĭg-zĕk´yə-tĭv brănch) the part of state government made up of the governor and various agencies, whose job it is to carry out state policy (p. 298).

expedition (ĕk´spĭ-dĭsh´ən) a trip that is made for a special reason, usually to find or explore a certain place (p. 59).

experiment (ĭk-spĕr´ə-mənt) a test designed to investigate an idea or to gather information (p. 186).

export (ĕk´-spôrt) a product that is sent to another country to be sold (p. 285).

F

forty-niner (fôr´tē-nī´nər) the name given to a person mining for gold during California's gold rush (p. 123).

frontier (frŭn-tîr´) that part of a country where people have not yet settled (p. 110).

G

geography (jē-ŏg´rə-fē) the mountains, valleys, lakes, rivers, and other physical elements that make up an area (p. 13).

globe (glōb) a ball-shaped object that has all of the earth's land masses and bodies of water drawn on it (p. 5).

gold rush (gōld rŭsh) a period from 1848 to 1856 when thousands of people came to California in order to search for gold (p. 122).

governor (gŭv´ər-nər) the highest ranking official in a state government (p. 298).

Great Depression (grāt dĭ-prĕsh´ən) the period from 1929 to 1940 when many banks and industries went out of business and millions of Americans lost their jobs and all of their savings (p. 243).

H

human resource (hyōō´mən rē´sôrs´) anyone who has abilities and talents that make that person valuable to the community (p. 22).

I

immigrant (ĭm´ĭ-grənt) a person who moves to another country, usually to find a better life (p. 204).

import (ĭm´-pôrt) a product that is bought from another country (p. 287).

independence (ĭn´dĭ-pĕn´dəns) when the people of a country or area govern themselves instead of being ruled by another country (p. 87).

industry (ĭn´də-strē) the making and selling of a good or service (p. 191).

invest (ĭn-vĕst´) to give money, such as to a business, in hopes of making more money in return (p. 170).

irrigation (ĭr´ĭ-gā´shən) the use of trenches and canals to bring water to a dry area (p. 196).

isthmus (ĭs´məs) a narrow strip of land that connects two greater areas of land (p. 124).

J

judicial branch (jōō-dĭsh´əl brănch) the part of government made up of the courts and judges (p. 298).

justice (jŭs´tĭs) the fair and equal treatment of all people (p. 147).

L

labor union (lā´bər yōōn´yən) a group of workers who join together to protect their interests (p. 274).

laborers (lā´bər-ərz) the men and women who do the physical work on a job (p. 175).

land grant (lănd grănt) a gift of land given to a Californio by the Mexican government (p. 91).

landmark (lănd´märk´) a structure, building, or spot in nature that becomes an important place to a country or region (p. 214).

law (lô) a rule or set of rules that citizens live by (p. 147).

legend (lĕj´ənd) a story handed down through the years that explains people and the way they see their world (p. 37).

legislative branch (lĕj´ĭ-slā´tĭv) the part of the government that is made up of legislators who make laws (p. 297).

levee (lĕv´ee) a high piece of land built up along a riverbank to keep flood waters from overflowing (p. 197).

M

manufacturing (măn´yə-făk´chər-ĭng) the process of turning raw materials into finished products (p. 251).

migrant laborer (mī´grənt lā´bər-ər) a worker who moves from one farm to another, picking ripe crops (p. 199).

mineral (mĭn´ər-əl) a substance, such as gold and copper, that is found in nature, often underground (p. 22).

minority (mə-nôr´ĭ-tē) a small group of people with similar characteristics within a large population (p. 272).

mission (mĭsh´ən) a settlement formed by Catholic priests in order to bring their religious beliefs to the local people (p. 66).

mountain range (mōun´tən rānj) a row of mountains (p. 16).

N

nation (nā´shən) a group of people who live in the same area and are ruled by one central government (p. 117).

natural resource (năch´ər-əl rē´sôrs´) a useful material found in nature, such as water, forests, or minerals (p. 22).

New Deal (nōō dēl) the programs created by President Franklin Delano Roosevelt to lift the United States out of the Great Depression (p. 245).

P

padre (pä´drā) a priest of the Spanish missions in California (p. 73).

peninsula (pə-nĭn´syə-lə) a small piece of land that sticks off from a larger piece of land and has water on three sides (p. 66).

pioneer (pī´ə-nîr´) a person who first explores or settles a new region, leading the way for others to follow (p. 109).

plaza (plä´zə) the town square, usually found in the center of a pueblo (p. 98).

pollution (pə-lōō´shən) the destruction of land, air, and water due to the dumping of garbage and other harmful substances (p. 299).

presidio (prĭ-sē´dē-ō´) fort built by the Spanish in California (p. 73).

product (prŏd´əkt) an item that is made by people, machines, or nature (p. 88).

production (prə-dŭk´shən) the process of grow-ing and manufacturing goods, and the total amount made in a given period (p. 186).

Progressives (prə-grĕs´ĭvz) a group of people who worked in the early 1900s to improve the government and society of the United States (p. 234).

protest (prə-tĕst´) to publicly complain or dis-approve of something (p. 272).

pueblo (pwĕb´lō) the towns built close to the missions, for Mexican settlers (p. 73).

R

ranchero (răn-châr´ō) the owner and person in charge of the Californio rancho (p. 91).

rancho (răn´chō) the livestock farm or ranch of the Californios (p. 90).

rebel (rĕb´əl) a person who fights against the government in power (p. 117).

refrigeration (rĭ-frĭj´ə-rā´shən) the use of ice or cold air to keep food fresh (p. 187).

refugee (rĕf´yōō-jē) a person who leaves one region in order to find safety or freedom in another region (p. 277).

region (rē´jən) an area of land that is different from other areas due to its physical features, climate, people, or industries (p. 13).

reservation (rĕz´ər-vā´shən) a land area set aside by the United States government for the Native Americans (p. 210).

revolt (rĭ-vōlt´) to fight against the government in power in order to change some of their rules or to become free from that government (p. 79).

rodeo (rō´dē-ō´) the round-up of a rancho's cattle for branding or sale (p. 95).

S

shipyards (shĭp´yärd´) a place where ships are built or repaired (p. 252).

slavery (slā´və-rē) a system where one person is allowed to own and control another person (p. 144).

squatter (skwŏ´tər) a person who settles on and begins farming another person's land (p. 156).

strait (strāt) a narrow passage of water that connects two larger bodies of water (p. 33).

strike (strīk) the stopping of work by laborers in order to receive better pay or working conditions (p. 274).

suburb (sŭb´ûrb´) a town or an area that grows up outside of a larger city (p. 261).

survey (sər-vā´) to measure the height or boundary of an area or natural feature such as a mountain or lake (p. 169).

T

technology (tĕk-nŏl´ə-jē) the scientific methods and ideas used in industry, agriculture, and trade (p. 128).

tenant (tĕn´ənt) a person who pays rent to live in a building or on a piece of land (p. 199).

tourism (tōōr´ĭz´əm) the business and the prac-tice of traveling for pleasure (p. 242).

town council (toun koun´səl) a group of elected officials who make the important decisions for a town (p. 98).

trade (trād) the exchange of one good or ser-vice for another good or service (p. 38).

tradition (trə-dĭsh´ən) a belief or a way of doing things that is passed down from one genera-tion to the next (p. 47).

transcontinental (trăns´kŏn-tə-nĕn´tl) some-thing that stretches from one side of a conti-nent to the other (p. 166).

transportation (trăns´pər-tā´shən) the move-ment of people and goods from one place to another (p. 165).

treaty (trē´tē) an official agreement between two or more countries (p. 119).

tribe (trīb) a group of people from nearby vil-lages who share the same languages, culture, and customs (p. 36).

V

vaquero (vä-kâr´ō) a cowboy who works on a rancho (p. 91).

vigilante (vĭj´ə-lăn´tē) a person who takes the law into his or her own hands, capturing and punishing people without having the right to do so (p. 147).

INDEX

Italic numbers refer to pages on which illustrations appear; *quoted* refers to a quotation from a speech or writings of the person listed.

North America, 6, 12, 22, 33, 34
North Pole, 22, 63

O

Obsidian, 44
O'Connor, Sandra Day, 148, *148*
Octopus, The (Norris), 184, 197
Oil, 22, 227, *227*
　industry, 226, *226*
　uses of, 39, 227
Olive oil production, 75, *75*
Oral directions, giving, 99, *99*
Oranges, 190, 191, *191*, 192, *192*
Oregon, 7
O'Shaughnessy Dam, 27
Owens River, 228, 229, 295
Owens Valley, 229, 293, *293*, 295

P

Pacific Ocean, 6, 33, 60, 62
Padres, 73, 76, 79
Panama Canal, 60, 230, 314
Panama route, 124
Panoche Pass, 146
Parks, Rosa, 271
Patty Reed's Doll (Laurgaard),
　114-115
Pearl Harbor, 250, 251
Peninsula, 66
Peralta family, 156-157
Philippines, 60
Pigtail ordinance, 209
Pioneers, 109-111, *110, 123*
Plaza, 98
Polk, James K., 122
Pollution, 299
Pony Express, 164, *164,* 166
Population
　decline of Indian, 79
　growth of, in California, 134-
　　136, 253, 261
Portolá, Gaspar de, 66-67, 68, 71
Precipitation, 19-20
Presidios, 73
Prime meridian, 63-64
Produce, 188-189, *188, 189*
Production, 186
Products, 88
Progressives, 234, 235
Project, planning, 306
Protest, 272
Pueblos, 73, 74, 95, 98, *98*

R

Railroads, 168-171
　building of, 173-177
　Big Four, 170-171, *171,* 175
　competition between, 193
　and growth of southern
　　California, 191, *191,* 193
　and refrigeration, 187
　song about, 177
　transcontinental, 165, 173-177,
　　173, 177
Rancheros, 91, 92-93, 98
Ranchos, 91, 92-93, *92*
　end of, *155,* 156-157
　life on, 96, *96*
Rancho San Antonio, 156-157,
　156
Reading, identifying main ideas,
　9
Rebels, 117
Redwood National Park, 14
Redwood trees, *25, 38, 38,* 39
Reference books, using, 301
Refrigeration, 187
Refugee, 277
Regions, 13
　Central Valley, 15, *15*
　coast, 14, *14*
　deserts, 17, *17*
　identifying, 19-20
　mountains, 16, *16*
　of United States, 316-317
Representation, 298
Reservations, 210
Revolt, 79
Ride, Sally, 4
Riley, Bennett, 137
Ring of Fire, 21, 313
Rivera, Fernando, 66, 67
Rodeo, 95
Roosevelt, Franklin Delano,
　245, 252
Roosevelt, Theodore, *26,* 233
"Roughing It" (Twain), 294
Royce, Sarah, 145
Russia, 66, 87

S

Sacramento, 110, 136, 164
Sacramento River, 15, 44, 196-
　197
Salinas, 81
San Bernardino Mountains, 296
San Diego, 14, *14,* 66, 68, 71, 73

early explorations of, 67-69
San Diego Mission, 79
San Diego Zoo, 302, *302*
San Francisco, 14, *135, 144*
　corruption in, 233, 234
　during the gold rush, 134-135
　crime in, 147, *147*
　earthquakes in, 232, *232,* 233,
　　236-239
　Golden Gate Bridge in, 245,
　　245
　immigrant contributions to,
　　216, *216*
　population growth in, 134-135
San Francisco Bay, 6, 14, *67, 135,*
　144
San Gabriel Valley, 196
San Joaquin River, 15
San Joaquin Valley, 108, 109,
　226, 227
San Luis Obispo, 142
San Miguel, 60
San Pasqual, 118
San Pedro, *14,* 118
San Pedro Bay, 296
San Pedro Harbor, 230
Santa Barbara, 39, 227
Santa Clara Valley, 284
Santa Fe Railroad, 193
Santa Rosa, 187
Satellites, 5
Schmitz, Eugene, 233
Semple, Robert, 141
Sequoia, 23
Seropian, Garabed, 205
Seropian, Hagop, 205
Serra, Junípero, 66-67, 68, *72,* 79
　quoted, 67
　starting missions, 71-73
Seven Cities of Cibola, 59
Shepard, Francis, 257
Shipyards, 252, 253
Sierra Nevada, 16, *16,* 22, 126,
　168
　crossing of, 108, 109, 111, 164,
　　166, 168
　gold in, 126
　tunneling through, 174, *174,*
　　175, 229, *229*
Silicon Valley, 284, 285
Slavery, 144, 145
Smith, Jedediah, 108-110, *110,*
　136
Smith, Robert, 145
Smog, 296, 297, *296,* 299, 300
Smokejumpers, 23, 24, *24*

Text *(continued from page iv)*

xvi–xvii, 114, 115 from *Patty Reed's Doll* by Rachel K. Laurgaard. Copyright © 1965 by The Caxton Printers, Ltd. Reprinted by permission of The Caxton Printers, Ltd. **4** Quote from Sally Ride, as seen in *Air & Space*, April/May 1986. Used by permission. **8** Quote by Robert Crippen from *National Geographic*, Oct. 1981. **10** Excerpt from *Mojave* by Diane Siebert Copyright © 1988 by Diane Siebert. Reprinted by permission of Harper & Row, Publishers, Inc. **12** From *New York World*, Sept. 16, 1894. **13** Quote by Luther Burbank from Burbank, Luther, and Wilbur Hall. *The Harvest of the Years.* Boston and New York, 1927. **35** Excerpt from *Koster: Americans in Search of Their Prehistoric Past* by Stuart Streuver and Felicia Antonelli Holton. Reprinted by permission of Doubleday, a division of Bantam Doubleday Dell Publishing Group Inc. **37** from *California Indian Days* by Helen Bauer. Published by Doubleday and Co., Inc. NY. **45** "Acorn Song" from *The Natural World of the California Indians* by Robert F. Heizer and Albert B. Elsasser. Copyright © 1980 by The Regents of the University of California. Reprinted by permission of University of California Press. **48** "How Coyote Put Fish in Clear Lake" from *Stories California Indians Told* by Anne B. Fisher. Copyright © 1957 by Anne B. Fisher, renewed 1985 by Parnassus Press. Reprinted by permission of Herman Schein. **58** From *Aztecs and Spaniards: Cortes and the Conquest of Mexico* by Albert Marrin. Copyright © 1986 Albert Marrin. Reprinted with permission of Atheneum Publishers, an imprint of Macmillan Publishing Company. **67** From *In His Footsteps, The Life of Junípero Serra* told by Gertrude Ann Sullivan, B.V.M. Reprinted by permission of The Education Division of the California Catholic Conference. **69** From *Big Ride* by Dorothy Ward Erskine. Copyright © 1958 by Thomas Y. Crowell. Reprinted by permission of John M. Erskine. **76** Quote by Pedro Fages from Sprietsmo, Leo C. *Mission San Antonio De Padua, Part One: The Mission Period, 1771–1835.* 1988. **79** Quote by Toypurina from Temple, Thomas Workman. "Toypurina the Witch." *Masterkey*, Sept.–Oct. 1958. **100** Excerpt from *Carlota* by Scott O'Dell. Copyright © 1977 by Scott O'Dell. Reprinted by permission of Houghton Mifflin Company. **124** From Jackson, Joseph Henry. *Gold Rush Album.* Charles Scribner's Sons, 1949. **135** Excerpt from *By the Great Horn Spoon!* by Sid Fleischman Copyright © 1963 by Albert S. Fleischman. By permission of Little, Brown and Company. **143** Quote by Pablo de la Guerra from Heizer, Robert F. and Alan J. Almquist. *The Other Californians: Prejudice and Discrimination Under Spain, Mexico, and the United States to 1920.* University of California Press, 1971. **145** Excerpt from *A Frontier Lady* by Sarah Royce, edited by Ralph Henry Gabriel. Copyright © 1932 by Yale University Press. Reprinted by permission of Yale University Press. **150** Excerpt from *By the Great Horn Spoon!* by Sid Fleischman © 1963 by Albert S. Fleischman. By permission of Little, Brown and Company. **155** Quote by Pablo de la Guerra from Pitt, Leonard. *The Decline of the Californios.* University of California Press, 1966. **177** "Huzza For the Railroad." Extensive efforts to locate a rights holder have been unsuccessful. If the rights holder sees this notice, he or she should contact School Division, Permissions Department, Houghton Mifflin Company, One Beacon Street, Boston, MA 02108. **179** "The Flower-Fed Buffaloes" from *Going–To–the–Stars* by Vachel Lindsay. Copyright © 1926, by D. Appleton & Co., renewed, 1954 by Elizabeth C. Lindsay. A Meredith Book. Reprinted by permission of Dutton, an imprint of New American Library, a division of Penguin Books USA Inc. **184, 197** Excerpts from *The Octopus: A Story of California* by Frank Norris. Copyright © 1958 by Kenneth S. Lynn. Reprinted by permission of Houghton Mifflin Company. **186** from page 182 of *California for Travellers and Settlers* by Charles Nordhoff. Copyright © 1973 by Ten Speed Press. Reprinted by permission of Ten Speed Press, P.O. Box 7123, Berkeley, CA 94707. **208** Quote by Yuki Torigoe from Nakane, Kazuko. *Nothing Left in My Hands.* Young Pine Press, 1985. **208** From *Issei, Nisei, War Bride* by Evelyn Nakano Glenn, © 1986 by Temple University. Reprinted by permission of Temple University Press. **212** Poem on page 40 from *Island Poetry and History of Chinese Immigrants on Angel Island: 1910-1940* by Him Mark Lai, Genny Lim, Judy Yung. Copyright © 1980 by Hoc Doi Project. Reprinted by permission of Hoc Doi Project/San Francisco Study Center. **212** Text excerpt from pp. 18–19 from *Dragonwings* by Laurence Yep. Copyright © 1975 by Laurence Yep. Reprinted by permission of Harper & Row, Publishers,

Inc. **236** Quote by Jesse Cook from Thomas, Gordon and Max Morgan Witts. *The San Francisco Earthquake.* Stein and Day Publishers, 1971. **236** Excerpt from "The Great Earthquake: A Little Girl's Record" by Eleanor Deering Mathews in *The San Francisco Chronicle*, April 15, 1984. Copyright © 1984 by *The San Francisco Chronicle*. Reprinted by permission of *The San Francisco Chronicle*. **239** From Gilman, Charlotte Perkins. "To the Wise: A Bargain." *Public*, Feb. 22, 1908. **244** Adapted from *Blue Willow* by Doris Gates. Copyright 1940, renewed © 1968 by Doris Gates. Reprinted by permission of Viking Penguin, a division of Penguin Books USA Inc. **245** Quote by Harold McClain from Van Der Zee, John. *The Gate.* Simon and Schuster, 1986. **250** From *Prejudice: Japanese-Americans: Symbol of Racial Intolerance* by Carey McWilliams. **253** Quote by Marguerite Hoffman from Jensen, Joan M., and Gloria Ricci Lothrop. *California Women: A History.* Boyd & Fraser Publishing Company, 1987. **255** from *Yeager: An Autobiography* by General Chuck Yeager and Leo Janos, Copyright © 1985 by Yeager, Inc. Used by permission of Bantam Books, a division of Bantam Doubleday Dell Publishing Group, Inc. **257** Quote by Francis P. Shepard from Scripps Institution of Oceanography, La Jolla, California. **272** Quote by Yvonne Brathwaite Burke from "The Kind of World I Want for My Children." *Ebony*, Mar. 1974. **274** Excerpt from *César Chavez, Autobiography of La Causa* by Jacques Levy. Copyright © 1975 by Jacques Levy. Reprinted by permission of W.W. Norton & Company, Inc., 500 Fifth Avenue, N.Y., NY 10110. **278** From Stone, Scott C.S., and John McGowan. *Wrapped in the Wind's Shawl.* Presidio Press, 1980. **280** Reprinted with permission of Margaret K. McElderry Books, an imprint of Macmillan Publishing Company from *A Jar of Dreams* by Yoshiko Uchida. Copyright © 1981 Yoshiko Uchida. **299** From "Los Angeles: City in Search of Self." *National Geographic*, Jan. 1979. **343** Pronunciation Key, Copyright © 1985 by Houghton Mifflin Company adapted and reprinted by permission from the *American Heritage Dictionary*, *Second College Edition*.

Illustrations

Literature border design by Peggy Skycraft

Ligature 27, 34 (b), 35 (b), 265 **Precision Graphics** 18, 20, 28, 42, 52, 53, 63, 64, 70, 77 (tl), 79, 82, 83, 94, 102, 126 (tl), 130, 137, 140, 158, 159, 166, 170, 172, 173, 175, 176, 177, 180, 181, 194, 196, 197, 200, 210, 218, 219, 220, 221, 231, 243, 246, 247, 262, 266, 267, 274, 275, 284, 288, 289, 292, 294, 301, 304, 307 **Brian Battles** 34 (inl), 35 (inr) **John Burgoyne** 61 **Kirk Caldwell** 89 **Susan Johnston Carlson** 229 **Tony Chen** 14, 15, 16, 17, 98, 165 **Susan David** 33, 39, 212 **Pat & Robin Dewitt** 69, 108 **Ruth Flanigan** 216 **Randall Fleck** 126 (br) **Simon Galkin** 45, 99 **Al Lorenz** 174 **Kathy Mitchell** 91, 73 **Yoshi Miyake** 97 **Jim Needham** 204, 299 **Rick Porter** 12, 24, 90, 95, 127, 146 **Mike Rodericks** 286 **Kim Root** 76, 86, 111 **Joseph Scrofani** 279 **Scott Snow** 77 (b) **Susan Swan** 297 **Dahl Taylor** 206 **Gary Toressi** 332, 333 **Johnathan Wright** 257

Maps

Caldwell & Associates 5, 7, 8, 13, 21, 22, 36, 40, 59, 68, 74, 93, 136, 170, 187, 193 **R.R. Donnelley & Sons Company Cartographic Services** 518–533 **Mapping Specialists** 6, 119, 142, 167, 230, 243, 258, 303 **Reineck & Reineck** 19, 33, 112, 113, 207, 277

Photographs

BL—Courtesy the Bancroft Library, University of California at Berkeley; **CSL**—California State Library, Sacramento; **GH**—Grant Heilman Photography; **MPA**—Courtesy Meyers Photo-Art; **OMA**—Courtesy the Oakland Museum Art Department, Oakland, CA; **OMH**— Courtesy the Oakland Museum History Department, Oakland, CA; **PH**—Courtesy the Pat Hathaway Collection of California Views; **PR**—Photo Researchers, Inc.; **RJB**—Ralph J. Brunke; **SB**—Stock Boston; **SC**—Seaver Center for Western History Research, Los Angeles